INTERMEDIATE MICROECONOMICS

WILLIAM S. NEILSON
DEPARTMENT OF ECONOMICS
TEXAS A&M UNIVERSITY

HAROLD WINTER
DEPARTMENT OF ECONOMICS
OHIO UNIVERSITY

SOUTH-WESTERN College Publishing

An International Thomson Publishing Company

Publisher/Team Director: Jack W. Calhoun
Acquisitions Editor: John Alessi
Developmental Editor: Dennis Hanseman
Production Editor: Sharon L. Smith
Production House: WordCrafters Editorial Services, Inc.
Internal Design: Lotus Wittkopf
Marketing Manager: Lisa L. Lysne

Library of Congress Cataloging-in-Publication Data
Neilson, William S.
    Intermediate microeconomics / William S. Neilson, Harold Winter.
        p.   cm.
    Includes index.
    ISBN 0-538-84582-1
    1. Microeconomics.   I. Winter, Harold   . II. Title.
    HB172.N43   1998
    338.5—DC21   97-15185
                                                                         CIP

    2 3 4 5 6 7 8 D1 3 2 1 0 9 8

Printed in the United States of America

I(T)P®
International Thomson Publishing
South-Western College Publishing is an ITP Company.
The ITP trademark is used under license.

To Beth and Henry
William S. Neilson

To Carol
Harold Winter

PREFACE

One of the primary challenges in teaching intermediate microeconomics is that students enroll in the course for so many different reasons. At one end of the spectrum, students majoring in economics need to learn skills and tools for field courses. At the other end, students who are in their last required economics course just want to learn something useful and not be bored. So, the course should not just be a technically more sophisticated rerun of the principles course. Instructors would like to teach students how to think like economists and get them to understand how economists use optimization and equilibrium concepts to analyze problems.

To complicate matters further, microeconomics has also undergone a drastic change over the past 25 years. First, advances in the theory of risk and uncertainty have allowed economists to analyze traditional problems more realistically, and have allowed them to use the standard analytic tools to study such areas as insurance and portfolio choice. Second, and much more visibly, game theory has greatly expanded the scope of economics, allowing it to address many important but previously untouched problems.

In writing this book, we have used the following guidelines. The standard neoclassical material is vital to any intermediate micro course, but is not the be-all and end-all of microeconomics. Consequently, we present a thorough but concise treatment of the neoclassical material. Risk and uncertainty is added using the familiar indifference curve–budget line approach, so that it reinforces the standard material while adding realism and interest. Finally, game-theoretic topics are covered extensively as the preferred approach to equilibrium analysis.

As a consequence, this book has far more coverage of risk and uncertainty than any other intermediate micro text and more game theoretic coverage than almost any other undergraduate text. Because it covers all of the tools, and not just the neoclassical ones, it provides a great background for economics majors preparing for field courses. And, because so many of the risk and game theory applications, such as portfolio choice, bargaining, job search, and contracts, have direct relevance to them, those students who do not continue in further economics courses will find the course to be both new and interesting.

WHAT IS DIFFERENT ABOUT THIS BOOK?

Many new intermediate micro texts aren't really new at all. Instead, they cover the same material as all the other texts, but each does it in a slightly different way. The only place that most books can legitimately claim to be "new" is in the last few chapters, most of which are completely independent from the rest of the text. In contrast, almost every chapter in this book covers a major topic that is not covered in other intermediate micro texts. For example:

Chapter 2. Preferences This chapter presents the properties of preference orderings and the indifference maps that represent them. It also covers utility function representations of preferences. Finally, it discusses time preferences, which other texts do not discuss. This is important because the idea of discounting is used later in the text in the discussion of durable good monopoly in Chapter 8, in the discussion of collusion and repeated games in Chapter 11, and in the discussion of bargaining in Chapter 12.

Chapter 3. Consumer Choice This chapter covers the standard analysis of budget lines and consumer optimization, including discussions of demand functions and their comparative statics, and elasticities. But it goes beyond the traditional to include a detailed analysis of the borrowing-saving decision and a review of an experiment revealing Giffen-like behavior for smokers.

Chapter 4. Risk One of the main features of Chapter 4 is the use of the state-preference approach rather than the mean-variance approach for analyzing problems of risk. This allows students to use traditional indifference curve–budget line analytical techniques, and it turns out to be very powerful. For example, we show that if insurance companies use proportional loading to set premiums, the optimal insurance policy involves only partial coverage. One interpretation is that the optimal insurance policy has a deductible. A second application is that the optimal portfolio cannot contain only the riskless asset when the risky asset has higher expected return than the riskless asset.

Chapter 5. Production This is a fairly traditional chapter, devoting most of its attention to properties of production functions and differences between the short and long runs.

Chapter 6. Cost and Profit This chapter is also traditional, except that it introduces profit along with cost. After all, the primary economic reason for analyzing cost is because it is useful in analyzing profit maximization, so it makes sense to introduce cost and profit together.

Chapter 7. Perfect Competition and Welfare This chapter covers standard topics but goes beyond them to study the competitive firm facing price uncertainty. For example, a small farmer might be risk averse, and the price at which he can sell his crops is uncertain at the time of planting. We demonstrate that uncertainty causes risk-averse, competitive firms to reduce their output.

Chapter 8. Monopoly Power This chapter works through the monopolist's optimization problem, then compares monopoly to perfect competition. Sections on measuring and maintaining monopoly power are then presented. Next, we offer an extended discussion of price discrimination, including all-or-nothing pricing and two-part tariffs. The main innovation in this chapter is a discussion of the durable good monopolist.

Chapter 9. Game Theory Most texts cover pure-strategy Nash equilibrium in normal-form games. Some also cover backward induction in extensive-form games. Our chapter covers both of those topics, as well as mixed-strategy Nash equilibrium and subgame-perfect equilibrium. These concepts are then applied in the remaining chapters of the book.

Chapter 10. Oligopoly Our short chapter on oligopoly focuses on the Cournot and Stackelberg duopoly models and also provides a brief discussion of the dominant firm model and monopolistic competition. Oligopoly theory is one of the major applications of game-theoretic analysis. Because we have already covered the basics, we can take full advantage of game-theoretic language and ideas.

Chapter 11. Collusion We offer a separate chapter on collusion in order to clearly emphasize the problems associated with joint-profit maximization. After a standard analysis of cartels, we employ rigorous game-theoretic tools to examine infinitely and finitely repeated games. Our goal is to introduce strategies that lead firms to credibly commit to the joint-profit maximizing outcome that is not a Nash equilibrium in a single-stage playing of the game. Grim (trigger) strategies are discussed in the infinitely repeated games section, and the Cournot duopoly example introduced in Chapter 10 is revisited here. The problem of backward unraveling in finite games is then discussed. Finally, finite games with the possibility of credible cooperation are reviewed.

Chapter 12. Labor Markets Almost all intermediate micro texts cover labor supply and labor demand explicitly, and most also cover other issues arising in labor markets. What is added in this book is the consideration of uncertainty and strategic behavior. In particular, we address bargaining between an employer and a prospective employee and the problem of searching for the best job. Students will find both of these new sections valuable for obvious reasons. The bargaining model employed is the alternating-offers model, which relies on subgame-perfect equilibrium as a solution concept.

Chapter 13. Information Economics Many intermediate micro texts include a chapter on information economics. Typically these chapters introduce adverse selection using the "market for lemons," moral hazard, and the concept of education as a signal. All of this is done here as well. In addition, however, the market for lemons model is changed a bit so that the adverse selection problem can be solved through the use of middlemen. Moral hazard is addressed in the context of contracts, and ways of avoiding moral hazard problems are discussed. Finally, all of the information problems are related to issues arising in health care. We are able to address the problem of adverse selection in insurance markets because of the way risk was treated (through the state-preference approach) in Chapter 4.

Chapter 14. Auctions No other intermediate micro text has a chapter on auctions. In our chapter, the four standard types of private-value auctions are introduced, and equilibrium bidding strategies are characterized. The winner's curse problem in common-value auctions is described, along with a method for avoiding it. Finally, lessons from spectrum auctions both in the United States and abroad are provided.

Chapter 15. Negative Externalities and Public Goods Our final chapter begins by discussing the Coase theorem in great detail. Following the law and economics literature, we compare property rules and liability rules in low and high transactions costs settings. A section on pollution control then introduces regulatory standards and fines as possible alternatives to property and liability rules. An application of the Coase theorem to pollution control is discussed in a marketable permits section. The chapter concludes with a standard discussion of public goods, but the Clarke tax as a preference revelation mechanism is presented in greater detail than in other texts.

WHO SHOULD ADOPT THIS BOOK?

This book is designed for instructors who are comfortable with the modern tools of microeconomic analysis and who believe that these tools have an important place in the curriculum. The main idea underlying the design of this text is that Nash equilibrium in games is a much more useful approach to teaching the concept of equilibrium than general equilibrium theory is, and that game theoretic applications are both interesting and teachable at the intermediate level. Until now, intermediate microeconomics texts have not reflected the content of graduate microeconomics sequences, as exemplified, say, in *Microeconomic Theory* by Andreu Mas-Colell, Michael Whinston, and Jerry Green (Oxford University Press, 1995). So, we expect that this text will appeal to instructors who are familiar with modern microeconomic theory and believe that it belongs in an intermediate course.

LEVEL AND STYLE

We have tried hard to present material in a form that is accessible to students without shying away from difficult topics. This means using language that is concise, easy to read, and entertaining. Frankly, we have written to students, not professors. Arguments were chosen for their simplicity, and they could be, depending on the case, verbal, graphical, or mathematical.

While the book is analytically simple, it is conceptually challenging. For example, while other texts avoid formal treatments of mixed-strategy equilibria, *Intermediate Microeconomics* presents it formally and in great detail. It teaches an elementary algorithm for computing mixed strategies, and the computed mixed strategies are then used to analyze economic problems. Students who have seen the algorithm in class find it very easy to use, and they rarely apply it incorrectly on exams. Other topics that fall into this category include formal treatments of discounting, search, and folk theorems, to name just a few.

Microeconomics is useless if it does not explain real-world phenomena. To illustrate just how useful theory can be, we have included many examples and applications. Some are short, while others are much longer, sometimes taking entire sections. Most applications have a foundation in the real world, and most will appeal to both economics and business economics students. The longest application extends game theory to the study of auctions and requires an entire chapter, while the shortest applications take only a paragraph and are mixed in with the body of the text.

Every chapter ends with a summary and homework problems. Some of the homework problems are designed to make students repeat the steps that they learned in the chapter, while others are designed to make them think about the material and extend the analysis to new types of problems.

ORGANIZATION

The text consists of two broad sections. The first presents standard neoclassical material, but it does not simply repeat material found in other texts. The material is augmented with some "designer" topics. For example, the chapter on preferences contains a discussion of subjective discounting, the chapter on perfect competition covers price uncertainty, the monopoly chapter discusses durable good monopoly, and the externality chapter covers the differences between property rules and liability rules.

The second section concentrates on strategic behavior. Game theory has advanced from being a supplementary topic to being a core topic, so a single chapter on game theory is no longer sufficient. *Intermediate Microeconomics* provides seven chapters on game theory, asymmetric information, and their applications. There is enough material to allow instructors to choose applied topics from a list including oligopoly, collusion, information economics, bargaining, auctions, and public good provision.

The intent of these chapters is to teach students both to think strategically and to analyze strategic interactions. Although competitive and monopolistic markets are attractive ideals from an analytical perspective, most real-world situations violate the assumptions of these models. By leaving these idealized settings, it is possible to address many important economic problems. And by presenting a comprehensive introduction to game theory, it is possible to address them correctly. This allows *Intermediate Microeco-*

nomics to devote full chapters to such issues as collusion and auctions, where other texts cover these topics in a single section, if at all.

Even though it devotes a considerable amount of space to game-theoretic treatments, this is not a game theory book. Instead, it is a microeconomics text, but many of the economics topics that it covers require game theory to analyze. Only Chapter 9 is explicitly about game theory. The remaining chapters use game theory as needed to address real and interesting economic problems.

The text is integrated in the sense that every analytical tool is used in multiple applications, and in different chapters if possible. When students come back to a topic, they come back with a fresh perspective and can learn new things. Also, by returning to a topic they are convinced of the topic's relevance. So, for example, uncertainty theory is applied with an analysis of a competitive firm facing price uncertainty in the perfect competition chapter and with an analysis of risk-averse bidding behavior in the auction chapter. Through this method, students learn that microeconomics operates through a unified treatment of economic problems, and they learn to use all of the techniques.

CONCLUSION

Intermediate Microeconomics provides students with a solid foundation.

- Students are taught to think like modern economists.
- Students are prepared for field courses.
- Material is presented in a manner that makes micro theory, in and of itself, interesting to students.
- Examples and applications equip students with the skills needed to apply the analysis to real-world situations in a variety of settings.

ACKNOWLEDGMENTS

We appreciate the work of everyone at South-Western College Publishing for turning our ideas into a book. We are grateful to Ken King for getting us started on this project, and to Dennis Hanseman for seeing it through. Susan Schwartz provided valuable editorial advice in the early stages of the process. Ann Mohan of WordCrafters did a wonderful job of copyediting the book and getting it ready for production. She made it very easy on us.

We would like to take the opportunity to thank the many reviewers whose helpful suggestions have improved this book. They include:

Chursong Ai   University of Florida
Michael Brien   University of Virginia
Jonathan Burke   University of Texas, Austin

James Cobbe   Florida State University
Vincy Fon   The George Washington University
Maxim Engers   University of Virginia
William Evans   University of Maryland
Paul Farnham   Georgia State University
Richard Fowles   University of Utah
Amy Glass   Ohio State University
Sumit Joshi   The George Washington University
Subbiah Kannappan   Michigan State University
Fahad Khalil   University of Washington
Subal Kumbhakar   University of Texas, Austin
Charles Mason   University of Wyoming
Rick McGrath   College of William and Mary
Craig MacPhee   University of Nebraska
Catherine Morrison   Tufts University
Julianne Nelson   The American University
Cliff Nowell   Weber State University
Eun-Soo Park   West Virginia University
Jeffrey Pliskin   Hamilton College
John Pomery   Purdue University
James Ratliff   University of Arizona
Lisa Takeyama   Amherst College
Helen Tauchen   University of North Carolina
Joel Watson   University of California, San Diego

William Neilson

Harold Winter

ABOUT THE AUTHORS

William S. Neilson is an Associate Professor in both the Economics Department and the George Bush School of Government and Public Service at Texas A&M University and is Editor of *Economic Inquiry*. He received his Ph.D. from the University of California-San Diego. Professor Neilson is a specialist in economic theory and has published widely in major professional journals including *Journal of Economic Theory*, *Rand Journal of Economics*, *Econometrica*, *Journal of Mathematical Economics*, *Economic Inquiry*, and *Journal of Economic Behavior and Organization*.

Harold Winter is Assistant Professor of Economics at Ohio University. He received his Ph.D. from the University of Rochester and taught at Texas A&M University before assuming his present position. Professor Winter is a specialist in applied microeconomic theory. He has published in major professional journals such as *Rand Journal of Economics*, *International Review of Law and Economics*, *Review of Industrial Organization*, *Jurimetric Journal*, and *Economics Letters*.

BRIEF CONTENTS

CONTENTS

CHAPTER 9   Game Theory   264

CHAPTER 10   Oligopoly   295

CHAPTER 14   Auctions   390

CHAPTER 15   Negative Externalities and Public Goods   412

SELECTED APPLICATIONS

1

INTRODUCTION

Overview

Microeconomics is the study of individual decisions. The individuals could be people, households, or firms. For example, people must decide how to spend their incomes on different consumer goods. Firms must decide how much of a good to produce and what combinations of inputs to use to produce it. These are standard economic decisions, and they will receive considerable attention in this book. Other decisions can also be studied using the methods of microeconomics. For example, we could study the decision of how fast to drive, or where to locate a business, or how best to punish a criminal.

Sometimes the decisions of one individual, or a group of individuals, have an effect on what another individual does. A simple example of this is when a customer and a car dealer negotiate over the price of an automobile: The offer the dealer decides to make has an effect on the counteroffer the customer decides to make. A different type of interaction is exemplified by the effect the choices of all people who buy gasoline have on the production and distribution decisions of oil companies. Microeconomics is also concerned with the study of how decisions interact.

The task of this book is to teach you to recognize microeconomic problems and to show you a method of thinking about them. To get you started, this chapter presents some of the basic concepts involved in analyzing decisions and provides some examples. You will also learn:

- How to analyze decisions about whether or not to take some specific action.

- How to analyze decisions about how much of some activity to undertake.

- How to distinguish between different types of costs.

- How to use supply and demand analysis to find equilibrium prices and quantities.

- How to apply supply and demand analysis to study real-world situations.

1.1 INDIVIDUAL CHOICE: WEIGHING COSTS AND BENEFITS

People make economic decisions all the time. For example, every time students try to decide whether or not to go to class, they make decisions that are of interest to economists. There are some obvious benefits from going to class. Going to class provides another opportunity to learn the material better, exposes students to different examples and different explanations, and helps students prepare for examinations. Sometimes part of the course grade is based on attendance, so going to class results in a slightly higher grade.

There are costs associated with attending class, too. One expense is the cost of transportation. For students who live away from campus, this cost could be quite high. If, on the other hand, students are already on campus, this cost is low. There is also another cost associated with going to class. If students decide not to attend class, they can use the time to do something else, such as studying for another course, doing laundry, or sleeping. These activities also provide benefits. When students decide whether or not to attend class, they must weigh the benefits of attendance against the costs.

Should students attend class or not? The answer depends on the benefits and costs, which, of course, depend on the situation. This book does not provide any definite answers to such questions. What it does, though, is provide a way of thinking about them systematically. In this section we look at different types of benefits and costs and which types are relevant for different kinds of decisions. In later chapters we look at particular decisions in more detail.

"Either-Or" Decisions

One type of decision is the "either-or" decision. Should you go to class or not? Should you buy a new car or not? Should you get a job or not? There are some related decisions that are not either-or decisions. For example, if you decide to buy a new car, what kind should you buy? If you decide to get a job, how much should you work? These other decisions are "how much" decisions, and the two types of decisions require different analytic techniques. Here we focus on either-or decisions.

To illustrate the issues, let's begin with a specific example. Tony's car is ten years old and needs some major repairs. He can either repair his old car or buy a new one. The either-or decision is, should he buy a new car or not? How would Tony answer this question? He would probably figure out the price of the new car and also the added tax, registration, and insurance charges. He would then compare this total to the repair bill for his current car and look at the difference. If the new car is worth this amount of money, he buys the new car. If the new car is not worth this amount of money, he keeps the old car and repairs it.

Let's rephrase some of this reasoning. What are the benefits of buying a new car? The obvious ones are lower repair bills, more reliable transportation, and the satisfaction of driving a newer car. What about the costs? These include the price of the car, the associated taxes, license and registration fees, and increased insurance costs. Tony also gets to avoid the repair bill for his old car. If Tony compares benefits to costs, he compares the satisfaction of the new car to the price of the new car minus the repair bill, as we said before.

But look again at what question Tony finally asked. Is owning the new car worth the price of the new car minus the repair bill? The only way to answer this is by looking at what Tony would do with the money if he did not buy the new car. In other words, he must look at what purchases he gives up when he buys a new car. The value of the best forgone alternative is called the **opportunity cost.** In this case, the opportunity cost of buying the new car is the satisfaction Tony would have received by fixing his old car and spending the leftover money on something else. Tony buys the new car if he receives more satisfaction from a new car than he could get by fixing the old car and spending the rest of the money on something else. Otherwise, he does not buy the new car.

What we have done is compare the benefits of purchasing a new car to the opportunity cost of buying the car. Looking at the problem this way yields a prediction about behavior. It predicts that people tend to buy new cars when their old cars have problems, not when their old cars are working well. Why is this? A higher repair bill for the old car means a lower opportunity cost of buying a new car. This is because if the person does not buy a new car, the old car must be fixed, leaving less money to spend on other goods. A higher repair bill, then, means that the person is more likely to buy a new car. Because of this, car dealers should be (and are) suspicious of trade-ins, because people are more likely to trade their cars in when the cars need major repairs.

Opportunity Costs Versus Sunk Costs

One item that was not considered in the preceding example was the original purchase price of the old car. Tony instead considered the price of the new car and the value of his old car. There is no reason he should have considered the original purchase price, because there is no way he could sell his car for that much. There are, however, some circumstances in which people consider original purchase prices in their decisions. For example, suppose Barbara bought some shares of stock at $70 per share, and, subsequently, the price fell to $65 per share. One tendency of some investors is to hold on to the shares until the price goes back up above $70. In other words, investors hold on to the stock to avoid taking a loss. In light of the decision process discussed earlier, does this behavior make any sense?

When the price of the stock is $65, Barbara must decide whether to hold on to the stock or sell it at a loss. The either-or decision is whether to hold the stock or not. If she holds it, she receives some future stream of payoffs from both dividends and possible increases in the price of the shares. If she sells it, she can then invest the money in a different stock or a different type of asset. From the new investment she receives a different future stream of payoffs. The opportunity cost of holding the stock, then, is the value of the future income stream generated by the best alternative investment. Barbara should hold the stock if she expects the income stream generated by the stock to be better than the income stream generated by the next best alternative. Nowhere in this reasoning does she consider what she originally paid for the stock. The purchase price of the stock is a **sunk cost;** that is, it is a cost that is irretrievable and, therefore, of no concern for her present decision.

Consider another example in which sunk costs arise. Suppose that you buy tickets for a football game in an outdoor stadium and it rains the day of the game. Also, since you bought the tickets the game has been picked up for a television broadcast. Should you go to the game or watch it on TV? At first glance, a typical response is that since you already bought the tickets, you shouldn't waste them. However, if you ignore the sunk cost, the correct reasoning is to weigh the benefits of attending the game in the rain against the costs of attending the game in the rain. The opportunity cost of attending the game is the value of whatever you would do if you didn't go to the game, which probably includes staying dry and watching it on TV. The opportunity cost does *not* include the price of the tickets. You have already spent that money, and you can't get it back. If you are able to resell the tickets, then you can get some of the money back, and that reduces the opportunity cost. But notice that this is the *current* value of the tickets, not the original purchase price of the tickets.

"How Much" Decisions

Many situations entail not only deciding whether or not to do something, but also how much of it to do. For example, when people exercise, they must decide how much to exercise. When firms make production decisions, they must decide not only what product to produce, but also how much of it to produce. The "how much" decisions require a different method of analysis.

Consider the case of a firm that installs car stereos. The customers buy the stereos somewhere else and then bring them to this firm for installation. How many stereos should this firm install? First let's look at benefits and costs. The benefit to the firm from installing car stereos is the money customers pay for the installation. The total amount paid by all the firm's customers is the firm's **revenue.** The costs of installation are the amounts the firm must pay for labor, electricity, rent, supplies, tools, and so on. There is also the opportunity cost of the owners' investment. It is the amount the owners of the firm could earn if they invested their money somewhere else. The firm's **profit** is revenue minus cost.

We assume that the firm installs the right number of stereos to maximize profit. This answers the question of how much the firm should produce. But how do we know whether the firm is maximizing profit or not? We can figure it out by looking at one unit of output at a time. Suppose that the firm has already installed a number of stereos and is deciding whether or not to install one more. If the additional revenue from installing one more stereo exceeds the cost of installing one more stereo, the firm should install it. If the additional revenue from installing one more stereo is less than the cost of installing one more, the firm would lose money on that installation and should not install it. If the additional revenue and cost from installing one more stereo are the same, the firm breaks even on that installation and doesn't care whether it installs the stereo or not.

The extra revenue generated by one more unit of output is called **marginal revenue. (MR)** In this case, marginal revenue is the amount the customer pays for one more installation. The extra cost of producing one more unit of output is called **marginal cost (MC).** In this case, marginal cost is the cost of installing one more stereo. Comparing marginal revenue and marginal cost tells us whether the firm is maximizing profit. If marginal revenue is above marginal cost, the firm should produce more because the firm makes money on the extra installations. If marginal revenue is below marginal cost, the firm should produce less because it lost money on the last installation. If marginal revenue is exactly equal to marginal cost, the firm should not change its production level in either direction. At that point, it is maximizing profit.

It is possible to use this same technique to analyze decisions made by entities other than firms. In the general setting, though, instead of comparing marginal revenue with marginal cost, we compare marginal benefit with marginal cost. **Marginal benefit (MB)** is the extra benefit generated by producing or consuming one more unit of the good. In the case where the decision maker is a firm, marginal benefit is exactly the same as marginal revenue. Marginal cost is the extra cost induced by producing or consuming one more unit of the good. The optimal amount of the good is the amount that makes marginal benefit equal to marginal cost.

Marginal analysis, the comparison of marginal benefits and marginal costs, is useful in a variety of settings, and it is employed extensively throughout this book. We use it in studying the behavior of consumers deciding how much of a particular good to buy, and we use an extension of the idea to study how consumers choose between combinations of goods. We use marginal analysis when studying the behavior of producers, in the context of both maximizing profit and minimizing cost. We use it in the study of labor markets, for determining both how much employees want to work and how much labor employers want to hire.

APPLICATION
The Effects of Automobile Safety Regulations

Marginal analysis is even useful in settings that some may not think are within the scope of economics. For example, it can be used to study how automobile safety regulations affect the number of accidents. A simplified view of the world is that drivers care about two things—how safe they are and how fast they get where they're going. This ignores such things as the likelihood of getting a speeding ticket and the resulting effect on insurance rates, but it keeps the analysis simple. The benefit of driving faster is that drivers get where they're going sooner, but the cost of driving faster is that it is more dangerous.

The marginal benefit and marginal cost of driving different speeds are shown in Figure 1-1. There are two marginal cost curves. The top marginal cost curve, labeled "no reg" for "no regulation," corresponds to the marginal cost when there are no safety devices on cars. The bottom marginal cost curve, labeled "reg," corresponds to the case where cars have mandated safety features. If cars are safer, accidents are less frequent and less severe. The marginal cost of driving at a specific speed is the additional cost incurred by driving 1 mile per hour faster. Let's compare the marginal cost of driving 70 mph with the marginal cost of driving 15 mph. When the speed increases from 15 mph to 16 mph, accidents become a little more likely, but they will not be very severe. But, when the speed increases from 70 to 71 mph, accidents become more likely, and they can be very severe. So marginal cost increases with speed, whether cars have mandated safety features or not. This is why the marginal cost curve is upward sloping in the figure, and having a positive slope is a typical feature of marginal cost curves.

The marginal benefit of driving a certain speed is the additional benefit derived from driving 1 mph faster, and the marginal benefit curve shown in the figure is downward sloping. This is because an increase from 15 to 16 mph provides more benefit than an increase from 70 to 71 mph, which makes sense. It is tedious to drive 15 mph, and a 1 mph increase is more noticeable when the original speed is 15 than when the original speed is 70. It is typical for marginal benefit curves to be downward sloping.

Drivers choose their speeds to equalize marginal benefit and marginal cost. This means that they choose the speed corresponding to the intersection of the marginal benefit and marginal cost curves. When cars do not have safety features, the marginal benefit curve intersects the relevant marginal cost curve at point A, and the speed is $s_{\text{no reg}}$. When cars do have safety features, the speed is s_{reg}, which is higher. So when cars have safety features, drivers go faster. And since driving faster is more dangerous, there are more accidents. Because of the safety features, the accidents are not as bad, but there are more of them.

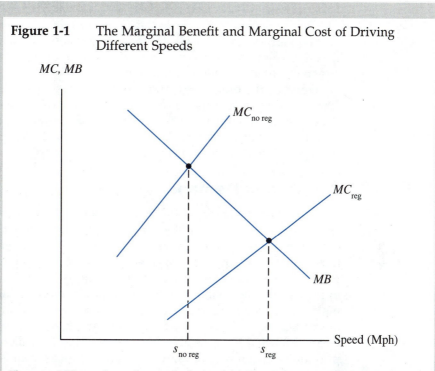

Figure 1-1 The Marginal Benefit and Marginal Cost of Driving Different Speeds

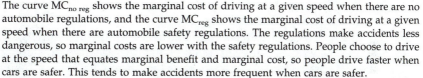

The curve $MC_{no\ reg}$ shows the marginal cost of driving at a given speed when there are no automobile regulations, and the curve MC_{reg} shows the marginal cost of driving at a given speed when there are automobile safety regulations. The regulations make accidents less dangerous, so marginal costs are lower with the safety regulations. People choose to drive at the speed that equates marginal benefit and marginal cost, so people drive faster when cars are safer. This tends to make accidents more frequent when cars are safer.

The reason that marginal analysis is so important is that it is used when somebody is maximizing something. Economists usually try to break problems into a benefit component and a cost component. Marginal analysis is used when an individual wants to maximize the difference between benefits and costs. The solution to a maximization problem can take two forms. If the problem involves an either-or decision, so that the individual decides whether or not to take a particular action, the maximum is achieved by comparing the benefit of the action to the cost of the action. If the benefit outweighs the cost, the action should be taken. If, instead, the problem involves a how-much decision, so that the individual chooses the amount of activity to undertake, the individual should undertake the action until its marginal benefit equals its marginal cost. This maximizes the difference between benefit and cost.

1.2 THE CONCEPT OF EQUILIBRIUM

In the preceding section we studied the decisions of isolated individuals. This is a major topic in microeconomics, and so it represents a large part of this book. But it does not cover all of economics. For example, it is not enough to determine the price in a market, and it is not enough to tell us the price that arises when two individuals bargain with each other. To determine prices, we need another concept, that of equilibrium. An **equilibrium** is a situation in which no individual has any reason to change behavior. This concept can be illustrated using supply and demand.

Supply and Demand

Consider the market for ice cream. Firms determine how much ice cream to produce at different prices by comparing marginal benefits and marginal costs. We can add up the amount produced by the different firms to determine the **market supply** at the given price. When we graph the market supply for every conceivable price, we get a **supply curve,** such as the curve S in Figure 1-2. The quantity of ice cream produced by all firms combined is measured on the horizontal axis, and the price of ice cream is measured on the vertical axis. To see how to read the graph, at point A the price of ice cream is $3, and the quantity of ice cream is 400,000 gallons. At point B the price of ice cream is $3.50, and the quantity of ice cream is 500,000 gallons. The amount of ice cream produced at a particular price is called the **quantity supplied** at that price.

    The supply curve in Figure 1-2 is upward sloping. This property holds as long as firms' marginal cost curves are upward sloping. (Firms' marginal cost curves are discussed at length in Chapter 6.) Taking this on faith for now, let's see why upward-sloping marginal cost leads to upward-sloping supply. If a firm produces more output, its marginal cost increases. Also, when the firm maximizes profit, it sets output at the point where marginal benefit equals marginal cost. So the firm will increase output only if its marginal benefit increases. A price increase causes marginal benefit to rise, since the firm now gets more money for every unit it sells. Putting this all together, the reason that supply curves are upward sloping is that to entice firms to incur higher costs and produce more, the price must rise.

    Now we turn our attention to demand. Consumers, using marginal analysis, decide how much ice cream to consume at different prices. The total amount of ice cream consumed by all consumers is the **quantity demanded** by the market at that price. Graphing the quantity demanded at every price yields a **market demand curve,** as shown in Figure 1-3. It is downward sloping, a property that holds when consumers have downward-sloping marginal benefit curves. As people increase their consumption of ice cream, each additional scoop of ice cream generates less additional benefit than previous scoops did. Phrased differently, the more ice cream they con-

Figure 1-2   The Supply Curve for Ice Cream

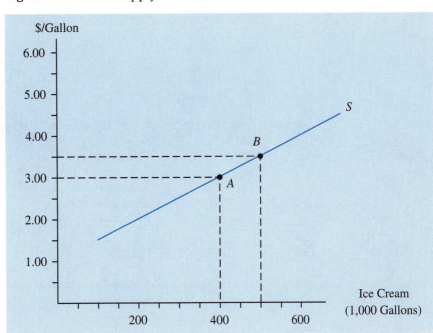

The curve S is a supply curve, and it shows how much ice cream firms produce at each price level. When the price is $3.00 per gallon, for example, firms produce 400,000 gallons of ice cream. Supply curves slope upward, reflecting the fact that to entice firms to produce more ice cream, the price must rise.

sume, the lower the marginal benefit of additional ice cream. If marginal benefit declines with consumption, consumers will buy more ice cream only if the marginal cost of consuming it declines, too. One way for the marginal cost to decline is for the price to fall. So, putting it all together, demand curves are downward sloping because a lower price is needed to entice consumers to purchase more ice cream.

Equilibrium

What we have done so far is find how much firms are willing to supply when the price is given (the supply curve) and how much consumers demand when the price is given (the demand curve). We can put these two curves together to find the price. Suppose that the price is p_1 in Figure 1-3. At price p_1, the quantity firms wish to supply is s_1, and quantity demanded is d_1. Note that $s_1 > d_1$—that is, the quantity firms wish to supply is greater than quantity demanded. In this case we say there is **excess supply.** Could this be an equilibrium? Remember that an equilibrium is a situation in which no one has any reason to change behavior. If there is excess supply, firms

Figure 1-3   Equilibrium at the Intersection of Supply and Demand

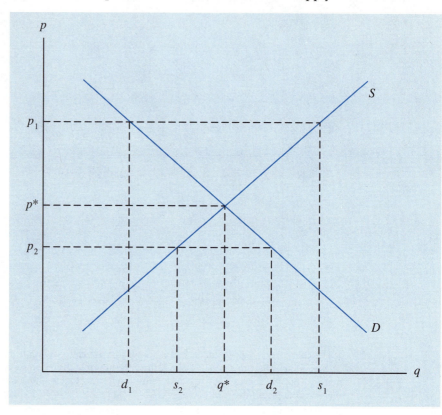

The demand curve shows how much consumers want to purchase at a given price, and the supply curve shows how much firms produce at a given price. At price p_1, the quantity supplied, s_1, is higher than the quantity demanded, d_1, which cannot be an equilibrium. At price p_2, the quantity demanded, d_2, is higher than the quantity supplied, s_2, which again cannot be an equilibrium. An equilibrium occurs when quantity supplied and quantity demanded are equal, which is at price p^* and at quantity q^*.

want to produce more output than consumers want to buy at the going price, so some firms are unable to sell as much as they want to at the going price. The firms that find themselves unable to sell the desired output have an incentive to lower the price, which will attract more buyers. Since firms have an incentive to change, p_1 cannot be an equilibrium price. In fact, no price that generates excess supply can be an equilibrium price.

What about price p_2? At this price quantity supplied is s_2 and quantity demanded is $d_2 > s_2$. In this case we say there is **excess demand.** This situation is not an equilibrium, either. When there is excess demand, there are consumers who wish to buy the item at the going price but who cannot find the item for sale. These consumers have an incentive to offer slightly more money for the item, in which case firms would rather sell the item to them at a higher price. Since consumers have an incentive to change their behavior, there is no equilibrium with price p_2. In fact, there is no equilibrium when quantity demanded is greater than quantity supplied.

The only remaining possibility is price p^*. At this price quantity demanded and quantity supplied are both equal to q^*, so there is neither excess demand nor excess supply. Is this an equilibrium? The answer is yes. Firms produce q^* and sell all of it, and they have no incentive to either raise or lower their prices. If any firm raises its price, it will not be able to sell any of its output, because consumers can buy all they want to at price p^*. If a firm lowers its price, it can sell as much as it wants to at the reduced price, but it could have sold as much as it wanted to at p^*. So firms earn less profit if they charge any price other than p^*, and, therefore, firms have no incentive to change their actions. What about consumers? When the price is p^*, consumers can buy as much of the good as they desire. If consumers offer a higher price for the good, they can buy as much as they want to, but they could already buy as much as they wanted to at price p^*. If consumers offer a price below p^*, they will not be able to buy anything at all, since firms can sell as much as they want to at price p^*. Thus, consumers have no incentive to change their actions either. This means that the price p^* is an equilibrium price.

Other Types of Interactions

The example we just studied involved the interaction of groups of participants on two sides of a market, and we found that equilibrium was the appropriate concept to use in determining the final **allocation,** or assignment, of goods. It is also possible to use the same concept to analyze situations in which two individuals interact. There is an important difference between the two cases. In the market setting it is unlikely that a single consumer could have much effect on the price prevailing in the market. If the consumer tries to pay a lower price, no one will sell to him. And, if there are many firms, it is unlikely that a single firm can have much impact on the market price. If it tries to charge a higher price, no one will buy from it. But if there is only one consumer and only one firm, if the buyer offers a lower price, the firm has no one else to sell to. This makes things more complicated. It is also a realistic situation, especially for expensive items such as the sale of a house or the sale of a business.

Analysis of situations in which interactions are more personal requires different techniques than the usual supply and demand situation does. The main idea is the same, though. In supply and demand analysis, the supply curve shows how firms react to every possible market price offered by consumers. The demand curve shows how consumers react to every possible market price offered by firms. In equilibrium, the firms' reaction to the market price exactly matches the consumers' reaction, so no one has any incentive to change their actions. We can use this same thinking to talk about personal interactions. We first determine the optimal reaction of each individual to all the possible actions of the other individuals. We then find an equilibrium in which no one has an incentive to change behavior.

In the first part of the book (Chapters 2 through 8), we study the decisions of consumers and firms, eventually leading to an analysis of market behavior and equilibrium prices. You can think of this material as providing the fundamentals behind supply and demand. It also provides more detail than simple supply and demand analysis. The material has two main components: the study of the optimizing behavior of individuals and the study of equilibrium in market settings. The second part of the book (chapters 9 through 15) examines situations in which interactions are more personal. Again, the material has an optimizing component and an equilibrium component. It is helpful to keep optimization and equilibrium separate in your mind as you read the text.

1.3 USING SUPPLY AND DEMAND

Supply and demand analysis can be used in a variety of settings, from explaining prices to figuring out the implications of a tax policy. This section provides some examples.

Cigarette Taxes and Health Care

One of the proposed methods of paying for a national health care program is by increasing the tax on cigarettes. The proposed tax increase could be as high as 75¢ per pack, and the government would collect it from the tobacco companies. One effect of this tax would be to reduce the number of packs of cigarettes that are smoked. Figure 1-4 shows the relevant supply and demand graph. The supply curve labeled S is the supply curve before the increased tax, and the supply curve labeled S' is the supply curve after the tax hike. Curve S' is higher than S by 75¢, the amount of the tax. To see why, suppose that a tobacco company was willing to sell, say, 400,000 packs of cigarettes at $1.25 each before the tax hike. It would get the same amount of revenue by selling 400,000 packs at $2.00 each after the tax. The upward shift in the supply curve causes the number of packs of cigarettes sold to decrease. Since smoking is considered bad, this effect of the tax increase is desirable.

There is a complication, though. If the primary purpose of the tax is to raise money for the government, any decrease in cigarette consumption also reduces tax revenue. The effectiveness of this program as a *tax policy*, then, depends on how much cigarette consumption is reduced. If there is a big reduction in consumption, the tax will not raise much money for the gov-

Figure 1-4   The Effect of a Tax on the Supply Curve

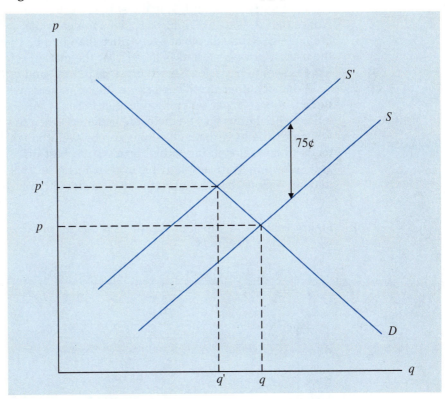

A 75¢ per pack tax on cigarettes shifts the supply curve up by 75¢, from curve *S* to curve *S'*. If the demand curve does not shift, the new equilibrium has a higher price and a lower quantity of cigarettes than before.

ernment. On the other hand, if the tax increase results in only a small decrease in cigarette sales, the tax will raise a large amount of money. Most estimates suggest that a tax hike of this magnitude would result in a rather substantial decrease in cigarette consumption (on the order of a 30 percent reduction), which raises the question of whether or not this policy will be able to raise enough money to pay for the health care program.

Agricultural Prices and Weather

Prices of agricultural products fluctuate greatly from year to year, and most of the fluctuations are caused by differences in the weather from one year to the next. There might be too much rain one year and too little rain the next. Extreme temperatures at the wrong time in the growing season can also cause problems. Let's compare supply and demand curves in a year with good weather with supply and demand curves in a year with bad weather. In Figure 1-5, the supply curve labeled S_g is the supply curve when the weather is good, and S_b is the supply curve when the weather is bad. Notice that S_g is to the right of S_b, which means that in a good year there are more goods available at every price than in a bad year. In a good year the market price is p_g, and in a bad year the market price is p_b. Consumers like farmers to have good weather, since $p_g < p_b$ and $q_g > q_b$.

What about farmers? The price is higher in years with bad weather, but the quantity is lower when the weather is bad. Consequently, it is hard to tell whether farmers, as a whole, are better off when the weather is good or when the weather is bad. One thing can be said, though. Since bad weather tends to be regional, individual farmers are best off when the weather is good where they are and horrible everywhere else. This reduces the supply in other regions, but the farmer under consideration has had good weather

Figure 1-5   The Effect of Weather on the Supply Curve for Farm Products

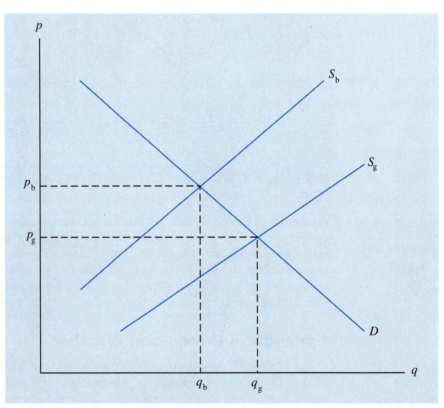

When the weather is good, there is a greater supply of farm products at every price than when the weather is bad. Thus, the supply curve S_g, which corresponds to good weather, is farther to the right than the supply curve S_b, which corresponds to bad weather. The equilibrium price is higher when the weather is bad and lower when the weather is good.

and has a large crop to sell. Since the market price is high, this farmer does very well. Of course, farmers in regions with bad weather are hurt.

Anti-Price-Gouging Laws

After one earthquake in Los Angeles, prices of many supplies shot up. For example, bottled water prices rose to more than five times the pre-

Figure 1-6   The Effect of an Earthquake on the Demand for Bottled Water

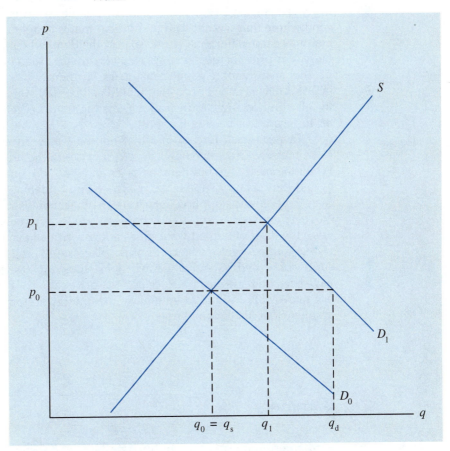

As a result of an earthquake, demand for bottled water in Los Angeles shifts outward from D_0 to D_1. Assuming no shift in supply, the price rises substantially, from p_0 to p_1. One effect of the higher price is to attract more bottled water to Los Angeles, where it is needed, and the quantity of water consumed also rises, from q_0 to q_1. Politicians saw the price increase as an attempt by merchants to gouge consumers, however, so they required merchants to return the price to p_0. With demand still given by D_1, there is a tremendous excess demand, given by $q_d - q_0$. Furthermore, there is no increase in the quantity supplied. Thus, the politicians' policy helps consumers who are able to buy water but hurts consumers who cannot find bottled water in stores.

earthquake price. In response, California created a task force to find and eliminate these instances of "price gouging," under the theory that the price increases were caused by greedy merchants trying to take advantage of the people hurt by a natural disaster. Let's see whether this interpretation of events makes sense.

For the case of bottled water, one explanation of the dramatic price increase is a large shift in the demand curve, as in Figure 1-6. When the demand curve shifts to the right, from D_0 to D_1, the price increases from p_0 to p_1. Why would the demand curve shift so far to the right? Earthquakes always present the possibility of some toxic substance leaking into the drinking water supply, so it is prudent for people to drink bottled water that comes from some other source. With so many people using bottled water instead of tap water, one would expect the demand curve to shift substantially. The price increase is simply an adjustment to equate demand and supply, not an attempt to gouge consumers. Furthermore, the high water prices in Los Angeles entice firms that would sell bottled water in other locations to sell it in Los Angeles instead. So, the higher price gets extra bottled water to where it is needed the most.

When the task force found that bottled water prices rose so dramatically, they required merchants to return prices to the pre-earthquake levels. When the price is p_0 but demand is given by D_1, the quantity demanded is q_d and the quantity supplied is q_s. The quantity demanded is much larger than the quantity supplied, which means that there is a shortage of water. Not everyone who wants to buy bottled water can find bottled water to buy. Since the price of bottled water does not rise, firms have no incentive to sell water in Los Angeles instead of other places, so there is no increase in the supply of bottled water. For many people in Los Angeles, the situation would have been better if the task force had left prices alone. The water was cheap, but impossible to find. In summary, then, anti-price-gouging laws lead to an inefficient allocation of goods.

Summary

- **Microeconomics** is the study of individual decisions made by people, firms, households, and others, and how these decisions interact.

- An **opportunity cost** is the value of the best forgone alternative. Part of the cost of any activity undertaken includes the opportunity cost of the next best activity that is *not* undertaken.

- A **sunk cost** is a cost that is irretrievable. Once incurred, a sunk cost is not part of the opportunity cost of an activity.

- When making an either-or decision, an individual compares the **total benefit** of an activity with the **total cost** of the activity. The activity is undertaken if the total benefit exceeds the total cost.

- The **marginal benefit** of an activity is how much the total benefit changes when the activity level is increased by one unit. The **marginal cost** of an activity is how much the total cost of an activity changes when the activity level is increased by one unit.

- When making a how-much decision, an individual compares the marginal benefit of one additional unit of an activity to the marginal cost of one additional unit. This is known as **marginal analysis.** If the marginal benefit exceeds the marginal cost, it is in the individual's best interest to increase the activity level. The activity level will be increased until the marginal benefit equals the marginal cost.

- An **equilibrium** is a situation in which no individual has any reason to change his behavior. In a market setting, an equilibrium price is found where the market demand curve intersects the market supply curve. At the equilibrium price, the quantity demanded by consumers is equal to the quantity supplied by producers.

- If the market price is greater than the equilibrium price, the quantity producers are willing to supply exceeds the quantity demanded by consumers. This is a situation known as **excess supply.**

- If the market price is less than the equilibrium price, the quantity demanded by consumers exceeds the quantity producers are willing to supply. This is a situation known as **excess demand.**

- The tools of supply and demand can be used to analyze a variety of settings, as illustrated by the cigarette taxes, agricultural prices, and price gouging examples in Section 1.3. In all these examples, an equilibrium price equates quantity supplied with quantity demanded. In equilibrium, there is no excess supply or excess demand.

Problems

1. An accounting firm is trying to decide whether or not to upgrade its computers. The new computers cost $3,000 each, and the firm would need five of them. The five old computers originally cost $4,000 each, but they are now worth only $300 each. The five new computers would allow the firm to process data faster and would save the firm a total of $14,000 over the next four years. In four years the firm expects to upgrade its computers again. Should the firm upgrade now or not? Explain your answer.

2. Candy machines have elaborate mechanisms to ensure that the candy buyer gets only the number of candy bars paid for, but newspaper machines let the buyer take as many newspapers as he wants. Use marginal analysis to explain why no one takes all of the newspapers at once.

3. Some parents choose to send their children to private schools instead of public schools. List the costs involved with sending a student to private school, making sure to include the opportunity costs.

4. Frequent flier programs were introduced to entice people to fly more often and with a single airline. Use marginal analysis to show the effect of frequent flier programs on the number of flights a consumer takes with a single airline.

5. The federal government supports dairy farmers by setting milk prices higher than they would be in equilibrium. In other words, there is a price below which no one is allowed to sell milk. Use a supply and demand graph to show the effects of the milk price regulations. Do people consume more milk or less milk than they would in equilibrium? Do farmers produce more milk or less milk than they would in equilibrium? Is the government's price regulation program efficient? Why or why not?

6. In 1996 Ford redesigned its big pickup trucks, making them more expensive to produce.
   a. If the new design makes the trucks more attractive to customers, what happens to the equilibrium price and quantity of Ford trucks sold?
   b. If the new design is just as attractive to consumers as the old one, what happens to the equilibrium price and quantity of Ford trucks sold?
   c. If consumers dislike the new design, so that Ford trucks are less attractive than before, what happens to the equilibrium price and quantity of Ford trucks sold?

7. The market for used compact discs has grown substantially in the last several years. The major recording companies are trying to get sales of used compact discs outlawed. Use supply and demand analysis to explain why the recording companies want to do this.

8. Evaluate the following statement: Assuming that the supply curve for gasoline does not shift, as cars become more fuel efficient the price of gasoline falls.

2

PREFERENCES

Overview

In deciding what goods and services to offer, retailers must pay attention to the tastes and incomes of their customers. One retail chain that does this successfully is Target.[1] In 1995 there were more than 600 Target stores, but no two carried exactly the same sets of merchandise. Some examples of the differences are pretty obvious: More winter coats are carried in Minnesota than in Southern California, and team-logo athletic apparel is sold in the same markets where the teams' fans live. But even two stores eight miles apart near Phoenix, Arizona, have differences. A store in a heavily Catholic and Spanish-speaking area stocks religious candles and Spanish-language compact discs, while the other store, in a Protestant and English-speaking neighborhood, stocks few religious candles and carries more country-and-western CDs. This trend of customizing the product line to the clientele, known as *micromarketing*, is becoming more and more common in retailing.

The reason that retailers are paying attention to tastes is because they are an important determinant of demand, as we saw in Chapter 1. As prevailing tastes change, perhaps because of demographic trends, demand curves shift. So, for example, during the 1980s, as people became aware of the dangers of eating too much red meat, many people began to substitute chicken for beef. This caused the demand for beef to fall and the demand for chicken to rise. American farmers are understandably concerned with how preferences for beef and chicken evolve, since the preferences have an impact on what the farmers should produce. Similarly, soft drink companies are concerned with people's preferences for regular and diet soft drinks, since these preferences affect the mix of products that should be produced. When buying cars, people decide about the size, style, and other features of the cars, and their preferences regarding these attributes determine how well particular models sell. This chapter discusses preferences in detail, and Chapter 3 shows the role played by preferences in determining demand.

---

1 *The Wall Street Journal,* May 31, 1995, p. A1.

In this chapter and Chapter 3, we study consumer choice. We will see that consumers' choices are governed by two basic considerations—the set of available alternatives and their tastes regarding these alternatives. In this chapter we study tastes, and in Chapter 3 we will add the consideration of the set of available alternatives. We begin by showing how economists represent and analyze people's preferences, with the goal of constructing a meaningful language that can be used to discuss tastes. The tools presented in this chapter are then used in Chapter 3 to analyze situations in which people have limited options and must choose among them.

The main ideas in this chapter all pertain to how economists think about preferences. The three main points covered are as follows:

- How to discuss preferences graphically and mathematically.
- How to characterize preferences using a measure of a person's willingness to trade one good for another.
- How to use these tools to discuss another phenomenon—impatience.

2.1 PREFERENCES

Consider the following example. Greg needs a new wardrobe for work and is considering different combinations of shirts and pants. One alternative is to get 10 shirts and 5 pairs of pants. A second alternative is to get 9 shirts and 6 pairs of pants. Which alternative does Greg prefer, or is he **indifferent,** that is, does he find them equally appealing? The answer, of course, depends on his tastes, but how do we model tastes? If we can devise a good model of his tastes, the model will tell us something about how he chooses among alternatives like these.

The Pairwise Choice Setting

It is convenient to represent Greg's alternatives as ordered pairs, with the number of shirts as the first element of the pair and the number of pairs of pants as the second element of the pair. The bundle (or combination) of 10 shirts and 5 pairs of pants is represented as (10,5), and the bundle of 9 shirts and 6 pairs of pants is represented as (9,6). There are three possible ways that Greg could answer the question "How would you rank these two alternatives?" The first is that he prefers the first alternative to the second. In this case we write $(10,5) > (9,6)$, which is read "the bundle with 10 shirts and 5 pairs of pants is preferred to the bundle with 9 shirts and 6 pairs of pants" ("$>$" is the symbol economists use to denote "is preferred to"; it is not the same as the symbol "$>$," which means "greater than"). A second possibility is that Greg prefers the second alternative to the first, that is, $(9,6) > (10,5)$. The third possibility is that he is indifferent between the two;

that is, he likes both bundles exactly the same. We write this as $(10,5) \sim (9,6)$, with the symbol "$\sim$" meaning "is indifferent to." We have discussed Greg's preferences regarding a single pair of alternatives. It is entirely possible that Greg will have the opportunity to decide among still more alternatives, so it would be nice to be able to talk about Greg's preferences regarding other pairs of alternatives, not just the two that we have already considered. To do this we need to discuss Greg's **preference ordering** over bundles of shirts and pants, which can be thought of as a list containing every conceivable pair of combinations of shirts and pants and states Greg's preferences for each pair. As with the first pair of alternatives we discussed, there are three possibilities for each pair: Either he prefers the first member of the pair, he prefers the second, or he is indifferent.

You may have noticed that the choice setting we are discussing is a greatly simplified version of any actual preferences. Greg would not just consider shirts and pants, but would also consider such things as shoes and ties and even movies, compact discs, haircuts, electricity, and food. Nothing about what we have done is specific to there being only two goods in each bundle. If there are more than two items under consideration, we simply represent them by a vector (or list) of the form $(x_1, x_2, \ldots, x_n)$. The individual still has a preference ordering over these larger bundles.

Properties of Preference Orderings

Suppose that you are presented with a long list of pairs of alternatives and asked to circle your favorite alternative in each pair. It is likely that the resulting preference ordering would naturally follow some simple rules. First, your preferences would probably be **complete;** that is, you would be able to state that you prefer one alternative to the other or that you are indifferent between the alternatives. There would not be any pairs of alternatives that you could not rank. Second, your preferences would probably be **transitive.** Preferences are transitive if, when alternative A is preferred to alternative B, and alternative B is preferred to alternative C, it is the case that A is preferred to C. In symbols, this is written as $A > B$ and $B > C$ implies $A > C$. Transitivity also requires that if $A \sim B$ and $B \sim C$, then $A \sim C$. In words, if the individual likes A and B equally well and likes B and C equally well, the individual must also like A and C equally well. Most people do satisfy transitivity, and economists consider it to be one of the most fundamental requirements for consumers to be rational. Why is transitivity such a big deal? Let's examine a case in which preferences are not transitive and see what happens.

Suppose that Greg's preferences are $A > B$, $B > C$, and $C > A$. With these preferences, it is possible for someone to take all of Greg's money away from him. Suppose Greg already has alternative C, and Jill comes along with alternative B. Since Greg prefers B to C, he would be willing to trade with Jill and would even be willing to give Jill a little money to induce her to trade. Now Greg is holding B, and Jill is holding C and some of Greg's money. She then offers alternative A to Greg. Greg prefers A to B, so he again offers Jill a little bit of money to trade. Jill now has B, C, and more of Greg's money, and Greg has A. Jill then offers to give C back to Greg. Since he prefers C to A, he again gives her a little money to entice her to trade. Where are we now? Greg is holding C, just as he was in the beginning, but he now has less money than before, having paid it to Jill.

This process is called a **money pump,** and it could go on forever, or at least until Jill gets all of Greg's money. It is also possible to construct money pumps if transitivity is violated in other ways. So, for example, if $A \sim B$ and $B \sim C$, it must be the case that $A \sim C$. If not, it is possible to construct a money pump. The appeal of the transitivity requirement, then, is that it eliminates situations in which people can lose all their money to a money pump. This is why transitivity is considered a requirement for preferences to be rational.

The third property, after completeness and transitivity, is **monotonicity.** Monotonicity simply states that more is better. For example, suppose Greg is given a choice between a combination of 10 shirts and 5 pairs of pants and a combination of 10 shirts and 6 pairs of pants. We would predict that Greg would take the second combination. The second combination has the same number of shirts but more pants, and if Greg's preferences are **monotone,** he prefers the second bundle to the first. Formally, suppose that a consumer is faced with a choice between $x = (x_1, \ldots, x_n)$ and $y = (y_1, \ldots, y_n)$, and that there is at least as much of each commodity in bundle y as there is in bundle x; that is, $y_i \geq x_i$ for each i. Furthermore, assume that for at least one of the commodities—for instance, commodity j—there is strictly more of that commodity in bundle y than in bundle x; that is, $y_j > x_j$. Preferences are monotone if $y > x$ in this case. In words, in comparing two consumption bundles, if one bundle contains at least as much of every good and more of at least one good, that bundle is preferred to the other. It is important to note that the amounts of each good must be compared separately; if one bundle has more of one good and the other bundle has more of a different good, monotonicity cannot be used to determine which bundle is preferred.

Preferences need not be monotone, but it makes the analysis in this and later chapters much simpler if they are. Consequently, we just assume that preferences are monotone and ignore cases in which they are not. There are two main cases in which preferences are not monotone. The first is when choices involve an **economic bad**—that is, a commodity that people prefer *not* to consume. Examples include loud music from a neighboring apartment, secondhand smoke, radon, and insomnia. In these cases less is preferred to more, so monotonicity is not satisfied. What economists usually do in these cases is to restate the problem so that the individual can eliminate economic bads rather than consume them. So, for example, if we consider *reductions* in the exposure to secondhand smoke, a bigger reduction is preferred to a smaller reduction, so these preferences are monotone. A second failure of monotonicity occurs when the consumer reaches a **satiation point,**

APPLICATION
Problems with Transitivity: Ranking College Football Teams

The current systems of ranking college football teams are rife with controversy. Why is it so hard to rank football teams? If a natural preference ordering over football teams can be found, and if it satisfies the properties of completeness and transitivity, then ranking football teams is a fairly straightforward exercise. In particular, the top-ranked team is just the team that is preferred to every other team. So what's the problem?

The problem is that the natural ordering over football teams is neither complete nor transitive. The natural ordering arises when one team beats another on the field. Because teams don't play every other team, this does not result in a complete ordering; some teams cannot be compared by how they fared against each other in a game. Furthermore, it occasionally happens that team A beats team B, team B beats team C, and team C beats team A, which is a violation of the transitivity property. Of these three teams, then, which should be ranked highest? The failure of these two properties is the reason that it is difficult, and even controversial, to rank college football teams.

and this occurs when the individual consumes the amount of a commodity that is *most preferred*. At the satiation point, either an increase or a decrease in the amount consumed makes the individual worse off. For example, some people consider the satiation point for spouses to be one (at least at a time). To keep things simple in this chapter and the rest of the book, we ignore situations in which people reach their satiation points.

2.2 GRAPHICAL REPRESENTATIONS OF PREFERENCES

We have now defined preference orderings and restricted them to satisfy the properties of completeness, transitivity, and monotonicity. This still does not tell us much about preferences or behavior; all we have is a list of pairs of possible alternatives and the preferred alternative in each pair. In principle, this list is sufficient to tell us everything we need to know about how a person behaves, but it is not very useful. Being able to graph preferences helps.

In our initial example, Greg was considering different combinations of shirts and pants. The set of possible combinations of shirts and pants is easy to show in a graph. Let the horizontal axis measure the number of shirts and the vertical axis measure the number of pairs of pants, as shown in Figure 2-1. Now we have an infinite collection of possible consumption alternatives for Greg, and our ultimate objective is to somehow depict his entire preference ordering over these alternatives. This is quite a task, so let's begin with something simpler. Let's start with point *A*, which is a combination of 10 shirts and 5 pairs of pants, and determine which points are preferred to *A*, which points are not preferred to *A*, and which points are indifferent to *A*.

Constructing Indifference Maps

Monotonicity helps determine some of the points that are preferred to *A*. Monotonicity states that bundles that have at least 10 shirts and 5 pairs of pants, and more of one of them, are preferred to *A*. Points with 10 or more shirts are to the right (east) of *A*, and points with 5 or more pairs of pants are above (north of) *A*. Consequently, points to the northeast of *A* have more of both of the things that Greg cares about, so monotonicity implies that he prefers all of these points to *A*. Points directly north or directly east of *A*

Figure 2-1   Preference Ordering Over Pairwise Choices

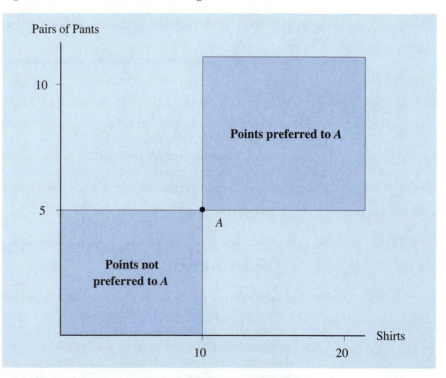

Point *A* represents a consumption bundle with 10 shirts and 5 pairs of pants. The points in the shaded region to the northeast of *A* are preferred to point *A*, because these points represent bundles with more shirts *and* more pants. Point *A* is preferred to points in the shaded region to the southwest of *A* because these points have fewer shirts *and* fewer pairs of pants.

have more of one good and the same amount of the other good, so monotonicity also implies that Greg prefers these points to A. Similarly, monotonicity states that A is preferred to all of the points to the southwest of A. Figure 2-1 shows the sets of points over which Greg's preferences relative to A can be determined by monotonicity. This takes care of some of the alternatives, but not all of them. In particular, what about the points to the northwest and southeast of A?

Monotonicity does not help with these points, so we need to use a different approach. Let's begin by finding a point that is indifferent to A. Monotonicity tells us that it cannot be to the northeast of A, since all those points are preferred to A, nor can it be to the southwest of A, since A is preferred to points to the southwest. Any point that is indifferent to A must be either to the northwest or the southeast. Which of these points actually are indifferent to A depends on Greg's preferences. Suppose that point B is northwest of A, and Greg tells us that point B in Figure 2-2 is indifferent to A; that is, given the choice between A and B, he finds them equally attractive. By continuing to search for points that are indifferent to A, we trace out a

Figure 2-2   An Indifference Curve

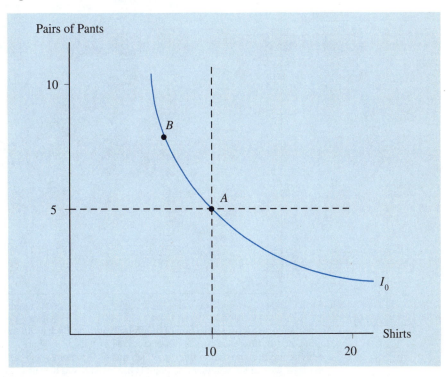

Point B is indifferent to point A. The curve labelled I_0 is an indifference curve, and it shows all of the points that are indifferent to A. The monotonicity assumption causes indifference curves to be downward sloping, as shown.

curve such as the one through points A and B in Figure 2-2. This curve (I_0) is known as an **indifference curve,** and it shows all the points that are indifferent to point A. Points to the northeast of the indifference curve must be preferred to A, and A is preferred to points to the southwest of the indifference curve. Knowing the indifference curve allows us to fully characterize Greg's preferences relative to point A, so an indifference curve conveys a considerable amount of information.

We now know that for any particular point, such as A, we can find an indifference curve through that point, and, therefore, we can also find the sets of points that are preferred to A and those that are not preferred to A. There is nothing special about A, so we can find an indifference curve through any, and every, point. Figure 2-3 shows a set of indifference curves

Figure 2-3   An Indifference Map

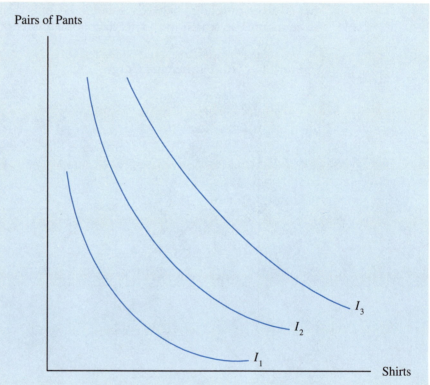

An indifference map is a collection of indifference curves. Each indifference curve is downward sloping, and indifference curves never cross, as explained in Figure 2-4. Indifference curve I_3 is a higher indifference curve than I_2, which means that points on I_3 are preferred to points on I_2. Because we can tell whether one point is preferred to another by comparing the indifference curves through the two points, an indifference map contains all the information in the individual's preference ordering.

called an **indifference map.** The indifference map depicts Greg's entire preference ordering. Given any two points, it is possible to tell which point Greg prefers or whether he is indifferent, simply by seeing whether the two points are on different or the same indifference curves.

There are two important restrictions to remember when drawing indifference maps. The first is that if preferences satisfy monotonicity, all indifference curves must be downward sloping. This was shown in Figure 2-2, where we saw that if one point is on an indifference curve, other points to the northeast or southwest cannot be on the same indifference curve. That means indifference curves must connect points from northwest to southeast; that is, they must be downward sloping. The second important restriction is that indifference curves must never cross. To demonstrate why, Figure 2-4 shows a case in which two indifference curves intersect at point *A*. Points

Figure 2-4   Intersecting Indifference Curves

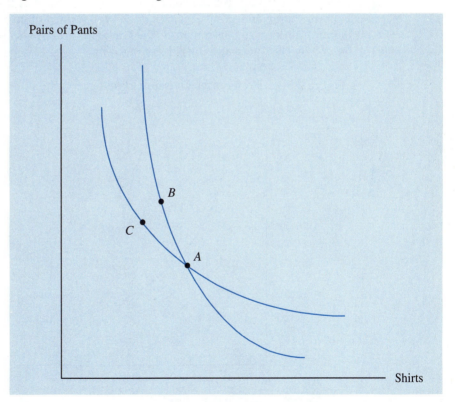

Indifference curves can never cross. To see why, suppose two indifference curves cross at point *A*. Because *A* and *B* are on the same indifference curve, *A* is indifferent to *B*. Since *A* and *C* are on the same indifference curve, *A* is indifferent to *C*. By transitivity, *B* and *C* must be indifferent too. But *B* has both more shirts *and* more pants than *C*, which violates monotonicity. To avoid these violations, indifference curves must not cross.

APPLICATION

Preferences Over Job Offers

It is possible to use indifference maps to depict preference orderings over other pairs of consumption items, even some that might not be so obvious. For example, suppose that Diane has just graduated from college and is trying to decide what type of job she wants. More specifically, she is trying to decide about different components of two job offers. Both jobs are with accounting firms in the same city. Coopers and Lybrand has offered her $40,000 a year and 3 weeks of vacation. Price-Waterhouse has offered her $50,000 a year but only 1 week of vacation. We can see which offer she prefers by consulting her indifference map, which is shown in Figure 2-5. The horizontal axis measures the amount of vacation time (in days) and the vertical axis measures the salary (in thousands of dollars). Point A is the Coopers and Lybrand offer, and point B is the Price-Waterhouse offer. Since A is on a higher indifference curve than B, she prefers the Coopers and Lybrand offer of $40,000 a year and 3 weeks of vacation.

Figure 2-5   Preferences Over Job Offers

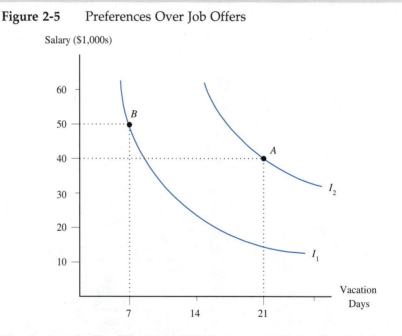

Diane has two job offers. Offer A is for $40,000 per year with 15 days (3 weeks) of vacation. Offer B is for $50,000 per year but only 5 days (1 week) of vacation. She prefers the job offer that is on the higher indifference curve. She takes offer A, which has less money but more vacation.

B and C are both indifferent to point A in Figure 2-4, and transitivity tells us that if $A \sim B$ and $A \sim C$, then $B \sim C$. But B is northeast of C, so B must be preferred to C (by monotonicity). This means that if indifference curves cross, preferences cannot satisfy both monotonicity and transitivity.

2.3 INTERPRETING INDIFFERENCE CURVES

Indifference maps have been introduced as a way of representing preferences. It is certainly easier to draw a few curves than to make a list of all possible preference pairs, but this is not the only reason indifference maps are useful. The slopes and shapes of indifference curves also provide information about people's underlying preferences in a surprisingly wide variety of circumstances. In this section we discuss how the slope and shape of an indifference curve should be interpreted and use these ideas to discuss some common behavioral patterns.

Interpreting the Slopes of Indifference Curves

To find the slope of an indifference curve at any point, first draw a line tangent to the curve at that point. (A line is tangent to the curve at a point if the line has the same slope as the curve and intersects the curve at that point. The idea of a tangent line is usually first introduced in geometry classes using circles. A line is tangent to a circle if it lies in the plane of the circle and intersects the circle at only one point.) The slope of the tangent line is measured by dividing the change in the variable on the vertical axis by the change in the variable on the horizontal axis. Figure 2-6 shows the case where the good on the horizontal axis is beef, the good on the vertical axis is fish, and the curve is an indifference curve. The change in the amount of beef is denoted Δb and, in this case, it corresponds to an increase of 2 ounces of beef. The change in the amount of fish is denoted Δf, and it is a decrease of 4 ounces of fish. The slope of the curve is $\Delta f / \Delta b = -4/2 = -2$. The slope is negative because the indifference curve is downward sloping.

In taking this measurement of the slope of an indifference curve, something strange happens. When we increase the amount of beef by 2 ounces and decrease the amount of fish by 4 ounces, we move the individual off of the indifference curve, as shown in Figure 2-6. In fact, the individual becomes worse off as a result of the change. Why, then, do we use the resulting number as the slope of the indifference curve? We can use it as the slope under two conditions. First, we must be careful to use the tangent line to take the measurement. Second, we must recognize that the tangent line is an *approximation* of the indifference curve. Unless the indifference curve is a straight line, any movement along the tangent line moves away from the indifference curve. For small movements along the tangent line, though, we will not move very far from the indifference curve.

Figure 2-6   The Marginal Rate of Substitution

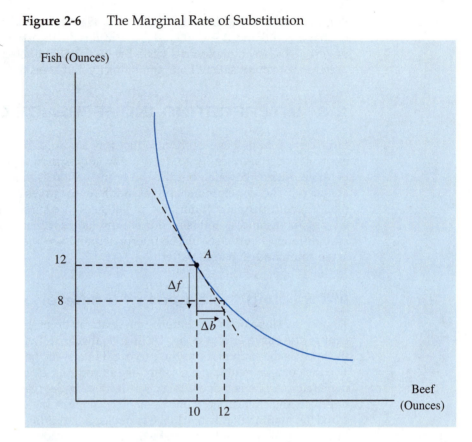

To find the slope of an indifference curve, draw a line tangent to the curve. For example, to find the slope of the indifference curve at point *A*, draw the dashed line that just touches the indifference curve at point *A*. The slope of the dashed line is the vertical change, Δf, divided by the horizontal change, Δb. As drawn, the amount of beef increases, so Δb is positive. The amount of fish decreases, so Δf is negative. This makes the slope negative, and equal to $-4/2 = -2$.

The negative of the slope of an indifference curve is known as the *marginal rate of substitution*. The interpretation of the marginal rate of substitution is the amount of fish given up to leave the individual indifferent when consumption of beef increases by 1 unit.

Economists have a name for the negative of the slope of an indifference curve—the **marginal rate of substitution (MRS).** The name is meaningful. The indifference curve in Figure 2-6 identifies all combinations of beef and fish that are indifferent to the bundle at point *A*. As the individual moves to the southeast along the indifference curve, he increases his consumption of beef and decreases his consumption of fish. Put another way, he *substitutes* beef for fish. The slope of the indifference curve tells how much beef must be substituted for fish to leave the individual indifferent, which is why the slope measures a "rate of substitution." The word "marginal" is used because, to be accurate, the changes must be small. Otherwise the tangent line and the indifference curve become far apart, and the slope of the line is not a good measure of the movement of the curve. Since indifference curves are downward sloping, their slopes are negative. It is generally easier to work with positive numbers, so economists take the negative of the slope.

The marginal rate of substitution is interpreted as the size of the reduction in the variable on the vertical axis that leaves the individual indifferent following a 1-unit increase in the variable on the horizontal axis. If the amounts of both beef and fish are measured in ounces, the marginal rate of substitution is interpreted as the size of the reduction in the number of ounces of fish needed to leave the individual indifferent when he consumes 1 more ounce of beef. We want the size of the *reduction* in fish consumption because we want the *negative* of the slope of the indifference curve. So, in Figure 2-6, the marginal rate of substitution at point *A* is 2. When beef consumption is increased by 1 ounce, fish consumption must decrease by 2 ounces to leave the individual indifferent.

The marginal rate of substitution can be interpreted in one more way. It is the largest amount of fish the individual is willing to give up to consume 1 more ounce of beef. In our example, the individual is left indifferent when he increases his beef consumption by 1 ounce and decreases his fish consumption by 2 ounces. If, instead, he increases his beef consumption by 1 ounce and decreases his fish consumption by less than 2 ounces, he is made better off. He would strictly prefer this new consumption bundle. On the other hand, if he increases his beef consumption by 1 ounce and decreases his fish consumption by more than 2 ounces, he is made worse off. The most fish he is willing to give up in exchange for a 1-ounce increase in beef is 2 ounces of fish. This is his marginal rate of substitution.

It may be tempting to say that the marginal rate of substitution between beef and fish should be low because fish is more expensive than beef, so a person would not be willing to give up much expensive fish for 1 more ounce of cheap beef. Prices are important for making decisions, but this chapter does not deal with prices. To think about marginal rates of substitution, you should ignore the prices of the two goods, and instead concentrate on what decisions people would make if someone were just handing them combinations of goods. Also, you should not think that people should want more beef just so they can resell it. You should only think about individuals *consuming* the goods, not *investing* in them.

This said, can we make guesses about whether the marginal rate of substitution between beef and fish is high or low? It depends on the person. A stereotypical Texan might like beef quite a bit better than fish, so he would probably give up a substantial amount of fish for just a little more beef, which means that the *MRS* is high. This Texan's indifference map is shown in Figure 2-7(a), with relatively steep indifference curves. Outside of Texas, though, you might find people who limit their consumption of red meat for health reasons. These people would probably be less willing to relinquish fish to get more beef. Since their *MRS* is lower, their indifference curves are

Figure 2-7   Different Marginal Rates of Substitution

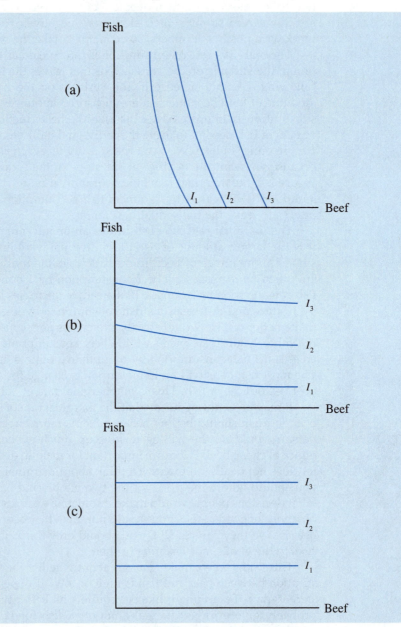

The indifference maps shown in this figure depict different preferences toward beef and fish. In panel (a) the indifference curves are steep, indicating that the person with these preferences is willing to give up a large amount of fish for a small amount of beef. The person in panel (b) likes fish, or beef less, than the person in panel (a). In panel (c) the indifference curves are horizontal, meaning the person is not willing to give up any fish for some extra beef. This person does not eat beef at all.

APPLICATION
Brand Loyalty

Many people are indifferent between a glass of Pepsi Cola and an equal amount of Coca Cola. Others, however, are very loyal to one brand or the other. Whenever possible, they choose a particular brand. How does brand loyalty show up in indifference maps? Imagine a graph like those in Figure 2-7, but with the amount of Coke measured on the horizontal axis and the amount of Pepsi measured on the vertical axis. Someone who is indifferent between an amount of Pepsi and an equal amount of Coke would have a marginal rate of substitution of 1; that is, she would be willing to give up 1 unit of Pepsi for an equal unit of Coke. A loyal Coke drinker would have steeper indifference curves. A loyal Coke drinker is willing to give up a large amount of Pepsi for a small amount of Coke, which makes the marginal rate of substitution high. In contrast, a loyal Pepsi drinker would have relatively flat indifference curves. He would not be willing to give up very much Pepsi in exchange for some more Coke.

flatter, as in Figure 2-7(b). Finally, a person who completely avoids red meat would not give up any fish for even a large amount of beef, so the *MRS* for this person is zero. Such an indifference map is shown in Figure 2-7(c). The indifference curves are horizontal, reflecting the fact that the slope is zero. Thus, knowing some characteristics of decision makers enables us to make predictions about their marginal rates of substitution, and vice versa. Consequently, it is possible to talk about people's tastes in terms of marginal rates of substitution.

Interpreting the Shapes of Indifference Curves

As we have already seen, the slope of an indifference curve measures the individual's willingness to trade one item for another. In the example we have been using, it measures how much fish the individual is willing to give up in exchange for 1 more ounce of beef. It is likely, though, that when the individual consumes a lot of beef but not much fish, his marginal rate of substitution is small; that is, he is not willing to give up much fish to get another ounce of beef. On the other hand, if he consumes plenty of fish but not much beef, a little less fish does not have much impact on his well-being, but an extra ounce of beef does. Consequently, he would be willing to relinquish a large amount of fish in order to get 1 more ounce of beef. That is, when one good is relatively scarce and the other is relatively abundant, the individual is unwilling to give up very much of the scarce good in exchange for another unit of the abundant good.

What does this imply about the shape of an indifference curve? In Figure 2-8, two points, A and B, are labeled on the indifference curve. At point A the individual has lots of fish but not much beef, and at point B the individual has not much fish but lots of beef. At point A fish is abundant relative to beef, so the individual is willing to give up a considerable amount of fish for a little more beef. In other words, the marginal rate of substitution at point A is high, which means that the indifference curve is steep. At point B beef is abundant relative to fish, so the individual is only willing to give up a small amount of fish for additional beef. The MRS at point B is low,

Figure 2-8   Diminishing Marginal Rate of Substitution

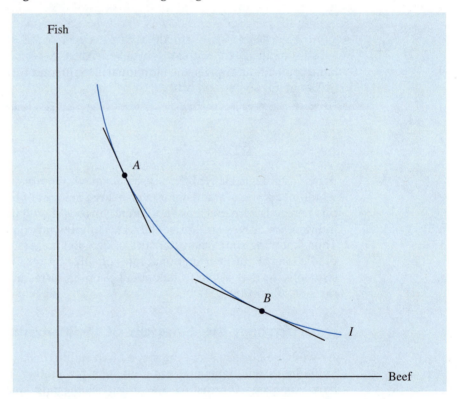

The marginal rate of substitution at point B is lower than at point A. This is the property of diminishing marginal rate of substitution, which means that the MRS declines with movements to the southeast along an indifference curve. To understand why diminishing MRS is a reasonable property, consider point A. Relative to point B, fish is abundant and beef is scarce. At point A the individual is willing to give up more of the abundant good, fish, for more of the scarce good, beef, compared to point B. At point B beef is abundant, and the person is willing to give up less of the scarce good for more of the abundant good, compared to point A.

and the indifference curve is relatively flat. Graphically, as you move to the southeast along the indifference curve, it gets flatter. Put another way, the indifference curve is bowed toward the origin. This property is known as the property of **diminishing marginal rate of substitution,** and it is a commonly made assumption when discussing preferences.

How much does the marginal rate of substitution change as we move along indifference curves? The answer depends on the goods being considered. In some cases indifference curves are extremely bowed toward the origin. One such example is eyeglass frames and lenses. Most people consume exactly two lenses per set of frames, at least at any given time. Frames are not of much use without lenses, and lenses are not of much use without frames to put them in. Indifference curves for frames and lenses look like those shown in Figure 2-9. They are L-shaped, with the vertices (corners) of the "L" lying at points with a 2:1 ratio of lenses to frames. To see why this is so, consider point A, which is a vertex point with two sets of frames and four lenses. At point B, which lies directly to the right of point A, the individual has the same number of frames but more lenses. Since the lenses are of no use without frames, the individual is indifferent between points A and B. The marginal rate of substitution at B is zero, since the individual is not willing to give up any frames for an additional lens. If she did, she would have even fewer frames than before and even more extra, and therefore useless, lenses. Point C lies directly above point A, and there the individual has extra frames. Since the frames are of no use without lenses to put in them, the individual is indifferent between points A and C. The marginal rate of substitution is infinite at point C. To see this, ask how many additional frames the individual would need to compensate for the loss of 1 lens. (Note that this is backward from the usual question of how many frames the individual would be willing to give up for an additional lens.) Since the loss of a lens makes her worse off, and extra frames are useless and cannot make her better off, she would need an infinite number of frames to compensate her for the loss of one lens. Pairs of goods with L-shaped indifference curves are called **perfect complements,** since they must be consumed together in a fixed proportion and one is never consumed without the other.

Now let's look at the case in which the marginal rate of substitution does not diminish along an indifference curve. The two goods are red and yellow M&Ms. The only difference between red and yellow M&Ms is the color; there is no difference in taste, size, chocolate content, or nutritional value. For a person who consumes M&Ms to eat them, not look at them, the mix of colors is irrelevant. Asked to state a preference over two combinations of red and yellow M&Ms, the person would choose the combination with more M&Ms. Furthermore, the marginal rate of substitution between red and yellow M&Ms is always the same; the person would be willing to give up no more than 1 red M&M for 1 more yellow M&M. Because the marginal rate of substitution is always the same, the person's indifference curves are straight lines, as shown in Figure 2-10. The slope of the indifference curve

Figure 2-9   Indifference Curves for Perfect Complements

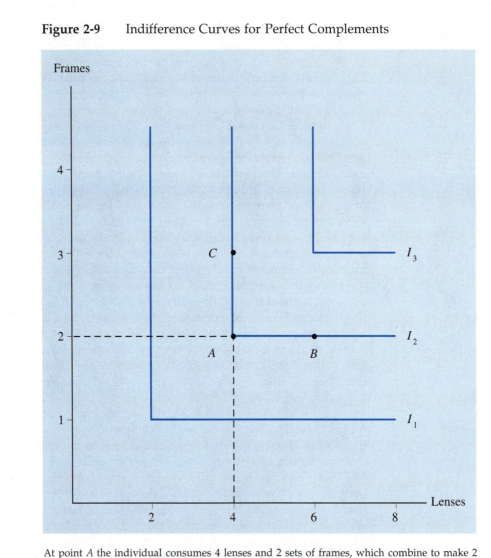

At point *A* the individual consumes 4 lenses and 2 sets of frames, which combine to make 2 complete pairs of glasses. If there are additional lenses, as at point *B*, the additional lenses are useless. They do not make the individual any better off, and so the individual is indifferent between points *A* and *B*. Likewise, extra frames are not of any use, and the individual is indifferent between points *A* and *C*. The indifference curves are L-shaped. Goods that generate L-shaped indifference curves are known as *perfect complements*.

is −1. When a person is always willing to exchange two goods in the same fixed ratio, as in this case, the goods are called **perfect substitutes.**

To summarize, we have identified many properties that indifference curves usually have: They are downward sloping, they never cross, and they get flatter with movements from left to right. The negative of the slope of

Figure 2-10   Indifference Curves for Perfect Substitutes

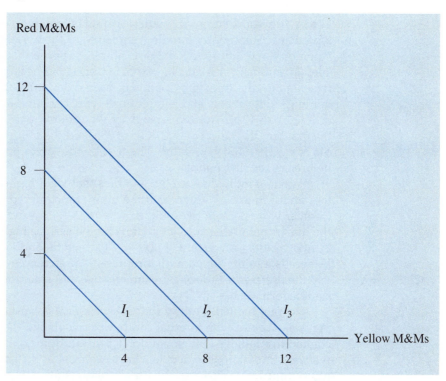

When indifference curves are straight lines, the marginal rate of substitution is the same at every point. In the case shown, the individual is always willing to trade 1 red M&M for 1 yellow M&M, no matter what mixture of red and yellow M&Ms the individual already consumes. When the trade-off between two goods is constant and does not depend on how much of the goods the individual has, the goods are known as *perfect substitutes*.

the indifference curve is the marginal rate of substitution, which measures the largest amount of one good the individual is willing to give up to get one more unit of the other good. The property that indifference curves get flatter with movements to the right reflects the property that individuals are less willing to give up a good when it becomes relatively more scarce.

2.4   UTILITY

So far in this chapter we have used preference orderings and indifference maps to discuss tastes. A third way to represent tastes is through utility functions, which are introduced in this section.

Do People Have Utility Functions?

Utility functions are mathematical formulas telling how much people like a particular commodity bundle. People prefer the bundle assigned a higher value by the utility function. For example, suppose that Greg's utility over beef (b) and fish (f) is $u(b,f) = 4b^3f^2$. Suppose that he is given the choice between a bundle containing 2 units of beef and 3 units of fish, and one containing 3 units of beef and 1 unit of fish. The first bundle is described by the ordered pair (2,3), and the second by the ordered pair (3,1). The utility of the first bundle is $u(2,3) = 4(2)^3(3)^2 = 288$, and the utility of the second bundle is $u(3,1) = 4(3)^3(1)^2 = 108$. The first bundle gives him higher utility, so he prefers the first bundle.

When an individual prefers bundles that yield higher values according to a utility function, we say that the utility function represents preferences. In other words, given two bundles $x = (x_1, \ldots, x_n)$ and $y = (y_1, \ldots, y_n)$, if the individual prefers x to y ($x > y$), then he assigns higher utility to x, that is, $u(x) > u(y)$. Conversely, if $u(x) > u(y)$, then the individual prefers x to y. If there is a utility function that represents preferences, the utility function and the preference ordering are interchangeable, since they both provide the same information.

The problem with utility functions is that it is hard to believe that people walk around with internal computers calculating the utility of different commodity bundles. Since we don't constantly make complicated mathematical computations to decide what to do, what is the point of talking about utility functions? There are two main reasons for doing so. First, they give a simple mathematical characterization of preference orderings that enables us to tell the individual's preferences over *any* pair of commodity bundles, simply by computing the utility values of the different bundles. The second reason for using utility functions is that most people, even if they don't calculate their preferences mathematically, do have preferences that can be represented by utility functions. In fact, if it is possible to draw indifference curves for a person it is also possible to find a utility function that represents the preferences.

Let's see how this is done. Figure 2-11 presents an indifference map, and our goal is to construct a utility function that represents these preferences. Remember that a utility function is just a rule assigning numbers to commodity bundles, with the preferred bundle in a pair being assigned a higher number. If the individual is indifferent between two bundles, those two bundles are assigned the same number. Once we are given an indifference map, all that has to be done to construct a utility function is assign a number to each indifference curve, with the numbers increasing with movements to higher indifference curves. Figure 2-11 shows an example of such a numbering system. Because each indifference curve is assigned a single number, if two bundles are indifferent they have the same utility value. Because points on higher indifference curves are assigned a higher number than

Figure 2-11   Indifference Curves and Ordinal Utility

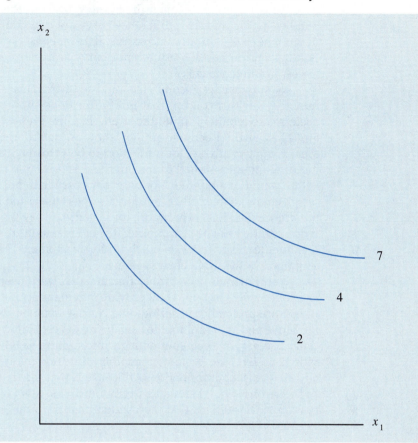

A utility function assigns numerical values to indifference curves. The only rule is that higher indifference curves must be assigned higher numbers.

points on lower indifference curves, if one bundle is preferred to a second, the first bundle has a higher utility value.

The two things a utility function can do are (1) tell you when two bundles are indifferent, and (2) tell you when one bundle is preferred to another. Something a utility function *cannot* do is tell you *how much more* the individual likes one bundle than another. In Figure 2-11, the middle indifference curve is assigned a utility value of 4, while the lowest indifference curve is assigned a utility value of 2. It might be tempting to say, then, that bundles on the middle indifference curve are twice as good as bundles on the lowest indifference curve. That would be a mistake. Remember that the utility function is an arbitrary assignment of numbers to indifference curves. A different assignment would work just as well, as long as higher indifference curves are assigned higher numbers. So, for example, the middle indifference curve could be assigned the number 20, and the highest indifference curve could be assigned the number 100. But this does not mean that bundles on the middle indifference curve are now 5 times better than bundles on the lowest indifference curve. It just means the same thing as before: Bundles on the middle indifference curve are preferred to bundles on the lowest indifference curve.

Not surprisingly, economists (and mathematicians) have a special terminology for this concept that utility functions show whether one good is preferred to another but not the strength of the preference. Utility functions are called **ordinal** because all they show is the ordering between two bundles. The alternative is for a function to be **cardinal,** that is, to have meaningful numbers assigned to the bundles. An example of a cardinal function is the weight of a bundle. Not only is it possible to tell whether one bundle weighs more than another, but it is also possible to tell how much more one bundle weighs. It is meaningful, for instance, to say that one bundle weighs twice as much as another bundle. It is *not* meaningful, however, to say that one bundle yields twice as much utility as another. That information is not contained in the preference ordering.

To summarize, then, utility functions are very useful, but they must be employed with caution. They provide a tremendous amount of information (the entire preference ordering) in a concise manner, which makes them an attractive and practical tool for analyzing tastes. Unfortunately, utility functions also *appear* to contain enough information to tell how much an individual prefers one bundle to another. The preference ordering, however, contains no such information. All it says is that the first bundle is preferred to the second. So, when using utility functions, it is important to restrict attention to those items that *can* be identified from the preference ordering.

Finding Marginal Rates of Substitution Using Utility Functions

As we have already seen, the marginal rate of substitution is an extremely useful tool for analyzing preferences, since it allows us to discuss both the slope and the shape of indifference curves. We now demonstrate how to find the *MRS* using utility functions. Suppose there are two goods, x and y. The marginal rate of substitution is the largest amount of y the individual is willing to give up for an additional unit of x, holding utility constant. In other words, when the individual is given one more unit of x, the *MRS* is the magnitude of the decrease in y that leaves the individual indifferent.

When the individual consumes one more unit of x, her utility rises. The extra utility generated by 1 additional unit of a good is called the **marginal utility (*MU*)** of the good. So, if the individual consumes 1 more unit of x, her utility rises by MU_x, which is the marginal utility of good x. If, instead, consumption of x rises by Δx units, utility rises by $MU_x \cdot \Delta x$. Similarly, if consumption of y changes by Δy units, utility changes by $MU_y \cdot \Delta y$. To find the marginal rate of substitution, x and y must change in a way that leaves the individual indifferent. That is,

$$MU_x \Delta x + MU_y \Delta y = 0.$$

The first term on the left-hand side is the change in utility caused by the change in x, and the second term on the left-hand side is the change in utility caused by the change in y. The left-hand side, then, is the total change in utility. For the changes in x and y to leave the individual indifferent, the total change in utility must be zero.

The next step in finding the marginal rate of substitution is remembering that the *MRS* is simply the negative of the slope of the indifference curve, or $-\Delta y / \Delta x$. By rearranging the equation shown previously, we get

$$MRS = -\frac{\Delta y}{\Delta x} = \frac{MU_x}{MU_y}.$$

Thus, the marginal rate of substitution between x and y is simply the ratio of marginal utilities.

To summarize, the principal advantages of utility functions are that they are easy to work with and that they are able to generate the main analytical tool for discussing preferences—the marginal rate of substitution. The principal disadvantage is that numerical changes in utility are meaningless, so we must be careful not to use utility functions in this way. In most cases, though, using a utility function is equivalent to using an indifference map or using a preference ordering. Which one should be used depends on which is easiest for addressing the problem at hand. In the next section we examine a problem in which using utility functions greatly simplifies the analysis.

2.5   MODELING IMPATIENCE

People tend to be impatient. To economists, this means that they prefer to consume now rather than later. This is true for everything from food to education, sleep, or income. However, people also tend not to consume things all at once. Thus, there is a tension between spreading consumption out and consuming everything immediately. A successful model of impatience must illustrate this tension. The task for this section, then, is to develop such a model.

An Approach Using Indifference Maps

In order to discuss impatience, we need some way to deal with time. Economists usually measure time in periods. In the simplest case, there are two periods, numbered 0 and 1. Period 0, the current period, lasts some length of time, and when it ends period 1 begins. Periods could be any length, from minutes to generations. Here we will think about them as years.

Becky is thinking about taking vacations both this summer and next summer. To represent her preferences graphically, we use a diagram in which the horizontal axis measures the number of days spent on vacation this year, denoted v_0, and the vertical axis measures the number of days spent on vacation next year, denoted v_1, as in Figure 2-12. What do her indifference curves look like? We know they should be downward sloping, of course, but what other features should they have? To begin answering this question, first consider point A, which is on the 45-degree line. The 45-degree line shows the set of points where Becky takes two vacations of the same length, so at point A both vacations are the same.

Impatience affects Becky's *MRS* at point A, and therefore the slope of her indifference curve at point A. The *MRS* measures how much she is willing to decrease next year's vacation in order to get 1 more day of vacation this year. Remember that when discussing preferences and marginal rates of substitution, we are only interested in what she is *willing* to give up, not what she *has* to give up. If she is impatient, she wants to enjoy the vacation now and is not willing to wait until next year. So she should be willing to sacrifice more vacation time next year than she gains this year; that is, her $MRS > 1$. The higher her *MRS*, the more future vacation days she is willing to sacrifice for 1 more vacation day this year, which can be interpreted as a higher degree of impatience.

So far we have been able to identify two properties of her indifference curves. First, they are downward sloping. Second, if Becky is impatient, her marginal rate of substitution is greater than 1 at points on the 45-degree line. What about the shape of her indifference curves? Vacations in different years are not perfect substitutes, implying that indifference curves must be bowed toward the origin, as in Figure 2-12, and marginal rates of substitution diminish as a vacation gets longer. This turns out to be true in general: Preferences over time exhibit diminishing marginal rates of substitution.

Utility Functions and Discounting

A very useful representation of preferences generates the indifference curves shown in Figure 2-12. Remember that Becky is choosing among pairs of vacations, (v_0,v_1) and that she dislikes waiting. A utility function that generates the indifference curves shown in Figure 2-12 is

$$u(v_0,v_1) = a(v_0) + \delta \cdot a(v_1).$$

This expression needs some interpretation. First, $u(v_0,v_1)$ is the utility Becky receives today when she takes a vacation of length v_0 this year and a vaca-

Figure 2-12   Indifference Map Over Days of Vacation This Year and
Next Year

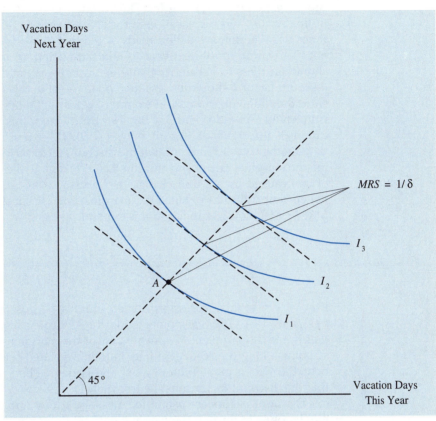

This graph shows Becky's indifference map over days of vacation this year, v_0, and days of
vacation next year, v_1. Points along the 45-degree line represent the same number of vacation
days both years. If Becky is impatient, she would rather have more vacation now, so her
marginal rate of substitution along the 45-degree line is greater than one. That is, she is willing
to give up more than a day of vacation next year to extend her vacation this year by one day.
The marginal rate of substitution at points on the 45-degree line is $1/\delta$, where δ is the discount
factor.

tion of length v_1 next year. Second, the function $a(v_i)$ denotes the utility she
receives from a vacation of length v in the current year i. So, in particular,
if she takes a vacation of length v_0 this year, she receives $a(v_0)$ in utility *this
year*; if she takes a vacation of length v_1 next year, she receives $a(v_1)$ in utility *next year*. Finally, δ (the lower case form of the Greek letter *delta*) is called
the **discount factor,** and it measures how much utility is changed by waiting for one year. By using the discount factor, we can transform next year's
utility into this year's utility.

To see how the discount factor works, suppose that Becky takes two equal-length vacations, $v_0 = v_1 = v$. Her utility from this combination of vacations is $u(v,v) = a(v) + \delta a(v)$. The vacation in the first year increases her utility by $a(v)$, and the vacation in the second year increases her utility by δ times this amount. We have already noted that Becky is impatient and does not like waiting until next year to take a vacation, so next year's vacation should add less to her utility than this year's vacation. In other words, the discount factor δ should be less than one. To make this more concrete, consider the following numerical example. Take $v_0 = v_1 = 9$, the function $a(v)$ is given by $a(v) = v^{1/2}$, and $\delta = 0.9$. Her utility from this combination of vacations is $u(v,v) = a(v) + \delta a(v) = 9^{1/2} + (0.9) \cdot (9)^{1/2} = 3 + 2.7 = 5.7$.

Another way to find out that the discount factor is less than 1 is by finding the marginal rate of substitution. Let $a'(v)$ denote the change in the value of $a(v)$ caused by a 1-unit change in the value of v. So, $a'(v)$ is the marginal current utility of v. Since the marginal rate of substitution is given by $MRS = MU_x/MU_y$, applied to this situation we get

$$MRS = \frac{1}{\delta} \cdot \frac{a'(v_0)}{a'(v_1)}.$$

If $v_0 = v_1 = v$, this expression is even simpler, because then $a'(v_0)/a'(v_1) = a'(v)/a'(v) = 1$. Thus, at points along the 45-drgree line, $MRS(v,v) = 1/\delta$, that is, the discount factor is the inverse of the marginal rate of substitution at points along the 45-degree line. Earlier we stated that if Becky is impatient, the MRS is greater than 1 along the 45-degree line, so this again means that the discount factor must be less than 1.

Discount factors are useful for measuring how impatient people are. If the discount factor is 1, they are patient and do not care whether they consume this year or next year. If the discount factor is 0, they are not patient at all, and future consumption gives them no utility whatsoever. So, how patient are people? Professor Emily Lawrance measured an average discount factor for people in the United States.[2] She found that the average discount factor for the entire U.S. population is about 0.89. On average, people in the United States are impatient.

Representing utility through discount factors is very convenient, especially when there are more than two periods. Suppose that Becky is considering vacations for three years, not two. There are now three vacations to discuss—v_0, v_1, and v_2. Her utility function is

---

2 Emily C. Lawrance, "Poverty and the Rate of Time Preference: Evidence from Panel Data," *Journal of Political Economy*, February 1991.

$$u(v_0,v_1,v_2) = a(v_0) + \delta a(v_1) + \delta^2 a(v_2).$$

Why is this the correct utility function? More specifically, why is her vacation two years from now discounted by δ^2? To answer this question, suppose that it is next year, and Becky is thinking about that year's vacation, v_1, and the vacation for the year after that, v_2. Next year's utility function covers just two vacations, and it is given by $u_1(v_1,v_2) = a(v_1) + \delta a(v_2)$. But Becky is impatient, so if she gets utility of u_1 next year, she discounts it by δ and it is only worth δu_1 today. Consequently, her utility today is $a(v_0) + \delta u_1$, which can be rewritten in the form above. The general formula for representing utility over time is

$$(2.1) \qquad u(v_0, \ldots, v_n) = \sum_{t=0}^{n} \delta^t a(v_n).$$

What if there are an infinite number of periods? Even though Becky will not live forever, it is still sometimes useful to know how to figure out this type of problem.[3] The result would be a problem with an infinite number of periods. With an infinite number of periods, the utility function is given by the formula

$$u(v_0,v_1, \ldots) = \sum_{t=0}^{\infty} \delta^t a(v_t).$$

This looks difficult, and in most cases it is. There is one case that can be handled rather simply, though, and it is the case in which Becky takes the same length vacation every year, so that $v_0 = v_1 = v_2 = \ldots$. If we denote this constant vacation length by v, so that we are trying to find $u(v,v, \ldots)$, it turns out that utility is given by the formula[4]

$$(2.2) \qquad u(v,v, \ldots) = \frac{a(v)}{1 - \delta}$$

---

3 For example, Becky might live for another period with some probability, and that probability could replace the discount factor in the problem.

4 Figuring out why this is the formula is a good mathematical exercise, and you may even have seen it in a math class during a discussion of geometric progressions. To get the desired result, multiply $u(v,v, \ldots)$ by δ and subtract the result from $u(v,v, \ldots)$. Solving the ensuing expression for $u(v,v, \ldots)$ gives the desired result. Try it.

APPLICATION
The Value of Future Income

The formula in equation (2.2) can be applied not only to the calculation of the utility of a never-ending flow of services, but also to the calculation of the monetary value of a never-ending flow of income. Suppose that Irma and her heirs are entitled to receive $10,000 per year forever. How much is this income stream worth? First, receiving $10,000 today is worth more to Irma right now than receiving $10,000 next year, because the future is discounted. Suppose that Irma's discount factor is 0.9. Then $10,000 a year from now is worth the same as (0.9)($10,000) = $9,000 today, and $10,000 two years from now is worth the same as only (0.9)(0.9)($10,000) = $8,100 today. The checks for $10,000 she receives three, four, and five years from now are worth only $7,290, $6,561, and $5,905, respectively.

What is the value of the entire future income stream? Using equation (2.2), and substituting $a(v) = \$10,000$, we get that the value of the future income stream is $10,000/(1 − 0.9) = $100,000. This is the most Irma would be willing to pay right now for the opportunity to receive $10,000 this year and every year in the future.

The utility of taking the same length vacation every year forever is simply the utility of taking a vacation of length v this year divided by $1 − \delta$. As long as $\delta < 1$, the utility is finite, even though the individual takes an infinite number of vacations.

The value in today's dollars of a future income stream is called the **present value** of the future income stream. If an individual receives v_0 today, v_1 in a year, v_2 in two years, and so on for n years, and if the individual's discount factor is δ, the present value of the future income stream is given by the formula

$$PV(v_0, \dots, v_n) = \sum_{t=0}^{n} \delta^t v_n.$$

The difference between the present value formula and equation (2.1) is that equation (2.1) uses utility values and the present value formula does not. So, equation (2.1) can be thought of as the *present utility value* of a future consumption stream.

Summary

- In a pairwise choice setting, an individual compares any two bundles of goods. If there are two bundles A and B, the individual can prefer A to B, or prefer B to A, or be **indifferent** between the two bundles. With many bundles to choose from, an individual's **preference ordering** over all the bundles can be determined through a series of pairwise choices.

- Three properties of preference orderings are: (1) **Completeness**—for any two bundles being compared, an individual can always state a preference for one bundle over the other, or be indifferent between the two bundles; (2) **Transitivity**—if an individual prefers bundle A to bundle B, and bundle B to bundle C, then transitivity implies that the individual prefers bundle A to bundle C; (3) **Monotonicity**—if bundle A contains at least as much of every good and more of at least one good compared to bundle B, an individual prefers bundle A to bundle B.

- When graphing preferences, points on an **indifference curve** represent bundles that an individual is perfectly indifferent between. An **indifference map** shows an individual's complete set of indifference curves. With an indifference map, an individual's preference ordering over all bundles can be seen graphically. Indifference curves cannot intersect.

- The slope of an indifference curve at any given point is the **marginal rate of substitution (MRS)** between the two goods included in each bundle. The MRS measures how much of one good an individual is willing to give up to get one more unit of the other good while remaining on the same indifference curve.

- When an indifference curve is downward sloping and bowed toward the origin, it exhibits the property of **diminishing marginal rate of substitution.** This property implies that as an individual has more and more units of one good, he is willing to give up fewer and fewer units of the other good to remain on the same indifference curve.

- **Utility functions** are mathematical formulas that represent how much a person likes a particular bundle of goods. Bundles with higher levels of utility are preferred to bundles with lower levels of utility. A utility function is **ordinal.** This means that utility functions are only used to rank bundles in order of preference.

- **Marginal utility** is how utility changes with one additional unit of a good, holding all else constant. The marginal rate of substitution between two goods is the ratio of their marginal utilities.

- The **discount factor** measures how impatient a person is by discounting future payoffs (utility or income). If the discount factor is equal to 1, a person is perfectly patient (that is, no discounting occurs). If the discount factor is less than 1, the person is impatient in the sense that a dollar tomorrow is worth less to that person than a dollar today.

- The **present value** of a future income stream is the value of that stream presented in today's dollars.

Problems

1. Suppose that an individual's preference ordering displays the following intransitivity: $x \sim y$, $y \sim z$, and $z > x$. Construct a money pump for this individual.
2. Gordon is allergic to nuts, and if he eats any nuts his face swells like a balloon. It is his only food allergy. Draw his indifference map over nuts and popcorn.
3. Draw an indifference map for a typical person's preferences over five-dollar bills and ten-dollar bills. Explain why the marginal rate of substitution is what you say it is.
4. Some people give a lot of money to charity, while other people give almost none. Draw two graphs with contributions to charity on the horizontal axis and selfish consumption on the vertical axis, and draw indifference curves for a charitable person on one of the graphs and for a selfish person on the other graph. Comment on why the slopes and shapes are the way you draw them.
5. People in the United States tend to eat bread with pasta, while people in Italy do not. (Italians do not understand this particular American dietary habit since pasta and bread are made from the same ingredients.) Draw indifference curves over bread and pasta in the two countries, and comment on the shapes of the indifference curves you have drawn.
6. College basketball decides on a national champion using a 64-team single-elimination tournament. If a team loses a game, it is out of the tournament, and the last team remaining is the national champion. Using winning as the preference relation, explain how the tournament *assumes* transitivity in declaring a champion.
7. A fad occurs when someone's desire to buy a good is enhanced by the fact that many other people buy the good. Suppose that there are two goods, x and y, and x is a fad good. That is, when more people buy good x, it makes the individual want good x more. Draw a pair of graphs showing what happens to the shape of the individual's indifference curves when more people buy good x.
8. Emily gets utility from compact discs (c), movies (m), and pizza (p). If her utility function is $u(c,m,p) = 2cm^2 + 4p + cp^2$, which of the following bundles of compact discs, movies, and pizza does Emily prefer?

    a. (2,3,4)

    b. (5,1,2)

    c. (3,3,0)

    d. (0,10,0)

9. Jason stays in shape by jogging. He would like to run the same amount every day, and the farther he runs every day, the better. If he runs x miles in a day, his utility from running is $2x^{1/2}$. His daily discount factor is .9995. Find his marginal rate of substitution between running today and running tomorrow. Find his utility if he is able to run 1 mile today, 4 miles tomorrow, and 9 miles the third day. Would his utility be higher if he ran 4 miles each of the three days?

10. How would you interpret a discount factor greater than 1? Can you think of any commodities whose consumption would generate a discount factor greater than 1?

11. An individual's discount factor is $\delta = 0.9$, and the function $a(v)$ is given by $a(v) = v^{1/2}$.

    a. What is the level of utility when $v_0 = 100$ and $v_1 = 64$?

    b. What is the level of utility when $v_0 = 64$ and $v_1 = 100$?

    c. In both (a) and (b), the individual eventually receives 164. Based on your answers, would you say that the individual would rather have the money sooner, or would he rather have it later (or does the timing not matter)? How is this related to impatience?

3

CONSUMER CHOICE

Overview

Businesses use many methods to increase sales of a product, and most of them are familiar. For example, some stores reduce prices of selected items to get customers to shop there instead of at a competitor. Some stores hold sales to get rid of merchandise at the end of a selling season. Many companies offer discount coupons for their goods, airlines have frequent flyer programs, and restaurants have frequent diner programs. Other business actions may just seem sensible: Stores in wealthy neighborhoods, for example, sell different merchandise than stores in poorer neighborhoods.

It is not difficult to think of reasons why these policies are effective. Analyzing policies like these formally, however, provides some additional insight. For example, a sale on Nike shoes at one store not only affects the number of Nikes purchased there, but it also affects the purchases of Reeboks at that store, purchases of clothing at that store, and purchases of shoes and clothing at other, competing stores. Going a bit further, for a store to figure out how much to reduce the price of Nikes, it must be able to quantify how price reductions affect sales.

This chapter provides the tools needed to analyze these and other problems. More specifically, the purpose of this chapter is to determine how choices are governed by preferences and constraints. Preferences were already introduced in Chapter 2. What is new here is that now the set of items an individual can choose is restricted: There are only certain combinations of goods that the individual can afford. We go on to address several aspects of consumer decision making:

- How to represent the set of alternatives available to consumers.

- How to find the optimal consumption choice, given a particular preference ordering.

- How to analyze the effects of changes in prices and income on a consumer's choices.

- How to analyze people's decisions about whether to borrow or save money.

- How to represent the effects of changes in prices and income in a manner useful to managers of firms and to government policy-makers.

3.1 BUDGET LINES

Jim is a college student who gets utility from just two things that he must pay for—long distance telephone calls and compact discs. His parents graciously provide for all his other needs. Both compact discs and telephone calls cost money, though, and Jim must decide how to divide his expenditures between the two goods. How do we model Jim's choice? We do it in two steps. In this section we characterize the set of combinations of telephone calls and compact discs that he can afford, and then in the next section we determine which of these combinations he wants to buy.

Before we proceed, we must first be more explicit about the problem. In particular, we must state the prices of the two goods and how much Jim has to spend. Let's assume that compact discs cost $p_c = \$15$ each and that long distance calls cost $p_t = \$10$ per hour. To pay for these things, Jim has a part-time job at which he earns \$300 per month after taxes. Which combinations of telephone calls and compact discs can he afford? The set of affordable alternatives is known as the **budget set.**

The budget set can be represented using a combination of math and graphs. To graph the budget set, we measure Jim's monthly consumption of compact discs on the horizontal axis and his consumption of telephone calls (in hours) on the vertical axis, as in Figure 3-1. He can afford any combination of phone calls and CDs that costs no more than \$300. If he consumes c compact discs, which cost \$15 each, he spends $15c$ on CDs. If he consumes t telephone calls at \$10 per hour, he spends $10t$ on phone calls. The combined expenditure cannot exceed \$300, that is,

$$15c + 10t \leq 300.$$

To graph this expression, it is helpful to rearrange it so that t is isolated on the left hand side:

$$t \leq 30 - 1.5c.$$

To graph this new expression, first graph the line $t = 30 - 1.5c$. It has vertical intercept 30 and slope -1.5, as shown by line A in Figure 3-1. The vertical intercept corresponds to Jim's consumption when he spends all his money on telephone calls, or 30 hours of calls. The horizontal intercept corresponds to the situation in which he spends all his money on compact discs, in which case he gets 20 CDs. The line connecting these two points is known

Figure 3-1   Budget Sets for Compact Discs and Telephone Calls

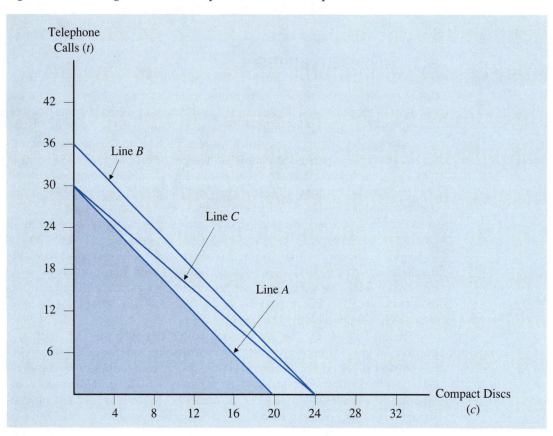

Initially Jim has $300 to spend, compact discs (c) cost $15 each, and telephone calls (t) cost $10 per hour. Line A and the shaded region show the combinations of CDs and phone calls he can afford. If his income rises to $360, keeping prices the same, his budget line shifts outward and parallel from line A to line B. If the price of telephone calls then rises to $12 per hour, the budget line rotates inward from line B to line C.

as the **budget line,** and it shows the set of combinations for which Jim spends all his income. Jim can also afford combinations to the southwest of the budget line, as shown by the shaded region in the figure, since these cost less than $300. The shaded region, together with the budget line, is Jim's budget set.

The slope of the budget line has a useful interpretation. To buy an additional CD Jim needs $15. He can get $15 by cutting his telephone calls by an hour and a half, since phone calls cost $10 per hour. To get an extra CD, then, Jim must give up 1.5 hours of phone calls, so a CD "costs" Jim 1.5 phone calls. When economists measure the cost of a good in units of a forgone alternative, it is called an **opportunity cost.** Formally, the opportunity cost of a good is the value of the best forgone alternative. In this case, the best alternative to consuming an extra CD is consuming 1.5 hours of phone calls, so the opportunity cost of a CD is 1.5 hours of phone calls.

If Jim's salary increases, his budget set changes. The easiest way to talk about changes in the budget set is by talking about changes in the budget line. Suppose that Jim gets a raise of $60 per month. The equation for the budget line is now

$$15c + 10t = 360,$$

which can be rewritten as

$$t = 36 - 1.5c.$$

The vertical intercept is now 36, the horizontal intercept is now 24, but the slope is still $p_c/p_t = -1.5$ because neither price has changed. As shown by the shift from line A to line B in Figure 3-1, when income increases the budget line shifts outward in a parallel fashion.

What happens if long distance rates go up to $12 per hour? Assume that income is still at $360 per month. The equation for the budget line is

$$15c + 12t = 360,$$

which can be rewritten as

$$t = 30 - 1.25c.$$

The horizontal intercept does not change, since Jim can still afford 24 CDs if he spends all his money on CDs. The vertical intercept does change, however, because of the increase in the price of telephone calls. The vertical intercept decreases from 36 down to 30, and the slope changes from -1.5 to -1.25. As shown by the shift from line B to line C in Figure 3-1, when a price increases, the budget line rotates inward.

A General Characterization

Instead of using a specific numerical example, let's think about budget lines more generally. Suppose there is an individual who gets utility from two goods, x and y, with prices p_x and p_y respectively. The individual's income is I. What is the budget line for this general case? The budget line is the set of combinations of x and y that cost exactly I to consume. If he consumes x units of good x, his expenditure on x is $p_x x$, and if he consumes y units of good y, he spends an additional $p_y y$. Total expenditure is $p_x x + p_y y$, and this must be exactly equal to his income, or

$$p_x x + p_y y = I.$$

To get this in a form that can be readily graphed, isolate y on the left hand side to get

$$y = \frac{I}{p_y} - \frac{p_x}{p_y}\, x.$$

In (x,y) space, the budget line corresponding to income I has vertical intercept I/p_y, horizontal intercept I/p_x, and slope $-p_x/p_y$.

3.2 CONSUMER OPTIMIZATION

We finally have enough tools to analyze the consumer's decision problem, about how much of each good to purchase, given prices and income. In Sec-

APPLICATION
Waldenbooks' Preferred Reader Program

Waldenbooks, a national bookstore chain, encourages customers to join its Preferred Reader program. For a $10 annual fee, customers save 10 percent on books purchased at Waldenbooks. This program changes the budget constraint faced by Waldenbooks customers. Consider an individual who has $190 dollars to spend, and the two goods available are long distance telephone calls for $10 per hour and books for $5 each. If the individual joins the Preferred Reader program, the price of books falls to $4.50 each, but now the individual only has $180 to spend on books and CDs.

Figure 3-2 shows how the budget set changes. The horizontal axis measures the number of books, and the vertical axis measures hours of telephone calls. The thin line is the budget constraint when the individual is not a member of the Preferred Reader program. If the individual spends the entire $190 on books, she can buy 38 books, which is the horizontal intercept. If, instead, she spends all her money on long distance calls, she can buy 19 hours of calls, which is the vertical intercept. What if the individual joins the Preferred Reader program? Now the individual has only $180 to spend, but books are only $4.50 each. The horizontal intercept, which corresponds to spending all $180 on books, is 40. This means that if the individual spends all her money on books, joining the Preferred Reader program allows her to buy more books. The vertical intercept, which corresponds to spending all $180 on telephone calls, is 18. So, as can be seen from the figure, the new (thick) budget line is flatter than the old (thin) budget line, and its vertical intercept is lower.

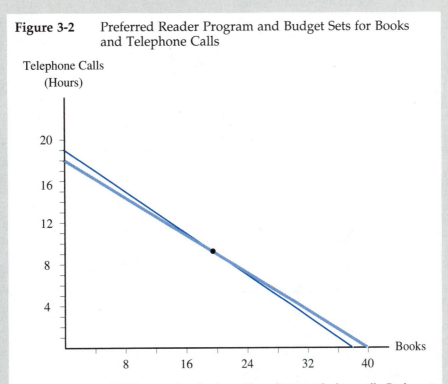

Figure 3-2   Preferred Reader Program and Budget Sets for Books and Telephone Calls

A person begins with $190 to spend on books and long distance telephone calls. Books cost $5 each, and telephone calls cost $10 per hour. The budget line is shown by the dark blue line. Waldenbooks offers a program in which, for a $10 annual membership fee, the consumer can save 10% on all purchases. Joining the program reduces the amount that can be spent to $180 and reduces the price of books to $4.50 each. The budget line shifts to the light blue line.

tion 3.1, we worked out the set of consumption bundles that an individual can afford, and in Chapter 2 we discussed ways to describe an individual's preferences between alternative bundles. All we have to do now is combine the two.

Choosing Points in the Budget Set

Let's look back at Jim, who has to decide between compact discs and telephone calls. He has $300 to spend, compact discs cost $15 each, and phone calls cost $10 per hour. What should he do? His budget line is shown again in Figure 3-3, and it is the same as the budget line depicted in Figure 3-1. The budget set is the set of alternatives that Jim can afford, so he must re-

Figure 3-3   Consumer Optimization

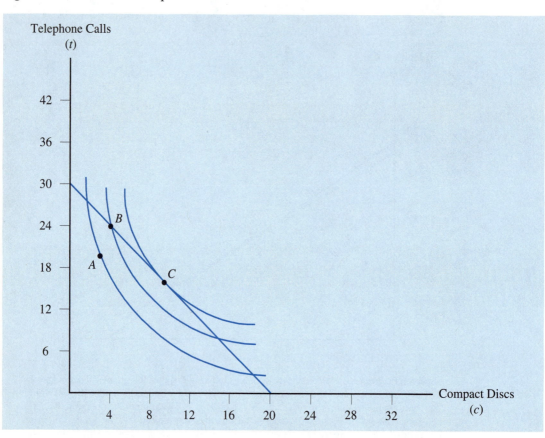

The budget line shows the set of points that Jim can afford, and we want to find the point on or under the budget line that makes Jim as well off as possible. Point *A* is in this set, but points *B* and *C* are on higher indifference curves. Consequently, point *A* cannot be an optimum. By the same reasoning, point *B* cannot be an optimum either. The optimal point is *C*. There is no other point in the budget set that is on a higher indifference curve than point *C*. The indifference curve is tangent to the budget line at the optimum.

strict his choice to these alternatives. The problem becomes one of figuring out which of these combinations of CDs and phone calls he should buy.

The idea behind the solution is that Jim should purchase the combination of CDs and phone calls that makes him as well off as possible. In particular, he should prefer the optimal combination to every other combination that he can afford. Let's look at combination *A* in Figure 3-3 and see if it fits this requirement. Jim's indifference curve through combination *A* is also drawn in the figure. Could *A* be Jim's optimal consumption bundle? The answer is no, because there is another affordable bundle, bundle *B*, that he prefers to bundle *A*. We know this because bundle *B* has more of both goods, so, by the monotonicity assumption, it is on a higher indifference curve than bundle *A*.

One problem with bundle A is that it lies inside the budget set, instead of on the budget line. For any point inside the budget set, it is possible to find a point on the budget line with more of both goods. Consequently, it is not optimal for Jim to spend less than his full income when monotonicity holds. Just because a bundle lies on the budget line—as B does—does not mean that it is the optimal bundle. Notice that there is another bundle, C, that lies on a higher indifference curve than bundle B. Is bundle C the optimal bundle? It is. Notice that the only points that are preferred to bundle C, that is, that lie to the northeast of the indifference curve through C, are points that Jim cannot afford. There is no point in the budget set that Jim prefers to bundle C, so C is the optimal consumption point.

Point C has two special features. First, it lies on the budget line, so that Jim spends all his money. Second, the indifference curve through C lies entirely on or above the budget line. In Figure 3-3, the indifference curve and the budget line intersect at point C and they have the same slope, so the indifference curve is **tangent** to the budget line at point C. Both the slope of the budget line and the slope of the indifference curve have economic interpretations.

The slope of the budget line is the negative of the price ratio, $-p_c/p_t$, and it can be interpreted as the opportunity cost of compact discs in terms of forgone telephone calls. The slope of the indifference curve is the marginal rate of substitution, which is the highest number of telephone calls Jim is willing to give up in exchange for one more compact disc. If the marginal rate of substitution is equal to the opportunity cost, the number of calls Jim is just willing to give up to get one more CD is exactly the same as the number of calls he *has* to give up to keep his budget balanced. In general, the optimality condition can be written

$$MRS = \frac{p_c}{p_t}.$$

At the optimum, the marginal rate of substitution is equal to the price ratio.

What happens if the marginal rate of substitution does not equal the price ratio? We have already looked at one case, the case of point B in Figure 3-3. At point B the indifference curve is steeper than the budget line, which means that the marginal rate of substitution is higher than the price ratio, that is,

$$MRS_B > \frac{p_c}{p_t} = 1.5,$$

using $p_c = 15$ and $p_t = 10$. If Jim buys one more compact disc, he must pay \$15, and he must give up 1.5 hours of phone calls to keep his budget balanced. Since his marginal rate of substitution is greater than 1.5, however, he is willing to give up more than 1.5 hours of long distance calls in exchange for one more compact disc, so he is happy to make this change. Consequently, B cannot be an optimum, and Jim would prefer to purchase more compact discs and fewer phone calls, which is what he does at point C.

A Utility Function Approach

Further intuition about the optimality condition, that the marginal rate of substitution equals the price ratio, can be gained by using utility functions. In Section 2.4 it was shown that the marginal rate of substitution equals the ratio of marginal utilities,

$$MRS = \frac{MU_x}{MU_y}.$$

The optimality condition states that the marginal rate of substitution equals the price ratio,

$$MRS = \frac{p_x}{p_y}.$$

Combining these yields

$$\frac{MU_x}{MU_y} = \frac{p_x}{p_y},$$

which can be rearranged to form the equation

$$\frac{MU_x}{p_x} = \frac{MU_y}{p_y},$$

which has a useful interpretation. The marginal utility of x is the extra utility generated by consuming one more unit of good x, and the price of x is the number of dollars needed to purchase an additional unit of x. The ratio MU_x/p_x is then the additional utility per unit of x divided by the number of dollars per unit of x, or the additional utility per dollar spent on good x. Similarly, MU_y/p_y is the additional utility per dollar spent on good y. The optimality condition states that spending an additional dollar on good x generates the same amount of utility as spending an additional dollar on good y.

Suppose that this were not the case. Specifically, suppose that $MU_x/p_x > MU_y/p_y$. Then the individual should spend more on good x and less on good y. Spending an additional dollar on good x yields additional utility equal to MU_x/p_x, while spending one less dollar on good y reduces utility by MU_y/p_y. By spending one dollar less on y and one dollar more on x, the individual raises utility by $MU_x/p_x - MU_y/p_y$, which is greater than zero. The individual can make himself better off by reallocating his budget between the two goods.

By phrasing the optimization condition in terms of utility per dollar, the individual's optimization problem is transformed into a simple comparison. Given some combination of x and y, he compares how his utility would change if he spent one more dollar on x compared to spending one more dollar on y. If his utility rises more when he spends one more dollar on x, he spends an extra dollar on x and one dollar less on y. If, instead, his utility rises more when he spends one more dollar on y, he spends an extra dollar on y and a dollar less on x. He continues this comparison until an additional dollar spent on x adds as much utility as an additional dollar spent on y. At this point it is impossible for the individual to increase his utility by reallocating his budget, so he is at the optimum.

Corner Solutions

As we have already stated, the optimal consumption point is on the budget line, and the indifference curve through that point lies above the budget line except at the point of tangency. While it may be the case that the indifference curve and the budget line have the same slope, as in Figure 3-3, it does not have to be this way. An exception is shown in Figure 3-4. Here the indifference curves are everywhere flatter than the budget line, so the budget line and the indifference curve could not possibly have the same slope. This does not mean, however, that there is no optimal consumption point. The problem Jim must solve (if these are now his indifference curves) is still the same: He must still find his favorite point in the budget set. In Figure 3-4 his favorite point entails consuming only telephone calls and no CDs, at point A. The optimal consumption point in Figure 3-4 is called a **corner solution.** Corner solutions occur when indifference curves either are everywhere flatter than the budget line, as in the figure, or they are everywhere steeper than the budget line. In either case, the consumer spends all his money on a single good, and the optimal consumption point is at a corner of the budget set.

In Figure 3-4 the indifference curve is flatter than the budget line at the optimal consumption point. This means that the marginal rate of substitution at that point is less than the price ratio. How can this be? Using the same prices as before, the price ratio is 1.5, so if Jim wants to consume a compact disc he must give up 1.5 hours of telephone calls. His marginal rate of substitution tells how many calls he is willing to give up, and because the marginal rate of substitution is less than the price ratio, he is not willing to give up 1.5 calls in exchange for one more compact disc. Consequently, Jim does not want to purchase any CDs. He would like to spend even more on phone calls and even less on CDs, but that would mean consuming a negative number of CDs, which is impossible. The best Jim can do is purchase no compact discs and spend all his money on long distance calls.

Figure 3-4   A Corner Solution

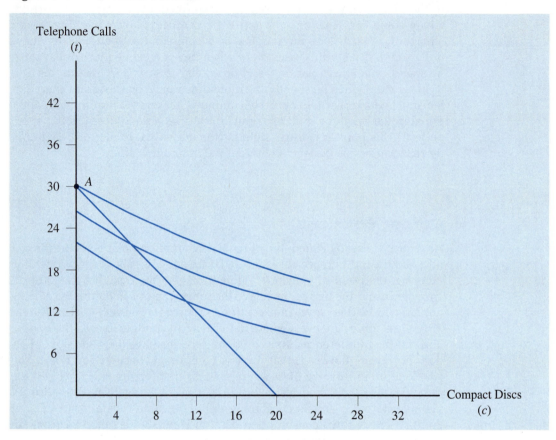

In this case the optimal consumption point is a corner solution. Point *A*, where Jim consumes no compact discs and 30 hours of telephone calls, is the best he can do. Here the indifference curve is not tangent to the budget line, but even so there is no way that Jim can afford to be better off than at point *A*.

3.3.   INCOME CHANGES

The ability to analyze the effects of changes in income is vital for both firms and government policymakers. If the government is considering raising the income tax rate, the effect on consumers is the same as the effect of a decrease in income. To assess the impact of the tax, policymakers must know how it affects consumption. For some goods consumption decreases when income decreases, while for other goods consumption actually increases when income decreases. Managers of firms would be interested in the impact of the tax on their own industry. They must know whether the change in income will cause sales of their products to rise or fall. This section demonstrates how to systematically analyze the effects of changes in income.

Figure 3-5   The Income Effects for a Normal Good and an Inferior
Good

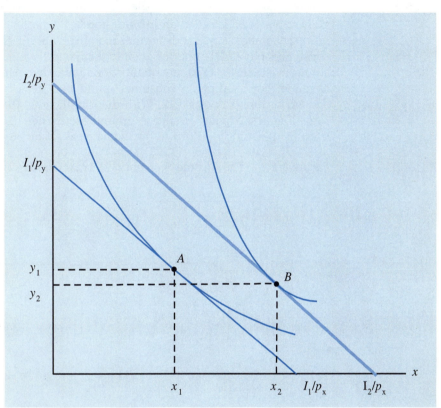

When income rises, the budget line shifts outward and parallel from the dark blue line to the
light blue line. The consumer switches from consuming at point *A* to consuming at point *B*. At
point *B* the individual consumes more of good *x* but less of good *y*. In this case good *x* is normal,
since the individual buys more of it when income rises, and good *y* is inferior, since the
individual buys less of it when income rises.

Normal and Inferior Goods

Consider the case in which a consumer makes choices between bundles of
two goods, *x* and *y*. The price of *x* is p_x, the price of *y* is p_y, and income is
I_1. The initial budget line is the thin line in Figure 3-5. The consumer chooses
bundle (x_1, y_1), which is determined at point *A* where an indifference curve
is tangent to the budget line.

Now consider what happens when income increases to I_2. The budget
line shifts outward and parallel to the thick line in Figure 3-5. The consumer's
new optimum is at the bundle (x_2, y_2), where an indifference curve is tangent
to the new budget line. Notice that $x_2 > x_1$. This means that the consumer
purchases more of good *x* when income rises. On the other hand, $y_2 < y_1$.

The consumer purchases less of good y when income rises. When consumption of a good rises as income rises, as with good x, the good is called a **normal good.** When consumption of a good falls as income rises, as with good y, the good is called an **inferior good.**

What makes some goods normal and others inferior? When income rises, consumers have more options open to them and have more latitude to substitute an expensive or higher quality good for an inexpensive or lower quality good. For example, a consumer might like steak but might not have enough income to buy steak. With the low income, the person has to eat something less expensive, such as ground beef. When his income rises, however, the person can afford to buy some steak. If he buys steak, he doesn't

Figure 3-6   The Income Effect and Normal Goods

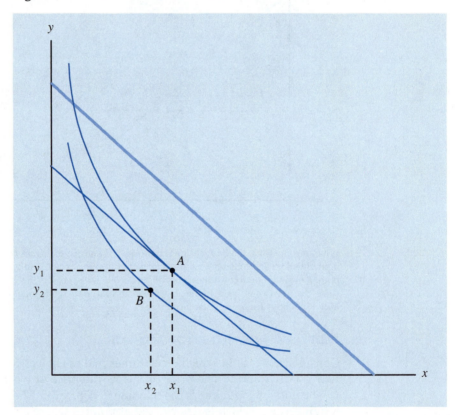

When there are only two goods, it is impossible for them both to be inferior. Suppose that the original budget line is the dark blue line, and an income increase shifts it outward and parallel to the light blue line. If good x is inferior, the new consumption point B must be to the left of the original consumption point A. Similarly, if y is inferior, the new consumption point must also be below the original consumption point. If both of these are true, as shown, then point B has less of both goods than point A, and B cannot possibly be the optimum because point A is affordable and preferred to B.

need as much ground beef, so ground beef purchases fall. In this case we would observe that steak is a normal good and ground beef is inferior.

When there are only two goods, three possibilities arise when income changes. Either x is normal and y is inferior, y is normal and x is inferior, or both goods are normal. Figure 3-5 shows the first of these, and you should try to draw the other two. It is impossible for both goods to be inferior. Figure 3-6 shows why. Once again, the initial budget line is the thin line, and

APPLICATION
Income Taxes

Income tax laws state that for each dollar a person earns, a certain percentage of that dollar must be paid to the government in taxes. What effect do income taxes have on consumption behavior? It may seem that income taxes cause people to buy less of everything, but this is not necessarily the case. An increase in income tax rates are like a decrease in income. When income decreases, consumption of normal goods falls, but consumption of inferior goods rises. So, some companies may actually benefit from increases in income tax rates.

For example, consider the choice between two modes of transportation for travel purposes—buses and airplanes. One might expect that when income rises people buy more airline tickets and fewer bus tickets, making airline tickets a normal good and bus tickets an inferior good. How will an income tax increase affect the demand for these two goods? The income tax increase should be thought of as a decrease in income, and the decrease in income reduces the quantity of airline tickets demanded. Consequently, the income tax increase hurts the airline industry. What about the bus transportation industry? Some people who were buying airline tickets before the income tax increase switch to bus transportation, increasing their demand for bus tickets. This is consistent with bus tickets being an inferior good. Bus tickets are probably not inferior for everyone, though. There might be some people who were buying only bus tickets and no airline tickets before the income tax increase, and who reduce their amount of travel after the income tax increase. The tax increase, then, reduces their demand for bus tickets. The total impact of the income tax increase on the bus transportation industry is ambiguous, since bus tickets are probably normal goods for some travellers and inferior goods for others. We can unambiguously predict, however, that the demand for airline tickets falls as a result of the income tax.

Figure 3-7   The Effect of a Price Change on Consumer Optimization

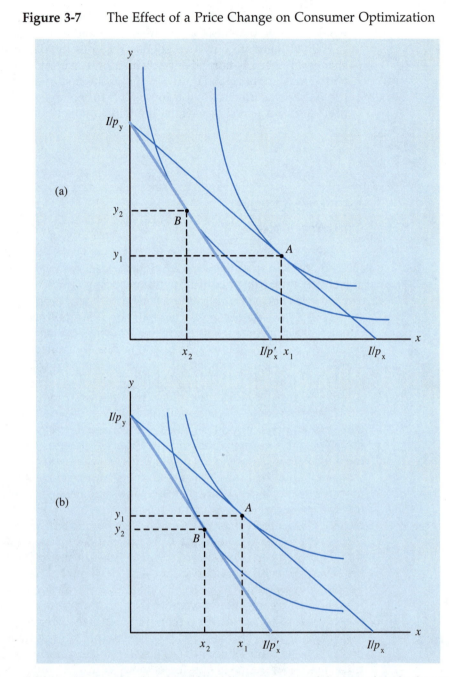

In both panels the price of good x increases, leaving income and the price of good y the same. In both panels the budget line rotates inward from the dark blue line to the light blue line. In panel (a) the individual consumes less of good x and more of good y as a result of the price increase. In panel (b) the individual consumes less x and less y.

the initial consumption point is (x_1,y_1). Income rises, and the budget line shifts to the thick budget line. If x is inferior, it means that the consumer buys less of good x when income rises. If y is also inferior, the consumer buys less of good y as well. So the consumer buys less of both goods, such as at point (x_2,y_2) in the figure. But (x_2,y_2) is on a lower indifference curve than (x_1,y_1), which means that the increase in income makes the consumer worse off, and (x_2,y_2) cannot be an optimum.

3.4 PRICE CHANGES

If managers of firms are interested in how income changes affect consumption, they are even more interested in how consumption reacts to changes in prices. Managers of firms have no control over their customers' incomes, but they do have control over prices. Government policymakers also care about price changes. If the government raises the tax on gasoline, that effectively raises the price of gasoline, and policymakers must know how gasoline consumption and the consumption of other goods will react to the tax. This section examines how price changes affect consumption. In the process, we develop one of the standard tools of economic analysis—the demand curve.

Price Changes and Budget Lines

As in the previous section, consider the case in which a consumer makes choices between bundles of two goods, x and y. The price of x is p_x, the price of y is p_y, and income is I_1. The initial budget line is the thin line in Figure 3-7(a). The consumer chooses bundle (x_1,y_1), which is the point where an indifference curve is tangent to the budget line.

Now let the price of x increase to p'_x. The budget line rotates inward around the y-intercept to the thick line in Figure 3-7(a). The new consumption point is (x_2,y_2). In the figure, $x_2 < x_1$, and $y_2 > y_1$. The individual consumes less of good x and more of good y when x becomes more expensive. This might occur if the goods are, for example, movies and videos. If movies at theaters become more expensive, it is likely that people will go to theaters less often and will rent movies instead. This causes consumption of movies to fall but consumption of videos to rise. Falling consumption of x and rising consumption of y is not the only possibility, though. Figure 3-7(b) shows a case in which consumption of both goods falls. An example that fits this scenario is when good x is gasoline and good y is food. When gasoline prices rise, people cut back gasoline consumption, but not by much. Because they reduce gasoline purchases only a little, and because the gasoline they buy is now more expensive, their expenditure on gasoline actually rises. This leaves less money to spend on other goods, such as food, so food consumption falls, too.

Demand Curves

We have now seen how to use budget lines and indifference curves to determine how consumption of a good reacts to price changes. In Chapter 1 we used a different approach to organize the same information—a demand curve. Demand curves show the consumption of a good at every possible price for that good, holding all other relevant factors (including tastes) constant. For example, the demand curve for movie tickets relates the number of movie tickets consumed to the price of movie tickets, holding such things as income and the rental price of video cassettes constant. We now show how to derive demand curves from budget line/indifference curve graphs.

Figure 3-7 shows how to find consumption of a good at two different prices, and it shows that consumption changes depend both on shifts in the budget lines and on the consumers' preferences. Demand curves show consumption at all possible prices, not just two. How do we get demand curves from budget line/indifference curve graphs? Figure 3-9 illustrates the pro-

Figure 3-8   Clearance Sales and Consumer Optimization

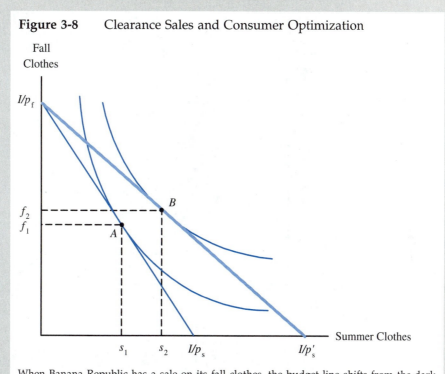

When Banana Republic has a sale on its fall clothes, the budget line shifts from the dark blue line to the light blue line. The individual shown changes from consuming at point A to consuming at point B. At point B the person buys more of both types of clothes.

cedure. The top panel of the graph shows a budget line/indifference curve graph, and the lower panel shows a demand curve graph. Demand curves measure the amount of good x consumed at different prices for good x, so the horizontal axis shows the quantity of good x and the vertical axis measures its price. Income and the price of good y (and the prices of all other goods) are held constant when constructing the demand curve. The top panel has the same horizontal axis—the amount of good x—but a different vertical axis—the amount of good y.

There are three different budget lines in the top panel of Figure 3-9, corresponding to prices p_1, p_2, and p_3 for good x. Price p_1 is the lowest price, so it corresponds to the budget line farthest to the right, and p_3 is the highest price, so it corresponds to the budget line farthest to the left. The three prices are also shown along the vertical axis of the demand curve graph in the lower panel of the figure. Let's begin with price p_1. The optimal consumption point is A in the upper panel, where an indifference curve is tangent to the budget line. At point A, consumption of good x is x_1. In the lower panel,

Figure 3-9   Deriving a Demand Curve

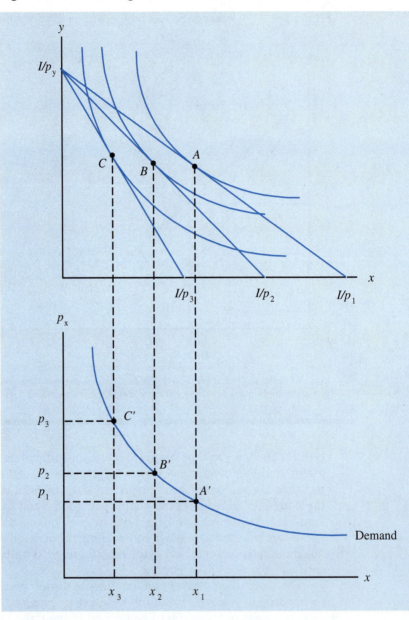

This figure shows how to construct a demand curve. In the top panel there are budget lines for three different prices of good x: $p_1 < p_2 < p_3$. The individual consumes at points A, B, and C, respectively. The bottom panel depicts the same information in a different way. It graphs the price of good x on the vertical axis and consumption of x on the horizontal axis. Point A' shows how much of good x the individual consumes when the price is p_1. Similarly for points B' and C'. The demand curve shows how much the individual consumes at each possible price of the good, holding income and the prices of other goods constant.

then, we have one point on the demand curve: When the price of x is p_1, the quantity demanded of x is x_1. This point is labeled A' in the lower panel.

When the price of good x rises to p_2, consumption switches to point B in the upper panel. Consumption of x is now x_2, which is less than x_1. Moving to the lower panel, the point (x_2, p_2) is another point on the demand curve, since when the price of x is p_2, the quantity demanded for x is x_2. This point is labeled B' in the lower panel. The same procedure can be used to find points C and C' for price p_3. In principle, we could do this for every possible price of good x and get a series of points in both panels. This would be both time consuming and messy, but the result would be the curve connecting points A', B', and C' in the lower panel. This curve is the demand curve for good x.

While individual demand curves are important to economists, they are not of much concern to firms. When considering how much to produce and what price to charge, firms rarely worry about the demand curve for a single individual. Instead, they consider the effects of price changes on all individuals at the same time. They are interested in the **market demand curve,** which is the horizontal sum of all the individual demand curves. The market demand curve measures the total quantity demanded for a particular good at a specified price. Market demand curves can be derived from individual demand curves by adding the individual demand curves horizontally. In Figure 3-10 there are three individuals in the market. When the price is $10, individual 1 consumes 5 units, individual 2 consumes 8 units, and individual 3 consumes 12 units. The total market demand at $10 is $5 + 8 + 12 = 25$ units, as shown. When we horizontally sum the quantities demanded at each price, we have the complete market demand curve.

Shifts in Demand

In constructing the individual's demand curve, only the price of the good was allowed to change. Income and the prices of other goods were held constant. What happens if there is a change in one of these other variables? Let's begin with the case of an income change. We explored this problem in Section 3.3, and learned that how income changes affect consumption depends on whether the good is normal or inferior. If income increases and the good is normal, consumption of the good increases. This case is shown in the top panel of Figure 3-11, where the increase in income changes the consumption point from A to B. The effect on the demand curve is that at the same price the individual consumes more of the good. The original demand curve passed through point A', but the new demand curve passes through point B'. By repeating this analysis for a variety of different prices of good x, we could trace out a new demand curve that lies to the right of the old demand curve.

For a normal good, then, an increase in income causes the demand curve to shift to the right. Likewise, a decrease in income causes the demand curve

Figure 3-10   Constructing the Market Demand Curve

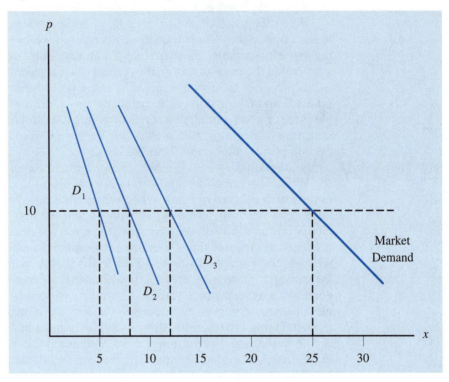

The market demand curve is found by adding individual demand curves horizontally. In this case there are three individuals with three different demand curves, labeled D_1, D_2, and D_3. Market demand shows the total quantity demanded by all three individuals at each price. To find the market demand when the price of the good is \$10, notice that the first individual consumes 5 units, the second individual consumes 8 units, and the third individual consumes 12 units. Together they consume 25 units, which is the market demand when the price is \$10. The market demand curve can be found by repeating this exercise at every price.

to shift to the left. The opposite occurs when the good is inferior. An increase in income causes demand to shift to the left, while a decrease in income causes demand to shift to the right.

Now consider the impact on the demand for good x of a change in the price of good y. If the price of y increases, the budget line rotates inward about the horizontal intercept, as in the top panel of Figure 3-12. The new consumption point is B, and, in this case, it corresponds to lower consumption of good x. In the lower panel, the new demand curve must pass through point B', which is to the left of A'. In other words, at the same price for good x, the increase in the price of y causes the individual to consume less x, so the demand for good x declines. We say that these two goods are **complements.** Two goods are complements when an increase in the price of one good causes a decrease in the demand for the other good. An example of

Figure 3-11   The Effect of a Change in Income on the Demand Curve

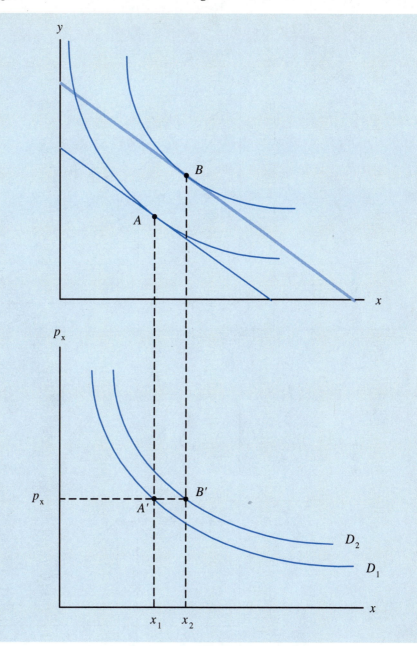

This figure shows how demand curves shift when there is a change in income. In the top panel there are two budget lines. The light blue budget line corresponds to higher income but the same prices as the dark blue budget line. When income increases the optimal consumption point shifts from A to B. The bottom panel shows how much the individual consumes at each price level. Since the price of good x does not change in this example, both points A' and B' must be on the same horizontal line. Because of the income increase, the individual consumes more of good x (x is normal). If x is normal at all price levels, the entire demand curve shifts to the right, from D_1 to D_2.

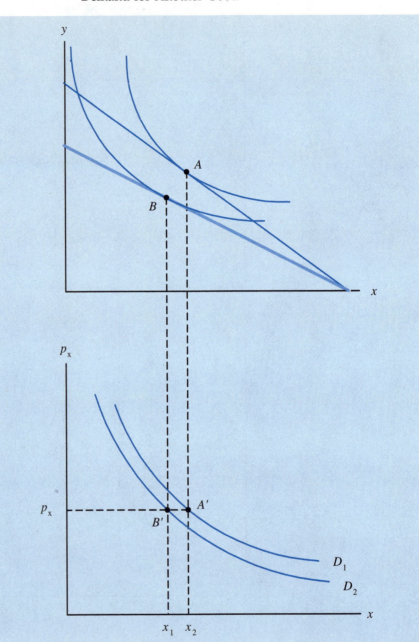

If the price of good y increases, the budget line rotates inward from the dark blue line to the
light blue line in the top panel. The optimal consumption points shifts from A to B. Because
the price of good x did not change but the optimal consumption of x did change (because of
the increase in the price of y), the demand curve shifts. In this case the demand curve shifts to
the left, so that the individual consumes less x at every price. If consumption of x falls when
the price of y rises, as shown, the goods are complements.

complements is hot dogs and hot dog buns. If hot dogs become more expensive, people typically buy fewer hot dogs, and they also buy fewer hot dog buns. Demand shifts to the left when the price of a complement rises, and demand shifts to the right when the price of a complement falls.

The opposite case is **substitutes.** Two goods are substitutes when an increase in the price of one good causes an increase in the demand for the other good. For example, if Coke becomes more expensive, many consumers will stop buying Coke and start buying Pepsi. Thus, demand shifts to the right when the price of a substitute rises and shifts to the left when the price of a substitute falls.

3.5   INCOME AND SUBSTITUTION EFFECTS

An increase in the price of a particular good has two effects on consumption. First, it increases the price of that good relative to the price of other goods, so it changes the rate at which consumers may exchange one good for another. Since consumers optimize by setting the marginal rate of substitution equal to the price ratio, this means that consumers will choose different bundles after the price change. The second effect of a price increase is that it rotates the budget line inward, so that consumers can no longer afford to buy as much as they did before. This, too, causes consumers to choose different bundles than they chose before the price increase. The analysis of the previous section combined these two effects. This section separates them.

Separating the Two Effects

When a price increases, how much of the resulting change in consumption is caused by the change in the price ratio, and how much of the change is caused by the change in the purchasing power of the consumer? We can answer this question through the following mental exercise: Suppose that when the price increases, the consumer is given enough extra income so that the price increase leaves him indifferent. This is shown in Figure 3-13. The original budget line is the thin line, and the initial consumption point is A, which is on indifference curve I_0. The price of x increases, and income increases enough to shift the budget line to the dashed budget line (ignore the thick budget line for now). The dashed budget line is tangent to the same indifference curve, I_0, and the point of tangency is C. Since the shift in the budget line left the individual indifferent, the individual can afford to make himself exactly as well off as before. When the price ratio changes but the individual remains indifferent, the change in consumption is known as the **substitution effect.** The substitution effect measures the change in consumption of a good when the price of that good changes but the individual is left indifferent. In Figure 3-13, the substitution effect for good x is $x_C - x_A$. The effect is to reduce the consumption of good x.

Figure 3-13   The Income and Substitution Effects of a Change in
Price of a Normal Good

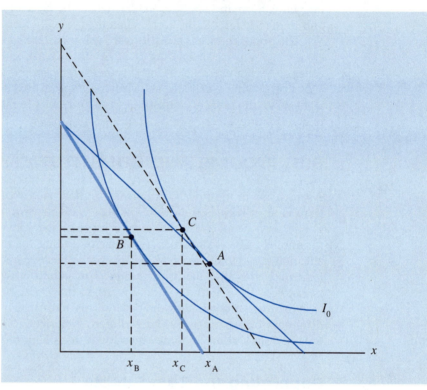

An increase in the price of x causes the budget line to rotate inward from the solid dark blue
line to the solid light blue line. The optimal consumption point changes from A to B. It is
possible, however, to separate this change into two parts: the part caused solely by the change
in relative prices and the part caused solely by the change in purchasing power.

Consider first the shift from the original budget line (the solid dark blue line) to the dashed
line. Since both lines are tangent to the same indifference curve, the individual is made neither
better nor worse off by the budget line shift. The dashed line is steeper, reflecting the fact that
the good x is now relatively more expensive. The consumption point moves from A to C, and
the individual buys less of good x. The amount $x_C - x_A$ is the substitution effect.

Now consider the shift from the dashed budget line to the solid light blue line. Both lines
have the same slope, so the price ratio remains the same. In the case shown, when the
consumption point moves from C to B, the individual consumes less of good x, so x is a normal
good. The amount $x_B - x_C$ is the income effect.

What happens if we now take away the extra income that made the consumer indifferent to the price ratio change? The budget line shifts inward
and parallel from the dashed line to the thick line. Consumption changes
from point C to point B, and this is the **income effect.** A price increase causes
a decrease in purchasing power, and the income effect measures the change
in consumption caused by the change in purchasing power with the price

ratio held constant. In Figure 3-13, the income effect for good x is $x_B - x_C$. The total effect on good x is $x_B - x_A$.

Figure 3-13 shows that the substitution effect is always in the direction opposite the price change. When the price of x rises, x becomes more expensive relative to y, and the consumer's substitution effect is to decrease consumption of x and increase consumption of y. This change is caused entirely by the shape of the indifference curve. The indifference curve exhibits a diminishing marginal rate of substitution, which means that when the slope of the budget line increases, it must be tangent to the indifference curve at a point to the left of the original point, as shown.

Figure 3-14   The Income and Substitution Effects of a Change in Price of an Inferior Good

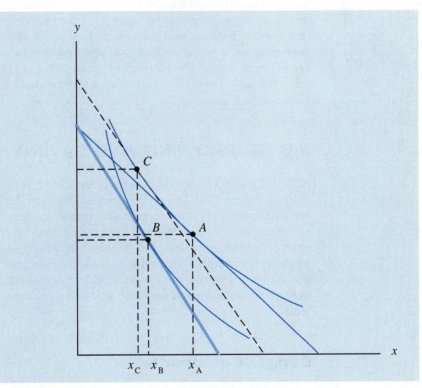

This figure is exactly the same as Figure 3-13, except for the direction of the income effect. The substitution effect is $x_C - x_A$, as before, and the income effect is $x_B - x_C$. The income effect involves the shift from the dashed budget line to the solid light blue line, which is like a decrease in income. The consumption point moves from C to B. This time, though x_B is larger than x_C, which means that the individual would consume more x when income falls. Thus, in this case x is an inferior good.

The direction of the income effect is determined by whether the good is normal or inferior. In Figure 3-13, x is a normal good, so the decline in income causes the consumer to purchase less x. When a good is normal and its price changes, the income and substitution effects both work in the direction opposite the price change.

Figure 3-14 shows another case. As before, the price of x rises, and to separate the income and substitution effects we draw an imaginary budget line tangent to the original indifference curve and parallel to the new budget line. The substitution effect works exactly as before. This time, however, the income effect works in the opposite direction. Point B is to the right of point C, which means that the consumer purchases more x when income falls. Consequently, x is an inferior good.

Figure 3-15 shows one more case. As with the last example, B is to the right of point C, so x is inferior. But B is also to the right of point A, which means that the consumer purchases more x when the price of x rises. This behavior is extremely counterintuitive, since one would expect people to buy less of something when it becomes more expensive. Indeed, the lower panel of Figure 3-15 shows that the demand curve for good x is upward sloping. Nevertheless, it is theoretically possible to find cases in which consumers buy more of a good when its price rises or less of a good when its price falls. In such a case the good is known as a **Giffen good,** named after the economist Robert Giffen.

3.6   BORROWING AND SAVING

In all the examples we have used so far, individuals have consumed their entire incomes. This behavior is not overly realistic, though, since people regularly borrow or save money. The reason for borrowing or saving is tied to the preferences discussed in Chapter 2. There we discussed the fact that most people are impatient, but they also tend to consume things evenly over time. To study *actual* borrowing and saving behavior, we need to use these preferences in conjunction with a budget constraint. We can then discuss borrowing and saving in the same way that we discuss other consumer problems.

Budget Constraints

To discuss preferences over time and issues in borrowing and saving, we need to simplify the real world quite a bit. First, let's assume that there are only two periods, which we will think of as years. The assumption of only two periods allows us to analyze the decision to borrow or save graphically. Second, let's assume that there is only one good, food, which spoils. Consequently, anything the individual wants to consume in a given year must

Figure 3-15   Deriving the Demand Curve for a Giffen Good

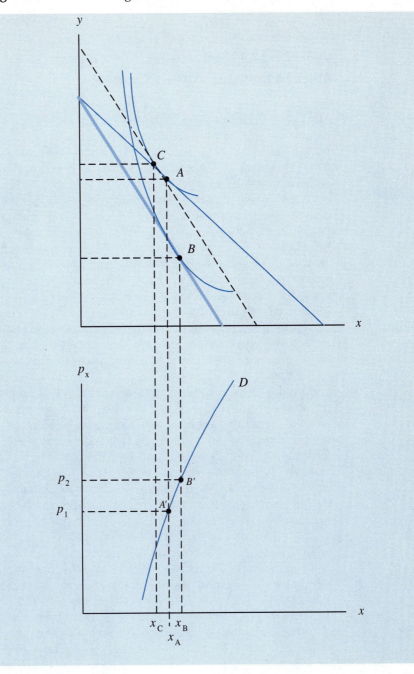

The top panel of this figure is similar to Figure 3.13. Since x_B is larger than x_C, good x is inferior. This time, though, the income effect, $x_B - x_C$, is larger in magnitude than the substitution effect, $x_C - x_A$, and the two effects are in opposite directions. The total effect is that when the price of x increases, consumption of x also increases. In such a case x is known as a *Giffen good*. The bottom panel constructs a demand curve for a Giffen good, and it is upward sloping.

APPLICATION
Cigarettes as Giffen Goods

The key to understanding Giffen goods is that they must be so inferior that the income effect outweighs the substitution effect. The most likely situation for a good to be that inferior is when income is very low, so that the consumer's choices are tightly constrained, and the good is necessary for the well-being of the consumer. One study used this intuition to detect a Giffen good in an experimental laboratory.* For experimental subjects they recruited seven nicotine-dependent cigarette smokers who smoked at least a pack a day. The subjects were instructed not to smoke for five or six hours before each experimental session, and the experimenters had equipment that enabled them to check whether or not the subjects had complied. This guaranteed that the subjects were nicotine deprived at the beginning of each session. Each experimental session lasted three hours, and during that time the subjects could buy puffs of cigarettes.

To find evidence of a Giffen good, the experimenters first had to find an inferior good. They did this by presenting the subjects with a list of different brands of cigarettes and asking them to rank the brands according to preference. The experimenters then used the subjects' most- and least-preferred brands to conduct the experiment. The less-preferred brand was hoped to be sufficiently inferior to cause it to be a Giffen good. The subjects were given an amount of money to spend (income), and were allowed to use this money to buy puffs of the two types of cigarettes. Initially, the preferred brand cost 25 cents a puff and the other brand cost 5 cents a puff. Then the price of the least-preferred brand was changed to see whether it was a Giffen good. Two of the seven subjects exhibited Giffen behavior; that is, they increased consumption of the least-preferred brand when its price increased.

Let's look at one particular subject's behavior in two sessions. In one session, income was $6.00, and the subject consumed 20 puffs of each brand. The budget line is shown in Figure 3-16, and the consumption point is shown as point A. In a second session, the price of the least-preferred brand was increased to 12.5 cents. The subject then consumed 24 puffs of the least-preferred brand and only 12 puffs of the most-preferred brand. Figure 3-16 also shows this new budget line, and the new consumption point is shown as point B. Since consumption of the least-preferred brand rose when its price increased, the least-preferred brand was a Giffen good.

* Richard J. DeGrandpre, Warren K. Bickel, S. Abu Turab Rizvi, and John R. Hughes, "Effects of Income on Drug Choice in Humans," *Journal of the Experimental Analysis of Behavior*, May 1993, pp. 483–500.

How can we rationalize this behavior? When the price of the least-preferred brand was low, the subject split consumption between the two brands so that he got 40 puffs during the three-hour session. This is close to the number needed to keep from experiencing withdrawal during the experiment. When the price rose, the subject would have had to change his consumption to maintain the same number of puffs. He could get 40 total puffs by cutting consumption of the most-preferred brand to 8 puffs and increasing consumption of the least-preferred brand to 32 puffs. As it was, the subject settled for only 36 total puffs. Even so, he still had to increase con-

Figure 3-16   A Giffen Good Experiment

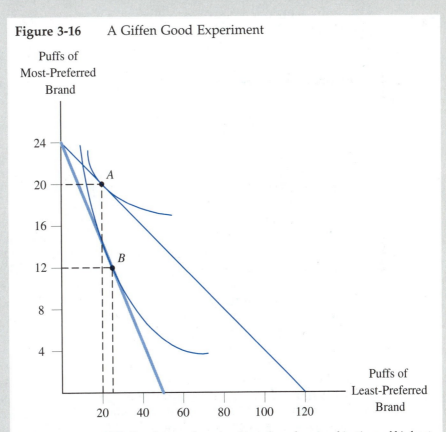

In the experiment of DeGrandpre et al., each subject chose from combinations of his least-preferred brand of cigarettes and his most-preferred brand. One subject's initial budget constraint is shown by the dark blue budget line. He chose point *A*, where he purchases 20 puffs on each type of cigarette. In another session he faced the light blue budget line and chose point *B*, purchasing 24 puffs of the least-preferred brand and 12 puffs of the most-preferred brand. Since consumption of the least-preferred brand rose when its price rose, the least-preferred brand was a Giffen good.

sumption of the least-preferred brand to get this many puffs. Even though the least-preferred brand was inferior, it was still necessary to consume it to avoid nicotine withdrawal, so the subject was forced to consume it. When the price of the least-preferred brand was lower, he could afford to smoke less of it.

The name "Giffen good" is a bit of a misnomer; a better name might be "Giffen behavior." The reason that the subject smokes the least-preferred cigarette at all is because income is so low. When income is higher he buys only the most-preferred brand, so the Giffen behavior disappears. Essentially, when income is higher the good is no longer necessary. Giffen goods are not commonly observed because it is unusual for income to be so constrained that one particular good becomes that necessary for survival. So far, the only observed Giffen behavior has come from laboratories.

be purchased that year. Third, let's consider a particular individual, Mary, who earns $35,000 this year and will earn $40,000 next year. Finally, we need an interest rate, which we will say is 10 percent.

To graph the budget constraint, measure this year's food consumption (in thousands of dollars worth of food) on the horizontal axis and next year's food consumption on the vertical axis, as in Figure 3-17. One point on the budget constraint is point E, at which Mary consumes $35,000 worth of food this year and $40,000 of food next year. In other words, she spends all her money on food in the year she receives the money. We call this point the **endowment,** or starting point. At the endowment point, Mary spends all her income in the period in which it is earned.

To find another point on the budget constraint, consider what happens if Mary consumes everything next year and nothing this year. Since she buys nothing this year, she saves her $35,000 income, and invests it at 10 percent interest. After a year, her investment has grown by 10 percent, which gives her a total of $38,500. Adding this amount to the $40,000 income next year, she can purchase $78,500 worth of food next year. This point is shown as point A in the figure, and it is a saving point.

What if she purchases all the food she can this year and purchases nothing next year? Since she will receive $40,000 next year and has no plans to spend it, she can get a loan from a bank. She pays back the loan with next year's income. How much can she borrow? She can repay $40,000, so she can borrow the amount that requires a $40,000 repayment. If she borrows x and pays 10 percent interest, at the end of the year she must repay the **prin-**

Figure 3-17   Budget Sets for Consumption Over Time

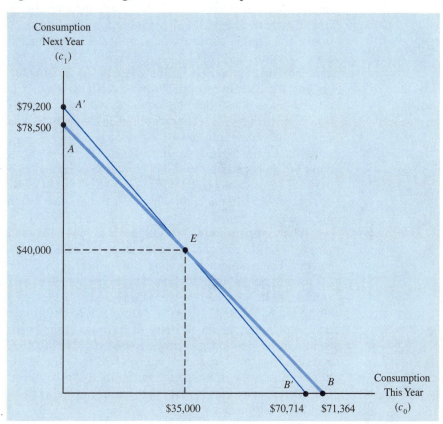

Mary earns $35,000 this year and $40,000 next year. The horizontal axis measures consumption this year, and the vertical axis measures consumption next year. If she neither borrows nor saves any money, she can consume $35,000 this year and $40,000 next year, as shown by point E, the endowment point. If she saves all her money at 10 percent interest, she will have a total of $78,500 to spend next year, and the resulting consumption point is point A. If, instead, she borrows as much as she can at 10 percent interest, she can spend a total of $71,364 this year, which is consumption point B. When the interest rate is 10 percent, her budget line is given by the line connecting points A, E, and B. If the interest rate rises, the budget line rotates about the endowment point E and becomes steeper. The budget line through points A', E, and B' corresponds to an interest rate of 12 percent.

cipal, or the amount she originally borrowed, x, plus the interest, which is 0.1 times x. In equation form this becomes

$$x + 0.1x = 40,000$$

or

$$x = 36,364.$$

She can borrow $36,364 dollars against next year's income of $40,000. Combining what she borrows with this year's income, she can spend $71,364 on food this year. This is shown as point B in the figure, and it is a borrowing point. The budget constraint is simply the line connecting points A, B, and E in Figure 3-17.

The slope of the budget line is -1.10. As is usual for the slope of a budget line, it measures an opportunity cost. In this case, it measures the amount of next year's consumption forgone to get one more dollar of consumption this year. If this year's consumption increases by one unit, Mary loses the interest that $1 would have earned, so she loses i in interest, where i denotes the interest rate. Since the interest rate is 10 percent, she loses 10 cents. Next year's consumption would have been higher by $1 plus the forgone interest, for a total of $1.10. The opportunity cost of this year's consumption, then, is $1.10 per unit, which is $1 + i$. In general, the slope of the budget line is $-(1 + i)$.

What happens to the budget line if the interest rate increases, say, to 12 percent from 10 percent? Since the slope is $-(1 + i)$, the budget line becomes steeper. The endowment point E stays where it was, since if Mary is neither borrowing nor saving, the interest rate has no effect on how much she consumes. If she saves all of her first-period income, her second-period consumption is $35,000(1.12) + $40,000 = $79,200. Consequently, the new vertical intercept A' is above point A. If, instead, she borrows as much as she can in the first period, she can spend $35,000 + $40,000/(1.12) = $70,714. As a result, the new horizontal intercept B' is to the left of point B. The new budget line is the line connecting points A', B', and E in Figure 3-17. When the interest rate rises, the budget line rotates about the endowment point and becomes steeper.

Optimal Borrowing and Saving

Let's return to the case of Mary, who receives $35,000 this year and $40,000 next year and faces a 10 percent interest rate. Figure 3-18 shows her budget line and an indifference curve. As usual, the point where an indifference curve is tangent to the budget line is the optimal point, and it is labeled A in the figure. The endowment point is labeled E. As drawn, point A is to the right of point E, which means that Mary consumes more than her income this year. Consequently, at point E Mary borrows money.

Also notice that point A is to the right of the 45-degree line. The 45-degree line is the set of points at which Mary consumes the same amount both years. At point A Mary consumes more this year than she does next year. When someone consumes more this year than next year, it tells us something about that person's discount factor. In Chapter 2 we saw that where an indifference curve crosses the 45-degree line, its slope is $-1/\delta$, where δ is the discount factor. Discount factors are between zero and one, with higher discount factors corresponding to more patient people and flatter indifference curves. Economists sometimes use another measure of people's impatience, the **discount rate,** which is denoted r.[1] The discount rate is related to the discount factor by the formula

$$\delta = \frac{1}{1 + r}.$$

The discount rate measures the percentage increase in utility needed to compensate an individual for putting off consumption for one period. A high discount rate corresponds to a low discount factor, and vice versa. The reason for using a discount rate instead of a discount factor is that the discount rate is of similar magnitude to the interest rate, and economists are used to interpreting interest rates. The discount rate is also related to the slope of the indifference curve at the 45-degree line: the slope of the indifference curve is $-(1 + r)$. To see why, remember that the slope of the indifference curve is $-1/\delta = -1/(1/(1 + r)) = -(1 + r)$.

In Figure 3-18, at the point where the indifference curve crosses the 45-degree line, the indifference curve is steeper than the budget line. The slope of the budget line is $-(1 + i)$, and the slope of the indifference curve is $-(1 + r)$. Since the indifference curve is steeper than the budget line, $r > i$. In other words, when a person consumes more this year than next year, that person's discount rate is higher than the interest rate. There is also some intuition behind this result. The discount rate is related to how much consumption next year the individual is willing to give up to increase this year's consumption by one unit. The interest rate is related to how much consumption next year the individual *must* give up to increase this year's consumption by one unit. If the discount rate is higher than the interest rate, the individual is willing to give up more consumption next year than she has to in order to increase this year's consumption by one unit. Consequently, when the discount rate is higher than the interest rate, people tend to consume more now than later. As we saw in Chapter 2, an average discount factor in the United States is about 0.89, which translates into a discount rate of 12 percent. Recent interest rates have been well below 10 percent. Because of this, people in the United States tend to consume more now than they plan to consume in the future.

Even if current consumption is higher than planned future consumption, it does not necessarily mean that people are borrowing money. Many people save money, usually for things like college or retirement. How can our model explain this? Let's consider the case of retirement planning. Suppose that Mary works this year, earning $60,000, and retires next year, earning nothing. Her budget line is shown in Figure 3-19, and the endowment

---

1 To help you remember which is the discount rate and which is the discount factor, we offer the following mnemonic: r is the first letter in rate, and δ is, well, Greek.

Figure 3-18   Consumer Optimization for Consumption Over Time

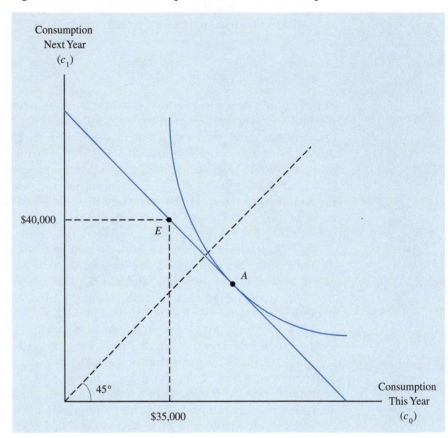

Mary earns $35,000 this year and $40,000 next year, as portrayed by the endowment point E. The 45-degree line shows the set of points at which she consumes the same amount in both years. Her indifference curve is tangent to the budget line at point A, which is to the right of the 45-degree line. This means that she consumes more this year than she does next year. Point A is also to the right of point E, which means that she borrows money to finance her extra consumption this year.

point is labeled E. Since all her income comes this year, point E is on the horizontal axis. Her consumption point is labeled A, and it is to the right of the 45-degree line. This time, though, A is to the left of E, so Mary saves money for retirement, spending less this year than she earns. Even though A is to the right of the 45-degree line, she is saving, not borrowing.

This discussion of borrowing and saving demonstrates how the tools of consumer theory—budget lines and indifference curves—can be used to determine individual borrowing and saving behavior. The three factors that determine whether a person borrows or saves are the discount rate, the interest rate, and the timing of income. When the discount rate is higher than

Figure 3-19   Consumer Optimization for Consumption Over Time

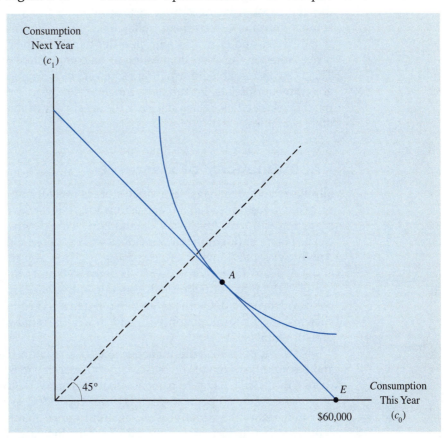

Mary earns \$60,000 this year and nothing next year, as portrayed by the endowment point E. Her optimal consumption point A is to the right of the 45-degree line, which means that she consumes more this year than she does next year. Point A is to the left of point E, which means that she saves money to finance next year's consumption.

the interest rate, people tend to consume more now rather than later. When the discount rate is lower than the interest rate, people tend to consume less now. When next year's income is higher than this year's income, people tend to borrow to consume more now. When next year's income is lower than this year's income, people tend to save so they can consume more later.

3.7 ELASTICITIES

Managers of firms and government policymakers all need to know about demand curves when making decisions. Managers of firms need to know the demand curve for their product to predict the effect of a change in price, and they also need to know how the demand curve shifts in order to predict the effect of changes in prices set by other firms and changes in consumers' income. Government policymakers need to know a variety of demand curves and how they shift in order to predict the effect of a change in taxes, either on the good in question or on complement or substitute goods. This is a considerable information requirement to impose on managers and government officials. Fortunately, much of the information can be summarized by **elasticities,** which measure the sensitivity of demand to changes in other variables.

Price Elasticity of Demand

Suppose that the manager of a video store is considering reducing the rental price of videos from $1 to 80 cents and wants to know what impact this price reduction will have on sales. Demand curves are downward sloping, so he can be fairly confident that more videos will be rented. But how many more? Another way of asking the same question is, "How sensitive to price changes is the demand for movie videos?" If demand is not very sensitive to price changes, the price reduction will generate only a small increase in the number of videos rented. On the other hand, if demand is quite sensitive to price changes, the price reduction will lead to a substantial increase in the volume of rentals.

Now suppose that the manager goes ahead with the price reduction, and the volume of rentals increases from 400 per day to 500 per day. In other words, the price falls by 20 percent—that is, from $1.00 to 80 cents, and volume increases by 25 percent—that is, from 400 to 500. We can use these figures to measure the sensitivity of demand to price changes. When a 20 percent decrease in price leads to a 25 percent increase in volume, we can calculate the effect of a 1 percent increase in price: Divide the percentage increase in quantity demanded by the percentage decrease in price. The percentage increase in quantity demanded is 25 percent, and the percentage decrease in price is 20 percent. Dividing one by the other gives us 1.25, and this is the **price elasticity of demand** for movie rentals.

The formula for a price elasticity of demand is

$$
\textbf{(3.1)} \qquad e_p = -\frac{\%\Delta q}{\%\Delta p} = -\frac{\dfrac{q_2 - q_1}{q_1}}{\dfrac{p_2 - p_1}{p_1}} = -\frac{q_2 - q_1}{p_2 - p_1} \cdot \frac{p_1}{q_1}
$$

First, the notation e_p denotes the elasticity of demand with respect to p, which is the price of the good. The second expression is simply the definition of price elasticity of demand, which is the negative of the percentage change in quantity demanded divided by the percentage change in price. The third expression shows how to calculate the elasticity using the percentage change in quantity demanded divided by the percentage change in price. In our example, the change in quantity is 100 movies and the original quantity is 400 movies, so the percentage change in quantity is (100 movies/400 movies) = 25 percent. Similarly, the percentage change in price is (−$0.20/$1.00) = −20 percent. The price elasticity of demand is −25/(−20) = 1.25. The last expression in equation (3.1) is an algebraic rearrangement of the third term that simplifies calculations.

The price elasticity of demand is useful to the store manager because it allows him to predict the effects of a wide variety of price changes. Instead of reducing the price by 20 cents, what if he reduces the price by 10 cents? This is a 10 percent price reduction. If the price elasticity of demand is 1.25, quantity demanded rises by (1.25)(10 percent) = 12.5 percent.

Price elasticities of demand have a graphical interpretation. Return to the last expression on the right in equation (3.1). The first term in the expression is the inverse of the slope of the demand curve. Recall that demand curves are graphed with price on the vertical axis and quantity on the horizontal axis. The slope of the demand curve is the change in the vertical axis variable, price, divided by the change in the horizontal axis variable, quantity. The second term in the expression is the ratio of the initial price to the initial quantity. Figure 3-20 shows two demand curves, both passing through point A. The elasticity of curve D_{AB} at point A is

$$e_P^{AB} = -\frac{q_B - q_A}{p_B - p_A} \cdot \frac{p_A}{q_A} = -\frac{7 - 10}{7 - 6} \cdot \frac{6}{10} = 1.8$$

The elasticity of curve D_{AC} at point A is

$$e_P^{AC} = -\frac{q_C - q_A}{p_C - p_A} \cdot \frac{p_A}{q_A} = -\frac{8 - 10}{8 - 6} \cdot \frac{6}{10} = 0.6$$

Demand curve D_{AB} is more elastic at point A than demand curve D_{AC}, that is, curve D_{AB}'s elasticity is higher than D_{AC}'s. In general, when you compare two demand curves at the same point, the flatter one is more elastic than the steeper one. To see that this makes sense, remember that elasticities measure the sensitivity of the quantity demanded to changes in price. When a demand curve is flat, it means that a small increase in price causes a large decrease in quantity demanded, which suggests that demand is relatively sensitive to price changes.

This does not mean that elasticities are the same things as slopes, though. The reason we were able to compare elasticities using the slope is because the comparison was made at a common point. To see that elasticities and slopes are really different, look at Figure 3-21. The demand curve is a straight line, so its slope is constant throughout. For the line drawn in the figure, the

Figure 3-20   Demand Curves and Price Elasticities of Demand

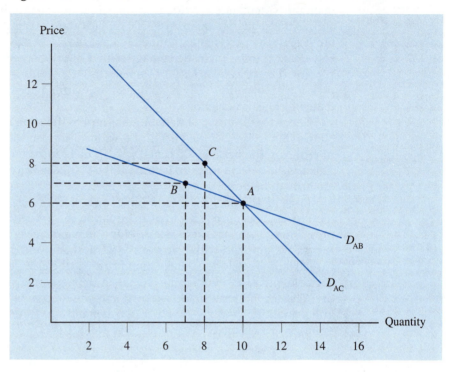

Two demand curves cross at point A. The demand curve connecting points A and B has a price elasticity at point A of 1.8, as calculated in the text. The demand curve connecting points A and C has a price elasticity at point A of 0.6. The demand curve D_{AB} is more elastic than the demand curve D_{AC} at point A.

slope is -5. The elasticity at a point is then $-(-1/5) \cdot (p/q)$, which clearly depends on the point being chosen. The elasticities at several points along the demand curve can be found in Table 3-1.

There are terms for elasticities of different magnitudes. When the elasticity is greater than 1, demand for the good is said to be **elastic** at that point. When demand is elastic at a point, quantity demanded is quite sensitive to price changes. When the elasticity is between 0 and 1, demand is said to be **inelastic** at that point, in which case quantity demanded is not very sensitive to price changes. When the elasticity is exactly equal to 1, demand is said to be **unit elastic.** In this case an increase in the price leads to exactly the same percentage change in quantity demanded. Figure 3-21 also shows two extreme cases. When the elasticity is ∞, demand is said to be **perfectly elastic.** Finally, when the elasticity is 0, demand is said to be **perfectly inelastic,** and quantity demanded is completely insensitive to changes in price. Price changes do not cause any change in quantity demanded.

Figure 3-21   Price Elasticities of Demand for a Linear Demand Curve

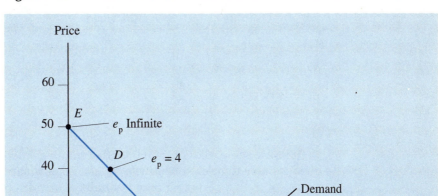

A linear demand curve has a different price elasticity at each point. The elasticities are shown in Table 3-1. At points above C demand is elastic, and at points below C demand is inelastic. This shows that the price elasticity does not just depend on the slope, but it also depends on the level of price and quantity demanded.

How elastic the demand for a good is depends on how many substitutes there are for the good. For example, the price elasticity for Pepsi is 2.08, so demand for Pepsi is elastic.[2] If the price of Pepsi increases, people can cut their consumption of Pepsi by switching to a different cola, such as Coke. Milk, on the other hand, is inelastic: There are not as many close substitutes for milk. If milk prices rise, it is possible to substitute other beverages for milk for drinking purposes, but not for cooking or for pouring on breakfast cereal. If all beverages are lumped together as a single good, the demand for beverages is even more inelastic than the demand for milk. There are simply no good substitutes for beverages.

---

2 See F. Gasmi, J.J. Laffont, and Q. Vuong, "Econometric Analysis of Collusive Behavior in a
   Soft-Drink Market," *Journal of Economics and Management Strategy*, Summer 1992, pp. 277–311.

Table 3.1   Price Elasticity of Demand Example

Point	Quantity	Price	Elasticity
A	10	0	0
B	8	10	.25
C	5	25	1
D	2	40	4
E	0	50	∞

There are some rules of thumb for determining whether the demand for a good is likely to be elastic or inelastic. If a good is narrowly defined, such as Pepsi, or even a particular brand of milk, demand is probably fairly elastic. If a good is more broadly defined, such as soft drinks, demand is less elastic. If a good is very broadly defined, such as beverages, demand is probably fairly inelastic. If there are substitutes available, demand is probably elastic, but if there are no substitutes available, demand is probably inelastic. One issue in the availability of substitutes is time. When gasoline prices skyrocketed in the mid-1970s, people were unable to cut their gasoline consumption by much at the time of the price increase. They could carpool, skip driving vacations, or take other measures to cut down on the amount of gasoline consumed, but there was not much immediate decrease in consumption. Over time, however, the demand for gasoline fell more sharply as automobile makers began building smaller, more fuel-efficient cars. As people bought fuel-efficient cars, the quantity of gasoline demanded declined. The short-run demand for gasoline was inelastic, but the long-run demand was much more elastic.

Income Elasticity of Demand

For managers to be able to predict demand, they must also know how demand changes in response to income changes. If incomes are rising, the manager must know how this trend affects sales. The sensitivity of demand to income changes is measured by the **income elasticity of demand.** It is calculated in much the same way as a price elasticity:

$$e_I = \frac{\%\Delta q}{\%\Delta I} = \frac{\Delta q/q}{\Delta I/I} = \frac{q_2 - q_1}{I_2 - I_1} \cdot \frac{I_1}{q_1}.$$

The income elasticity of demand is the percentage change in quantity demanded divided by the percentage change in income.

In an earlier section we categorized goods as either normal or inferior. **Normal goods** are goods for which consumption increases when income increases, and **inferior goods** are ones for which consumption decreases when income increases. For a normal good, the change in quantity is always in the same direction as the change in income, so the income elasticity is positive—that is, $e_I > 0$. For an inferior good, quantity moves in the direction opposite the income change, so $\Delta q / \Delta I < 0$. Thus, the income elasticity of an inferior good is negative.

Cross-Price Elasticities of Demand

The last type of elasticity to be considered in this chapter is the **cross-price elasticity of demand.** It measures the sensitivity of the quantity demanded of one good to changes in the price of another good. Its mathematical formula is

(3.6)
$$e_{x,y} = \frac{\% \Delta q_x}{\% \Delta p_y} = \frac{\Delta q_x / q_x}{\Delta p_y / p_y} = \frac{q_{x_2} - q_{x_1}}{p_{y_2} - p_{y_1}} \cdot \frac{p_{v_1}}{q_{x_1}}.$$

In this case, it measures the sensitivity of the demand for good x to a change in the price of good y.

Cross-price elasticities can be used to tell whether two goods are substitutes or complements. If they are substitutes, the quantity demanded of one good increases when the price of the other good rises, making the cross-price elasticity positive. If they are complements, the quantity demanded of one good rises when the price of the other good falls, making the cross-price elasticity negative.

The different elasticities are summarized in Table 3-2.

Table 3-2   Elasticities of Demand Summary

Elasticity	Range	Terminology
Price elasticity	$e_p = 0$	perfectly inelastic
	$0 < e_p < 1$	inelastic
	$e_p = 1$	unit elastic
	$1 < e_p < \infty$	elastic
	$e_p = \infty$	perfectly elastic
Income elasticity	$e_I > 0$	normal
	$e_I < 0$	inferior
Cross-price elasticity	$e_{x,y} > 0$	substitutes
	$e_{x,y} < 0$	complements

3.8 REVEALED PREFERENCE

In this chapter we have learned how people make choices. These choices depend on both the opportunities available to them and their preferences. Unfortunately, we can only observe the opportunities available to people, not

APPLICATION
Elasticities of Some Common Items

Economists have estimated demand elasticities for a variety of items, and we can use these estimates to determine whether our intuition about elasticities is sound. First consider two broad classes of goods, food and clothing. Their elasticities are reported in Table 3-3.*

Table 3-3   Food and Clothing Elasticities of Demand

	Food	Clothing
Price elasticity	0.56	0.62
Cross-price elasticity	−0.28	−0.20
Income elasticity	0.61	0.92

Both food and clothing have inelastic demands, which is not surprising. Since both categories are so broadly defined, neither good has a close substitute. The cross-price elasticity in the food column indicates that when the price of clothing rises by 1 percent, quantity demanded for food falls by 0.28 percent. This means that food and clothing are complements, but the elasticity is small enough to suggest that the two demands are not very closely related. Finally, both goods are normal, since their income elasticities are positive. The income elasticity for clothing is higher than the income elasticity for food, which means that clothing purchases are more sensitive to income changes than are food purchases. When incomes rise, people do not need to consume much more food, but they can buy more and better clothing.

*These estimates are from Richard Blundell, Panos Pashardes, and Guglielmo Weber, "What Do We Learn About Consumer Demand Patterns from Micro Data?" *American Economic Review*, June 1993, pp. 570–597.

their preferences. For example, we can observe an individual's income and the prices of the goods, but without knowing the individual's preferences, it is impossible to know what the optimal choice should be. This raises an important question. If we cannot observe preferences, how do we know whether people are acting the way we think they are?

Testing Consumer Theory for a Single Person

The theory of consumer behavior that we have developed is based on one simple yet crucial assumption: Consumers always choose the available con-

APPLICATION
Elasticities of Demand for Coke and Pepsi

Food and clothing are two broadly defined goods. Compare these elasticities to the corresponding elasticities for two narrowly defined goods, Coke and Pepsi. The elasticities for Coke and Pepsi are reported in Table 3-4.*

Table 3-4   Coke and Pepsi: Elasticities of Demand

	Coke	*Pepsi*
Price elasticity	1.71	2.08
Cross-price elasticity	0.61	0.80
Income elasticity	0.68	1.70

Some of these estimates are surprising, and some are not. First, demand for both goods is elastic, which makes sense because both goods have close substitutes. In fact, they are substitutes for each other, as suggested by the cross-price elasticities. The cross-price elasticities show that demand for Pepsi is more responsive to changes in the price of Coke than the demand for Coke is to changes in the price of Pepsi. This suggests that an unmatched increase in the price of Pepsi causes a larger number of Pepsi drinkers to switch to Coke than the same unmatched increase in the price of Coke would cause Coke drinkers to switch to Pepsi. On the other hand, it also suggests that an unmatched decrease in the price of Pepsi attracts more Coke drinkers to Pepsi than the same unmatched decrease in the price of Coke would attract Pepsi drinkers. So, the cross-price elasticities suggest that the price of Pepsi is a bigger determinant of the distribution of cola demand for the two colas than the price of Coke is. Finally, the income elasticities state that both of these soft drinks are normal goods. The surprising thing is that Pepsi's income elasticity is so much higher than Coke's. Pepsi consumption rises much more with income than Coke consumption, which suggests that Pepsi is the soft drink for wealthier people and Coke is the soft drink for less-wealthy people.

*These estimates can be found in F. Gasmi, J.J. Laffont, and Q. Vuong, "Econometric Analysis of Collusive Behavior in a Soft-Drink Market," *Journal of Economics and Management Strategy,* Summer 1992, pp. 277–311.

sumption bundle that makes them best off. In other words, they always consume on the highest indifference curve possible. Suppose that a consumer faces the thin budget line in Figure 3-22. The consumer can afford any point on or below that line. Let's say that we observe the consumer choosing point *A*. If the consumer behaves optimally, the choice of point *A* implies that *A* is (weakly) preferred to *B*, since the consumer is able to afford point *B* but chooses point *A* instead. Bundle *A* must also be preferred to every other

Figure 3-22   Budget Lines and Revealed Preference

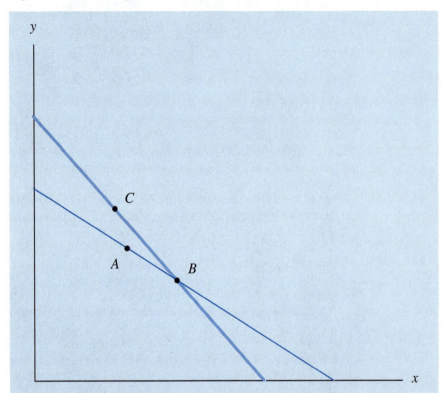

If an individual faces the dark blue budget line and chooses consumption point *A* instead of point *B*, we say that *A* is revealed preferred to *B*. If the budget line then shifts to the light blue line, it is rational for the individual to choose point *B*? The answer is no, because both *A* and *B* are in the budget set, and we have already determined that the individual would rather have *A* than *B*. Choosing point *C* is consistent with our model of consumer behavior, though, since with the dark blue budget line the individual could not afford *C*. This analysis gives us a method of testing our model of consumer behavior. If *A* is revealed preferred to *B* when the individual faces the dark blue budget line, and the individual chooses point *B* or a point to the right of point *B* when facing the light blue budget line, the individual's behavior is inconsistent with the theory. If, however, a point on the light blue budget line to the left of *B* is chosen, the behavior is not inconsistent with the theory.

point in the budget set. When one bundle is chosen over other available bundles, as *A* is chosen over *B* in Figure 3-22, we say that the chosen bundle is **revealed preferred** to the unchosen bundle. Information about preferences is revealed by the person's choice.

This suggests a test to tell whether or not an individual is behaving consistently with consumer theory. What if the budget line shifts to the thick budget line, which still contains point *B*? Point *A* is below the thick budget line. What can we say about the choice of a rational consumer faced with the new budget line? First, we expect that he will not choose point *B*, since we have already said that *A* is revealed preferred to *B*, and *A* is still a feasible alternative. The consumer can still afford *A* and, furthermore, can afford to do strictly better than *A*. Also, the consumer should not choose any point on the new budget line between *B* and the horizontal axis, since *A* is revealed preferred to all of these points as well. The only rational choices are points on the new budget line between *B* and the vertical axis, such as *C*. This, then, provides us with a way of testing the rationality of consumers. If two bundles, *A* and *B*, are affordable and *A* is chosen, then whenever prices and income change so that both *A* and *B* are affordable, *B* should not be chosen.

Interpersonal Comparisons

Revealed preference theory can also be used to make comparisons between people. Suppose that there are two people with identical preferences. Person 1 can afford both bundle *A* and bundle *B* and chooses bundle *A*. Person 2 can afford bundle *B* but not bundle *A*. Is person 1 better off than person 2? The answer is yes. Since person 1 could afford either bundle and chose *A*, he must prefer *A* to *B*. Since both people have the same preferences, person 2 also prefers *A* to *B*. But person 2 cannot afford *A* and must consume *B*. Consequently, person 1 consumes on a higher indifference curve than person 2.

Now suppose that we observe something different. Both bundles are affordable for both people, but person 1 chooses *A* and person 2 chooses *B*. In this case we can tell that the two people have different preferences. Since person 1 chooses *A* when he can also afford *B*, by revealed preference theory he must prefer *A* to *B*. Since person 2 chooses *B* when she can also afford *A*, it must be the case that she prefers *B* to *A*. Thus, their preferences are different.

To summarize, revealed preference theory allows us to test three ideas from consumer theory. First, it provides a method of testing whether or not a single individual is maximizing utility. Second, it equips us with a method of telling whether one individual is better off than another individual who has the same preferences. Third, it generates a method of testing whether or not two individuals have the same preferences.

APPLICATION
The Standard of Living

It is possible to use revealed preference theory to compare the well-being of citizens of different countries. For example, suppose that citizens of the United States consume only goods x and y, and that citizens of Ethiopia consume the same two goods. Because of income differences, the average American can afford the average Ethiopian consumption bundle (at American prices), but the average Ethiopian cannot afford the average American con-

Figure 3-23   Standards of Living and Revealed Preference

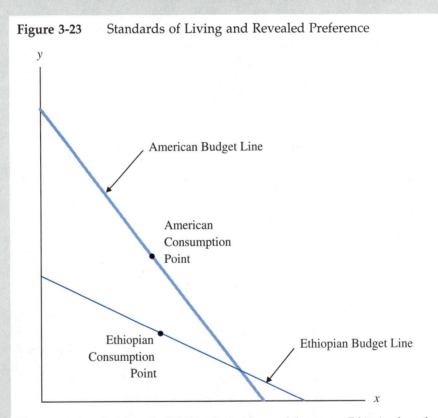

The average American faces the light blue budget line, and the average Ethiopian faces the dark blue budget line. The consumption bundles chosen by the average American and the average Ethiopian are shown. Since the Ethiopian consumption point is in the American budget set, the average American can afford the Ethiopian consumption bundle. However, since the American consumption point is not in the Ethiopian budget set, the average Ethiopian cannot afford the American consumption bundle. In this case we say that Americans have a higher standard of living than Ethiopians.

sumption bundle (at Ethiopian prices). This means that the average American consumption point is revealed preferred to the average Ethiopian consumption point, as shown in Figure 3-23. Since the average American can mimic the average Ethiopian if she wants to, but chooses to do better, we say that the average American is better off than the average Ethiopian. Put another way, the standard of living is higher in the United States than in Ethiopia. One study used this technique to rank standards of living in 60 countries, and the ranking of a subset of these countries can be found in Table 3-5.*

Table 3-5   Standards of Living in Different Countries

Countries Ranked by Standard of Living	Rank out of 60 Countries
Canada	1
United States	2
Germany	5
France	7
Japan	12
Poland	22
Korea	32
Nigeria	50
India	55
Ethiopia	60

*These data come from Steve Dowrick and John Quiggin, "International Comparisons of Living Standards and Tastes: A Revealed Preference Analysis," *American Economic Review*, March 1994, pp. 332–341.

Summary

- A **budget set** displays the set of affordable alternatives a consumer can purchase given his income and the prices of the goods. A **budget line** is the frontier of the budget set, and it displays the set of alternatives in which *all* of a consumer's income is spent.

- A consumer's optimization problem is to maximize utility subject to his budget constraint. At the optimum point, a consumer's indifference curve is *tangent* to his budget line. Thus, the consumer is on the indifference curve that is furthest from the origin, while still touching the budget line at a single point.

- At the point of tangency between the indifference curve and the budget line, the slope of the indifference curve (the marginal rate of substitution, *MRS*) is equal to the slope of the budget line (the ratio of prices). The *MRS* measures how many units of one good the consumer is *willing* to give up to get one more unit of another good while remaining on the same indifference curve. The ratio of prices measures how many units of one good the consumer *must* give up to purchase one more unit of the other good. When the *MRS* equals the ratio of prices, the consumer is at his point of optimization.

- If the demand for a good increases when a consumer's income increases, that good is said to be a **normal good.** Conversely, if the demand for a good decreases when a consumer's income increases, that good is said to be an **inferior good.**

- If an increase in the price of one good decreases the demand for another good, the goods are said to be **complements.** If an increase in the price of one good increases the demand for another good, the goods are said to be **substitutes.**

- The impact of a price change on consumption can be divided into two effects—the **substitution effect** and the **income effect.** The substitution effect measures the change in the consumption of a good when its price changes, holding constant the consumer's utility level. The income effect measures the change in consumption of a good when its price change affects the *real* income of the consumer, holding constant money income.

- A **price elasticity of demand** measures the percentage change in quantity demanded brought about by a percentage change in price. If demand is **elastic,** a 1 percent increase in price (for example) brings about a greater than 1 percent reduction in quantity demanded. If demand is **inelastic,** a 1 percent increase in price brings about a less than 1 percent decrease in quantity demanded.

- An **income elasticity of demand** measures the percentage change in quantity demanded brought about by a percentage change in income. If the income elasticity of demand is positive, the good is **normal,** since increases in income lead to increases in demand. If the income elasticity of demand is negative, the good is **inferior,** since increases in income lead to decreases in demand.

- A **cross-price elasticity of demand** measures the percentage change in the quantity demanded of one good brought about by a percentage change in the price of *another* good. If the cross-price elasticity of demand is positive, the two goods are **substitutes,** since an increase in the price of one good leads to an increase in the demand for the other good. If the cross-price elasticity of demand is negative, the two goods are **complements,** since an increase in the price of one good leads to a decrease in the demand for the other good.

Problems

1. The only two goods that give Bart utility are soap and calculators. When calculators cost $8 each and soap costs $2 per bar, his optimal consumption bundle is 8 bars of soap and 4 calculators. What is his income? Now the price of soap rises to $3 and the price of calculators falls to $6, so he can afford a combination of 10 soaps and 3 calculators if he so desires. Would it make any sense for him to consume this new combination? [*Hint:* Draw a graph.]

2. Abe's marginal utility of apples is 12 and his marginal utility of bananas is 5. If apples cost $2 each and bananas cost $1 each, is Abe consuming at an optimum? If not, which fruit should Abe consume more of?

3. If Frank spends all of his money on pizza, he can buy 12 pizzas, and if he spends all his money on movies, he can see 18 movies. His utility is maximized when he consumes 8 pizzas and sees 6 movies. What is his marginal rate of substitution at this point?

4. Seth and Michael are roommates, and they each have 20 hours a week that can be spent either cleaning their apartment or reading science fiction novels. Seth reads more than Michael. What can you say about their marginal rates of substitution?

5. Suppose that an individual has utility function $u(x,y) = 3x^3y^2$. The marginal rate of substitution at point (x,y) is given by $MRS(x,y) = 3y/2x$.
   a. If the price of x is 4, the price of y is 5, and income is 40, find the optimal bundle of x and y.
   b. Now suppose that income rises to 50. Find the new optimal bundle of x and y. Are the goods normal or inferior?
   c. Suppose that income returns to its original level, but that the price of y falls to 4. Find the new optimal bundle of x and y. Are the goods substitutes or complements?

6. The federal government allows people to deduct contributions to charity from their taxable income. Explain why this entices people to donate more to charity.

7. If the economy undergoes a general inflation, all prices and wages rise by the same percentage. Does a general inflation make consumers worse off? Why or why not?

8. Suppose that there are two individuals with identical preferences, except that one lives farther from town than the other. The one who lives far away has a round-trip travel cost of t_1 per trip, and the one who lives closer has a round-trip travel cost of t_2. The two individuals are deciding separately where to eat. Restaurant A charges price p_A, and restaurant B charges price p_B, with $p_A > p_B$. Both restaurants are in town.
   a. Find the total prices, including travel costs, of each restaurant for each individual.
   b. Find the relative total price of eating at restaurant A for each individual.

c. Suppose that the two individuals go to different restaurants. Which individual goes to restaurant A, the more expensive restaurant? Why?

d. Use a similar argument to explain why couples with small children go to more expensive restaurants when they leave the children at home than couples with no children do.

9. Suppose that an individual gets utility from two goods, x and y.

a. The government imposes an excise tax on good x—that is, a tax that is added to the purchase price of good x but not of good y. Show the consumer's budget lines before and after the tax.

b. Next the government imposes a sales tax that affects both goods. In a new graph, show the consumer's budget lines before and after the tax.

c. Typically, excise taxes are only imposed on goods whose consumption is considered harmful in some way. For example, excise taxes are imposed on alcohol and tobacco products. Why is it reasonable for the government to use excise taxes only on harmful products?

10. In Chapter 2 we defined the concepts of perfect complements and perfect substitutes. Suppose that there are two goods, x and y, with $p_y = 3$ and $I = 60$.

a. Find the demand curve for x if x and y are perfect complements.

b. Find the demand curve for x if x and y are perfect substitutes.

11. When a good has an income elasticity greater than one it is called a *luxury*, while if its income elasticity is less than one it is called a *necessity*. Explain why these terms make sense.

12. Figure 3-9 shows how to derive a demand curve by shifting the budget line when the price of good x changes. It is possible to use a similar technique to find a curve called the **Engel curve**. The Engel curve graph has consumption of x on the horizontal axis and income on the vertical axis, and the Engel curve shows how much x the individual consumes at different income levels, holding all prices constant.

a. Construct an Engel curve by drawing a two-panel diagram, as in Figure 3-9. Use three different levels of income to construct the Engel curve. Assume that x is normal.

b. Now construct an Engel curve when x is inferior.

13. Consider the borrowing–saving problem.

a. Banks generally charge higher interest rates to borrowers than they pay to savers. Show how this affects budget sets. Does this encourage or discourage saving? Why?

b. The government taxes interest income from savings but lets people deduct interest payments on loans. Show how this affects budget sets. Does this encourage or discourage saving? Why?

c. If the government wants to encourage people to save more, what sort of tax policy should it use?

14. When an individual has an income elasticity greater than one for a specific product, we call that product a **luxury** good. Explain why this name is appropriate.

15. The **revenue** a firm earns is equal to its total sales receipts. More formally, if it sells q units at price p per unit, its total revenue is pq.
    a. Suppose that a firm initially sells 2,000 units at $4 each. What is the firm's total revenue?
    b. Show that if the price elasticity of demand is 1.25 and the firm reduces its price by 10 percent, total revenue increases.
    c. Show that if the price elasticity of demand is .75 and the firm reduces its price by 10 percent, total revenue decreases.
16. Mr. Johnson works downtown and is looking for somewhere to live. He gets utility from housing h and other consumption m. For simplicity, assume that h measures the size of the house in square feet, and all Mr. Johnson cares about is how big his house is. The price of other consumption is $1 per unit. The price of housing depends on where the house is located. Specifically, it depends on how far the house is from downtown, so that the price of housing is $p_h(d)$, where d is the distance from downtown. Also, if Mr. Johnson lives away from downtown, he must pay a transportation cost to get to work. The transportation cost is td, where t is the per-mile cost and d is the distance from downtown in miles.

    Mr. Johnson's budget constraint is

    $$p_h(d)h + m = I - td.$$

    a. Draw a graph with house size on the horizontal axis and other consumption on the vertical axis. Draw a budget line corresponding to some fixed distance, say d_0, from downtown. Draw an indifference curve tangent to the budget line. Label the optimal point (h_0, m_0).
    b. Now draw a budget line corresponding to distance $d_1 - d_0$, assuming no change in the housing price.
    c. Suppose that $p_h(d_1)$ is set to just leave Mr. Johnson indifferent between living at distance d_1 and living at distance d_0. Is $p_h(d_1)$ greater than or less than $p_h(d_0)$? [*Hint:* Graph the new budget line.]
    d. Given that the housing price changes this way, find Mr. Johnson's new optimal consumption point, and label it (h_1, m_1). Is h_1 larger or smaller than h_0?

4

RISK

Overview

Up to this point, all of our analysis has been based on the premise that consumers know exactly what will happen when they make a choice. If they go to the grocery store and choose some bundle of goods, it is reasonable to assume that they know exactly what they are getting. But this is not always the case. Some people buy shares of corporate stock, and the future value of the stock is uncertain. How do people choose what combination of stocks to buy? Many personal finance experts suggest that small investors purchase a variety of different assets—large stocks, small stocks, foreign stocks, bonds, and so on. Why would people want to hold a diversified portfolio of assets? The answer depends on people's preferences when the outcomes of choices are uncertain.

We use the term **risky** to describe any situation in which the outcome of a choice is uncertain. Risk arises in a number of situations. Driving is risky because of the possibility of an accident. Waiting until the last minute to register for classes is risky because the classes may be full by then. Buying a lottery ticket is risky because you may or may not win money. This last example shows that there need not be a possibility of a loss for a situation to be risky. Once you own a lottery ticket, either you win nothing or you win something (the money spent on the lottery ticket is already gone). Since you do not know exactly what will happen with the ticket, you face some risk.

In this chapter we will look in depth at two situations in which risk arises—insurance and investing. People can avoid financial loss by purchasing insurance against losses. For example, they can buy homeowners insurance to pay for any losses caused by theft or fire. They can buy health insurance to pay medical bills if they become sick or injured. In this chapter we analyze the insurance decision formally. Should people buy insurance or not? If they do buy insurance, what policy should they buy? The other situation, investment, also entails risk. The stock market is risky because stock prices fluctuate fairly randomly. The prices of some types of stocks, such as those of new companies, fluctuate more than other types. There are also the alternatives of keeping money in a savings account or buying a certificate of deposit, both of which are less risky than the stock market. In this chapter we look at what portfolios, or combinations, of investments people purchase.

The main topics in this chapter are:

- How to represent preferences in risky situations.
- How to find the optimal insurance policy.
- How to find the optimal investment portfolio.
- How to decide whether or not the model we use is a good one.

4.1 REPRESENTING PREFERENCES

How do people decide whether or not to buy insurance against a possible loss? How do they decide on an investment portfolio? These are just two examples of questions involving risky decisions, and there are many others. If you are considering traveling to Britain next month, you will need British currency when you get there. You can either purchase some British pounds now, at the current exchange rate, or you can purchase some next month, at whatever exchange rate prevails then. Compared to what would have happened had you bought pounds immediately, waiting might cause you to lose money if the dollar becomes weaker compared to the pound, or you might gain money if the dollar becomes stronger. This is another situation involving risk. Of course, situations involving risk could also be more mundane. For example, when you get ready to leave home in the morning you must decide what to wear. You must consider the likelihoods of cold weather, rain, and warm weather, since each dictates a different type of dress. If we want to analyze any of these risky decision problems, we must take a preliminary step: We must devise a way to represent preferences, as we did in Chapter 2.

Indifference Maps

Suppose that you are faced with the following choice: You can receive $100 for sure, or your winnings can be determined by the toss of a fair coin. If the coin lands heads you win $150, but if the coin lands tails you win only $50. The first alternative is *riskless,* since it has only one possible outcome, and the second alternative is *risky,* since it has more than one possible outcome. Many people, but not everyone, would choose the riskless alternative in this situation.

If we want to represent preferences using an indifference map, we must first decide how to graph the alternatives. We can do this using the idea of **states of nature.** A state of nature is a randomly determined event, such as which side of a coin lands face up. In the case of a coin toss there are two states of nature, or *states,* corresponding to the two sides of the coin. In the case of a roll of a die, there are six states corresponding to the six sides of the die. If states are determined by the weather, there are a large number of states corresponding to the different combinations of temperature, precipitation, wind speed and direction, humidity, and so on.

In the example we are using, there are two states of nature: The coin lands either heads or tails. For the risky alternative the payoffs are $150 in one state and $50 in the other state. For the riskless alternative the payoff is $100 in both states. We can represent these two alternatives graphically by measuring the payoff in one state on the horizontal axis and the payoff in the other state on the vertical axis. Such a graph depicts what is known as **state-payoff space,** since it shows the payoffs in the different states. In Figure 4-1, the payoff when the coin lands heads is measured on the horizontal axis, and the payoff when the coin lands tails is measured on the verti-

Figure 4-1   Indifference Curves in State-Payoff Space

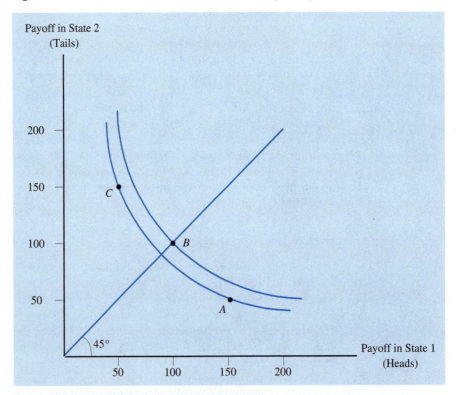

Risky choices can be depicted in state-payoff space. The horizontal axis measures the payoff in one state, and the vertical axis measures the payoff in the other state. Point *A*, then, pays $150 if the first state occurs and $50 if the second state occurs. The 45-degree line is the set of points that have the same payoff in both states, which means that they are riskless. The individual chooses the alternative on the highest attainable indifference curve, which is point *B*.

cal axis. The risky alternative is labeled point A, and the riskless alternative is labeled point B. The riskless alternative is on the 45-degree line, which is the set of points with the same payoff in both states. Points on the 45-degree line are riskless since the payoff does not depend on the state. The figure shows one other alternative, point C, in which the individual receives $50 if the coin lands heads and $150 if the coin lands tails.

We have already stated that many people prefer point B to point A. If the coin is truly fair, so that heads and tails are equally likely, people should also be indifferent between points A and C. If the coin is fair, the only difference between points A and C is whether the higher payoff occurs when the coin lands heads (point A) or tails (point B). If the coin is not fair, of course, people would prefer point A if heads are more likely and point C if tails are more likely. If A and C are indifferent, by transitivity B must be preferred to C. We now have enough information to ascertain the general shape of an indifference curve. Since A and C are indifferent, the curve passes through both points. This makes the indifference curve symmetric about the 45-degree line, which happens *only* when the states are equally likely, as with a fair coin toss. Since B is preferred to both these points, the indifference curve passes through A and C and to the southwest of B, so that B is on a higher indifference curve than A and C. These indifference curves have the same shape as the indifference curves studied in Chapters 2 and 3. In this case, though, the shape has a special interpretation, which we will discuss after we introduce a bit more terminology.

Expected Value

When the payoffs in risky alternatives are amounts of money, the alternatives are referred to as **prospects.** Every prospect has two components. The first is the set of possible outcomes. In the coin toss discussed in the previous example, there are two possible outcomes, $150 and $50. The second component is the set of probabilities that correspond to the possible payoffs. In our example the coin is fair, which means that each payoff occurs with probability 0.5.

One question we can ask about prospects is, "If we repeat the prospect over and over, what average payoff we should expect?" Half of the time, on average, the coin would land heads and the payoff would be $150. The other half of the time the coin would land tails and the payoff would be $50. Since the payoff is $150 half the time and $50 half the time, the average payoff is $100. We can arrive at the same amount by computing the **expected value** of the prospect, which is a mathematical measure of the average payoff from a prospect. Expected value is found in two steps. First, multiply each payoff by its probability, and then add each of these elements to get the expected value. The expected value of the coin toss is 0.5($150) + 0.5($50) = $100. Expected values can be calculated for more complicated prospects as well. Consider the situation in which you roll a fair die and receive $1 for each pip on the side facing up. Since the die is fair, the probability of any given side landing face up is 1/6, and the expected value of the prospect is

$$\$1/6 + \$2/6 + \$3/6 + \$4/6 + \$5/6 + \$6/6 = \$3.50.$$

Finally, expected value calculations do not require that all outcomes be equally likely. Suppose you flip a fair coin twice, and you receive $20 if it lands heads both times and $0 if not. The probability of heads landing twice is 0.25, and the expected value is 0.25($20) + 0.75($0) = $5.

To describe expected value more generally, some notation is needed. A prospect is represented by a sequence of pairs of numbers, with the first number in each pair representing the monetary payoff, and the second number representing the probability of that payoff. The coin toss, for example, can be represented by ($150,0.5; $50,0.5). The general representation when there are n possible payoffs takes the form $(x_1,p_1; x_2,p_2; \ldots; x_n,p_n)$. Expected value is calculated by multiplying the probability and payoff in each pair, and then adding up the n products. Thus, the expected value of the prospect $(x_1,p_1; x_2,p_2; \ldots; x_n,p_n)$ is

$$EV(x_1,p_1; x_2,p_2; \ldots; x_n,p_n) = p_1 x_1 + p_2 x_2 + \ldots + p_n x_n.$$

APPLICATION

The Expected Value of a Share of Corporate Stock

An investor is considering buying Office Depot stock on October 1. The current price of a share of stock that day is $30. A financial analyst advises her that on October 1 the following year there is a 20 percent chance that the stock will be worth $50, a 30 percent chance the stock will be worth $40, a 20 percent chance the stock will still be worth $30, a 25 percent chance the stock will be worth only $20, and a 5 percent chance the stock price will fall all the way to $10. What is the expected value of next year's stock price? The prospect can be written ($50,0.2; $40,0.3; $30,0.2; $25,0.25; $10,.05). The expected value of the future stock price is

$$EV = (0.2)(\$50) + (0.3)(\$40) + (0.3)(\$30) + (0.2)(\$25) + (.05)(\$10)$$
$$= \$10 + 12 + 9 + 5 + 0.5 = \$36.50.$$

The stock price is expected to rise by $6.50 during the next year.

For example: the expected value of the prospect ($100,0.3; $50,0.4; $10,0.3) is 0.3($100) + 0.4($50) + 0.3($10) = $53.

Risk Aversion

Let's return to our example in which the individual has a choice between the risky prospect ($150,0.5; $50,0.5) and the riskless prospect ($100,1). Note that these two prospects have the same expected value, $100, yet the individual in Figure 4-1 prefers the riskless prospect to the risky prospect. If the individual expects to earn the same amount from both prospects, why would he prefer one to the other? The answer is that one prospect is risky, while the other one is not, and the individual would rather avoid the risk. When an individual prefers a riskless prospect to a risky prospect with the same expected value, we say that the individual is **risk averse.**

Graphically, risk aversion arises when indifference curves in state-payoff space are bowed toward the origin. Figure 4-2 shows the same points A, B, and C as in Figure 4-1, and all three prospects have the same expected value, $100. The dashed line connecting them represents the set of all prospects with expected value equal to $100, and is known as an **iso-expected value line.**[1] The 45-degree line represents all the riskless prospects. If an individual is risk averse, he prefers the point on the 45-degree line to all the other points on the iso-expected value line. If indifference curves are bowed toward the origin, as shown, this preference pattern emerges.

The intuition behind risk aversion is that the individual would like to avoid risk and receive the expected value of the prospect instead. Risk arises when payoffs differ across states. A risk-averse person, then, when faced with different lotteries with the same expected value, would prefer to equalize his payoffs across states. This can be seen in Figure 4-2. The dashed line is an iso-expected value line, and four points are shown. Point B is riskless, and point D lies in between points A and B. At point D both payoffs are closer to the expected value than at point A, or, in other words, D's payoffs are "more nearly equal" than A's. Which point would a risk-averse individual prefer, D or A? The answer, as shown by the indifference map, is D.

Drawing an iso-expected value line was easy in Figure 4-2, because we already knew that points A, B, and C had the same expected value. To draw an iso-expected value line in general, suppose that the payoff in state 1 is w_1 and the payoff in state 2 is w_2. State 1 occurs with probability p, and state 2 occurs with probability $1 - p$, so that the probabilities sum to one, as they must. A prospect can be written $(w_1, p; w_2, 1 - p)$, and as has already been stated, the expected value of this prosect is $pw_1 + (1 - p)w_2$. An iso-expected

---

1 The prefix *iso* means same, and it is also used in the word *isosceles*, which refers to a triangle with two sides of equal length.

Figure 4-2   The Iso-Expected Value Line and Risk Aversion

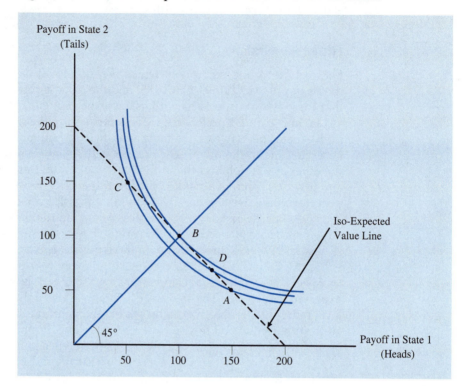

The iso-expected value line shows the set of points that have the same expected value, in this case $100. Points A, B, C, and D all have the same expected value. Point B is riskless, while the others are risky. The individual prefers the riskless alternative to risky alternatives with the same expected value, in which case we say that the individual is *risk averse*. Point D is less risky than point C, since D has the same expected value but lies closer to the 45-degree line, and the risk averse individual prefers the less risky alternative D to the riskier alternative A.

value line is a set of points in state-payoff space that all have the same expected value. To find an iso-expected value line, choose a level of expected value, such as y, and write down the equation for all of the prospects that have expected value y:

$$pw_1 + (1 - p)w_2 = y.$$

Rearranging this equation to isolate w_2 on the left-hand side, we get

$$w_2 = -\frac{p}{1 - p}\, w_1 + \frac{y}{1 - p}.$$

This is the equation of a line that can be graphed in state-payoff space, as in Figure 4-3. The slope of the iso-expected value line is $-p/(1 - p)$, or the

Figure 4-3   The Slope of the Iso-Expected Value Line

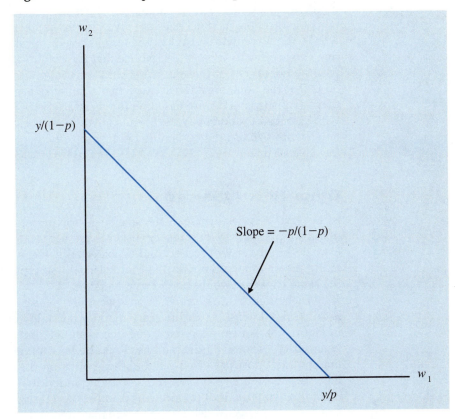

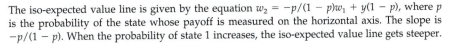

The iso-expected value line is given by the equation $w_2 = -p/(1 - p)w_1 + y(1 - p)$, where p is the probability of the state whose payoff is measured on the horizontal axis. The slope is $-p/(1 - p)$. When the probability of state 1 increases, the iso-expected value line gets steeper.

negative of the ratio of the probability of the horizontal axis state and the probability of the vertical axis state. When p increases, so that the first state becomes more likely, the iso-expected value line becomes steeper.

In our first example, the states were determined by the toss of a fair coin, so the probability of the first state was 0.5 and the probability of the second state was 0.5. The slope of the iso-expected value line was $-p/(1 - p) = -0.5/0.5 = -1$. For a different example, suppose that the probability of the first state is 0.75, and the probability of the second state is 0.25. The slope of the iso-expected value line is $-0.75/0.25 = -3$. This iso-expected value line is steeper than the one from our original example.

The ratio $p/(1 - p)$ has a name—the **odds ratio** for state 1 occurring. The odds ratio is the probability that state 1 occurs divided by the probability that state 1 does not occur. The higher the odds ratio, the more likely state 1 is. Odds are used often in gambling situations, such as at horse races. There, however, the odds ratio is read differently and calculated backwards.

For example, the favorite in a race (the horse judged most likely to win) might face 3:1 odds, read "three to one." If p is the probability that the horse wins the race, the *racetrack odds* are given by the ratio $(1 - p)$ to p. In other words, the horse with 3:1 odds wins the race with probability $p = 1/4$, so that $(1 - p):p = 3/4:1/4 = 3:1$. Notice that the racetrack odds are the odds that the horse *loses*, while the odds ratio we use would correspond to the odds that the horse *wins*. The reason that racetracks use racetrack odds are that payoffs from a bet are based on the racetrack odds: A \$2 bet on a horse with 3:1 racetrack odds pays \$6 (minus what the racetrack holds back) if the horse wins. We use the odds ratio because it is the negative of the slope of the iso-cost line.

Other Risk Attitudes

Not everyone is risk-averse. A risk-averse person prefers the expected value of a risky prospect to the prospect itself. Some people, though, are indifferent between the risky prospect and its expected value, and some people actually prefer to take the risk. We can discuss these types of preferences in the same way that we discussed risk aversion.

When an individual prefers a prospect to its expected value, the person is called **risk loving.** An indifference map for a risk-loving person is shown in Figure 4-4. An iso-expected value line is shown, but this time the point where it crosses the 45-degree line, B, is the least preferred point on that line, not the most preferred point. Other points on the iso-expected value line, such as A, are risky, and the risk-loving individual prefers A to B. For this to happen, the indifference curves must be concave, as shown. Unlike a risk-averse person, a risk-loving person likes unequal payoffs across states.

The final case is when an individual is indifferent between a prospect and its expected value. Such an individual is called **risk neutral,** since he does not care one way or the other about risk. Again consider points A and B in Figure 4-4. The two points are on the same iso-expected value line, so they have the same expected value. A risk-neutral individual is one who is indifferent between A and B and, in fact, is indifferent between any two prospects with the same expected value. Consequently, iso-expected value lines are indifference curves for a risk-neutral person.

4.2 EXPECTED UTILITY

In Chapter 2 we devised two useful methods of discussing preferences: indifference maps and utility functions. We have already represented risk preferences using indifference maps, and we now turn our attention to utility functions. In the case of risks, however, finding a utility function is complicated by the fact that we cannot just focus on payoffs, but we must also account for the probabilities of the different outcomes. The utility function

Figure 4-4   Risk Indifference Curves

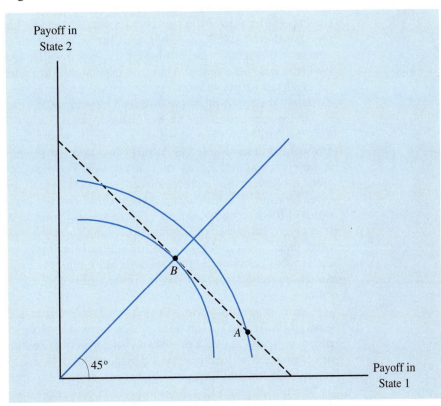

Points *A* and *B* have the same expected value, and point *A* is risky while point *B* is not. The individual with the indifference curves shown prefers point *A* to point *B*. Such an individual is called *risk loving*.

used in this section takes a very special form, which also turns out to have some intuitive appeal.

The Expected Utility Representation

As defined in Chapter 2, a utility function is a function that *represents* preferences, that is, a function that assigns a higher value to the preferred alternative in any pair. When the topic is behavior toward risk, people choose among prospects of the form $(x_1, p_1; \ldots; x_n, p_n)$. The focus of this section, then, is on a function V that represents preferences over prospects.

It is useful to write the function V in a particular way:

$$V(x_1, p_1; \ldots; x_n, p_n) = p_1 u(x_1) + \ldots + p_n u(x_n).$$

This expression needs some interpretation. To get the function V, we first transform each monetary payoff x_i into its *utility* value, $u(x_i)$. Then, we take the expected value of the prospect $(u[x_1], p_1; \ldots ; u[x_n], p_n)$. In other words, we take the expected value of the utility values of the payoffs. This representation of preferences is called the **expected utility** representation. An individual whose preferences have an expected utility representation is called an **expected utility maximizer.** Before we use expected utility, it is helpful to clarify the meaning of the "utility" function u.

In the expression just shown there are two "utility" functions: V and u. V is the "utility" of the prospect (x,p), and u is the "utility" of a payoff, x_i. Only one of these is the real "utility" function we are interested in; the other is simply a tool to help us analyze choices. The real "utility" function is V, since it represents preferences over prospects, which are the objects under consideration. The function u merely simplifies the discussion of the properties of the function V, such as risk aversion. Unfortunately, the function u was given the name "utility function" long ago by the economists who first used them, even though the term "utility function" would better fit V. To distinguish between the two, we will call V a *preference function,* since it represents preferences, and we will call u a utility function in keeping with tradition.

Now let's examine how the expected utility representation works. Suppose an individual is given a choice between two prospects. In the first prospect, there is a 0.25 probability of receiving $36 and a 0.75 probability of receiving $64. In the second prospect, there is a 0.50 probability of receiving $25 and a 0.50 probability of receiving $100. If the individual's utility function is given by $u(x) = x^{1/2}$, which prospect does she prefer? The expected utility of the first prospect is

$$V(36, 0.25; 64, 0.75) = 0.25(36)^{1/2} + 0.75(64)^{1/2} \doteq 0.25(6) + 0.75(8) = 7.5.$$

The expected utility of the second prospect is

$$V(16, 0.50; 100, 0.50) = 0.50(16)^{1/2} + .50(100)^{1/2} = 0.5(4) + 0.5(10) = 7.$$

The first prospect generates higher expected utility than the second prospect, so the first prospect is preferred.

Notice that she chooses the prospect with the lower expected value. The expected value of the first prospect is

$$EV(36, 0.25; 64, 0.75) = 0.25(36) + 0.75(64) = 57.$$

The expected value of the second prospect is

$$EV(16, 0.50; 100, 0.50) = 0.50(16) + 0.50(100) = 58.$$

In general, an expected utility maximizer may or may not choose the prospect with the higher expected value, depending on the prospects being compared and the utility function being used. In particular, the choice depends on the riskiness of the prospects and whether or not the individual is risk averse. It is possible to find a utility function that always chooses the prospect with the highest expected value. For example, the utility function $u(x) = x$ does just this, and you should write out the expected utility formula to figure out why. If an individual always chooses the prospect with the highest expected value, we say that she is an **expected value maximizer.** Expected value maximizers are also expected utility maximizers, but not necessarily the other way around.

The expected utility calculation has a fairly appealing rationale. For each outcome of a prospect, the individual determines how much utility would be generated by that outcome if it were to occur. Since the different outcomes are not certain, she figures out the average level of utility that she can expect. To make her choice among available alternatives, she compares the average amounts of utility generated by them. An expected value maximizer, in contrast, only cares about the levels of the different payoffs and not how much utility they generate.

Risk Aversion

In Section 4.1 we introduced *risk aversion* as describing an individual who prefers a riskless prospect to a risky prospect with the same expected value, and we demonstrated that risk-averse individuals have indifference curves that are bowed toward the origin, as in Figure 4-1. In this section we show how risk aversion determines the shape of the utility function in the expected utility formulation.

To do this, suppose that Gretchen begins with $200 in wealth. (We use *wealth* instead of *income* because wealth is the stock of money that the individual already owns, while income is the flow of money that the individual earns during some specific time period. Since individuals sometimes have to pay for losses in this chapter, we talk about wealth because it is the relevant source of money for making payments.) Further suppose that Gretchen has a choice between two prospects. The first prospect is a coin toss in which she wins $150 with probability 0.5 and loses $50 with probability 0.5. The expected value of this prospect is $50. The second prospect pays $50 for sure, so its expected value is $50. Both prospects have the same expected value, but only the coin toss is risky. If Gretchen is risk averse, she prefers the $50 for sure to the coin toss. What must her utility function look like? Look at the utility function in Figure 4-5. The horizontal axis measures her wealth in dollars, and the vertical axis measures her utility. The coin toss involves a 0.5 probability of wealth $200 + $150 = $350, and a 0.5 probability of wealth $200 − $50 = $150. Preferring the sure $50 to the coin toss is the

Figure 4-5   Utility Function for a Risk-Averse Individual

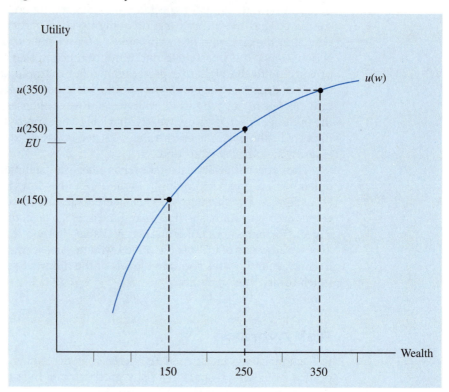

The utility function $u(w)$ can be used to find the expected utility of a prospect. The prospect pays $150 with probability 0.5 and $350 with probability 0.5. The expected value of the prospect is $250. The vertical axis shows the utility each of these values generates. Expected utility is $0.5u(350) + 0.5u(150)$, which is the point midway between $u(350)$ and $u(150)$ on the vertical axis. It is lower than the utility of the expected value, $u(250)$. This individual is risk averse, since she prefers the expected value of a prospect to the prospect itself. Risk-averse expected utility maximizers have concave utility functions, as shown.

same as preferring the sure wealth level of $250 to the 0.5 chance of $350 and the 0.5 chance of $150.

We want to use the figure to find the expected utility of the two prospects. Finding the expected utility of the sure $250 is simple; it is just $u(\$250)$. For the coin toss, with probability 0.5 her utility is $u(\$350)$, and with probability 0.5 her utility is $u(\$150)$. Her expected utility is $0.5u(\$350) + 0.5u(\$150)$, which is the midpoint on the vertical axis between $u(\$350)$ and $u(\$150)$, and it is labeled EU. Note that EU lies below $u(\$250)$, and since she chooses the alternative with the higher expected utility, she chooses the sure $250.

The same technique can be used even when the probabilities of the two outcomes are different from 0.5. Consider the prospect that pays $300 with probability 0.3 and pays nothing with probability 0.7. The expected value of this prospect is 0.3($300) + 0.7($0) = $90. Which would a risk-averse individual rather have, this prospect or $90 for sure? To answer this question, we first have to find the expected utility of the prospect. This is done in Figure 4-6(a), which shows a utility function for a person with initial wealth $100. With probability 0.3 she wins $300, so her wealth becomes $400, and with probability 0.7 she wins nothing, so her wealth remains at $100. One way to find her expected utility is to find the point three-tenths of the way from $u(\$100)$ to $u(\$400)$ on the vertical axis, and it is labeled EU in the figure. This is not the only way, though. A second, and more accurate, way to find expected utility is to draw a line segment connecting points A and B in the figure. Point A is the point on the utility function above the low wealth level, $100, and point B is the point on the utility function above the high wealth level, $400. Next find the expected wealth, which is $190 in this case, and find point C, which is the point on the line segment above $190. The height of point C is the expected utility of the prospect. Notice that in Figure 4-6(a) the individual would rather have the expected value of the prospect for sure than take the prospect, so the person is risk averse.

Not all utility functions imply risk aversion. Look at Figure 4-6(b), which shows an individual's choice over the same two prospects as in Figure 4-6(a). By repeating the steps of Figure 4-6(a) with this utility function, we find that this individual receives higher expected utility from the coin toss. In this case, the individual is risk loving. Why is the person in Figure 4-6(a) risk averse while the person in Figure 4-6(b) is risk loving? The key is that the utility function in Figure 4-6(a) is **concave,** which means that its slope decreases with movements to the right, and the utility function in Figure 4-6(b) is **convex,** which means that its slope increases with movements to the right. A risk-averse person must have a concave utility function.

What Expected Utility Implies About Indifference Curves

When the individual is an expected utility maximizer, we get one extra restriction on the shape of indifference curves in state-payoff space, and this restriction turns out to be important when we talk about insurance and investing. In Chapter 2 we used utility functions to find the marginal rate of substitution between two goods. Here we can use the expected utility preference function to find marginal rates of substitution, which can then be used to discuss the shapes of indifference curves in state-payoff space. First, though, we must decide which "commodities" the individual chooses between. Since the horizontal axis in state-payoff space measures wealth in state 1 and the vertical axis measures wealth in state 2, the "commodities" are state-1 wealth and state-2 wealth. The marginal rate of substitution we are looking for measures how much state-2 wealth the individual must forgo to remain indifferent after a $1 increase in state-1 wealth. As usual, the MRS is the negative of the slope of the indifference curve.

Figure 4-6   Finding Expected Utility Graphically

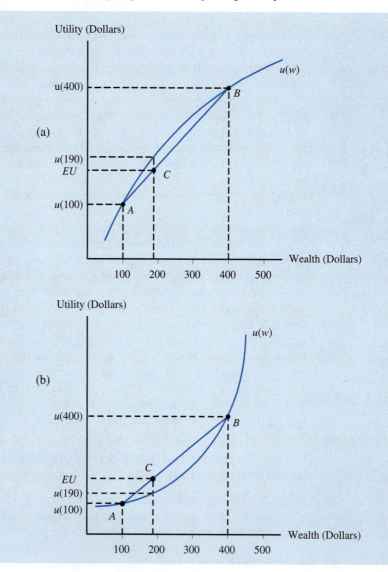

To find expected utility graphically when the two outcomes are not equally likely, use the following procedure. Find the points on the utility curve above the different outcomes, such as with points *A* and *B* in panel (a). Draw a line segment connecting these two points. Find the expected value of the prospect on the horizontal axis, and draw a line up from it to the line segment. This gives you point *C*. The height of point *C* is the expected utility of the prospect. In panel (a) the utility function is concave, so the individual is *risk averse* and the expected utility of the prospect is below the utility of the expected value, $u(190)$. In panel (b) the utility function is convex, so the individual is *risk loving* and the expected utility of the prospect is above the utility of the expected value.

Before finding the *MRS*, recall that marginal utility is the amount utility increases when wealth increases by $1. Notice that if wealth increases by $1 in state 1, utility in that state rises by $MU(w_1)$, and expected utility increases by $p_1MU(w_1)$. Likewise, a $1 decrease in w_2 decreases expected utility by $p_2MU(w_2)$. If the individual is to be left indifferent, expected utility cannot change; that is,

$$\Delta EU = p_1MU(w_1)\Delta w_1 + p_2MU(w_2)\Delta w_2 = 0.$$

Since the $MRS = -\Delta w_2/\Delta w_1$, as in Chapter 2, the marginal rate of substitution is

$$MRS = \frac{p_1}{p_2} \cdot \frac{MU(w_1)}{MU(w_2)}.$$

The marginal rate of substitution is a function of the probabilities of the states and the marginal utilities of state-dependent wealth.

Along the 45-degree line this expression can be further simplified. The 45-degree line is the set of points where $w_2 = w_1$. If wealth is the same in both states, marginal utility must be the same as well, which means that $MU(w_1)/MU(w_2) = 1$. The expression for *MRS* becomes

$$MRS = \frac{p_1}{p_2}.$$

But we have already seen the expression p_1/p_2 in Section 4.1—it is the odds ratio. The MRS is equal to the odds ratio at every point along the 45-degree line. This means that every indifference curve must have slope $-p_1/p_2$ where it intersects the 45-degree line, no matter what utility function is being used. As we saw in Section 4.1, the odds ratio is also the negative of the slope of the iso-expected value line. Putting these two facts together, *indifference curves must be tangent to iso-expected value lines along the 45-degree line.* This property of indifference curves becomes important in the next two sections.

4.3 INSURANCE

Many people buy insurance against possible losses. If a car is stolen, for example, the insurance company covers the loss by paying the victim the value of the car. Consumers regularly purchase insurance for their homes, cars, and health; doctors buy malpractice insurance; shipping companies purchase insurance against accidents and losses of cargo; and so on. We can use our characterization of risk preferences to determine how much people are willing to pay for insurance, and also what form insurance policies should take.

Fair Insurance

Consider the case of Dr. Quinn, a radiologist. She has done a little research and has determined that there is a 20 percent chance that she will be successfully sued for $100,000 for malpractice during the coming year. In other words, she faces a 20 percent chance of losing $100,000. Many doctors purchase malpractice insurance to avoid risks like this one. Malpractice insurance compensates doctors for any losses incurred in a malpractice suit, up to the amount of the insurance. For example, if Dr. Quinn purchases a $100,000 policy, the insurance company promises to pay her $100,000 if she loses a malpractice suit. If, instead, she only buys a $50,000 policy, she will only receive $50,000 from the insurance company if she loses a malpractice suit. The amount the insurance company promises to reimburse for a loss is known as the **coverage.**

Dr. Quinn must decide how large an insurance policy to buy. Suppose that the insurance company offers to sell her any amount of coverage up to $100,000. For any policy she buys, she must pay an insurance **premium** equal to the expected benefit payment. An insurance premium is simply the price of insurance, so it is the amount Dr. Quinn must pay for the insurance whether or not she loses a malpractice suit. The insurance **benefit** is the amount that the insurance company pays Dr. Quinn if she loses a malpractice case. For example, when she buys a policy with $100,000 of coverage, the insurance company promises to pay her a benefit of $100,000 if she loses a malpractice suit. Assuming that Dr. Quinn's probabilities are accurate, the insurance company pays the benefit of $100,000 with probability 0.2 and no benefit with probability 0.8. Thus, the expected benefit payment is $20,000, so the premium for this insurance policy would be $20,000. When the insurance premium is set equal to the expected benefit payment, the insurance is called **actuarially fair insurance.** If Dr. Quinn is risk averse, how much actuarially fair insurance should she buy?

We can solve this problem graphically using state-payoff space. Assume that Dr. Quinn begins with wealth of $150,000. She faces a 20 percent probability of losing $100,000 and an 80 percent probability of losing nothing. Let w_1 denote her wealth if she loses a malpractice case and w_2 denote her wealth if she does not. If we measure amounts in thousands of dollars, her initial wealth point without insurance is (50,150), which is shown as point A in Figure 4-7. State 1 occurs with probability $p_1 = 0.2$, and state 2 occurs with probability $p_2 = 0.8$. Her expected wealth is $130,000.

What if she buys a $100,000 insurance policy? As we have already noted, the premium is $20,000. In state 1 she begins with $150,000, pays the $20,000, loses a $100,000 malpractice suit, and receives a $100,000 benefit payment from the insurance company. Her final wealth position in state 1 is $130,000.

Figure 4-7   Actuarially Fair Insurance

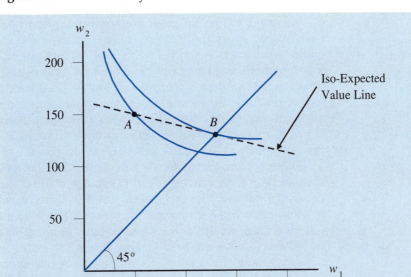

Dr. Quinn begins with wealth of $150,000 and faces a 0.2 probability of losing $100,000. The horizontal axis measures her wealth in the state in which she suffers a loss, and the vertical axis measures her wealth in the state with no loss. Her initial point is A. She is able to buy actuarially fair insurance, which means that she can choose any point betwen A and B on the iso-expected value line. Point A corresponds to buying no insurance, and point B corresponds to buying enough insurance to cover the entire loss. Since indifference curves are tangent to the iso-expected value line at points along the 45-degree line, her optimal point is B. So, when insurance is actuarially fair, she buys full insurance.

In state 2 she starts with $150,000 and pays the $20,000 premium. She suffers no loss and receives no insurance benefit, so her final wealth is again $130,000. If she buys a $100,000 policy, then, her wealth is $130,000 in both states, as shown by point B in Figure 4-7.

What about insurance policies with other levels of coverage? Suppose that she purchases an insurance policy with coverage of x. The premium is $0.2x$, and she pays the premium in both states. In state 1 she begins with wealth of $150,000, pays the insurance premium of $0.2x$, loses a $100,000 malpractice suit, and receives insurance benefits of x. Her state-1 wealth is $150,000 - 0.2x - \$100,000 + x = \$50,000 + 0.8x$. In state 2 she begins with wealth of $150,000 and pays the insurance premium, so her state-2 wealth is $150,000 - 0.2x$. Her expected wealth is

$$0.2(\$50,000 + 0.8x) + 0.8(\$150,000 - 0.2x) = \$10,000 + .16x + \$120,000 - .16x$$
$$= \$130,000$$

So, her expected wealth is the same with every actuarially fair insurance policy, and her choice set is the iso-expected value line.

As usual, to find the most-preferred point in the choice set we look for the point where an indifference curve is tangent to the choice set. Since the choice set is the iso-expected value line, it has slope $-p_1/p_2$. We must find a point where the slope of the indifference curve is also $-p_1/p_2$. In the previous section we found that for any individual whose preferences have an expected utility representation, the marginal rate of substitution is p_1/p_2 at all points on the 45-degree line. This solves our problem. The indifference curve is tangent to the iso-expected value line at point B in Figure 4-7, where the iso-expected value line crosses the 45-degree line.

Point B corresponds to the case where Dr. Quinn buys a \$100,000 insurance policy. So, she buys **full insurance;** that is, she buys a policy that covers the full loss. This is a general result: A risk-averse person always buys full insurance when insurance is actuarially fair. When the individual buys full insurance, wealth is the same in both states, so buying full insurance puts the individual on the 45-degree line. When insurance is actuarially fair, the choice set is the iso-expected value line. A risk-averse person's indifference curve is tangent to the iso-expected value line at the 45-degree line, which is the full-insurance point.

Insurance with Deductibles

People do not always buy full insurance. In many cases, people buy policies that have a **deductible.** For example, if someone has a \$100 deductible on his health insurance policy, he must pay the first \$100 of medical bills himself, and the insurance company pays any amount over \$100 up to the coverage of the policy. If someone has a \$500 deductible for his automobile insurance and gets in an accident causing \$3,000 of damage, he must pay \$500 himself and the insurance company pays \$2,500. In light of the previous section, the question arises as to why people buy insurance with deductibles. We have already seen that when insurance is actuarially fair, risk-averse people prefer full insurance. So why don't people buy full insurance? The answer is that the insurance available in the marketplace is not actuarially fair.

If insurance is actuarially fair, what does the insurance company get out of it? In Dr. Quinn's case, the policy brings in a premium of \$20,000, but it pays out an expected benefit of \$20,000. The insurance company's expected net earnings on this policy are zero. But we have ignored all the other costs the insurance company faces, such as labor costs, administrative costs, advertising, and so on. If we count all these costs, the insurance company expects to lose money on this policy. Consequently, insurance companies do not sell actuarially fair insurance. Instead, they charge premiums higher than the expected benefit payment.

One way that insurance companies set premiums is through **proportional loading.** If a policy has an expected benefit payment of Y, the insurance company charges a premium of $(1+L)Y$, where L is a **loading factor.** When insurance is actuarially fair, the loading factor is zero and the premium is equal to the expected benefit payment. If the insurance company is to avoid losing money on the policy, it must raise its premium to cover the other costs. According to the proportional loading formula, the insurance company increases the premium by a factor of L. For example, if L is 0.25 and if Dr. Quinn buys a $100,000 policy, the premium would be $(1.25)(\$20,000) = \$25,000$.

Graphically, proportional loading makes the budget line steeper, as in Figure 4-8. The initial wealth position before insurance is point A, and the choice set for actuarially fair insurance is the iso-expected value line. If Dr. Quinn buys full insurance when insurance is actuarially fair, she buys a $100,000 policy that costs $20,000. After buying the policy, her wealth is $130,000 in both states, as shown by point B. If, instead, insurance is only available with a 25 percent loading factor, a $100,000 policy costs $25,000. When she buys full insurance with loading, her wealth in both states is $125,000, which is point C in the figure. The slope of the actuarially fair insurance line can be calculated using the coordinates of points A and B, and the slope is $(150,000 - 130,000)/(50,000 - 130,000) = -1/4$. The slope of the proportional loading insurance line can be calculated using points A and C, and it is $(150,000 - 125,000)/(50,000 - 125,000) = -1/3$.

Dr. Quinn purchases the insurance policy that gets her to her most preferred point on the new, steeper choice set, which is line AC in Figure 4-8. Let's begin by seeing whether or not she wants to buy full insurance. By the definition of full insurance, the insurance company will compensate her for all her losses, so her wealth is the same in both states. Consequently, when she buys full insurance she must be on the 45-degree line, so point C has full insurance. At point C, though, her indifference curve has slope $-1/4$, since point C is on the 45-degree line and indifference curves have slope $-p_1/p_2$ where they cross the 45-degree line. (Remember that $p_1 = 0.2$ and $p_2 = 0.8$.) Since the choice set has slope $-1/3$ at point C, and the indifference curve has slope $-1/4$, the indifference curve is flatter than the choice set. Since indifference curves are steeper to the northwest of the 45-degree line and flatter to the southeast of the 45-degree line, the point of tangency must be to the northwest of the 45-degree line. In Figure 4-8, the optimal point is D.

The insurance policy purchased at point D has a natural interpretation in terms of deductibles. As shown in Figure 4-8, wealth in state 1 is $98,000 and wealth in state 2 is $134,000. We can figure out the insurance premium from state-2 wealth. In state 2 Dr. Quinn begins with $150,000 and pays the

Figure 4-8   Insurance with a Loading Factor

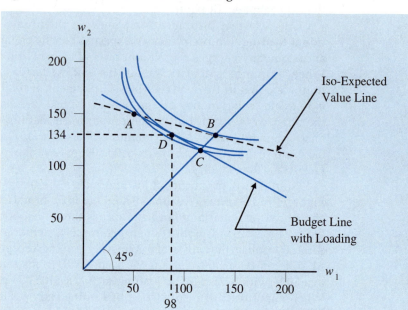

In this case insurance companies use a loading factor to set premiums above the actuarially fair rate. Dr. Quinn begins at point A, and she can choose any point along the solid downward-sloping line. Point C corresponds to full insurance, but it is not optimal because the indifference curve through C is flatter than the budget line at C. The optimal point is D, which does not have full coverage. This policy has a deductible: When Dr. Quinn suffers a loss, she pays for part of the loss and the insurance company covers the rest. In the case depicted here, the amount of coverage is $64,000 and the deductible is $36,000. Policies with deductible are optimal when the insurance company uses a loading factor.

premium. In order for her to end up with $134,000, the premium must be $16,000. State-1 wealth can now be used to find the deductible. She begins with $150,000, pays a $16,000 insurance premium, and loses $100,000 in a malpractice suit. She has $34,000 before she receives any insurance benefit. Since she ends up with $98,000, the benefit must be $64,000. The insurance policy covers all but $36,000 of her loss, so the deductible is $36,000.

Whether or not people buy full insurance, then, depends on whether or not insurance is actuarially fair. If it is actuarially fair, risk-averse people buy full insurance. If it is not actuarially fair, insurance with a deductible is optimal. This is not the only reason why insurance policies have deductibles, however. Chapter 14 provides another, completely different rationale for them.

4.4   INVESTMENT PORTFOLIOS

When people consider buying insurance, they decide how much risk to take. Another situation in which people decide how much risk to take is when they invest their money. Different financial assets have different levels of risk. For example, stocks are usually considered riskier than corporate bonds, since stock prices tend to fluctuate more than corporate bond prices. Corporate bonds are usually considered riskier than government bonds, which are usually considered riskier than certificates of deposit. The riskiness of assets also differs within categories, and some stocks are much riskier than others. When people decide which assets to invest in, they also decide between different levels of risk. This section looks at how these decisions are made.

Budget Sets

Consider the case of Stan, who has money he wishes to invest and two choices of where to invest it. One alternative is to put some money in a savings account in a bank, where it earns a fixed interest rate. The other is to buy stock in Really Realty, a large national realtor. How well the stock does depends on how well the underlying company does, and, as you might expect, the real estate market has good periods and bad. Consequently, the stock is risky, but the savings account is not. What should Stan do?

We need to determine Stan's budget set. First, though, we must be more concrete about the payoffs from the two alternatives. If Stan puts all of his money into a savings account, he receives a payoff of $1,000 for sure. If he puts all of his money in the risky asset, his payoff depends on what state occurs. Assume that there are only two states of the world, the high state H, which occurs with probability 0.4, and the low state L, which occurs with probability 0.6. During the high state the economy expands and there is a large amount of real estate activity, so the stock does well. During the low state the economy is in a recession and the stock does poorly. If Stan invests all his money in the stock and the high state occurs, his payoff is $1,400, but if the low state occurs his payoff is $900. The payoffs of the two assets are shown in state-payoff space in Figure 4-9, where the horizontal axis shows the payoff in state H and the vertical axis shows the payoff in state L. The payoff from the risky asset is labeled R, and the riskless (safe) asset is labeled S. Notice that point S is on the 45-degree line, the line corresponding to the set of riskless prospects.

The expected value of investing everything in the riskless asset is $1,000, and the expected value of investing everything in the risky asset is 0.4($900) + 0.6($1,400) = $1,200. These are not the only choices, though, because Stan may choose to divide his money between the risky asset and the riskless as-

Figure 4-9   Possible Payoffs for Investing in Risky and Riskless Assets

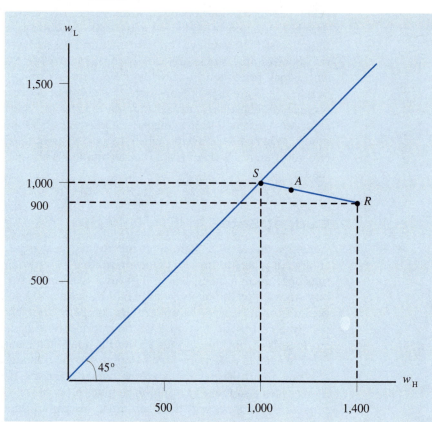

There are two assets available for investing. If Stan invests all of his money in a savings account, he receives $1,000 for sure. The payoff is shown by point S. If he invests all of his money in a risky asset, the payoff depends on the state of the world. In the high state H he receives $1,400, but in the low state L he receives only $900. State H occurs with probability 0.4. The payoff of the risky asset is shown as point R. By investing some of his money in the risky asset and putting the rest of it in the savings account, Stan can also get payoffs corresponding to points on the line segment between R and S. For example, point A is one-third of the distance from S to R, and Stan can earn this payoff by putting one-third of his money in the risky asset and two-thirds in the savings account.

set. This means that he can choose any point on the line segment connecting points R and S in the figure, and this segment is his budget line. To interpret the budget line, consider point A, which is one-third of the distance from S to R. Stan can reach point A by investing one-third of his wealth in the risky asset and two-thirds in the safe asset. The slope of the budget line is $(1,000 - 900)/(1,000 - 1,400) = -1/4$.

Before going on, it is helpful to make one comment about the way this problem was formulated. Notice that we never said how much money Stan has to invest. That number is completely irrelevant to the problem. All that matters for his choice is how much he can receive *after* he invests his wealth.

The Optimal Portfolio

The next step in solving the choice problem is to draw indifference curves. Recall that every indifference curve has slope $-p_1/p_2$ where it crosses the 45-degree line, with p_1 defined as the probability of the state on the horizontal axis and p_2 defined as the probability of the state on the vertical axis. In this case the slope is the negative of the probability of state H divided by the probability of state L, or $-0.4/0.6 = -2/3$. The indifference curve through point S has this slope, and it is shown in Figure 4-10(a). Notice that the indifference curve in the figure is for risk-averse preferences, since it is convex. Because the budget line has slope $-1/4$, the indifference curve is steeper at point S than the budget line, as shown, so point S cannot be an optimum.

To determine the optimal portfolio, we must find the point on the budget line that is on the highest possible indifference curve. It is point B in Figure 4-10(a). At this point the indifference curve is tangent to the budget line. How can we interpret this tangency? The slope of the indifference curve is the (negative of) the marginal rate of substitution, which tells how much wealth in state L Stan is willing to give up to get a $1 increase in wealth in state H. The slope of the budget line tells how much the payoff in state L falls when Stan puts enough money in the risky asset to increase the payoff in state H by $1. In essence, the marginal rate of substitution tells how much Stan is *willing* to pay for an increase in the payoff in state H, and the slope of the budget line tells how much he *must* pay. If he is willing to pay more than the budget line requires, so that the indifference curve is steeper than the budget line, he buys more of the risky asset. If he is willing to pay less than the budget line requires, so that the indifference curve is flatter than the budget line, he buys less of the risky asset. At the optimal point, he cannot do better by purchasing either more or less of the risky asset.

Figure 4-10(a) shows a case where Stan wants to put some of his money in the risky asset and some of his money in the riskless asset. We call such an investor a **diversifier,** since his optimal portfolio contains a variety of types of assets. Figure 4-10(b) shows a different case, where the investor only buys the risky asset. This investor is known as a **plunger,** since he puts all of his money in a single asset—the risky asset. Notice that under no circumstances will an investor put all of his money in the riskless asset, since all indifference curves have the same slope at points on the 45-degree line,

Figure 4-10   Choosing an Optimal Investment Point

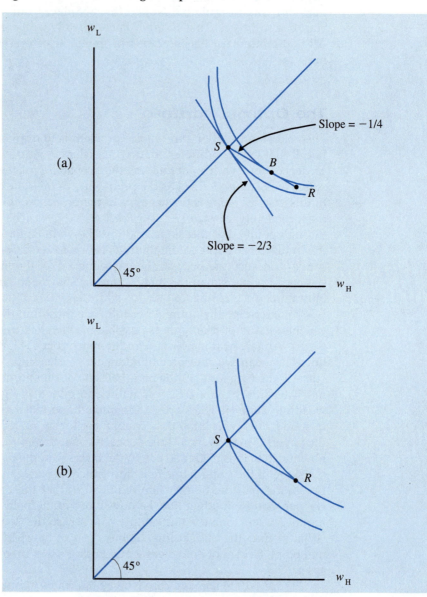

Stan can choose his favorite point on the budget line, which is the segment between *R* and *S*. In panel (a), the optimal point is *B*, which is between *R* and *S*. At point *B* Stan invests some of his money in both assets, and in this case Stan is known as a *diversifier*. In panel (b) the optimal point is *R*, and Stan only invests in the risky asset. In this case Stan is called a *plunger*.

and this slope is steeper than the slope of the budget line. This is an important result: When a risky asset with higher expected return than the riskless asset is available, it is never optimal for an investor to put all of his money in the riskless asset. Instead, he should always put at least some of it in a risky asset.

We can use the fact that some risk-averse investors desire diversified portfolios to discuss why there is such a large market for mutual funds. Investors place at least some of their wealth in risky assets, but it is by no means clear that they should invest in only one risky asset. Risk can be reduced by investing small amounts in many different stocks, for example, because the forces that change the price of one stock are often unrelated to the forces that change the price of a different stock. By investing small amounts in many different stocks, investors can avoid large increases or decreases in wealth. Brokerage fees make it too expensive to make a large number of small investments, though. Mutual funds pool together the contributions of a large number of investors and use this money to purchase a diversified portfolio of stocks (and sometimes other types of assets, too, such as bonds or money market instruments). People with relatively small amounts of wealth have only a few options for investing in the stock market. They can either pick a few individual stocks, which is risky, or they can invest in mutual funds. Since mutual funds are already diversified, they provide small, risk-averse investors with a way of obtaining a portfolio that is much more diversified than might otherwise be possible.

When investors choose among alternative assets, they face a trade-off between risk and expected return. Assets with higher expected return also

Table 4-1   Different Types of Assets

Highest risk and highest expected return	Commodities
	Rare coins
	Precious metals
	Options
	International stocks
	Small company stocks
	Common stocks
	Stock mutual funds
	Corporate bonds
	Municipal bonds
	Bond mutual funds
	Government bonds
Lowest risk and lowest expected return	Savings accounts
	Savings bonds
	Treasury bills

tend to be riskier. It is possible to get higher returns from investments, but only by taking greater risks. Most people, when formulating their investment portfolio, must decide how much risk they are willing to bear. Table 4-1 ranks several different types of assets from riskiest to least risky. Since expected return rises with riskiness, the table also ranks the different assets from highest expected return to lowest expected return.

Summary

- The term **risky** is used to describe any situation in which the outcome of a choice is uncertain. A **state of nature** is a randomly determined event. For example, when flipping a coin there are two states of nature—heads and tails.

- When payoffs in risky alternatives are amounts of money, the alternatives are referred to as **prospects.** Every prospect has two components—the set of possible outcomes and the set of probabilities that correspond to the possible payoffs.

- The **expected value** of a prospect is found by multiplying each possible payoff of the prospect by its respective probability and then summing each of these terms. For example, if you can win $10 if a coin flip comes out heads and win $20 if a coin flip comes out tails, the expected value of that prospect is 0.5($10) + 0.5($20) = $15.

- A person who is **risk averse** prefers the expected value of a risky prospect to the prospect itself. For example, a risk-averse person prefers the certainty of $1 to the expected value of $1 by winning $1.50 with probability 0.5 and 50 cents with probability 0.5.

- A person who is **risk loving** prefers the prospect itself to the expected value of a risky prospect. A person who is **risk neutral** is indifferent between the expected value of a risky prospect and the prospect itself.

- **Expected utility** is found by multiplying the utility in each possible state by its respective probability and then summing up these terms. As his objective, an **expected utility maximizer** maximizes expected utility.

- When an insurance premium is set equal to the expected insurance benefit payment, the insurance is called **actuarially fair insurance.** A risk-averse person always buys **full insurance** (a policy that covers the full loss) when insurance is actuarially fair.

Problems

1. Find the expected value of the following prospects:
   a. ($100, 0.3; $20, 0.7)
   b. ($50, 0.2; $10, 0.5; −$10, 0.3)
   c. Flipping a coin twice and receiving $1 for each head and $2 for each tail

2. Calculate the expected utility of the prospects in problem 1 when the utility function is $u(x) = x^{1/2}$. Calculate expected utility when the utility function is $u(x) = x^2$.

3. Suppose that an individual faces a choice between prospect A = ($20, 1) and prospect B = ($30, 0.2; $20, 0.7; $0, 0.1). He then faces a choice between prospect C = ($30, 0.7; $20, 0.3) and prospect D = ($30, 0.9; $0, 0.1). For each preference pattern listed below, state whether or not the pattern is consistent with expected utility maximization:
   a. A over B and C over D
   b. A over B and D over C
   c. B over A and C over D
   d. B over A and D over C

4. Determine whether or not the following preference patterns are consistent with risk aversion, or risk loving, or whether it is impossible to tell:
   a. ($50, 0.8; $0, 0.2) preferred to ($40, 1)
   b. ($50, 0.8; $0, 0.2) preferred to ($45, 1)
   c. ($45, 1) preferred to ($50, 0.8; $0, 0.2)
   d. ($35, 1) preferred to ($50, 0.8; $0, 0.2)
   e. ($65, 0.3; $40, 0.7) preferred to ($50, 0.8; $0, 0.2)

5. a. Suppose that the probability of state 1 is 0.8 and the probability of state 2 is 0.2. Draw an iso-expected value line and an indifference curve for a risk-averse expected utility maximizer.
   b. Now suppose that the probability of state 1 falls to 0.6. In the same graph, show how the iso-expected value line and the indifference curve change.

6. Suppose that there are two assets, a risky asset and a riskless asset.
   a. If the risky asset has lower expected return than the riskless asset, will anyone buy it?
   b. Using your answer to part a, explain why riskier assets must have higher expected payoff than less risky assets.
   c. Does this suggest a method to "beat the market"—that is, earn higher expected payoffs than the average investor? What is it?

7. Suppose that there are two equally likely states of the world and three assets. Asset A pays $1,000 in both states, asset B pays $1,600 in state 1 and $600 in state 2, and asset C pays $800 in state 1 and $1,400 in state 2.

a. Graph the three assets in state-payoff space.

b. Show that no one should invest in the riskless asset.

c. What investment strategy does this suggest?

8. Suppose that an insurance company sells policies to three different people. Each person has a 0.2 chance of losing $75, and each person pays $25 for full insurance. The losses are independent; that is, one person suffering a loss does not make it either more or less likely for any other person to suffer a loss.

a. Find the prospect faced by the insurance company. (*Hint:* there are eight states of the world, and it is suggested that you find the payoffs and probabilities in all eight.)

b. Find the expected value of the prospect in part a.

c. Compare the prospect in part a to the prospect faced by a company insuring just one person. Which company is more likely to lose money—that is, get earnings less than zero?

d. Based on the answer to part c, try to explain why insurance companies are willing to take on risks when they sell insurance to large numbers of people.

e. Explain why insurance companies might be reluctant to sell earthquake insurance.

9. Using a state-payoff space diagram, show what happens to the optimal insurance policy when the loading factor rises. Does the deductible get larger or smaller?

10. Many U.S. states require drivers to purchase a certain amount of auto insurance. Suppose, for example, that Mark faces a possible $100,000 loss and must buy at least $80,000 of coverage.

a. Show graphically how the law affects Mark's budget set, assuming that the law does not cause premiums to change?

b. Suppose that if there was no law Mark would only buy $50,000 of coverage. Draw his indifference curves showing the cases with and without the law. Does the law make him better off or worse off?

11. The residents of a certain city decide to build a new stadium in the hopes of luring a major league baseball team to the city. The stadium costs $80 million to build, and, if a team comes, the city will benefit by $150 million. If the city as a whole is risk neutral, what is the lowest probability of getting a team that makes the city want to build the stadium?

12. Stephanie has just invented a device that turns on her car stereo by remote control. If she turns the volume up really loud, it makes it easier to locate her car in a crowded parking lot. She calls the device Radiauto. She has patented the invention, and is preparing to mass-produce it. She can build either a small, medium, or large plant. Before deciding which size plant to build, she has estimated the probabilities of the success of the product. With probability 0.3 sales are high, and with probability 0.7 sales are low. Profits for the different levels of sales and the different plant sizes are given below.

	High	*Low*
Small	$20,000	$20,000
Medium	$40,000	$12,000
Large	$60,000	-$ 5,000

    a. If she is risk neutral, which plant size should she choose?

    b. If her utility function is $u(w) = w^{\frac{1}{2}}$, which plant size should she choose?

13. The highest amount an individual is willing to pay for full insurance is known as the **risk premium.**

    a. Suppose that the individual has $3,600 in state 1, which occurs with probability 0.25, and $10,000 in state 2. Draw a state-payoff diagram showing the initial wealth point, the full-insurance point, and the risk premium.

    b. Using the same numbers, if the individual's utility function is $u(x) = x^{\frac{1}{2}}$, calculate the risk premium.

5

PRODUCTION

Overview

In this chapter we move away from the consumer, or demand, side of the market and to the producer, or supply, side of the market. We begin by constructing a formal model of what it is that producers do. An individual producer is called a *firm*, and its basic task is to transform inputs into output. The goal of this chapter is to model that process, the production process. In later chapters we will use this model to discuss how the firm achieves its ultimate goal—maximizing profit.

Production processes are very different in different industries. For example, airlines produce passenger flights. Each time a passenger makes a flight on the airline, the airline is producing something. How does the airline produce passenger flights? It uses several inputs, such as planes, pilots, flight attendants, ground crews, fuel, food, and so on. The airline must transform all of these inputs into output (passenger flights). Now consider a completely different type of firm, a dentist's office. The output of the dentist's office can be loosely characterized as dental services. How does the firm produce dental services? It uses labor (including not only dentists but also hygienists and receptionists), equipment, office space, and dental supplies, among other things. Once again, the firm must combine these inputs to produce output.

In both of these very different firms, inputs are transformed into output. The purpose of this chapter is to model this transformation, and, in doing so, impart some understanding of the production process. In this chapter you will learn:

- How to model the production process mathematically.
- How to analyze the production process when the quantity of only one input can be varied.
- How to analyze the production process when the quantities of all of the inputs can be varied.
- How to model education and skills as inputs to the production process.

5.1 THE PRODUCTION PROCESS

Suppose that you are the manager of a potato chip firm. Your firm uses many different **inputs,** which are goods and services used in the production of another good or service. To make potato chips, you need the ingredients, which include potatoes, oil for frying, salt, and preservatives. Since these ingredients do not magically turn themselves into potato chips, you need machines to peel, slice, fry, salt, and bag the chips. Since most machines do not work completely by themselves, you need workers to run the machines and to perform tasks machines cannot perform. You need electricity and other utilities. You need a building to house this whole operation. All of these items are inputs for making potato chips, and the **output** is some number of bags of chips. While it is relatively easy to list inputs for a particular type of output, such as potato chips, it is not nearly as easy to identify ways in which inputs can be transformed into output. Modeling the production process is the purpose of this section.

Fixed Versus Variable Inputs

Suppose that the demand for your potato chips increases and you want to produce more chips. How would you go about it? You would need more ingredients, of course. You would have to run the machinery longer each day to produce the extra chips, which would require more electricity and probably more water. You would either have to entice workers to work longer hours or hire more workers to cover the extra time that the machines are running. It may even be the case that the machines are already running 24 hours a day, in which case you would need to buy more machines. If the building is already full, or if you are expanding the operation greatly, you would need to buy a new building to house the new machines.

Some of these changes can be brought about more quickly than others. For example, increasing the amount of ingredients can be accomplished with a call to a supplier. Workers are often willing to work extra hours, especially if they are paid extra for overtime. If overtime is not possible and new workers must be hired, the process would take longer. Advertising the positions, hiring the new workers, and training them could take a month or so. Buying a new machine could take some time, too. The machine would have to be ordered, manufactured, and then delivered, which could take months. If a new building is required, it could take years to increase output.

If you want to increase the amount of output quickly, adding machines and buildings is out of the question. You are constrained by the number of machines and the space you already have. Since it is a relatively quick process to increase the amount of ingredients and the number of hours worked, these are the only inputs that can be changed. The inputs that can be changed are called **variable inputs,** while the inputs that cannot be changed are called **fixed inputs.** Whether or not an input is fixed depends on the time frame being considered. For example, if you want to increase output over a three-year period, that would be sufficient time to buy new machines and build a new factory, so all inputs would be variable. If you want to increase the output in one month, only the ingredients and labor are variable.

In what follows, we want to discuss how firms behave when they are constrained by some fixed inputs and how they behave when they are not constrained by some fixed inputs. To do this, we make a distinction between the short run and the long run. In the **short run** some inputs are fixed, while others are variable. In the potato chip example, the ingredients, electricity, water, and labor would all be variable inputs in the short run. Machinery and buildings would be fixed inputs. In the **long run,** all inputs are variable. The difference between the short run and the long run, then, is not a specific amount of time. Instead, it depends on how long it takes to change the amounts of the fixed inputs. In some industries it takes very little time to change fixed inputs, while in others it takes a very long time. In the house-painting industry, for example, the inputs are paint, brushes, labor, ladders, and scaffolding. If a painter wanted to increase output, he could just work a little longer each day. If necessary, he could hire a helper, which would take a bit longer. Even so, it would not take very long to change all the inputs. In the nuclear power industry, on the other hand, it can take upwards of a decade to construct a new nuclear power plant. The long run is very long in this case.

Production Functions

Let's begin by simplifying the problem a bit. Let's assume that there are only two inputs; we'll call them capital and labor. Capital includes all of the equipment, machinery, buildings, and so on used in the production process. Capital is the fixed input in the short run. Labor is the number of hours worked on the project. Notice that we are leaving out such things as ingredients or components. This is done not to abandon reality, but to simplify the problem. Hopefully when we are through you will see how to extend the analysis to handle such things as ingredients.

When a specific amount of labor is combined with a specific amount of capital, a predictable amount of output is produced. (Remember that when we say that labor is combined with capital, what we mean is that a certain number of people work on a specific number of machines for a certain number of hours.) A **production function** tells how much output is produced for a given combination of capital and labor. A production function is denoted $F(L,K)$, where L is the amount of labor used, K is the amount of capital, and F is a mathematical function stating how much output is produced from different combinations of inputs. For example, if the production function is $F(L,K) = 10LK$ and the firm uses 20 units of labor and 4 units of capital, the firm produces $(10)(20)(4) = 800$ units of output. Production functions are a convenient mathematical description of how inputs are transformed into outputs.

5.2 PRODUCTION IN THE SHORT RUN

Suppose that a T-shirt printing company is asked to fill a large order within a very short time frame. If it wants to fill the order on time, it must increase its production. Ordinarily the firm would have three choices. One choice is to increase the amount of labor by either getting existing workers to work longer hours or hiring new workers to work on a separate shift. A second choice is to get either more printing equipment and have fewer workers per machine, or replace the old equipment with larger or faster machines. The third choice is to do some combination of the two, getting some new equipment and some additional labor. If the firm has a deadline for when the T-shirts must be made, however, getting new equipment is out of the question. Buying equipment takes time, and the firm doesn't have time. The only way it can produce more T-shirts is by using more labor. But how much more labor? This section examines how labor affects the amount of output when capital is fixed.

Total Product

In the short run, by definition, some of the inputs are fixed, while others can be varied. We want to see how different levels of output can be produced in this case. Since capital is fixed, denote the amount of capital by K_0. The production function is $F(L,K_0)$. Since capital is fixed and only labor can vary, the short-run production function can be graphed. Measure the amount of labor on the horizontal axis and the amount of output on the vertical axis, as in Figure 5-1. The graph of the production function is called a **total product curve,** and a common shape for it is shown in the figure. At very low levels of labor, between 0 and L_1, output increases at an increasing rate. That is, the slope of the curve gets steeper with movements to the right along the curve. As the amount of labor grows from L_1 to L_2, output continues to increase, but the rate at which it increases slows. Finally, when labor exceeds L_2, output decreases. How can we explain this shape? Consider a specific example. Suppose that the production process is to drill a hole in a piece of wood, and then file the wood around the hole until it is smooth. The capital available is one drill press and one file. If there were only one worker, the worker would have to drill holes, then file around the holes, then drill some more, then file some more, and so on. Since it takes time to move between tasks, and since it takes a while to get up to speed every time he switches tasks, his output would be pretty low. If a second worker were added, one could file while the other drilled, reducing the time lost because of switching tasks. Because of this, two workers could probably produce

Figure 5-1   Production Function with One Fixed Input

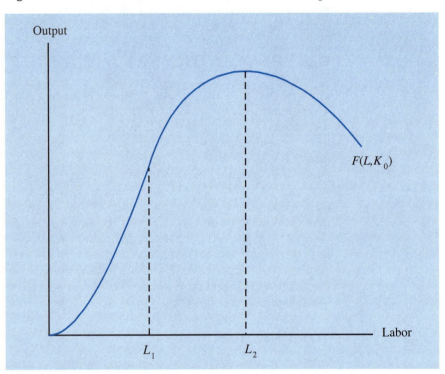

When the amount of one input is fixed, the production function can be drawn. In this case, the amount of capital is fixed at K_0 units, and the amount of labor can be varied. As labor increases, the amount of output changes. When fewer than L_1 units of labor are used, output increases at an increasing rate as labor increases. When the amount of labor is between L_1 and L_2, output increases when labor increases, but at a decreasing rate. When more than L_2 units of labor are used, output declines as the amount of labor is increased.

more than twice what one worker could produce, making the total product curve increase at an increasing rate. Adding a third worker would allow one worker to rest while the other two worked, and output would increase by a small amount because the workers would not get so tired. At this point the total product curve is increasing at a decreasing rate. Eventually, though, adding more workers would fail to increase output, because the machinery would be fully utilized. There would be nothing left for the new workers to do. Adding more workers might even distract the ones who were working, lowering their output. So, when the amount of equipment is fixed, output might even fall when the number of workers gets too large, and in this case the total product curve would be decreasing.

We have discussed the shape of the total product curve; now let's discuss its height. The amount of capital changes the height of the total prod-

uct curve. Consider the case of two firms with the same underly
duction function but with different levels of capital in the short run
1's fixed level of capital is K_1, and Firm 2's fixed level of capital is hi
at $K_2 > K_1$. Suppose that they both use the same amount of labor, L, as sho
in Figure 5-2. Since Firm 2 has more capital for the L workers to use, th
workers at Firm 2 are able to produce more than the same number of workers at Firm 1. This means that Firm 2's total product curve is higher than
Firm 1's at that level of labor. In general, extra capital makes workers more
productive, so the figure is drawn with Firm 2's total product curve everywhere above Firm 1's total product curve.

Average and Marginal Product

Sometimes it is more convenient to describe labor's effect on output using
the concepts of **average product of labor** and **marginal product of labor.**
The average product of labor is defined as the total output divided by the

Figure 5-2   A Shift in the Production Function

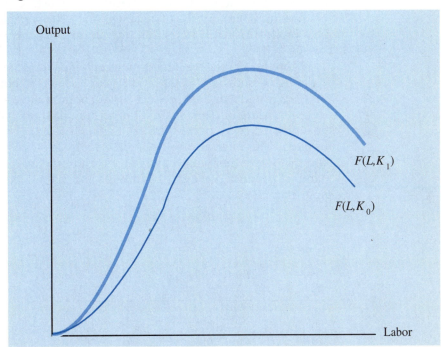

When the amount of capital increases from K_0 to K_1, labor becomes more productive. At each
level of labor, more is produced than before. Graphically, this means that the production
function shifts upward.

nt of labor, or, the average output per unit of labor. Mathematically, mula is

$$AP_L = \frac{TP}{L} = \frac{q}{L}$$

where AP_L denotes average product of labor and q is the output. The marginal product of labor is defined as the extra output generated as labor input increases by one unit. It is given by the formula

$$MP_L = \frac{\Delta TP}{\Delta L} = \frac{\Delta q}{\Delta L}.$$

A firm can use average product to measure the productivity of the entire work force, and it can use marginal product to measure the productivity of the *last* unit of labor hired.

Average and marginal products of labor can be calculated using information about total product. Table 5-1 lists different levels of output corresponding to different levels of labor, assuming that capital is fixed. It also lists the average product and the marginal product. Note that total product increases until the very end of the range, and both average product and marginal product increase at first but then decrease as the amount of labor increases.

Figure 5-3 graphs the information contained in Table 5-1. The top panel of the figure shows the total product curve, and the bottom figure shows the average and marginal product curves. Both average and marginal product are measured in terms of output per unit of labor. Notice that the marginal product curve passes through the highest point on the average product curve. This must always be the case, and you should be careful to make sure that every time you draw average and marginal product curves, the marginal product curve passes through the highest point on the average product curve.

Table 5-1

Labor (L)	Total Product (q)	Average Product (q/L)	Marginal Product (Δq/ΔL)
0	0	—	—
10	100	10	10
20	320	16	22
30	480	16	16
40	500	12.5	2
50	470	9.4	−3

Figure 5-3   Deriving Average Product and Marginal Product from Total Product

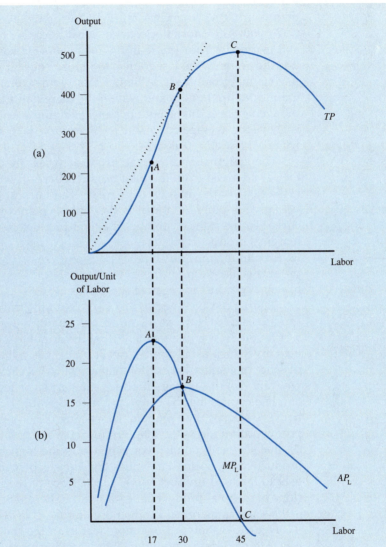

This figure graphs the information contained in Table 5-1. The height of the average product curve, labeled AP_L in panel (b), is the slope of the line segment connecting the origin to the total product curve in panel (a), such as the line segment connecting the origin to point B. The height of the marginal product curve, MP_L in panel (b), is the slope of the tangent to the total product curve. Note that at point B the dashed line segment is tangent to the total product curve and it connects the origin to the total product curve. This means that average product equals marginal product at this level of labor, as shown in panel (b). Also, the dashed line segment lies completely above the total product curve, so the average product curve reaches its peak at this level of labor.

This relationship between average and marginal might be easier to see with a different example. When you take a course and receive a grade higher than your grade point average, your GPA rises. If you receive a grade lower than your GPA, your GPA falls. If your grade is exactly the same as your GPA, your GPA does not change. What does this have to do with average and marginal? Your grade in the new course is your *marginal* grade, since it is the grade in the last course you took. Your GPA is your *average* grade. If your marginal grade is higher than your average grade, your average grade goes up. Put another way, if the marginal is higher than the average, the average rises. In the bottom panel of Figure 5-3, when the marginal curve is above the average curve, the average curve is upward sloping. Similarly, when $MP_L < AP_L$, AP_L falls.

The marginal and average product curves are also related by the way they are derived from the total product curve. The marginal product curve is the slope of the total product curve. The steepest point on the total product curve is point A, and it is the highest point on the marginal product curve. To the right of point A the total product curve flattens out and the marginal product curve declines. At point C the total product curve reaches its maximum, and the slope at point C is zero. This means that marginal product is also zero for this amount of labor. When total product is falling, marginal product is negative.

Finding the average product curve is a little trickier. Recall that average product is q/L. How can we find this quantity in the top panel of Figure 5-3? If you draw a line segment from the origin to a point on the total product curve, such as at point B, what you get is a line that covers a vertical distance of q and a horizontal distance of L. It's slope is q/L, which is what we want. So, the average product at a particular level of labor is the slope of a line connecting the origin to the total product curve at that level of labor. The steepest line segment connecting the origin to a point on the total product curve meets the total product curve at point B. Since it is the steepest line segment, point B corresponds to the highest point on the average product curve, as shown. Notice that the steepest line segment is also tangent to the total product curve, so the slope of the line segment is also the slope of the total product curve at point B. In other words, average product is the same as marginal product at point B.

Figure 5-3 shows us one more feature of the short-run production function. After a certain amount of labor is used, marginal product begins to fall. In Figure 5-3, the critical point is 17 units of labor. The property that marginal product falls after some point is known as the **law of diminishing returns.** It is caused by the fact that some inputs are fixed, which means that at some point the workers will gain all the advantages of optimal scheduling, specialization, and so on. After that point it is impossible for additional workers to match the way the old workers were behaving. As the number of workers increases, the firm gets less and less output from each additional worker. Put another way, the firm gets less and less return on its investment in workers, which is why it is called the law of diminishing *returns.*

5.3 PRODUCTION IN THE LONG RUN

In the long run all inputs are variable, and to handle a potentially large number of inputs we need an approach different from the one used to analyze short-run production. Specifically, we need to rephrase the underlying question. Instead of asking, "How much output is produced from a given combination of inputs?" we should ask, "What combinations of inputs can be used to produce a given level of output?" This may not seem like the natural question to ask. But consider the following. When General Motors chose to use robots in its plants instead of people, everyone was concerned about how many auto workers would lose their jobs. To frame this issue in terms of our analysis, GM initially used one combination of workers and robots to produce cars and later switched to a different combination of workers and robots. To get an idea of how many workers would be replaced by robots, we should find out what combinations of robots and workers can be used to produce GM's desired output of cars. Then, if we know how many robots GM plans to purchase, we can figure out how many fewer workers would be needed.

A Graphical Approach

Our task for analyzing long-run production is to find all of the combinations of labor and capital that can be used to produce a given amount of output. Before doing so, there is one slight technical problem that must be overcome. Suppose that the firm wants to produce q units of output and that it is possible for the firm to do this using L units of labor and K units of capital. Then it would also be possible to produce q units of output using more of both inputs. The firm could just throw away the extra inputs and achieve the same level of output. We want to ignore this possibility. Instead, we restrict attention to **efficient** combinations of inputs. That is, we only consider combinations of inputs for which $F(L,K) = q$, and not combinations of inputs for which $F(L,K) > q$. In the latter case the firm would waste inputs.

This said, we can begin to find all of the efficient combinations of inputs that can be used to produce, say, 100 units of output. We do this graphically. Figure 5-4 measures labor on the horizontal axis and capital on the vertical axis. We have to start somewhere, so assume that if the firm uses the combination of inputs given by point A, the firm can produce no more than 100 units of output. This means that point A is an efficient combination of inputs. If the firm uses more of both inputs, it should be able to produce more than 100 units of output; at least it can if both inputs have positive marginal products. So we can rule out all of the points to the northeast of A. If A is an efficient combination, the firm is unable to produce 100 units of output if it uses less of both inputs, so we can rule out all of the points to the southwest of A. This means that the only possible efficient combinations of inputs that produce 100 units of output lie either to the northwest or the southeast of point A.

Figure 5-4   An Isoquant

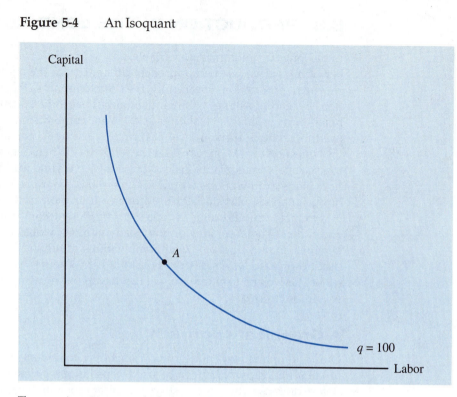

The curve is an isoquant, which shows all of the combinations of capital and labor that can be used to produce a given amount of output. In this case, the amount of output is 100 units. The isoquant is downward sloping because if the firm uses more of both inputs, it can produce more output. Similarly, if the firm uses less of both inputs, it can no longer produce 100 units of output. The only way to keep output at 100 units is to use more of one input and less of the other.

The curve in Figure 5-4 is the set of all efficient combinations of inputs that can be used to produce 100 units of output. Such a curve is called an **isoquant.** It is similar in appearance to the indifference curves of earlier chapters, and we discuss it in much the same way. Both the slope and the shape of isoquants have meaning. Begin with the slope. The slope of an isoquant shows how much less capital is needed to produce the same amount of output when labor is increased by one unit. Since the firm can use less capital when it uses more labor, the slope is a negative number. The negative of the slope of the isoquant, which is a positive number, is known as the **marginal rate of technical substitution,** which measures how much capital is needed to make up for the removal of one unit of labor when output is kept constant. The marginal rate of technical substitution, or *MRTS*, tells how the firm can substitute capital for labor. The higher the marginal rate of technical substitution, the more capital it takes to replace a unit of labor, while the lower the marginal rate of technical substitution, the less capital it takes to replace a unit of labor.

It is possible to relate the marginal rate of technical substitution to the marginal products of the inputs. To find the marginal rate of technical substitution, K and L must change in a way that leaves output unchanged. If the firm uses ΔL more units of labor, its output increases by $\Delta L \cdot MP_L$. If capital is increased by ΔK units, output rises by $\Delta K \cdot MP_K$. If both labor and capital change, but output does not change, then it must be the case that

$$MP_K \cdot \Delta K + MP_L \cdot \Delta L = 0.$$

The first term on the left-hand side is the change in output caused by the change in K, and the second term on the left-hand side is the change in output caused by the change in L. The left-hand side, then, is the total change in output. To remain on the isoquant, this total change in output must be zero. The next step in finding the marginal rate of technical substitution is remembering that the $MRTS$ is simply the negative of the slope of the isoquant, or $-\Delta K/\Delta L$. By rearranging the above equation we get

$$MRTS = -\frac{\Delta K}{\Delta L} = \frac{MP_L}{MP_K}.$$

Thus, the marginal rate of technical substitution is the ratio of the marginal products of the two inputs.

The shape of the isoquant tells something about how easily inputs can be substituted for each other. This is a different issue than how much of one input it takes to substitute for a unit of another input. For the isoquant shown in Figure 5-4, as the firm moves to the southwest along the isoquant, using less capital and more labor all the time, the $MRTS$ decreases. This means that as the firm uses more and more labor in its production process, it becomes easier and easier to replace labor with additional capital. As the amount of labor grows and the amount of capital falls, the remaining equipment becomes more crucial to the production process and the workers become less critical, making the remaining equipment and machinery more difficult to replace and the workers less difficult to replace.

An extreme case of this occurs in **fixed-proportion production functions,** as depicted in Figure 5-5. In a fixed-proportion production function, the inputs must be used in specific proportions, and it is impossible to substitute one input for another. The best example is a recipe. If the recipe calls for eggs and flour and you don't have enough eggs to make the entire recipe, it is not usually a good idea to substitute more flour for the missing eggs. Instead, you would cut down the recipe to accommodate the number of eggs you have, decreasing the rest of the ingredients in the right proportions. You can see that this is happening in Figure 5-5. At point A the firm has the in-

Figure 5-5   Fixed-Proportions Isoquant

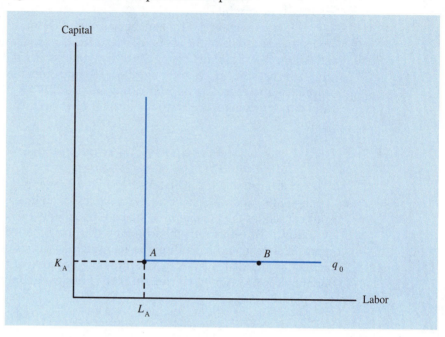

When an isoquant is L shaped, the firm must use the inputs in fixed proportions. Suppose that the firm has K_A units of capital and more than L_A units of labor. Then the firm is at a point like B, which is still on the same isoquant as point A, so the firm still produces the same amount as at point A. The extra labor is of no use to the firm. It cannot be substituted for capital in production.

puts in the right proportions. If the firm has more labor than it can use with K_A units of capital, it wastes the extra labor and produces the same amount of output. Similarly, if the firm has extra capital, it wastes the extra. When isoquants are L-shaped, as shown, there is no substitution between inputs. In general, the more L-shaped the isoquants, the harder it is to substitute one input for the other. The straighter the isoquants, the easier it is to substitute on input for the other.

There are different isoquants corresponding to different levels of output. Figure 5-6(a) shows an **isoquant map.** Movements to the northeast correspond to increases in output. An isoquant map provides a complete description of the production function and, hence, of technology. If technology changes, so does the isoquant map. For example, suppose that technology changes in a way that enables workers to be replaced by machines more easily. There could be an improvement in robot technology, for instance. Since it now takes less capital to replace a worker, the marginal rate of technical substitution falls, and the isoquants become flatter, as in Figure 5-6(b).

Figure 5-6   Isoquant Maps

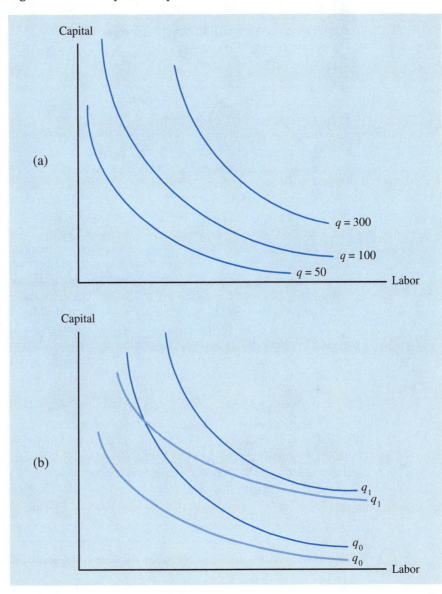

Panel (a) shows an isoquant map. The different isoquants correspond to different levels of output, with isoquants farther from the origin corresponding to higher levels of output. Panel (b) shows how a technology change can affect the isoquant map. The technology change causes the marginal rate of technical substitution to fall at every point, and the new, thick isoquants are flatter than the old, thin isoquants.

APPLICATION
An International Comparison of Productivity Growth

When technology improves, firms can produce more output using the same inputs. Graphically, the production function shifts upward. If technology improves in a country, every firm in that country benefits from the new technology and every firm can produce more using the same inputs. Technology can improve in a country for two reasons. First, the country can **innovate,** devising new production processes that allow firms to produce more output with the same inputs. Second, the country can adopt more advanced technology already in use in other countries. The country simply "catches up" to more technologically advanced countries.

Rolf Fare and his colleagues at Southern Illinois University measured productivity growth in seventeen industrialized countries from 1979 to 1988 and ascertained whether the growth was due to innovation or catching up.* Of the seventeen countries, the ones with the highest productivity growth rates were, in order from highest to lowest, Japan, Norway, Finland, Italy, and Canada. The United States was in about the middle of the group, and Ireland was at the bottom. Japan's productivity growth was split about evenly between innovation and catching up, while all of the United States' productivity growth came from innovation. Canada had quite a bit of innovation, but actually lost ground relative to the best technology in the rest of the world.

Fare and his colleagues also estimated a "world production function," which shows how much output can be produced using the best technology in the world. They found that throughout the 1980s, the world production function was the same as the United States' production function, meaning that the United States had the most advanced technology in the world. All of the U.S. innovations caused the world production function to shift upward.

* Rolf Fare et al., "Productivity Growth, Technical Progress, and Efficiency Change in Industrialized Countries," *American Economic Review*, March 1994, pp. 66–83.

Returns to Scale

In the long run, a firm can vary the level of all its inputs. When we consider a long-run production function, $F(L,K)$, we can now see how output is affected by changes in both labor and capital. Although the firm can vary the proportions of labor and capital in many different ways, there is a convenient approach to examining the properties of a production function: Vary labor and capital in the same proportion, and observe what happens to output. For example, if the firm doubles the quantities of both labor and capital, the new level of production can be written as $F(2L,2K)$. How does $F(L,K)$ compare to $F(2L,2K)$? The answer depends on the type of **returns to scale** exhibited by the production function. Put another way, it depends on how much output changes when the scale of the operation is doubled.

If the firm doubles all inputs, we expect more output to be produced. But exactly how much more depends on the underlying technology of the production process. There are three possibilities.

1. *Constant Returns to Scale.* If a doubling of all inputs leads to exactly a doubling of output, the production function is said to exhibit **constant returns to scale.** For example, if a steel mill is producing five tons of steel a day, and the owner builds a second mill that includes the same equipment and number and quality of workers as in the first mill, the second mill will also produce five tons of steel a day.

2. *Increasing Returns to Scale.* If a doubling of all inputs leads to a more than doubling of output, the production function is said to exhibit **increasing returns to scale.** For example, one house painter with one ladder may take 100 hours to paint a house, whereas two painters with two ladders may take only 40 hours. Thus, by doubling inputs, the painters can now complete two and one-half jobs in 100 hours.

3. *Decreasing Returns to Scale.* If a doubling of all inputs leads to a less than doubling of output, the production function is said to exhibit **decreasing returns to scale.** This may occur if, once a firm becomes very large, there are increased difficulties in organizing the production process.

Returns to scale are an important determinant of how many firms an industry should have. Consider first the case of increasing returns to scale. If two equal-sized firms combine to form one large firm, with increasing returns to scale the large firm can produce more than the total of the two smaller firms. It would make sense, then, to take advantage of this enhanced production capability by having large firms when the production function exhibits increasing returns to scale. In contrast, with decreasing returns to scale the large firm would produce less than the total of the two smaller firms. With decreasing returns to scale, then, firms should be relatively small. For the intermediate case of constant returns to scale, the large firm's output is the same as the combined output of the two smaller firms, so it does not matter how large the firm is.

One particular type of production function is useful for discussing returns to scale. It is the **Cobb-Douglas production function,** and it takes the form

$$F(L,K) = AL^aK^b.$$

For example, if $A = 100$, $a = 0.7$, and $b = 0.3$, the Cobb-Douglas production function takes the form $F(L,K) = 100L^{0.7}K^{0.3}$. The reason that this function is useful is that the two exponents, a and b, can be used to determine whether the function exhibits increasing, decreasing, or constant returns to scale. Remember that the function exhibits increasing returns to scale if $F(2L,2K) > 2F(L,K)$, that is, output more than doubles when the inputs are doubled. The function exhibits decreasing returns to scale if $F(2L,2K) < 2F(L,K)$, so that doubling the inputs less than doubles the output. Finally, under constant returns to scale, $F(2L,2K) = 2F(L,K)$, and doubling the inputs exactly doubles the output.

Let's determine what happens to output when inputs are doubled in the Cobb-Douglas production function:

$$F(2L,2K) = A(2L)^a(2K)^b = 2^{a+b}AL^aK^b = 2^{a+b}F(L,K).$$

The Cobb-Douglas production function exhibits increasing returns to scale if $F(2L,2K) > 2F(L,K)$; that is, if $2^{a+b}F(L,K) > 2F(L,K)$, which holds if $2^{a+b} > 2^1$. The condition for increasing returns to scale reduces to the inequality $a + b > 1$. If $a + b < 1$, the production function exhibits decreasing returns to scale, and if $a + b = 1$, the production function exhibits constant returns to scale. In the example given above, $a = 0.7$ and $b = 0.3$, so the example production function exhibits constant returns to scale.

5.4 HUMAN CAPITAL

As people work at their jobs, they acquire knowledge and skills that make them more proficient. For example, before they begin their jobs, sales representatives cannot anticipate every question customers might ask, but as customers ask new questions the sales reps learn more answers. Through experience, entrepreneurs gain a "feel" for their market, making them better able to anticipate changes. Pilots gain skills in different weather situations. Doctors learn more about particular ailments and accumulate personal experience to draw upon. People also gain knowledge and skills when they attend school. As workers gain knowledge and skills, they become more productive, but, as yet, our model does not account for this productivity change. In this section we take care of this omission.

Adding Human Capital to the Production Function

There are a couple of ways in which we could account for different knowledge and skill levels in the production function. One is to use a different type of labor for each different skill level, thereby adding a large number of independent variables to the production function. So, for example, we could model production as being a function of the number of hours provided by workers with one month of experience, workers with two months of experience, workers with three months of experience, and so on. We could also distinguish among workers with engineering degrees, business degrees, economics degrees, no degrees, and so on. This makes the production function rather complex, though, so it would be nice to have something simpler.

A second approach is to add a single variable accounting for the knowledge and skills accumulated by the workers. An increase in this variable would make labor more productive, just as an increase in capital tends to make labor more productive. As the firm acquires more capital, workers are able to produce more. Because the accumulated knowledge and skills variable behaves so much like capital, it is often termed **human capital.** When human capital is accounted for, the production function becomes $F(K,L,H)$, where H denotes human capital. To see how this works, suppose that the production function is $F(K,L,H) = 10KLH$. If $K = 2$, $L = 10$, and $H = 1$, then output is $F(2,10,1) = (10)(2)(10)(1) = 200$. If the amounts of capital and labor stay the same, but the amount of human capital rises to $H = 2$, output changes to $F(2,10,2) = (10)(2)(10)(2) = 400$. So, by increasing the knowledge and skill level of the workers, the firm's output increases.

Changing the Level of Human Capital

In the short run, is human capital a variable input, like labor, or a fixed input, like capital? To answer this question, we must determine how the firm can change the level of human capital. Recall that human capital is the accumulated knowledge and skills of the work force. To get a more knowledgeable and skillful work force, the firm can take two actions. One is to fire the old workers and hire new workers with more education and experience. This rarely happens. One reason firms are reluctant to use this approach is because some knowledge and skills are firm-specific. Workers must know the organization of the firm, workers in other parts of the firm, and so on. They must also know the firm's specific products. New workers would need time to gain this knowledge. A second reason a firm might not want to fire all its workers is because the firm would gain a bad reputation, which would make it more difficult for the firm to hire workers in the future. No one would want to work for a firm with a history of mass firings.

A better way for the firm to change knowledge and skill levels is to provide training for its workers. Many large firms provide a variety of training programs for their workers. For example, investment companies have long training programs for new workers to familiarize them with the firm's procedures, equipment, and products. Other companies have classes to teach workers to use new computer software, for example. Some companies even have media links so that employees can take college courses from remote locations. It is quite common for companies to pay for a worker to go back to college for an advanced degree. Why does a firm do this? By gaining more knowledge and skills, the employee becomes more productive for the firm. The firm *invests* in human capital.

Investing in human capital can either take a short amount of time or a long amount of time, depending on how big the investment is. Setting up a class to teach employees to use a new computer spreadsheet program does not take very long, so it can be thought of as a short-run change. Sending an employee back to college for an advanced degree takes much longer and should be thought of as a long-run change. There are also constant increases in human capital that just come naturally because of on-the-job experience. Nevertheless, large changes in human capital require time, so human capital is typically assumed to be fixed in the short run.

The Use of Temporary Workers

In the last several years there has been a growing trend toward firms using temporary workers instead of permanent workers for some positions. For example, many large companies hire temporary clerical workers. Some of the fastest-growing companies in the early 1990s were temporary service companies. Why do firms hire temporary workers, and which types of positions are most likely to be filled by temporary workers? Part of the answer comes from looking at human capital. Some positions require more human capital than others, especially firm-specific human capital. At one extreme, the chief executive officer of the company should have accumulated a large amount of human capital and should have considerable knowledge about the operations of the specific company. On the other hand, workers whose chief duties are typing and filing do not need much firm-specific human capital. It does not make sense for the firm to hire a temporary worker for a position that requires a great deal of firm-specific human capital, but it may make sense to hire a temporary worker for other, possibly skilled, jobs that do not require much firm-specific human capital. That is why the largest number of temporary workers can be found in clerical positions.

But why would firms want to hire temporary personnel? The answer comes from weighing costs and benefits. When a firm hires a permanent worker, the firm must provide insurance coverage, withhold taxes and social security, and so on. Insurance coverage has obvious costs, and providing the other benefits creates an administrative burden for the firm. The firm can reduce costs by hiring temporary workers and forgoing these costs. The temporary agency takes care of all the administrative details. The firm should hire a temporary worker if the cost reduction more than makes up for the worker's lack of firm-specific human capital. Otherwise, the firm should hire a permanent worker.

Summary

- **Inputs** are goods and services used in the production of another good or service, referred to as an **output.**

- Inputs that can be varied in the production process are called **variable inputs.** Inputs that cannot be varied are called **fixed inputs.**

- In the **short run,** at least one input is fixed. In the **long run,** all inputs are variable. The difference between the short run and long run, then, is not a specific amount of time. Instead, it depends on how long it takes to change the amounts of fixed inputs.

- A **production function** tells how much output is produced for a given combination of inputs.

- The **average product** of an input is defined as the total output divided by the amount of the input. The **marginal product** of an input is defined as the extra output generated by increasing the input by one unit.

- The **law of diminishing returns** refers to the point where the marginal product of an input begins to decrease. Beginning at this point, the firm gets less and less additional output from each additional unit of input.

- An **isoquant** is a curve that represents a constant amount of output for different combinations of inputs.

- The slope of an isoquant at any given point is the **marginal rate of technical substitution (MRTS)** between the two inputs used to produce a constant amount of output. The MRTS measures how much of one input is needed to make up for the removal of one unit of the other input, while remaining on the same isoquant.

- If the doubling of all inputs leads to exactly a doubling of output, the production function is said to exhibit **constant returns to scale.**

- If the doubling of all inputs leads to more than a doubling of output, the production function is said to exhibit **increasing returns to scale.**

- If the doubling of all inputs leads to less than a doubling of output, the production function is said to exhibit **decreasing returns to scale.**

- The knowledge and skills accumulated by workers is termed **human capital.** Human capital can be treated as an input to the production process along with the *quantity* of labor.

Problems

1. A firm's production function is given by $F(L,K) = 10LK$.
   a. How much output does the firm produce when it uses 6 units of capital and 40 units of labor?
   b. Assume that the amount of capital is fixed at 6 units in the short run. Graph the total product curve.
   c. Still assuming that capital is fixed at 6 units in the short run, graph the average and marginal product curves.
2. Complete the following table:

L	q	AP_L	MP_L
0	0	—	—
5	60		
10	140		
15	195		
20	240		
25	275		

3. Justin enters a room full of people. If Justin is older than the average person already in the room, does the average age of people in the room rise or fall when Justin enters? Why?
4. Consider your economics class as a firm, with students and your instructor's effort as inputs. The firm's product is average teaching evaluation scores. Holding the instructor's effort constant in the short run, draw what you think is a reasonable total product curve and explain its shape.
5. A restaurant uses radio and television advertising to attract customers. Draw an isoquant when the two types of advertising are inputs and explain its shape. How well do you think radio advertising substitutes for television advertising? How does this affect the slope of the isoquant?
6. Consider the production function $F(L,K) = 2000LK^{0.5}$. Does this production function exhibit increasing, constant, or decreasing returns to scale? Verify your answer using $L = K = 10$ and $L = K = 20$.
7. The concept of returns to scale was discussed in Section 5.3, which covered production in the long run. Why doesn't it make sense to talk about returns to scale in the short run?
8. Explain why it makes sense for education to be mandatory for children in the United States and why it makes sense for taxpayers to subsidize public education.
9. Imagine that the increased use of computers in public schools greatly increases the human capital of the population, making workers more productive, on average. If a firm's production function is given by $F(L,K,H)$, what happens to the firm's isoquants in capital-labor space when human capital increases? Explain your answer.

6

COSTS AND PROFIT

Overview

Suppose that IBM decides to produce 50,000 Thinkpad computers during a certain period of time. IBM would like to produce them as cheaply as possible, which means using the least expensive combination of inputs that can produce 50,000 Thinkpads. The production function tells which combinations of inputs can be used to produce 50,000 Thinkpads, but it does not tell which of the many possible combinations should be used. That is the task of this chapter.

Minimizing costs does not mean minimizing quality. For example, it is possible to talk about an upscale restaurant minimizing costs. If the restaurant minimizes costs, it does not mean that the restaurant buys low-quality ingredients, or hires a second-rate chef, or skimps on service. What it means is that the restaurant does not buy more ingredients than it will use, does not pay the chef too much, and does not have too many waiters at one time.

Three important points arise in this chapter. First, the manner in which firms minimize costs is important. We look at how firms minimize the cost of producing a given amount of output. Doing this requires use of the production functions from Chapter 5. The short and long runs must be treated separately, because the firm has more choices to make in long-run decisions than in short-run decisions. Second, after the cost-minimizing method of production has been found, we can talk about cost functions. Once we have the cost functions, we can move on to the third point, which is that once we have the cost function, we no longer need the production function for analyzing the firm's profit-maximization problem.

The basic tasks of this chapter can be further exemplified using the IBM example. First, IBM figures out the least costly way to produce 50,000 Thinkpads, as above. This gives IBM the cost of producing 50,000 Thinkpads. Then it figures out the least costly way to produce other numbers of Thinkpads. By doing this, IBM now knows how much it costs to produce a variety of numbers of Thinkpads. The last step is that IBM can look at the demand for Thinkpads and figure out how much revenue it can earn by selling different numbers of Thinkpads. Profit is revenue minus cost, so now IBM has all of the information it needs to decide how many Thinkpads to produce to maximize profit.

In this chapter you will learn:

- How firms minimize costs when the amount of at least one input is fixed (the short run).
- How firms minimize costs when all inputs can be varied (the long run).
- How short-run costs and long-run costs are related.
- How firms use costs in their profit-maximization decisions.

6.1 COSTS IN THE SHORT RUN

In order to get their money, credit card companies must employ workers to open envelopes and process payment checks. So, the credit card companies must bring in enough workers to process all of the payment checks they expect to receive on a given day. The number of checks that can be processed is fixed by the number of workers available that day. The credit card company does not want to bring in too many workers, because the workers must be paid regardless of how many checks are processed. Nor does it want to bring in too few workers, because then some payments go unprocessed, and the company is unable to earn interest on that money for a day. So, the problem the firm faces, for a given daily volume of payments, is how many workers should be used. This is a short-run cost-minimization problem.

The Cost-Minimization Problem

Let us begin by stating the firm's objective in more detail. Suppose that a firm has decided to produce q units of output. There are many ways in which the firm can combine its two inputs, capital and labor, to produce q units of output. In fact, any combination of K and L with $F(L,K) = q$ will do it. In order to maximize profit, though, the firm must choose the combination of K and L that costs the least. Suppose that L measures the number of hours of labor. Then for each unit of labor used the firm must pay the going wage, denoted w. When the firm uses L hours of labor at a cost of w per hour, the total expenditure on labor is wL. Similarly, for each unit of capital used, the firm must pay some amount of r per hour, which is the rental price of capital. If the firm uses K units of capital at r per unit, the total expenditure on capital is rK. The total cost of using L units of labor and K units of capital, then, is $wL + rK$.

Note that to calculate the total expenditure on capital, we used the *rental* price of capital. When the firm rents capital, it must pay a fee to the rental company, just as people pay fees when they rent cars. But what if the firm owns the capital? When a firm owns capital, it has two choices of what to do with it. One choice is to use the capital as part of the production process. The other choice is to let some other firm rent the capital for r per unit. If the firm uses the capital in its own production process, it *forgoes* the amount of money it could have earned by letting some other firm rent the capital. Thus, by using the capital itself, the firm forgoes r per unit. So, whether the firm owns its own capital or rents it from someone else, the firm still forgoes r per unit in cash. Put another way, the rental price of capital is the *opportunity cost* of capital. (Opportunity costs are discussed in more detail in Chapter 1.) This is why we can use the rental price of capital to calculate the firm's total expenditure on capital.

The firm's objective is to find the combination of L and K that (1) produces the right amount of output, that is, $F(L,K) = q$, and (2) minimizes the total cost, $wL + rK$. In the short run, this problem can be greatly simplified, because in the short run the firm does not choose the amount of capital. It is fixed at K_0. So, the firm's new problem is to find the amount of labor that (1) produces the right amount of output, that is, $F(L,K_0) = q$, and (2) minimizes total cost, $wL + rK_0$.

To find the optimal amount of labor, let's begin by looking at the production function in Figure 6-1. The firm wants to produce q units of output using as little labor as possible, which means using $L^*(q)$ units of labor. The total short-run cost associated with this choice is $TC(q) = wL^*(q) + rK_0$, where $TC(q)$ denotes the **short-run total cost function,** which measures the lowest possible total cost of producing different levels of output when the amount of capital is fixed at K_0.

Fixed and Variable Costs

The **total cost** of producing q units of output can be split into two components. First, there is the cost of the capital. The firm has a fixed level of K_0 units of capital in the short run, and the rental price of capital is r. The cost of capital, then, is rK_0, and it is the **total fixed cost (TFC).** In general, the total fixed cost is the cost of all combined fixed inputs, and the firm incurs that cost regardless of how much it produces, or even if it produces nothing at all. The second component of total cost is the cost of labor. To produce q units the firm uses $L^*(q)$ units of labor, at a wage rate of w per unit of labor. The total cost of labor is $wL^*(q)$, and, since labor is the variable input, this is called the **total variable cost (TVC).** Total variable cost measures the labor cost of producing the desired quantity of output. Note that total variable cost is a function of q, but total fixed cost is not. Thus, we can write the total cost function as

$$TC(q) = TVC(q) + TFC.$$

In Table 6-1 we calculate the various total costs of different levels of output based on the production figures given in the first three columns. To calculate the costs, we use a wage rate of $w = 5$ and a capital price of $r = 20$. Notice that when nothing is produced, that is, when $q = 0$, total cost is still pos-

Figure 6-1   The Optimal Amount of Labor in the Short Run

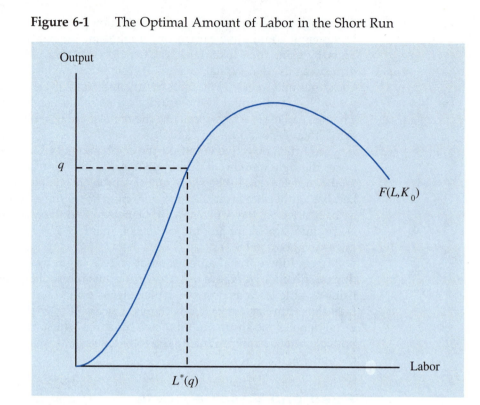

Suppose that the firm wants to produce q units of output. Its capital is fixed in the short run, so the only choice it must make is the amount of labor to use. The production function shows that the firm must use at least $L^*(q)$ units of labor to produce q units of output. If the firm uses more labor, it must pay for more labor. So, to keep costs at a minimum, the firm should use exactly $L^*(q)$ units of labor.

itive. This is because capital is fixed in the short run, and the firm must pay for it even if the firm doesn't use the capital to produce anything.

To graph the cost functions, it is best to begin with the component functions. Measure the amount of output, q, on the horizontal axis, and the cost, in dollars, on the vertical axis, as in Figure 6-2. The total fixed cost is the same at all levels of output, so its graph is just a horizontal line at height rK_0. To graph total variable cost, refer back to Figure 6-1. When capital is fixed at K_0, the firm must use $L^*(q)$ units of labor to produce q units of output. The total variable cost of producing q units of output is $wL^*(q)$. The shape of the total variable cost function, then, is the same as the shape of the function $wL^*(q)$ with output, q, on the horizontal axis and cost on the vertical axis. The total cost curve is obtained by adding the two component curves vertically, as in the figure. Notice that in Figure 6-2 the TC curve is a constant height above the TVC curve, and this height difference is the height of the TFC curve.

Table 6-1   Total Variable, Total Fixed, and Total Cost Example

Labor (L)	Capital (K)	Output (q)	Total Variable Cost (TVC)	Total Fixed Cost (TFC)	Total Cost (TC)
0	5	0	0	100	100
10	5	200	50	100	150
20	5	500	100	100	200
30	5	660	150	100	250
40	5	760	200	100	300
50	5	800	250	100	350

Figure 6-2   The Total Cost, Total Variable Cost, and Total Fixed Cost Curves

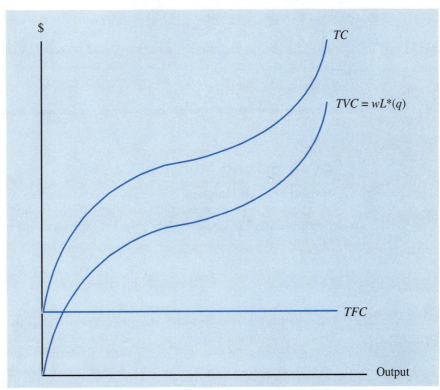

In the short run the firm has three different cost curves. The total cost curve, TC, shows the lowest possible cost of producing the desired level of output. It has two components. The total variable cost curve, TVC, shows the labor cost of producing the desired quantity of output. The total fixed cost curve, TFC, shows the cost of the fixed amount of capital. Since capital is fixed, this cost is the same no matter how much the firm produces, so the TFC curve is a horizontal line. It is possible to get the TC curve from the other two by adding the TVC and TFC curves vertically. In fact, the TC curve is a constant height above the TVC curve, and that constant height is exactly the height of the TFC curve.

APPLICATION
The Japanese Barrier Against Laying Off Workers

There are cultural barriers in Japan against laying off workers. According to the culture, employment is supposed to be for life, with no unintended spells of unemployment. If a firm adheres to this custom, it makes labor a somewhat fixed input. The firm is free to expand employment but is not free to reduce it. And, because of the cultural barrier, the firm may not be able to reduce its work force for a long time. A case in point is Nissan Motor Co. In the late 1980s Nissan expanded very quickly in an attempt to match the size of Toyota, Japan's largest car company. In the early 1990s Nissan found itself with low demand and an excessively large work force, but with no way to cut it because of the cultural barrier.* Consequently, Nissan was not able to reduce labor when it reduced output, and so total variable costs did not fall when output fell. This means that Nissan's total variable cost curve cannot fall below the current labor cost, and so the *TVC* curve has a horizontal component.

The Wall Street Journal, April 7, 1994, p. B4.

Average and Marginal Costs

Instead of discussing total costs, it is sometimes more convenient to discuss average costs. The **average total cost,** or *ATC,* is defined as the total cost per unit produced. In equation form, the average total cost of producing q units of output is

$$ATC(q) = \frac{TC(q)}{q}.$$

The reason it is convenient to discuss average cost is that average costs can be directly compared with prices. If the average cost is below the price of the output, the firm earns a profit. Why? Each unit that the firm sells brings in p in revenue, where p is the price, but only costs the firm *ATC* to produce. The firm earns a profit of $p - ATC$ per unit, and if the price is higher than average cost, the profit per unit is positive. If, on the other hand, the average cost is higher than the price, the firm loses money on each unit it sells, and its profit is negative.

Just as total cost can be broken down into variable and fixed costs, average costs can also be separated into variable and fixed components: **average variable cost** and **average fixed cost.** Average variable cost is given by the formula

$$AVC(q) = \frac{TVC(q)}{q},$$

and, in the two-input case we have been analyzing, the average variable cost is the labor cost per unit. Similarly, average fixed cost is given by the formula

$$AFC(q) = \frac{TFC}{q},$$

which can be interpreted as the capital cost per unit. As you might expect, adding $AVC(q)$ and $AFC(q)$ together yields $ATC(q)$.

There is one other type of cost that is important for analyzing the behavior of firms, and that is **marginal cost.** We already mentioned and used marginal costs in Chapter 1, but we did not say where they came from. With the cost functions we have already derived, it is now possible to calculate marginal costs. The marginal cost of the q-th unit of output, written $MC(q)$, is the additional cost of producing the q-th unit. Marginal cost is calculated using the formula

$$MC(q) = \frac{\Delta TC(q)}{\Delta q}.$$

The change in total cost is the same as the change in total variable cost, though, because only variable costs change as output changes. Thus, marginal cost can also be calculated according to the formula

$$MC(q) = \frac{\Delta TVC(q)}{\Delta q}.$$

It is possible to calculate average and marginal costs using the same figures as in Table 6-1. This is done in Table 6-2.

Table 6-2   Average and Marginal Costs Example

Output (q)	Average Variable Cost (AVC)	Average Fixed Cost (AFC)	Average Total Cost (ATC)	Marginal Cost (MC)
0	—	—	—	—
200	.25	.50	.75	.25
500	.20	.20	.40	.17
660	.23	.15	.38	.31
760	.26	.13	.39	.50
800	.31	.12	.43	1.25

Figure 6-3 graphs the information contained in Table 6-2. Notice that the average fixed cost curve is decreasing. To see why, recall that average fixed cost is defined as TFC/q. Since TFC is fixed, as q gets larger the denominator gets larger and the fraction gets smaller. The average variable and average total cost curves are U-shaped, as is the marginal cost curve. Notice, from both the table and the figure, that the average total cost curve reaches its minimum at a higher level of output than the average variable cost curve. This is because at the level of output where the average variable cost curve reaches its minimum, the slope of the average variable cost curve is zero, but the slope of the average fixed cost curve is negative. In fact, the average fixed cost curve always has a negative slope. Adding together the slopes of the average variable and average fixed cost curves gives you the slope of the average total cost curve. At the level of output where the average variable cost curve reaches its minimum, then, the average total cost curve must be downward sloping, as shown.

Figure 6-3 The Average Total Cost, Average Variable Cost, Average Fixed Cost, and Marginal Cost Curves

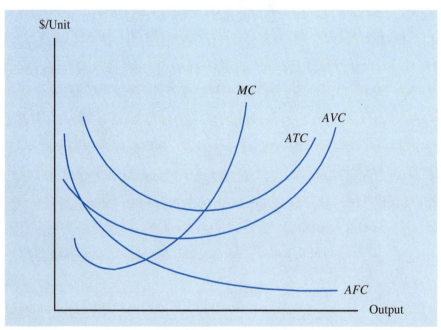

The average total cost (ATC) and average variable cost (AVC) curves are U-shaped. The marginal cost curve (MC) intersects both of these curves from below and passes through the minimum point of each of the two curves. The average fixed cost curve (AFC) is downward sloping, because as output increases, the fixed cost is being spread over a larger number of units, causing the average fixed cost to fall.

As with average product and marginal product curves, there is a relationship between average cost and marginal cost, and also between average variable cost and marginal cost. The marginal cost curve cuts through the lowest points of both the average cost and average variable cost curves. Also, when $MC < ATC$, ATC is decreasing, and when $MC > ATC$, ATC is increasing. Similarly, when $MC < AVC$, AVC is decreasing, and when $MC > AVC$, AVC is increasing. These relationships hold for the same reasons that the relationships between average and marginal product curves hold. To draw average and marginal cost curves correctly, you must be careful to make sure that the marginal cost curve passes through the minimum points of the ATC and AVC curves.

Figure 6-4 shows how to derive the average and marginal cost curves from the total cost curves. The technique is similar to that of finding the average and marginal product curves from the total product curve. The top panel of the figure shows total variable cost, total fixed cost, and total cost curves. The bottom panel shows the corresponding average cost curves and the marginal cost curve. The marginal cost curve is the slope of the total cost curve, which, at any given level of output, is the same as the slope of the total variable cost curve. The height of the average cost curve at a particular level of output is equal to the slope of a line connecting the origin to a point on the total cost curve. Point A generates the flattest line connecting the origin to the total cost curve, so it corresponds to the minimum point of the average cost curve in the lower panel. The height of the average variable cost curve at a particular level of output is the slope of a line connecting the average variable cost curve to the origin. Point B generates the flattest such line, so it corresponds to the minimum point of the average variable cost curve. Notice that at point A the line to the origin is tangent to the total cost curve, so average cost equals marginal cost at output q_A. At point B the line to the origin is tangent to the total variable cost curve, so average variable cost equals marginal cost at output q_B. Finally, the height of the average fixed cost curve at a particular level of output is the slope of a line from the total fixed cost curve to the origin. Notice that as output increases, the line from the origin to the total fixed cost curve gets flatter, so average fixed cost falls.

Changes in Input Prices

What happens to the cost curves if one of the inputs becomes more expensive? Let's begin by looking at what happens if capital becomes more expensive, that is, if r rises. Figure 6-5 shows what happens to the various cost curves. Panel (a) shows how total cost curves shift. The total fixed cost curve shifts upward because total fixed cost is rK_0, and if r rises, fixed costs must also rise. The total variable cost curve does not shift, because it depends only on the wage rate w and the amount of labor used, not r. The total cost curve shifts upward to reflect the upward shift in total fixed costs.

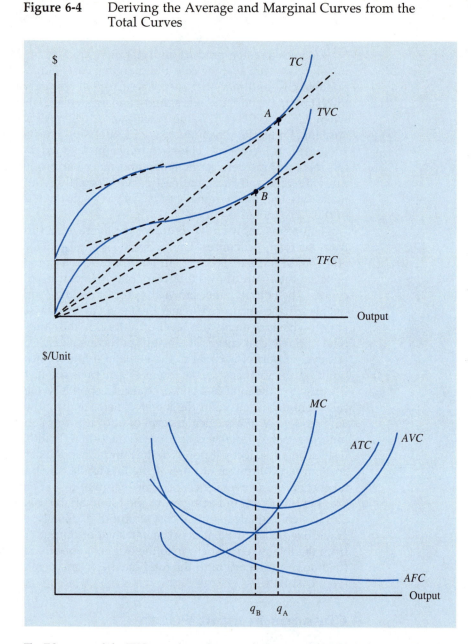

The *TC* curve and the *TVC* curve have the same slope at any given level of output. This slope is the height of the *MC* curve. The height of the *ATC* curve at a given level of output is the slope of the line segment connecting the origin to the *TC* curve at that level of output. The flattest line segment connecting the origin to the *TC* curve is tangent to the *TC* curve at point *A*, so q_A is the quantity corresponding to the minimum point of the *ATC* curve and is also where *MC* intersects *ATC*. Similarly, q_B is the quantity corresponding to the minimum point of the *AVC* curve and the intersection of *MC* with *AVC*. The line segments connecting the origin to the *TFC* curve get continually flatter as output increases, so the *AFC* curve is downward sloping.

Figure 6-5   The Effects of an Increase in the Price of a Fixed Input

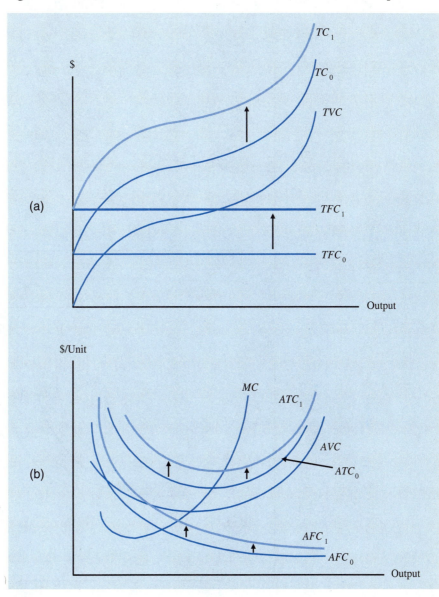

Panel (a) shows how the total cost curves shift when the price of capital rises. The *TFC* curve shifts upward because the fixed input, capital, now costs more. Since labor prices do not change, there is no shift in the *TVC* curve. The *TC* curve shifts upward to match the shift in the *TFC* curve. Panel (b) shows how the average and marginal cost curves shift. The *AFC* and *ATC* curves shift upward to reflect the increase in fixed costs. The *AVC* curve does not shift, because labor costs did not change. The *MC* curve is the slope of the *TC* curve, but it is also the slope of the *TVC* curve, which did not move. Consequently, the *MC* curve does not move.

Figure 6-6   The Effects of an Increase in the Price of a Variable Input

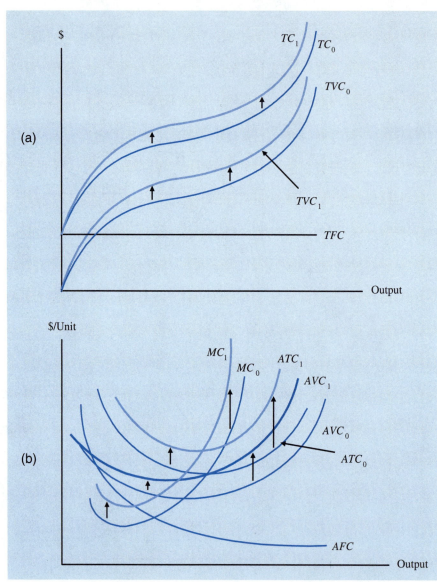

Panel (a) shows how the total cost curves change when the price of the variable input rises. The *TVC* and *TC* curves rotate upward because the variable input is more expensive. The *TFC* curve does not shift, though, because the price of the variable input has no impact on the cost of the fixed input. Panel (b) shows how the average and marginal cost curves shift. The *MC* curve shifts upward because when the *TC* curve rotated it became steeper, and the height of the *MC* curve is the slope of the *TC* curve. The *AVC* and *ATC* curves shift upward because the *TVC* and *TC* curves are higher than before. The *AFC* curve does not move because fixed costs are not affected by changes in the price of the variable input.

APPLICATION
A Rise in the Price of Newsprint

Newsprint prices increased 20 percent during 1994. Newsprint is only one of the inputs to publishing a newspaper, but the usage of paper is directly related to the usage of some of the firm's other inputs. If the firm hires more writers, or establishes more features (such as comic strips, community announcements, and so on), it must use more paper. When newsprint prices increased dramatically, newspaper publishers took steps to cut their costs. For example, the Green Bay (Wis.) *Press-Gazette* responded to the newsprint price increase by cutting news columns by 2 percent, or about a half a page per day. It also trimmed such features as church listings and international wire-service stories. It decided not to cut local news reporting.*

*The Wall Street Journal, February 15, 1995, p. B1.

Panel (b) shows what happens to average and marginal costs. First, average fixed cost rises because of the increase in *r*, but average variable cost does not shift. Average total cost rises because it is the sum of average fixed cost and average variable cost. Marginal cost does not shift because it is the slope of average total cost *and* the slope of average variable cost, and average variable cost did not shift. So, in summary, when capital becomes more expensive the total and average fixed cost curves shift upward, and the total and average cost curves shift upward, and that is all.

What about when labor becomes more expensive, that is, when the wage *w* rises? Figure 6-6 shows that answer. The total fixed cost curve does not shift because the cost of capital does not depend on the wage rate. The total variable cost curve rotates upward, though, becoming steeper. It still passes through the origin. The total cost curve also becomes steeper to reflect the increase in variable costs. The bottom panel shows what happens to the average and marginal cost curves. Since both the total cost and total variable cost curves rotate upward, the average total cost and average variable cost curves shift upward. Since the total cost and total variable cost curves are steeper than before, the marginal cost curve shifts upward, as shown. Thus, when labor costs rise, all of the curves shift upward *except* for the total fixed cost and average fixed cost curves, which are not affected by the change in labor costs.

6.2   COSTS IN THE LONG RUN

In 1987 the Owens-Corning Fiberglass plant in Jackson, Tennesee, produced 130 million pounds of fiberglass using 540 employees. The plant then closed for seven years. When it reopened in 1994, the old equipment had been either refurbished or replaced, and the plant incorporated all of the latest technological advances. The plant matched the old rate of production, 130 million pounds of fiberglass per year, but now it only used 80 employees.[1] Owens-Corning chose to substitute machinery for workers when it reopened the plant.

When Owens-Corning decided how to produce fiberglass at its new plant, it made a long-run decision. All of its inputs were variable. In the short run, on the other hand, it is assumed that only one input can be varied. The outcome of the long-run decision was to use more machinery and equipment but fewer workers. In the terminology of this chapter, it chose to use more capital and less labor. How did Owens-Corning make this decision? That is the question for this section.

The Long-Run Cost Minimization Problem

Suppose that the firm uses two inputs, capital and labor, to produce its output. In the short run, the firm can only adjust the amount of labor; the amount of capital is fixed. In the long run, however, the firm can adjust both inputs. We would like to derive a cost function, just as we did for the firm's short-run problem. In the short run, the firm finds the least expensive way of producing each level of output. This entails using as little labor as possible, since the amount of capital is fixed. In the long run, both inputs can be varied, so the firm's problem is slightly different. When the firm wants to produce a given level of output, it should choose the least expensive combination of inputs that can be used to produce the desired output. This is the firm's long-run cost minimization problem.

The problem can be solved graphically. First, we find the set of combinations of inputs that can be used to produce a given level of output, and graph it as shown in Figure 6-7. But this is just an isoquant. The firm's problem is to choose the point on the isoquant that costs the least. Now let's determine how much a particular combination costs. Suppose that if the firm uses 8 hours of labor and 2 units of capital, it can produce 20 units of output. If the wage rate is $10 per hour, and the cost of machinery is $20 per hour, how much does it cost the firm to produce 20 units of output? The firm spends $80 on labor and $40 on capital, so it costs $120 to produce 20 units of output.

Instead of focusing on a fixed amount of output, let's focus on a fixed level of costs. What other combinations of inputs cost $120? If the firm uses 12 hours of labor and no capital, it spends $120. If the firm uses no labor

---

1 "How an Outdated Plant Was Made New," *The Wall Street Journal*, October 21, 1994, p. B1.

Figure 6-7   The Firm's Cost-Minimization Problem

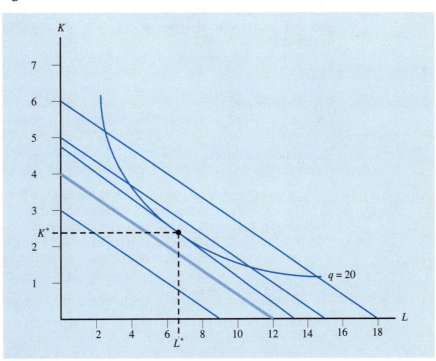

The isoquant shows all of the combinations of K and L that can combine to produce the desired level of output, q = 20. Each iso-cost line shows the combinations of K and L that yield the same total cost. The thick iso-cost line corresponds to a total cost of $120, given that capital costs $30 per unit and labor costs $10 per hour. The firm minimizes the cost of producing 20 units of output at the point where the isoquant is tangent to an iso-cost line. In this case, cost is minimized when the firm uses 6.3 hours of labor and 2.4 units of capital, and the total cost is 6.3($10) + 2.4($30) = $135.

and 6 units of capital, it spends $120. In general, the combinations of inputs that cost $120 are given by the equation

$$10L + 30K = 120.$$

The first term on the left-hand side is the labor cost, and the second term on the left-hand side is the capital cost. The equation says that the labor cost and the capital cost together add up to $120. If we rearrange this equation to isolate K on the left-hand side, we get

$$K = 4 - 0.33L.$$

The graph of this equation is the thick line in Figure 6-7. It is a downward-sloping straight line, and is called an **iso-cost line.** An iso-cost line shows all of the combinations of inputs that cost a set amount. It is different from the cost function, because the cost function tells the cost of producing some level of *output*, while the iso-cost line shows the cost of producing with some combination of *inputs*.

In general, an iso-cost line is derived from the formula

$$wL + rK = c,$$

where c is the set level of cost. Rearranging this equation yields

$$K = \frac{c}{r} - \frac{w}{r}L.$$

The slope of the line is $-w/r$, which is the ratio of input prices. Using this equation, it is a straightforward exercise to determine how the iso-cost line reacts to changes in the input prices or in the cost level c. If c increases, the iso-cost line shifts outward and parallel. If the wage rate w increases, the iso-cost line rotates inward, keeping the vertical intercept unchanged. Finally, if the price of capital r increases, the iso-cost line rotates inward, keeping the horizontal intercept the same.

Now let's return to the firm's cost-minimization problem. The firm wants to produce a fixed amount of output, q, at the lowest possible cost. Since the amount of output is fixed at q, the firm must choose a point on the isoquant. Since iso-cost lines shift upward when the cost increases, the firm wants to choose a point on the lowest possible iso-cost line. The solution to the cost minimization problem is shown in Figure 6-7. The problem is solved where the iso-cost line is tangent to the isoquant. Mathematically, the optimal input combination, (L^*, K^*), must satisfy two conditions. First, it must lie on the isoquant, which means that

$$F(L^*, K^*) = q.$$

Second, the isoquant and the iso-cost line must be tangent, which means that they must have the same slopes. As already noted, the slope of the iso-cost line is $-w/r$. In Chapter 5 we found that the slope of the isoquant is $-MRTS = -MP_L/MP_K$. Consequently, the tangency condition is

$$MRTS = \frac{MP_L}{MP_K} = \frac{w}{r}.$$

The tangency condition has an intuitive interpretation. Rearrange the last equality to get

$$\frac{MP_L}{w} = \frac{MP_K}{r}.$$

The marginal product of labor is the extra output produced by an extra unit of labor, and the wage rate is the cost, in dollars, of an extra unit of labor. The left-hand side, then, is the extra output produced by an additional dollar's worth of labor. Similarly, the right-hand side is the extra output produced by an additional dollar's worth of capital. To see why the two sides must be equal, suppose that the left-hand side is larger than the right-hand side. In that case, the firm could use one less dollar's worth of capital and spend the extra dollar on labor. Reducing capital by a dollar's worth reduces output by MP_K/r, and increasing labor by a dollar's worth increases output by MP_L/w. If $MP_L/w > MP_K/r$, the increase in labor raises output more than the decrease in capital lowers output. Thus, total output increases. The same argument shows that the left-hand side cannot be less than the right-hand side. If the two sides are not equal, the firm can produce more output for the same cost. Thus, if the two sides are not equal, the firm is not minimizing cost.

Changes in Input Prices

Suppose that labor becomes more expensive, that is, suppose that the wage rate w increases. What is the effect on the optimal combination of inputs? The problem is illustrated in Figure 6-8. The firm wishes to produce q units of output, which means that it must choose a point on the corresponding isoquant. With the initial wage rate, the iso-cost line is shown by the thin line, and the optimal input combination is (L_1,K_1). To find the effect of an increase in the wage rate, recall that the slope of an iso-cost line is $-w/r$. Consequently, if w increases, the iso-cost lines become steeper. The thick line is the new iso-cost line, and the new tangency point is at (L_2,K_2). The firm uses less labor and more capital.

The intuition behind this result is that when the price of labor rises, labor becomes more expensive relative to capital. When analyzing the firm's cost-minimization problem, it is enough to consider only changes in relative prices. If the relative price of labor rises, the firm uses less labor and more capital. If the relative price of labor falls, the firm uses more labor and less capital. If both prices change by the same percentage, so that the relative prices stay the same, the firm does not change its mix of inputs.

What happens to total cost when the wage rate rises? As one would expect, when one input becomes more expensive, total cost rises. To see this graphically, begin by looking at point A in Figure 6-8. Even though the firm does not choose point A after the wage increase, we can still determine the cost of producing there and use it as a benchmark to see whether total cost rises or falls as a result of the wage rate increase. Notice that point A and point C are both on the original iso-cost line, so that before the wage change both input combinations cost the same amount. But at point C the firm uses K_C units of capital and no labor. So, the cost of point C, and hence the cost of point A, is rK_C, which does not depend on the wage rate. Now look at the dashed iso-cost line through point C. It is parallel to the thick iso-cost

Figure 6-8   The Effect of an Increase in the Wage Rate on the Input
Combination Choice

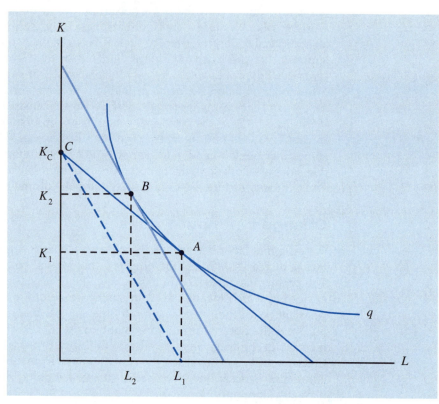

When the wage rate increases, iso-cost lines become steeper. Before the wage increase, the cost-minimizing input combination was at point A. After the wage increase, the new cost-minimizing combination is at point B, where the firm uses more capital and less labor. Total cost rises, as can be seen by comparing the thick iso-cost line to the thick, dashed iso-cost line. Both have the same slope, so both have the higher wage. However, points on the dashed line have the same cost, rK_C, as point A before the wage increase. Since B is on a higher iso-cost line than the dashed line, the total cost of producing q has risen.

line, so it is an iso-cost line after the wage increase. Because it goes through point C, and because the cost of point C is rK_C, which does not depend on the wage rate, the dashed iso-cost line represents input combinations that cost rK_C. Remember that point A also cost rK_C before the wage increase. So, points on the dashed iso-cost line cost the same after the wage increase as point A cost before the wage increase.

The dashed iso-cost line is not tangent to the isoquant, however. To reach the isoquant, the firm must move to a higher iso-cost line, the one through point B. Since it is a higher iso-cost line, point B costs more than point C after the wage increase. But point C cost the same as point A before the wage

APPLICATION
The Effects of Safety Regulation

OSHA (the Occupational Safety and Health Administration) is considering issuing guidelines for how firms should treat workers who must perform repetitive tasks with their hands, such as typing on a computer, because such tasks can lead to carpal tunnel syndrome. Studies have shown that workers who perform the same repetitive motions for two hours or more at a stretch are particularly susceptible to the ailment. What would happen if OSHA required a fifteen-minute break every two hours of the workday? Then it would take eight workers to complete the same amount of work as it used to take seven workers to complete. Essentially, then, the price of labor would rise by one-seventh.

What does this do to a firm's choice of how much labor to use? The answer can be found in Figure 6-8. When labor becomes more expensive, the firm substitutes capital for labor. The safety regulations would result in firms using fewer workers and more capital to produce output.

increase. Putting this all together, the firm's costs are higher after the wage increase, and this happens even though the firm reduces its use of labor and uses more capital.

We can use this knowledge of how firms respond to changes in relative prices to determine what must have happened with Owens-Corning Fiberglass, as discussed at the beginning of the section. Recall that Owens-Corning reduced the amount of labor and increased the amount of capital, keeping output unchanged. Based on the findings of Figure 6-8 we can surmise that either labor became more expensive, or capital became less expensive, or both. In fact, capital prices fell over the years, so it became profitable for Owens-Corning to substitute capital for labor.

Cost Curves

It is possible to draw long-run cost curves just as we drew short-run cost curves in Section 6.1. The progression is the same as before. First we derive a total cost curve, and then we use it to find average and marginal cost curves. Since there are no fixed costs in the long run, there is no need to separate out fixed and variable cost curves. Instead, all costs are variable, so we only need one set of curves.

The first step is to derive a total cost curve. A typical long-run total cost curve is shown in the top panel of Figure 6-9, and it is labeled *LTC* to distinguish it from the short-run total cost curve. Notice that the long-run to-

Figure 6-9 The Long-Run Total Cost, Long-Run Average Cost, and Long-Run Marginal Cost Curves

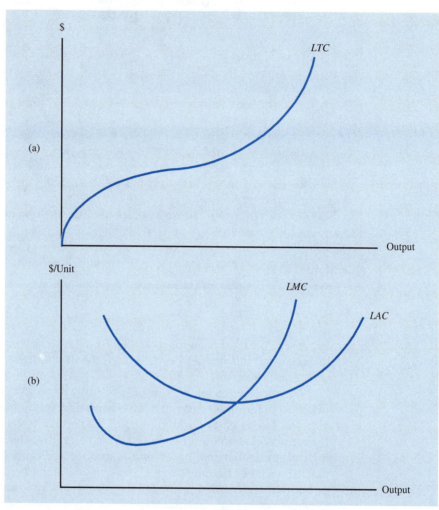

Panel (a) shows the long-run total cost curve. It begins at the origin because when the firm produces nothing in the long run, it uses no inputs at all, so its cost is zero. Panel (b) shows the long-run average and marginal cost curves. As with the short-run curves, the marginal cost curve passes through the minimum point of the average cost curve.

tal cost curve has the same shape as the short-run total variable cost curve in Figure 6-2. Also, since there are no fixed costs, the cost of producing zero output is zero, so the total cost curve begins at the origin. The average and marginal cost curves are shown in the bottom panel of the figure and are labeled *LAC* and *LMC*, respectively. Both are U-shaped, and the marginal cost curve cuts through the minimum point of the average cost curve.

Returns to Scale and Economies of Scale

Figure 6-9 shows what a typical long-run average cost curve is presumed to look like. It is downward sloping at low levels of output and upward sloping at high levels of output. But what determines the turning point? Or, equivalently, how does a manager of a firm know whether he is on the downward-sloping portion or the upward-sloping portion of the long-run average cost curve? A partial answer comes from looking at returns to scale, as discussed in Section 5.3.

According to the definition, a production function exhibits increasing returns to scale if doubling all of the inputs more than doubles output. Suppose that the firm begins by using L_1 units of labor and K_1 units of capital and that the wage rate is w and the rental price of capital is r. The firm produces $q_1 = F(L_1,K_1)$ units of output at a cost of $TC_1 = wL_1 + rK_1$. Average cost is TC_1/q_1. Now suppose that the firm doubles both inputs. Its new level of production is $q_2 = F(2L_1,2K_1)$ and its total cost is $TC_2 = 2w_1 + 2rK_1 = 2TC_1$. Since the production function exhibits increasing returns to scale, doubling the inputs more than doubles output, so $q_2 > 2q_1$. Doubling the inputs causes average cost to become

$$AC_2 = \frac{TC_2}{q_2} < \frac{2TC_1}{2q_1} = AC_1,$$

where the inequality comes from the fact that $TC_2 = 2TC_1$ but $q_2 > 2q_1$. The important point for our purposes is that when output grows from q_1 units to q_2 units, average cost falls. This is an implication of increasing returns to scale: When the production function exhibits increasing returns to scale, average cost falls when output increases. In terms of the shape of the long-run average cost curve, increasing returns to scale means that the long-run average cost curve is downward sloping.

Similar steps show that if the production function exhibits decreasing returns to scale, the long-run average cost curve is upward sloping, and if the production function exhibits constant returns to scale, the long-run average cost curve is horizontal (over some interval). Increasing returns to scale are usually caused by productivity gains from specialization or by beneficial interactions between similarly equipped workers. These gains can usually be realized when firms are small. Decreasing returns to scale are usually attributed to increased management problems when organizations become large. Therefore, analyzing returns to scale leads to the shape for the long-run average cost curve shown in Figure 6-9.

A different but similarly named issue is economies of scale. **Economies of scale** occur when a firm realizes cost advantages from producing more output. Increasing returns to scale is one cause of economies of scale, but there are others. If a firm uses a large volume of inputs, it might receive a volume discount when it purchases the inputs, reducing the average cost of the output. In some cases it only makes sense for firms to be large—for example, in the case of electricity generation. When a utility company builds a hydroelectric dam, it typically installs large generators. Most of the cost of generating the electricity is in the maintenance of the generators. When customers use more electricity, the total cost of providing the electricity does not change, but it is spread over a larger quantity of electricity. The average cost of electricity falls as the output increases.

The key difference between economies of scale and returns to scale is that returns to scale refers to what happens when the firm increases all inputs proportionately, while economies of scale refers to what happens when the firm increases output. For economies of scale, the firm may or may not choose to increase all inputs proportionately. In fact, the economies of scale may come from the ability of the firm to substitute one large machine for many workers, as might occur when a small farm adds acreage.

6.3   COMPARING LONG-RUN AND SHORT-RUN COSTS

Suppose that a firm wants to produce a particular amount of output, q. In the short run, it can choose the amount of labor, but the level of capital is fixed at K_0. By choosing labor appropriately, it minimizes the short-run cost of producing q. This is how we get the short-run total cost of producing q, $TC(q)$. In the long run, the firm not only can choose the amount of labor, but it can also choose the amount of capital. By choosing the optimal combination of inputs, it minimizes the long-run cost of producing q. This is how we get the long-run total cost of producing q, $LTC(q)$. Which is higher, $TC(q)$ or $LTC(q)$? The answer is the topic of this section.

This question, in and of itself, is not all that interesting. After all, the firm cannot choose whether it is operating in the long run or the short run. For the immediate future, at least, the firm must operate in the short run, with the amount of capital fixed. So, the answer to the question does not tell anything about how the firm should minimize cost. We ask the question anyway, because the answer demonstrates some important differences between short-run and long-run analysis.

Analysis Using Isoquants and Iso-Cost Lines

The task for the firm is to find the cost-minimizing method of producing output q. Figure 6-10 shows an isoquant corresponding to that output level. In the long run, the firm chooses both capital and labor to minimize cost, which occurs where an iso-cost line is tangent to the isoquant. The optimal long-run input levels are L^* and K^*. What about in the short run? The firm is stuck with a fixed level of capital, K_0, which may or may not be equal to

Figure 6-10   Short-Run Versus Long-Run Cost of Production

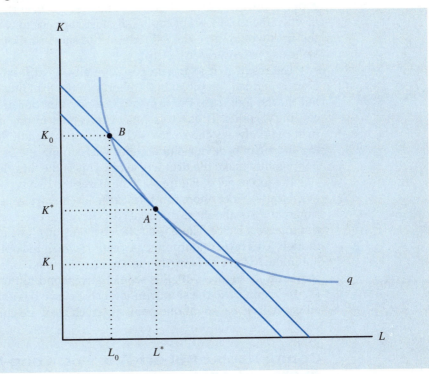

In the long run, when a firm wants to produce q units of output, it can choose the input combination that minimizes cost, that is, the point on the isoquant that is on the lowest possible iso-cost line. The firm shown here chooses point A, where labor is L^* and capital is K^*. In the short run, however, capital is fixed, and it may be fixed at a level different from K^*. Suppose that the capital stock is fixed at K_0. Now the best the firm can do is use L_0 units of labor and produce at point B. Since point B is on a higher iso-cost line than point A, the short-run cost is higher than the long-run cost. This is also true when the firm has a fixed capital stock of $K_1 < K^*$.

K^*. In the figure, K_0 is larger than K^*. The firm chooses the smallest amount of labor that enables it to produce q, which, in this case, is L_0 units of labor. We find L_0 at the point where the isoquant interesects the horizontal line corresponding to $K = K_0$. In this example, the firm uses less labor in the short run than it does in the long run.

Which method of producing q costs less? We can answer this by looking at the iso-cost lines. Recall that iso-cost lines farther from the origin correspond to higher levels of total cost. In the figure, notice that (L_0, K_0) lies on a higher iso-cost line than (L^*, K^*), so in this case costs are higher in the short run than in the long run. It turns out that short-run costs are always at least as high as long-run costs. The long-run input combination, (L^*, K^*), is the point on the isoquant that is on the lowest iso-cost line. The short-run input combination could not possibly be on a lower iso-cost line, because then the iso-cost line would not intersect the isoquant, and the firm would not be able to produce q units of output. The best the firm can do in the short run is when the fixed level of capital, K_0, just happens to correspond to K^*. Then the firm would choose $L_0 = L^*$, and the short-run total cost would be the same as the long-run total cost.

The result that short-run costs are always at least as high as long-run costs is perfectly sensible. In the short run the firm must use K_0 units of capital. In the long run, the firm can use any amount of capital it wants, including K_0 units. Thus, costs cannot be higher in the long run, because the firm could always choose to use K_0 units of capital in the long run, mimicking short-run behavior. Put another way, giving the firm more choices cannot possibly make the firm worse off. This is the intuition behind the result.

The top panel of Figure 6-11 compares the two types of total cost curves graphically. Since short-run total costs are always at least as high as long-run total costs, the short-run total cost curve lies everywhere above the long-run total cost curve. There is one level of output, q', where the two are equal, though. This level of output is the one for which the optimal amount of capital in the long run is exactly the same as the fixed amount of capital in the short run. In Figure 6-10, this would correspond to the case in which $K_0 = K^*$. To summarize, the short-run total cost curve lies above the long-run total cost curve, except at one point at which they are equal.

Comparison of Short-Run and Long-Run Average Costs

We have found that $TC(q) \geq LTC(q)$; that is, that short-run costs are at least as high as long-run costs. What about average costs? Average costs are found by dividing total cost by output. If we divide both sides of the inequality by q, we get

$$AC(q) = \frac{TC(q)}{q} \geq \frac{LTC(q)}{q} = LAC(q).$$

This means that the short-run average total cost curve must lie everywhere above the long-run average cost curve. In the top panel of Figure 6-11, though, there is one level of output, q', at which the two total cost curves are tangent. At this level of output, short-run average total cost is exactly equal to long-run average cost, because short-run total cost is exactly equal to long-run total cost. Thus, the short-run average total cost curve is tangent to the long-run average cost curve when output is q'.

Figure 6-11 reveals one more fact about the relationship between short-run average total cost and long-run average cost. It is *not* necessarily the case that the two are equal at the minimum point of the short-run average total cost curve. Recall that average costs are found by drawing lines from the

Figure 6-11   The Relationship Between Short-Run and Long-Run
Cost Curves

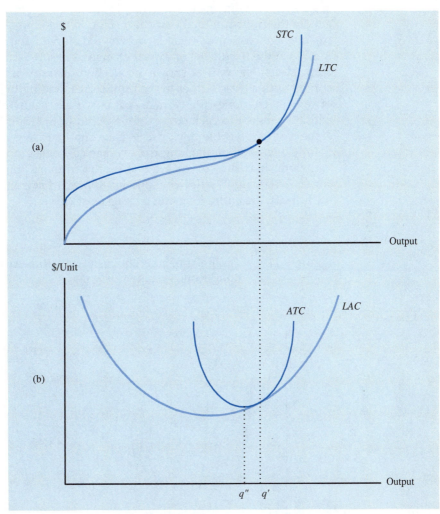

Panel (a) shows the relationship between the long-run total cost curve and a short-run total cost curve. Because short-run costs are always at least as high as long-run costs, the short-run cost curve is above the long-run cost curve. Since there is one level of output, q', at which the two are equal, though, the short-run total cost curve is tangent to the long-run total cost curve when output is q'. Panel (b) shows the corresponding relationship between long-run average cost and short-run average total cost. The short-run average total cost curve lies everywhere above the long-run average cost curve, and it is tangent to the long-run average cost curve when output is q'. Notice that the tangency does not necessarily occur at the minimum point of the short-run average total cost curve.

origin to the total cost curves. The slope of the line is the average cost at that level of output. The minimum point of the short-run average cost curve is at q'', where the line from the origin to the short-run total cost curve is tangent to the short-run total cost curve. Since q'' is to the right of q', the short-run average cost curve must be downward sloping at q', as shown.

When the fixed level of capital changes, the short-run average total cost curve shifts. Figure 6-12 shows a collection of short-run average total cost curves, with curves farther to the right corresponding to higher fixed levels of capital. The long-run average cost curve lies below all of these curves, and it is tangent to each curve at one point. In the figure, the long-run average cost curve is the thick curve. Each short-run average total cost curve defines one point on the long-run average cost curve, and if we draw more and more short-run curves, we find more and more points on the long-run curve. Eventually, by drawing enough short-run average total cost curves, we identify the entire long-run average cost curve.

Figure 6-12   The Relationship Between Short-Run Average Cost and Long-Run Average Cost

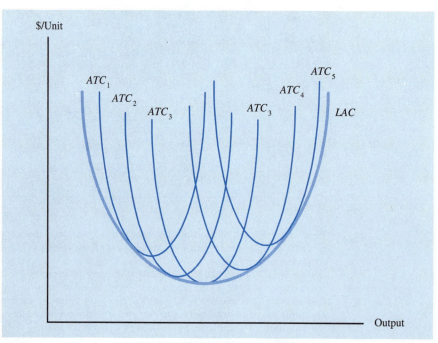

Each short-run average total cost curve corresponds to some fixed level of capital. In the figure, the thin curves are short-run average total cost curves, and the thick curve is a long-run average cost curve. *ATC* curves farther to the right have higher fixed level of capital. Each *ATC* curve defines one point on the *LAC* curve, and by drawing enough *ATC* curves we are able to find the entire *LAC* curve.

APPLICATION
Cost Cutting at Delta Airlines

Occasionally firms go through a major "cost-cutting" or "downsizing" period. When they do this, they are making a long-run cost-minimization decision. The recent cost-cutting efforts at Delta Airlines provides a good example.* In 1990, Delta spent 9.76 cents per airplane seat per mile of flight. That was the second highest average cost in the industry at the time. Since then, Delta has cut over 17,000 jobs, changed the food service, reduced inventory in the maintenance division, and reduced the number of flights. By doing this it reduced average cost to about 8.4 cents per airplane seat per mile of flight by the end of 1995, with a goal of reducing average cost to only 7.5 cents per airplane seat per mile of flight by June 1997, which would be the second *lowest* average cost in the industry.

How does this cost-cutting fit in with our analysis? In 1990, Delta was on a high short-run average cost curve to the right of the minimum point of the long-run average cost curve, such as curve ATC_5 in Figure 6-12. By reducing the number of routes they fly, Delta reduced output. With the reduced output, they were able to cut employment and other expenses. At the 8.4 cent average cost level, they were operating on a short-run average cost curve more like ATC_4. The goal is to reach an ATC curve even farther to the left, so that an average cost of 7.6 cents per seat per mile can be obtained.

Business Week, December 11, 1995, p. 106.

6.4 A FIRST LOOK AT PROFIT MAXIMIZATION

We began this chapter by identifying the ways in which a firm could produce different levels of output. We then found the least expensive way for the firm to produce each level of output, which gave us the firm's cost function. Both of these are intermediate results, however. Our goal from the beginning has been to model how the firm maximizes profit, which requires some additional considerations. For example, Nike's goal in manufacturing and distributing athletic shoes is to make as much profit as possible. To do this, it is not enough that Nike knows its production function—that is, the quantities of inputs it takes to produce a given number of shoes. It is also not enough that Nike knows its cost function—that is, how much it costs to produce a given number of shoes. Nike must also decide how many shoes to produce. This section discusses how much a firm should produce to maximize profit.

Total Revenue

What has been missing from the firm's analysis so far has been total revenue, or the amount of money the firm collects from selling its output. If the firm sells q units of output at a price of p per unit, the firm receives $TR(q) = pq$, where $TR(q)$ denotes the total revenue from selling q units of output. For example, if Nike sells 40 million pairs of athletic shoes for $50 each, its revenue is $2 billion. Nike would report this amount as *sales* in its annual report to stockholders.

Nike has control over how much revenue it collects. One way it can control revenue is by raising the price of its shoes. If people still buy 40 million pairs of shoes at the new price, Nike's revenue will rise. This is unlikely, though, because quantity demanded falls when the price rises. So Nike would still sell a large number of shoes, but less than 40 million pairs. The effect of the price increase on revenue depends on the amount of the price increase and the amount of the demand decline. Suppose that Nike raises the price to $60 per pair, and quantity demanded falls to 35 million pairs. Total revenue is now $2.1 billion, so the price increase increases revenue. If, on the other hand, quantity demanded falls to 30 million pairs when the price is $60, Nike's revenue is $1.8 billion, which is less than the $2 billion revenue generated by a $50 price. Thus, increasing the price can either raise or lower revenue.

The other way that Nike can affect its revenue is by producing more shoes and letting the market find a price at which all of the shoes sell. For example, suppose that Nike increases its production from 40 million pairs to 50 million pairs. If the price does not change from the initial $50 level, Nike's revenue will rise. But this, too, is unlikely because of downward-sloping demand curves. If Nike tries to sell an additional 10 million pairs of shoes, it will probably have to reduce the price. If the price falls to $45 per pair, revenue rises to $2.25 billion. If, on the other hand, the price falls to $35 per pair, revenue falls to $1.75 billion. This shows that increasing the quantity produced can either raise or lower revenue.

If Nike sets the price of its shoes, the quantity sold is determined by the demand curve. If, instead, Nike chooses how many pairs of shoes to produce, the price at which they all sell is determined by the demand curve. Thus, it does not matter whether we model Nike as setting price or setting quantity, since the other variable is determined by the demand curve. And since it does not matter, we will choose the one that is most convenient. Cost functions have the level of output as arguments, so we will focus on Nike choosing quantity, with the price determined by the market.

Now that we have made this choice, we can graph the total revenue curve with output on the horizontal axis. A demand curve is shown in the top panel of Figure 6-13, and the total revenue curve is shown in the bottom panel. The equation for the demand curve is $q = 10 - p$. At point A on the demand curve, the price is 10 but the quantity sold is zero. Since total revenue is price times quantity, total revenue is zero. The corresponding

Figure 6-13   Demand and Total Revenue

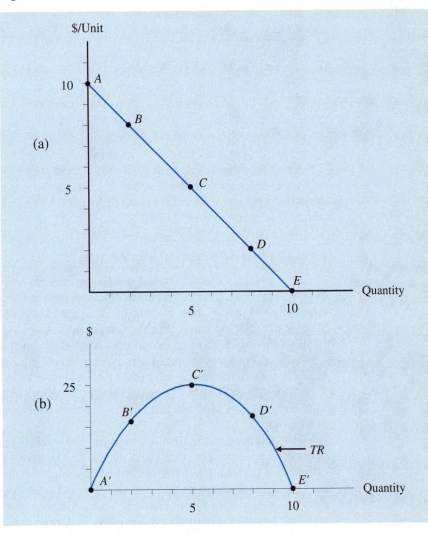

A firm faces a demand curve given by the function $q = 10 - p$. This curve is graphed in panel (a). When the firm sells q units at price p, its revenue is given by the formula $TR = pq$. This total revenue curve is drawn in panel (b). Revenue is maximized when the firm sells 5 units of the good.

point on the total revenue curve in the bottom panel is the origin, since quantity is zero and total revenue is zero. At point B on the demand curve, the price is 8 and the quantity is 2. Total revenue is 16, and the corresponding point on the total revenue curve is point B'. At point C on the demand curve, the price is 5 and the quantity is 5. Total revenue is 25, as shown by point C' on the total revenue curve. As the firm produces more, total revenue begins to fall. At point D on the demand curve, for example, the price is 2 and

Table 6-3   Total Revenue Example

Quantity	Price	Total Revenue
0	10	0
2	8	16
5	5	25
8	2	16
10	0	0

quantity is 8. Total revenue is 16, as shown by point D' in the bottom panel. Finally, if the firm wants to sell 10 units of output, the price must be zero, as shown by point E in the top panel. Total revenue is zero, and the corresponding point on the total revenue curve is E'. The information in this paragraph is summarized in Table 6-3.

Profit and Marginal Revenue

A firm's profit is the revenue it collects minus the costs it incurs; that is, $\pi(q) = TR(q) - TC(q)$, where $\pi(q)$ denotes the amount of profit the firm earns when it produces q units of output. Figure 6-14 shows the profit function graphically. The top panel graphs a total revenue curve and a total cost curve. In this case it is a short-run total cost curve (can you tell why?), although the same technique works for both the short and long runs. Profit is the vertical distance between the total revenue curve and the total cost curve, and it is shown in the bottom panel of the figure. When total revenue is above total cost, profit is positive, but when total revenue is below total cost, profit is negative.

The objective of the firm is to choose the level of profit at which profit is maximized. In the bottom panel of the figure, profit is maximized when output is q^*. In the top panel, profit is maximized when the total revenue curve is at its greatest distance above the total cost curve. At this level of output, the two curves must have the same slope, as shown. To think about why, suppose that the total revenue curve is steeper than the total cost curve. Then increasing output by one unit increases total revenue by more than it increases total cost, and so profit increases. Similarly, if the total revenue curve is flatter than the total cost curve, cutting output by one unit increases profit. So, at the profit-maximizing level of output, the total revenue and total cost curves must have the same slope. As we have already seen, the slope of the total cost curve is marginal cost. The slope of the total revenue curve is **marginal revenue,** which is defined as the extra revenue generated by producing one more unit of output. The **profit-maximization condition** for the firm is that marginal revenue equals marginal cost, or

$$MR(q) = MC(q).$$

Figure 6-14   Graphing the Profit Function

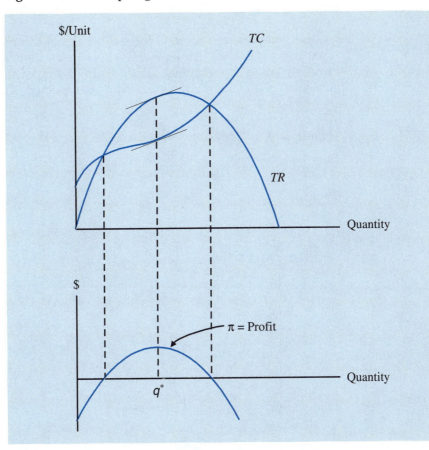

Profit is total revenue minus total cost. In the top panel, that translates as the vertical distance between the total revenue curve and the total cost curve. Profit is maximized when output is equal to q^*, which is the level of output at which *TR* is farthest above *TC*. You can tell where q^* is because if profit is maximized, both the *TR* and *TC* curves have the same slope at that level of output. The bottom panel shows the profit function. It is negative at low levels of output, reaches a maximum when $q = q^*$, and is negative again at high levels of output.

We will say more about this condition later, after we discuss marginal revenue in more detail.

The marginal revenue curve can be derived from the total revenue curve in the same way as marginal product is derived from total product and marginal cost is derived from total cost. We can also find **average revenue,** which is total revenue divided by the number of units of output. Let's begin with average revenue. Recall that the total revenue from selling q units of output is $TR(q) = pq$, where p is the price read off the demand curve. Average revenue is $AR(q) = pq/q = p$. If we graph average revenue with output on the horizontal axis, as in Figure 6-15, we find that the height of the average revenue curve is exactly the same as the height of the demand curve. So, average revenue and demand coincide.

Since the average revenue curve is the demand curve, the average revenue curve is downward sloping. Our conclusion about the relationship between average and marginal curves states that when the average curve is declining, the marginal curve lies below the average curve. Thus, the mar-

Figure 6-15   The Profit-Maximizing Price and Output

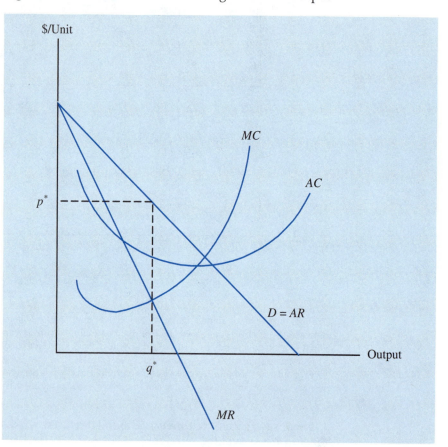

The demand curve faced by a firm is also the firm's average revenue curve. As we have seen, when an average curve is downward sloping, the corresponding marginal curve must lie below it. So, in this case, the marginal revenue curve lies below the demand curve. When the demand curve is a downward-sloping straight line, we can say even more: The marginal revenue curve is a straight line that is twice as steep as the demand curve.

The firm maximizes profit by choosing output to make $MR = MC$. This is point q^* in the graph. The firm then sets the price according to the height of the demand curve at that level of output. The optimal price is p^*.

ginal revenue curve lies below the average revenue curve, as shown in Figure 6-15. Also notice that the marginal revenue curve cuts below the horizontal axis, meaning that marginal revenue can be negative. Marginal revenue is negative when the total revenue curve is downward sloping, so that additional output actually decreases revenue. The marginal revenue curve has two additional useful properties that hold only when the demand curve is a downward-sloping straight line. These are mathematical properties, and we do not go into their derivation here. The first property is that the marginal revenue curve is a downward-sloping straight line, and the second is that the marginal revenue curve's horizontal intercept is half of the demand curve's horizontal intercept. It turns out that when the demand curve is a straight line, the marginal revenue curve is also a straight line, but with twice the slope of the demand curve.[2] Both of these properties are exhibited in Figure 6-15.

As we have already stated, the profit-maximization condition for the firm is that marginal revenue equals marginal cost, or, in equation form, that $MR(q) = MC(q)$. Marginal revenue is the extra revenue generated by one more unit of output. Marginal cost is the cost of producing one additional unit of output. If the additional unit of output generates more revenue than it costs to produce it, the firm can increase its profit by producing the extra unit of output. Therefore, the firm should produce more output. In equation form, if $MR(q) > MC(q)$, the firm should produce more output. On the other hand, if $MR(q) < MC(q)$, it costs more to produce the extra output than the firm receives in additional revenue. The firm loses money on the extra output, so it should not produce the extra output. In fact, by the same reasoning, the firm should reduce its output in this case. When it reduces output by one unit, costs are reduced by $MC(q)$, and revenue is decreased by $MR(q)$. Since $MC(q) > MR(q)$, the cost reduction is more than the revenue reduction, so profit increases. The firm makes as much profit as possible when the extra revenue from producing another unit just covers the cost of producing it. In other words, the firm maximizes profit when marginal revenue equals marginal cost.

The profit-maximization condition gives us a convenient graphical method for finding the optimal level of output. Figure 6-15 has both a marginal revenue and a marginal cost curve. Profit is maximized at the level of output where marginal revenue equals marginal cost, which is where the two curves cross. The optimal level of output is q^*.

---

2 If you must know, a downward-sloping straight line demand curve can be specified by an equation of the form $p(q) = a - bq$. Its horizontal intercept is the value of q that solves $pq = 0$, or $q = a/b$. Total revenue is given by $TR(q) = p(q) \cdot q = aq - bq^2$. Marginal revenue is the derivative of this expression, which is $MR(q) = a - 2bq$, which is the equation of a downward-sloping line with the same vertical intercept and twice the slope. The horizontal intercept is the value of q that solves $MR(q) = 0$, or $q = a/2b$.

The Profit-Maximizing Price

We have now found the firm's optimal output, which is q^* in Figure 6-15. How much should the firm charge for its product? Given that the firm produces q^* units of output, it should set the highest price possible at which all q^* units sell. This is just the price at which quantity demanded is equal to q^*, denoted p* in Figure 6-15. The graph shows that when the firm behaves optimally, price is above marginal cost. There is an important exception to this rule, which is discussed in the next chapter. The exception occurs when demand is horizontal instead of downward sloping. For the time being, though, we work with downward-sloping demand curves, so that marginal revenue is below demand and price is above marginal cost. We want to see how far above marginal cost the optimal price is.

To figure this out, we take a somewhat roundabout method, eventually getting to the relationship between the price and marginal revenue. Then, since marginal revenue equals marginal cost at the optimum, we also have the relationship between the price and marginal cost. The first step in the process is to reexamine the definition of marginal revenue, which is the change in revenue caused by a change in output. Since revenue is given by the formula $TR(q) = p \cdot q$, we need to figure out how the product pq changes when q changes There are two components to the change, and we can find them by looking at how revenue changes when the firm moves from producing $q - \Delta q$ units to producing q units. When the firm sells Δq more units of output, it receives the price p for each extra unit, or $p\Delta q$ for the extra Δq units. This is the first component of marginal revenue. But, when the firm sells one more unit of output, the fact that demand is downward sloping means that the firm receives a lower price *for every unit it sells*. It sells q units, and the price changes by Δp, so the second component of marginal revenue is $q\Delta p$. Adding the two components up, the combined change in total revenue is

$$\Delta TR = p\Delta q + q\Delta p.$$

Recalling that marginal revenue is given by the formula $MR = \Delta TR/\Delta q$, we get

$$MR = \frac{\Delta TR}{\Delta q} = p + q\,\frac{\Delta p}{\Delta q}$$

by dividing the expression for ΔTR by Δq. Rearrange this expression as

(6.1) $$MR(q) = p\left(1 + \frac{q}{p}\,\frac{\Delta p}{\Delta q}\right).$$

Now recall that the price elasticity of demand is defined as

$$e_p = -\frac{\%\Delta q}{\%\Delta p} = -\frac{p}{q}\frac{\Delta q}{\Delta p}.$$

Thus, equation (6.1) can be rewritten as

(6.2)
$$MR(q) = p\left(1 - \frac{1}{e_p}\right).$$

So, marginal revenue is related to the price elasticity of the demand curve.

For equation (6.2) to make any sense, demand must be elastic; that is, e_p must be greater than one. To see why, remember that $MR(q) = MC(q)$ at the optimum, and since $MC(q)$ is positive, $MR(q)$ must also be positive. This implies that the term in parentheses must be positive, which means that e_p must be greater than one. In other words, demand must be elastic.

What we are doing is finding a formula for the optimal price in terms of marginal cost. We are almost there. Remember that at the optimal level of output, marginal revenue is equal to marginal cost, so we can substitute MC for MR in equation (6.2). The final step is to rearrange equation (6.2) to get

(6.3)
$$\frac{p - MC}{p} = \frac{1}{e_p}.$$

This is known as the **markup pricing formula.** It tells how much the firm should increase price over marginal cost. Remember that price elasticities are positive numbers, so price is higher than marginal cost. How much higher depends on how elastic demand is. If, for example, the price elasticity of demand is 2, then the markup pricing formula reduces to $(p - MC)/p = .05$, meaning that half of the price is a markup over marginal cost. If the price elasticity is 1.5, then two-thirds of the price is a markup over marginal cost. If the price elasticity is 4, then only a quarter of the price is a markup over marginal cost. So, the more elastic demand is, the less the price is marked up over marginal cost.

Summary

- **Total fixed cost (*TFC*)** is the cost, in the short run, of all combined fixed inputs. The firm incurs its TFC regardless of how much it produces, even if it produces nothing at all.

- **Total variable cost (*TVC*)** is the cost of all combined variable inputs.
- **Total cost (*TC*)** in the short run is the sum of total fixed cost and total variable cost.
- **Average total cost (*ATC*)** is total cost divided by output. Similarly defined, **average variable cost** is total variable cost divided by output, and **average fixed cost** is total fixed cost divided by output.
- **Marginal cost (*MC*)** is the change in total cost that is brought about by the production of just one more unit of the good.
- The relationship between marginal cost and average cost is as follows: When $MC > AC$, AC is increasing; when $MC < AC$, AC is decreasing; and, when $MC = AC$, AC is constant. The same relationship holds between marginal cost and average variable cost: When $MC > AVC$, AVC is increasing; when $MC < AVC$, AVC is decreasing; and, when $MC = AVC$, AVC is constant.
- Since there are no fixed inputs in the long run, there are no fixed costs in the long run.
- An **iso-cost line** shows all the combinations of inputs that cost a set amount. Each iso-cost line, then, represents a different long-run total cost of production. The slope of an iso-cost line is the ratio of input prices.
- To minimize cost for a fixed amount of output, a firm's optimal input combination is found where the isoquant is tangent to the iso-cost line. At the point of tangency, the slope of the isoquant is equal to the slope of the iso-cost line. Thus, optimality requires that the marginal rate of technical substitution be equal to the ratio of input prices.
- **Economies of scale** occur when the average cost of production decreases with increases in output.
- **Total revenue** is the amount of money a firm collects from selling its output. **Marginal revenue** is the change in total revenue brought about by selling one more unit of output.
- **Profit** is defined as total revenue minus total cost. To maximize profit, a firm produces its output at the point where its marginal revenue equals its marginal cost.

Problems

1. Complete the following table using the facts that $w = \$8$ and $r = \$75$.

L	K	q	TVC	TFC	TC	AVC	AFC	ATC	MC
0	10	0				—	—	—	—
5	10	60							
10	10	140							
15	10	195							
20	10	240							
25	10	275							

2. When a firm uses $K_0 = 100$ units of capital, its short-run production function is given by $F(L,K_0) = 2L^{1/2}$. If the wage rate is $40 and the rental price of capital is $60, find the short-run fixed, variable, and total cost functions.

3. Draw a graph showing what happens to the different short-run cost curves when the wage rate falls.

4. Feed is the variable input of beef production, and cattle is the fixed input. Interpret what the different total, average, and marginal cost curves mean in the context of beef production. During the drought of 1996, feed prices soared. Show the effect of rising feed prices on the different cost curves.

5. Consider a long-run cost-minimization problem. Show graphically what happens to the cost-minimizing input combination for a given level of output when the rental price of capital falls. What happens to long-run total cost in this case?

6. Periodically Congress raises the minimum wage. Suppose that a firm uses both high-skilled workers, who get paid more than the minimum wage, and low-skilled workers, who get paid the minimum wage. Show how an increase in the minimum wage changes the firm's optimal mixture of high- and low-skilled workers for a given level of output. What does this imply about the unemployment effects of raising the minimum wage? Next show what happens to the firm's profit-maximizing level of output and profit-maximizing price when the minimum wage rises.

7. Show mathematically that if the production function exhibits increasing returns to scale, the long-run average cost curve is downward sloping.

8. If a production function exhibits increasing returns to scale, does the long-run marginal cost curve lie above or below the long-run average cost curve? Explain why.

9. A firm uses both capital and labor in production, and the amount of capital is fixed in the short run. Suppose that the rental price of capital falls. Explain why short-run total cost falls. What about short-run average total cost and short-run marginal cost? In the long run the firm adjusts the amount of capital and labor it employs in response to the drop in the price of capital. Explain why long-run total cost falls. Which falls more, short-run total cost or long-run total cost?

10. In Section 3.7 we introduced the concept of price elasticities of demand. Whether or not demand is elastic is related to whether or not revenue increases when the price increases. Construct an example to show that if demand is elastic, an increase in the price of the good causes total revenue to fall. Construct a different example to show that if demand is inelastic, an increase in the price of the good causes total revenue to rise.

11. The increasing frequency of product liability lawsuits has the effect of raising producers' cost curves. For example, if McDonald's is more likely to be sued for serving coffee that is too hot, it raises both the marginal cost of producing one more cup of coffee and the average cost of all cups of coffee sold. Show that the increased likelihood of being sued decreases the number of cups of coffee sold by McDonald's and raises the price customers pay for coffee.

12. Consider the case of a firm operating in the short run. If the price of the fixed input rises, what happens to the profit-maximizing level of output and the profit-maximizing price?

13. Suppose that the demand for Harley-Davidson motorcycles shifts outward. Draw a graph showing how the optimal output and price of Harleys should change.

7

COMPETITION

Overview

So far (in Chapters 2 through 4), we have discussed the behavior of consumers without taking the behavior of firms into account. And (in Chapters 5 and 6), we have discussed the behavior of firms without taking the behavior of consumers into account. It is time to stop treating the two sides of the market separately. We have found that, on the consumption side of the market, we can use the market demand curve to show the total amount consumers buy at any given price. If we had a market supply curve, we could use it to show the total amount firms produce at any given price. The problem is that we have not yet constructed a market supply curve. There is a very good reason for this: The behavior of firms depends on how many other firms there are in the market. So, we must analyze different numbers of firms (different types of market structure) separately.

In this chapter we assume that a large number of firms each produce exactly the same good. We call this case *perfect competition.* Alternatives include the cases of monopoly (just one large firm) and oligopoly (several large firms). These are studied in later chapters. There are several reasons for studying perfect competition first. To begin with, the fact that there are many firms allows us to simplify each individual's profit-maximization problem significantly. Added to this, the case of many firms provides the rationale for why markets "work." This issue is explored further in Chapter 8. Finally, the case of many firms describes many actual industries pretty well, especially agricultural industries and financial markets.

Consider, for example, the case of navel oranges. Most people who buy oranges care whether they are navel or some other type of orange, but they do not care who the grower was. From the standpoint of consumers, all growers produce the same kind of navel orange. Moreover, no single grower produces a large fraction of the country's navel oranges. So, this industry fits the requirement of having a large number of small firms producing exactly the same commodity. The same is true of cut diamonds. While it is true that a single company controls most of the world's uncut diamond supply, the number of diamond cutters is large. Most consumers care about the size and quality of the diamond, but not about who cut it. So, diamond cutting is also a competitive industry.

The primary purpose of this chapter is to analyze the behavior of competitive firms. While doing this, we will also be able to analyze the characteristics of the market price that arises in perfect competition. In this chapter you will learn:

- How much competitive firms produce in the short run and in the long run.

- What an equilibrium is and what conditions must hold for a competitive industry to be in long-run equilibrium.

- How the analysis changes when prices fluctuate and the owners of firms are risk-averse.

7.1   SHORT-RUN COMPETITION

We learned in Chapters 5 and 6 that it is important to distinguish between the short run and the long run. In the short run at least one input is fixed, and in the long run all inputs are variable. We begin our analysis of perfect competition with the short run. Before doing so, however, it is important to explain exactly what we mean by perfect competition.

The Competitive Assumptions

In this chapter we analyze both a competitive *industry* and a competitive *firm.* Accordingly, we should begin by distinguishing between the two. A **firm** is a single entity producing goods or services from inputs. Examples of firms include corporations, such as Exxon or Microsoft; small businesses, such as local restaurants; and even family businesses, such as farms. An **industry** is the collection of all firms producing a single good or service. Industries have particular characteristics, and the firms in the industry must respond to these characteristics. This chapter is devoted to one particular set of characteristics, and later chapters consider other types of industries.

The important characteristics of a **competitive industry** are as follows:

1. All firms produce exactly the same product.
2. Consumers know the prices charged by every firm in the industry.
3. Each firm's output is small relative to the total output of the industry.
4. Firms may enter and exit the industry freely.

Each of these characteristics is crucial in the analysis of the behavior of firms. Characteristic 1 implies that consumers do not care who produces the good, since every firm produces exactly the same good. The only way that consumers distinguish between goods is by price. Characteristic 2 states that consumers can identify the firm with the lowest price, so if one firm charges a lower price than every other firm, all of the consumers want to buy from that firm. Or, more important, if one firm charges a higher price than other firms, no one would want to buy from the high-priced firm. Characteristic 3 states that each firm is small relative to the size of the industry. What this means is that if consumers decide not to buy from one of the firms, the other firms can easily handle the extra demand without raising their prices. Characteristic 4 is not used until the next section.

We want to show that if characteristics 1, 2, and 3 hold, then there is a **market price** with the properties that each firm can sell as much output as it wants to at or below the market price but nothing at all above the market price. Suppose first that firm 1 decides to charge a price higher than the market price. Characteristic 2 says that all consumers instantly know that firm 1 is charging a high price. Characteristic 1 says that no consumers buy from a high-priced firm; instead, the consumers try to buy from the other firms charging the market price. Characteristic 3 says that the other firms can easily handle the increased demand, so no consumers are forced to buy from firm 1. So, when firm 1 raises its price above the market price, it cannot sell any of its output.

So far we have shown that if a firm charges more than the market price, it cannot sell anything, and if it charges less than the market price, it can sell as much as it wants. What's left is to show that the firm can also sell as much as it wants if it charges the market price. This demonstration requires a different sort of argument, one using the concept of equilibrium. In general, an *equilibrium* is a situation in which nothing has any pressure to change, and this definition applies in biology, physics, chemistry, and meteorology as well as in economics. For example, in biology, a population of organisms is in equilibrium if there is no pressure causing the population to either increase or decrease. In the case of perfectly competitive firms, an equilibrium is a situation in which no firm has any incentive to change its price. We claim that if every firm charging the market price is an equilibrium, every firm must be able to sell as much as it wants to at the market price. For if some firm is not able to sell as much as it wants to at the market price, it would be able to increase its profit by cutting its price a tiny amount. When it reduces its price even a little bit, every consumer wants to buy from it, and it can sell as much as it wants to. The only way firms won't want to lower their prices, then, is if they are already selling as much as they want to.

These facts that perfectly competitive firms can sell as much as they want to at or below the market price but nothing at all above the market price are reflected in the shape of the demand curve faced by the firm, as shown in Figure 7-1(a). The demand curve is horizontal at the market price p. The way to interpret this demand curve is as follows. If the firm charges a price at or below p, it can sell all of its output. If it charges a price above p, all of the customers buy from other firms, and the demand for the firm's output is zero. Figure 7-1(b) shows the demand curve facing the industry as a whole.

Figure 7-1   Demand Curves for a Competitive Firm and a
                   Competitive Industry

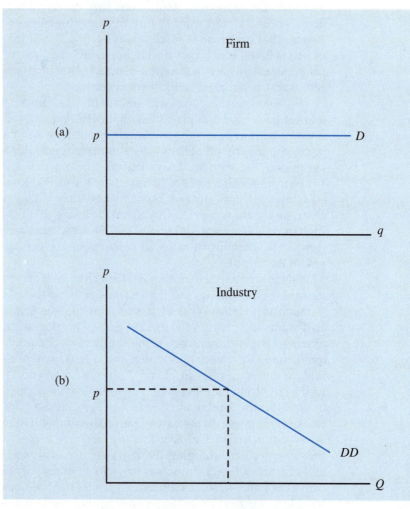

Panel (a) shows the demand curve faced by an individual competitive firm. It is horizontal at
the market price *p*. If the firm sets a price higher than *p*, it cannot sell any of its output, because
consumers can buy the identical good from a different firm for a lower price. The firm can sell
as much as it wants at the price *p*. Panel (b) shows the demand curve faced by the industry as
a whole. It is downward sloping. If all of the firms in the industry increase their prices, the
total amount purchased by consumers falls.

It is important to distinguish between the two demand curves. The industry demand curve is downward sloping, because if all firms raise their prices,
consumers wish to buy less of the good. The firm's demand curve is horizontal, because if a single firm raises its price while all other firms leave

their prices unchanged, no consumers wish to buy the good from the high-priced firm.

To further distinguish between the demand for a firm's output and demand for the industry's output, we use a lower case q to denote the output of a single firm and an upper case Q to denote the output of the industry. Industry output Q is simply the sum of the outputs of the individual firms. More specifically, if there are N firms in the industry and q_i denotes the output of firm i, then industry output $Q = q_1 + q_2 + \ldots + q_n$. Also, we label the firm's demand curve D and the industry demand curve DD.

The most important feature of short-run competition is that individual firms' demand curves are horizontal at the going market price. Firms can sell as much as they want to at the market price, but nothing at all above the market price. Because of this, all firms charge the market price, and they have no incentive to charge any other price. Because of this, we say that competitive firms are **price takers;** the price is determined by the market, and firms must take the price determined by the market.

Behavior of a Single Firm in the Short Run

Given that a firm faces a horizontal demand curve, what is its optimal level of output? The firm chooses output to maximize profit, which is the firm's revenue minus its cost. We saw in Chapter 6 that when a firm produces, it maximizes its profit by setting output so that marginal revenue equals marginal cost. We discussed marginal costs in detail in Chapter 6, and the firm's cost curves are shown in Figure 7-2. All that is left, then, is to figure out what marginal revenue is.

Marginal revenue is defined as the extra revenue a firm receives when it produces one more unit of output. For the competitive firm, every unit sells for the same price, p, so the extra revenue generated by producing one more unit is just p. Therefore the marginal revenue curve is a horizontal line of height p, and it coincides with the firm's demand curve. Be sure to note that the fact that the marginal revenue curve and the demand curve are identical is a property that is particular to competitive firms, and it does not hold in other types of industries.

We have now established that marginal revenue is equal to price and that if a firm produces it maximizes profit by setting output so that marginal revenue equals marginal cost. Combining these concepts, we can see that if a competitive firm produces, it maximizes profit by setting output so that marginal cost is equal to the price, or

$$MC(q) = p.$$

This is point A in Figure 7-2, and the corresponding level of output is q^*. The condition that marginal cost equals price has some intuition behind it. Suppose, to begin with, that the marginal cost of producing the last unit is $5,

Figure 7-2   The Short-Run Production Decision of a Competitive Firm

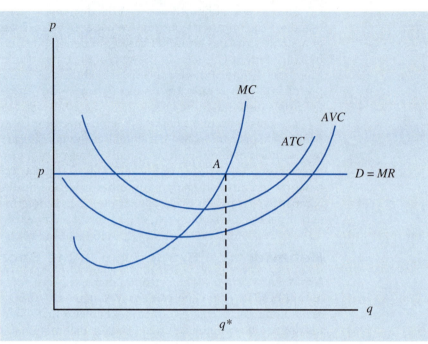

If a competitive firm produces, it should set output to make marginal cost equal to the price. This is output level q^*, where the MC curve crosses the price line. The firm still faces a decision of whether to produce q^* or nothing. It should produce q^* if the price is above AVC at q^*, and it should shut down if the price is below AVC at q^*. The firm shown here should produce, not shut down.

and that the going price is $4. Here marginal cost is greater than the price. If it costs $5 to produce a unit and the firm can only sell the unit for $4, it loses $1 on that unit. The firm's profit would be higher if it produced less. Now suppose that the marginal cost of producing one more unit is $3 and that the going price is $4. In this case the firm's profit is higher if it produces more. Putting these two examples together, we see that if marginal cost is not equal to price, it is possible for the firm to change its output and increase profit. If the firm is maximizing profit by producing, there cannot be a way for the firm to increase its profit, so it must be the case that $MC(q) = p$.

We now know how much the firm produces *if* it produces, but there is still the issue of whether or not the firm should produce at all. Which way does the firm earn more profit, by producing q^* units or by shutting down and producing zero units? If the firm shuts down, its revenue is zero and its total cost is $TC(q) = TVC(q) + TFC$. But, since $q = 0$ when the firm shuts down, total variable cost is zero (that is, $TVC(0) = 0$), so total cost is just total fixed cost, which does not depend on output. The firm's profit π from producing zero, then, is

$$\pi(0) = TR(0) - TC(0) = -TFC.$$

Note that if the firm shuts down it loses an amount equal to its fixed cost. The reason the firm loses money is that in the short run capital is fixed, so the firm must pay for its capital whether it uses the capital or not.

What about when the firm produces q^*? In this case the firm's revenue is $TR(q^*) = pq^*$, since the firm sells q^* units at the price p each. The total cost is $TC(q^*) = TVC(q^*) + TFC$. The firm's profit from producing q^*, then, is

$$\pi(q^*) = TR(q^*) - TC(q^*) = pq^* - TVC(q^*) - TFC.$$

Which way does the firm earn more profit? Producing q^* earns at least as much profit as shutting down if $\pi(q^*) \geq \pi(0)$, or, rearranging, if $\pi(q^*) - \pi(0) \geq 0$. Subtracting the two expressions yields

$$\pi(q^*) - \pi(0) = pq^* - TVC(q^*) - TFC - [-TFC] = pq^* - TVC(q^*) \geq 0,$$

or

$$pq^* \geq TVC(q^*).$$

The fixed-cost term cancels out, since the firm must pay fixed cost whether it produces or not. The expression just shown says that the firm should produce q^* if the revenue from doing so is larger than the total variable cost. This makes sense, because the firm pays fixed costs no matter what, so fixed cost is irrelevant to the production decision. The only extra cost the firm must pay if it produces is the variable cost, so it should produce if revenue exceeds variable cost.

It is possible to rearrange the expression so that it can be shown graphically. The firm produces if $pq^* \geq TVC(q^*)$. Divide through by q^* to get

$$p \geq \frac{TVC(q^*)}{q^*} = AVC(q^*)$$

The firm produces if the price exceeds the average variable cost at the optimal level of output. In Figure 7-2, the test to see whether or not the firm produces is to see whether point A (where the price line crosses the marginal cost curve) lies above or below the average variable cost curve. If it is above the curve, the firm produces. If it is below the curve, the firm shuts down and just pays its fixed cost. In Figure 7-2, point A is above the average variable cost curve, so the firm produces q^*. The figure also shows another way of thinking about this condition. Point A is above the average variable cost

APPLICATION
The Effect of a Decline in the Price of Beef

In choosing beef, consumers might recognize such things as the region where the cattle were raised and what they were fed, but, beyond this, consumers do not usually recognize individual ranches. So, for example, Kansas corn-fed beef is a product grown by many different firms. The competitive model describes the behavior of ranchers fairly well. We can think of beef firms using two basic inputs, cattle and land. In the short run the amount of land is fixed, but cattle can be bought and sold, so cattle constitute the variable input.

What happens to ranchers as the nation becomes more health conscious and begins to eat less beef, causing beef prices to fall? Let's consider the ranch shown in Figure 7-3, in which the firm was producing q_0 before the price decline. If the price falls from p_0 to p_1, the ranch reduces its output from q_0 to q_1. If, instead, the price falls from p_0 to p_3, the ranch shuts down and produces no beef. Either way, the ranch produces less beef than it did before. When does the ranch shut down? It shuts down when the market price is below average variable cost; that is, when the price falls to p_2 or less.

curve if the price line is above the average variable cost curve when output is equal to q^*.

Short-Run Supply Curves

The firm's **supply curve** shows how much it will produce at each different price level. We have seen that if the firm produces, it sets output to equate price and marginal cost. The firm produces if the price is above average variable cost at this level of output; otherwise, it shuts down.

Let's begin by finding the set of prices at which the firm produces and the set of prices at which it shuts down. The firm produces where price equals marginal cost, as long as that price is above average variable cost. Therefore, we can say that the firm produces if marginal cost is above average variable cost. In Figure 7-4, the firm produces whenever the price is above $\underline{p}$, where the marginal cost curve crosses the average variable cost curve. At any price below $\underline{p}$, the firm shuts down.

For prices above $\underline{p}$, how much does the firm produce? Consider price p in Figure 7-4. As we have already seen, the optimal output makes price equal to marginal cost. So, the optimal amount of output is read off the marginal cost curve. Since the firm's supply curve shows the optimal output at each

Figure 7-3   The Effect of a Decline in the Price of Beef

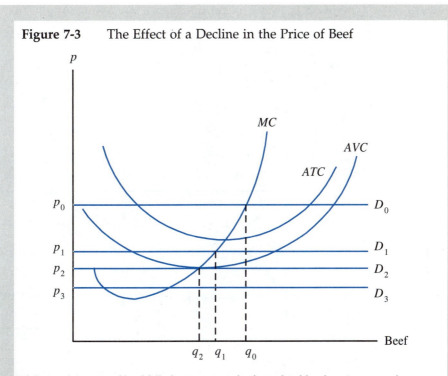

If the market price of beef falls from p_0 to p_1, the farm should reduce its output from q_0 to q_1. The farm should continue to produce, because p_1 is still above the AVC curve when output is q_1. If the price falls further to p_3, though, the farm should shut down and not produce anything, because the demand curve lies below the AVC curve. The firm should shut down at any price below p_2 and produce whenever the price is above p_2.

price, the supply curve coincides with the marginal cost curve for prices above $\underline{p}$, as shown in the figure. The supply curve is labeled S. When the price is below $\underline{p}$, the firm shuts down and produces zero, so the supply curve coincides with the vertical axis for prices below $\underline{p}$. When the price is exactly $\underline{p}$, the standard convention is to say that the firm produces $\underline{q}$,

Short-Run Profit

One last issue to discuss for short-run competitive firms is the profit they earn. In particular, we want to know how to measure profit graphically. Before doing so, let's look at profit mathematically. The formula for profit is

$$\pi = TR - TC.$$

Figure 7-4   A Competitive Firm's Short-Run Supply Curve

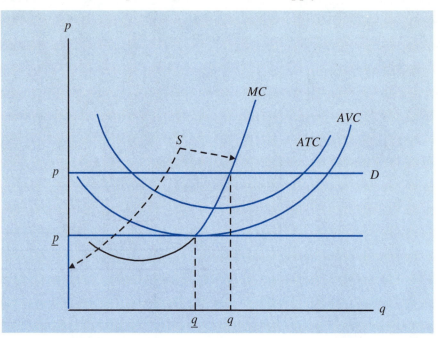

The firm's supply curve has two pieces. If the market price is below $\underline{p}$, the lowest point on the *AVC* curve, the firm shuts down and produces nothing. Consequently, the supply curve corresponds to the vertical axis below the price $\underline{p}$. When the price is above $\underline{p}$, the firm maximizes profit by producing where $p = MC$. So, the second portion of the supply curve coincides with the portion of the *MC* curve above the *AVC* curve.

Since a competitive firm faces the same price no matter how many units it sells, total revenue is given by $TR = pq$. The reason for this is if the firm's output is q units, and it sells them at price p per unit, the total dollar value of the sales is pq. So, we have

$$\pi = pq - TC.$$

We can multiply and divide TC by q without changing this expression, which gives us

$$\pi = pq - (TC/q)q.$$

Now remember that TC/q is just average total cost, so

$$\pi = p{\cdot}q - ATC{\cdot}q = (p - ATC){\cdot}q.$$

Let's use this formula to find profit graphically. Figure 7-5 shows two cases. Let's look at panel (a) first. The price is given by p, and the firm's op-

Figure 7-5   Graphically Determining a Firm's Profit or Loss

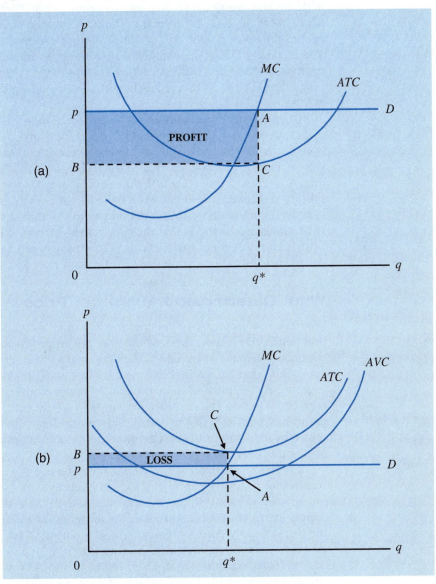

This figure shows how to graphically determine the firm's profit or loss. In both cases the area of the shaded region is the firm's profit. In panel (a), the firm receives revenue p for each unit, but must pay cost B per unit. The firm earns $p - B$ per unit, and, since q^* units are produced, the firm's profit is the area of the rectangle $BpAC$. In panel (b), the average cost, B, is greater than the average revenue p, so the firm *loses* $B - p$ per unit. The firm's total *loss* is the area of the rectangle $BpAC$.

timal output is q^*. The firm's revenue is given by the area of a rectangle of height p and width q^*, so that total revenue is $p \cdot q$. The rectangle with vertices $OpAq^*$ fits this requirement. The firm's total cost is given by the area of a rectangle of height $ATC(q^*)$ and width q^*, so that total cost is $ATC \cdot q^*$. The rectangle $OBCq^*$ has height $ATC(q^*)$ and width q^*, so it works. Total profit is given by the difference between these two areas, or the area of rectangle $BpAC$. This rectangle has height $p - ATC(q^*)$ and width q^*, so profit is $\pi = [p - ATC(q^*)] \cdot q^*$.

In panel (a) the price is above the average total cost curve at the optimal output level, so profit is positive. Panel (b) shows a case in which profit is negative. The total revenue and total cost rectangles are found in the same way as before, but now the total cost rectangle ($OBCq^*$) is bigger than the total revenue rectangle ($OpAq^*$). Since total cost is greater than total revenue, profit is negative, or in other words, the firm makes a loss. It is entirely possible for a competitive firm to lose money in the short run. The requirement to continue producing is that the firm covers variable costs; that is, that the price is above average variable cost. The firm may not be able to cover fixed costs in addition to variable costs, so the firm may lose money.

What Determines the Market Price?

We have now determined the method by which a competitive firm decides how much to produce, and whether or not to produce, given the price of the good. We have even determined the firm's profit, given the price of the good. But what determines the price of the good? In general, prices are determined by supply and demand; that is, prices adjust to make the quantity supplied equal to the quantity demanded. We introduced supply and demand in Chapter 1. In the specific case considered here, prices are determined by *industry* supply and demand. So, we must construct a supply curve for the industry.

The firms' short-run supply curves can be used to construct the short-run **industry supply curve.** The industry supply curve shows the total output produced by all of the firms in the industry at every price. The firm's supply curve shows the output of an individual firm at every price. Once the firms' supply curves are available, the output of each firm at a particular price can be read off those. Adding up these levels of output yields the total industry output at that price. Thus, the industry supply curve simply shows the sum of the firms' output at each price.

Graphically, we can use the same technique we used in Chapter 3 to construct the market demand curve. Suppose that the industry contains three firms. (This is not consistent with the industry's being competitive, but using more firms makes the graph too hard to draw.) In Figure 7-6, the firms' supply curves are labeled S_A, S_B, and S_C. The industry supply curve is labeled SS. At price p, firm A produces 6 units of output, firm B produces 7 units of output, and firm C produces 9 units of output. Total industry out-

Figure 7-6   The Competitive Industry Supply Curve

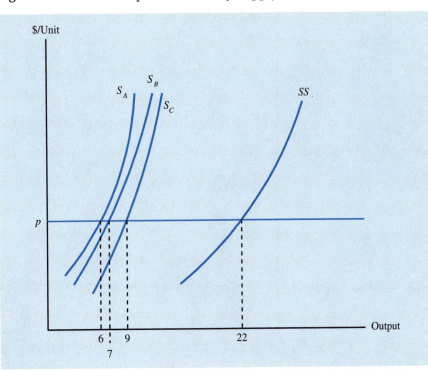

The industry supply curve is found by adding up the individual firms' supply curves horizontally. In the case shown, at price p firm A supplies 6 units, firm B supplies 7 units, and firm C supplies 9 units. The total industry supply at price p is then $6 + 7 + 9 = 22$ units.

put when the price is p is $6 + 7 + 9 = 22$ units, which yields a point on the industry supply curve SS. Repeating this process for other prices completes the construction of the curve.

The market price of the good is determined by the intersection of the industry supply and demand curves. A pair of curves is shown in Figure 7-7. The supply curve is drawn as upward sloping because it is the sum of the marginal cost curves of all the firms in the industry, and marginal cost is generally upward sloping. The market demand curve shows how much of the good consumers wish to purchase from firms in the industry. It is downward sloping for all of the reasons given in Chapter 3.

For the sake of completeness, let's review how the market price in Figure 7-7 translates into the firm's demand curve in Figure 7-1. If the market price is p, consumers wish to buy Q, as shown by the market demand curve. If all firms charge the same price p, then the total amount supplied by the industry is Q, as shown by the industry short-run supply curve. But what happens if one firm decides to charge a price different from p? If it charges

Figure 7-7 Finding the Market Price

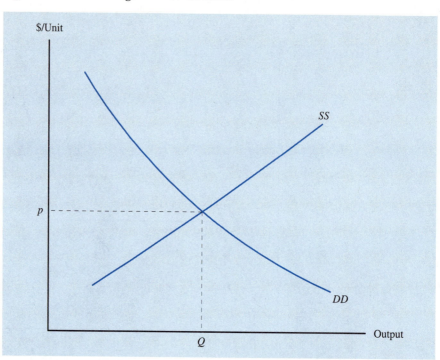

The market price equates the quantity supplied and the quantity demanded. In the figure, the market price p is determined at the intersection of the industry supply curve, SS, and market demand curve, DD. The total output of the industry is Q.

a price higher than p, none of the consumers will buy from that firm, because they can get the identical good at a lower price from other firms. If the firm charges a price lower than p, the firm can sell as much as it wants. But it can already sell as much as it wants at price p, because the total amount produced by the industry is exactly equal to the total amount purchased by consumers. So, the firm can sell as much as it wants at price p, and nothing at all at prices above p. The demand curve for a single firm's output, then, is horizontal at price p, consistent with Figure 7-1.

7.2 LONG-RUN EQUILIBRIUM

Recall that in the short run one or more inputs are fixed, and in the long run all inputs are variable. In the short run, if a firm shuts down it must still pay its fixed costs. In the long run, however, if a firm shuts down it can sell all of its capital and exit the industry. By the same token, new firms can enter the industry. The importance of studying the long run, then, is that it allows us to analyze exit from and entry into the industry. So, for example, we can discuss why farmers might switch from growing soybeans to growing cotton; that is, we can discuss why they exit the soybean industry and enter the cotton industry.

Entry, Exit, and Profit

The first step in analyzing a competitive firm in the long run is to determine how much it produces, given the market price. To do this, we follow the same steps as with the short-run analysis. Consider the firm depicted in Figure 7-8. This time there is no average variable cost curve, because in the long run all inputs, and hence all costs, are variable. Just as in the short run,

Figure 7-8   The Long-Run Competitive Equilibrium Price

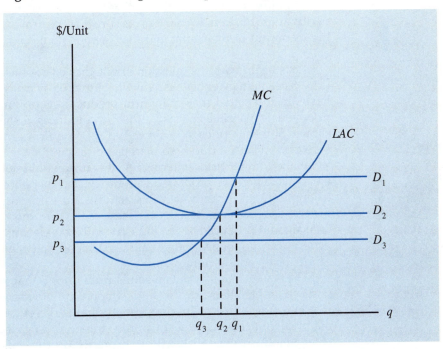

This figure illustrates the characteristics of a long-run equilibrium price. The highest price p_1 cannot be a long-run equilibrium price because the price line is above the long-run average cost curve, LAC, at the firm's optimal output q_1. This means that the firm earns a positive economic profit when the price is p_1. Other firms will enter the industry, driving up the total quantity supplied in the industry and driving down the market price. Since there is a force causing the price to change, p_1 cannot be an equilibrium price. Similarly, p_3 cannot be an equilibrium price. Economic profits are negative when the price is p_3, and firms exit the industry, placing upward pressure on the market price. The only situation in which there is no pressure for the price to change is when the price is p_2, which corresponds to the minimum point of the LAC curve. Economic profits are zero at this price, so firms neither enter nor exit the industry.

though, the firm faces a horizontal demand curve: It can sell any amount at a price at or below the market price, but it cannot sell anything at all at a higher price. And, just as before, the firm maximizes profit by setting output to equate price and marginal cost.

In Figure 7-8, there are three different demand curves corresponding to three different market prices. Let's begin with price p_1, which is the highest of the three prices. The firm's optimal output is q_1, where marginal cost is equal to price. If this were the short run, we would know that the firm would wish to produce and would even make a profit. (Can you determine how much?) But this is the long run, so we need to consider some additional issues. In particular, we must decide whether or not the price p_1 is consistent with an equilibrium. As always, an equilibrium is a situation in which there is no pressure to change. What could possibly change? The firm in question could change its output, or it could exit the industry. Other firms could enter the industry. To see whether the price p_1 is consistent with **long-run competitive equilibrium,** we must make sure that the firm cannot gain by changing its output or by exiting and that there is no incentive for new firms to enter.

Let's begin with the question of whether or not the firm shown in Figure 7-8 can gain by either changing its output or by exiting the industry. We have already stated that if the firm produces, its optimal output is where price equals marginal cost. So, if the firm produces, it should produce q_1, as shown. Since the price p_1 is above $LAC(q_1)$, the firm earns a positive profit on every unit it produces, so there is no reason for the firm to shut down. What about other firms entering? A new firm would notice that it is possible to make positive profit in this industry, and therefore it has an incentive to duplicate an incumbent firm's actions and earn positive profit. If new firms enter, producing exactly the same as the firm shown in Figure 7-8, the total amount produced by the industry will increase. But this means that the price p_1 can no longer equate market demand and industry supply, so p_1 cannot be an equilibrium price.

The reason that p_1 is not an equilibrium price is that at p_1 the firm makes positive profit. Other firms want the opportunity to make positive profit, so they enter the industry. This increases the industry's output and drives down the price. But this might seem a little strange. Why is it that firms want to enter an industry that makes positive profit? More specifically, why is profit above zero enough? The world is filled with firms that are just barely profitable, but we do not see new firms trying to come in and compete against them. When economists talk about profit, they talk about **economic profit.** Economic profit is different from accounting profit, because economic profit explicitly subtracts opportunity costs, while accounting profit does not. As discussed in Section 6.1, the capital that the owner of the firm provides to this production process could also be used in some other production process. The profit that could be made by using the capital in its next best alternative use is the opportunity cost of capital. If the incumbent firms earn positive profit, it means that capital earns more in this industry than in its next best alternative use. Put another way, the capital earns more accounting profit in this industry than anywhere else. By duplicating the actions of incumbent firms, new owners can bring in new capital and earn positive economic profit, or, equivalently, they can earn more accounting profit in this industry than they can elsewhere.

Now let's consider price p_3, which is the lowest price of the three shown in Figure 7-8. If the firm produced, its optimal output would be q_3. But in this case the price is below the average cost curve at output q_3, so the firm would lose money on every unit it produced. Its total economic profit would be negative. This means that it could earn more profit by employing its capital in its next best alternative use, so the firm exits the industry. When a firm exits the industry, total industry output declines. After the firm exits, if the market price does not change, consumers demand more of the good than is produced by the industry, causing the price to rise. Therefore, p_3 cannot be an equilibrium price.

So far we have found that if a competitive firm earns positive economic profit, other firms enter the industry, driving down the price. If firms earn negative profits, some of them exit the industry, driving up the price. The only remaining candidate for a long-run equilibrium is a price that is equal to average cost, so that economic profit is zero. In the figure, p_2 is such a price. Since the firm produces where price is equal to marginal cost, and since profit is zero when price is equal to average cost, the firm's demand curve must pass through the intersection of the marginal cost curve and the average cost curve, as shown. In Chapter 6 we saw that the marginal cost curve intersects the average cost curve at the minimum point of the average cost curve. In the figure, the price is equal to the minimum level of long-run average cost.

Is p_2 a long-run equilibrium price? We must check that the firm does not want to change its output, that it does not want to exit the industry, and that no new firms want to enter. The firm produces q_2, which maximizes its profit. Therefore, it does not want to change its output. Moreover, since $p_2 = LAC(q_2)$, the firm's profit is zero. This means that there is no reason for the firm to exit the industry since it is earning enough to cover the opportunity cost of capital, and there is no reason for new firms to enter. The price p_2 is consistent with a long-run equilibrium.

It is helpful to summarize what we have done. We have looked for a long-run equilibrium price. For it to be an equilibrium price, several conditions must be satisfied:

1. Every firm must produce where price equals marginal cost; that is, every firm must produce its optimal output given the price.
2. Every firm in the industry must earn zero profit. This implies that the price line intersects the minimum point of the long-run average cost curve, and it rules out entry and exit.

3. The total output produced by the industry must equal the total quantity demanded by consumers.

Long-Run Supply

The next step is to construct a supply curve for the industry in the long run. If we have an industry long-run supply curve, we can find the long-run equilibrium price at the intersection of the long-run supply curve and the market demand curve. There is a difficulty in constructing the long-run supply curve, though. When the market price rises, every firm produces more, *and* more firms enter. So, constructing the long-run supply curve is more complicated than constructing the short-run supply curve.

The **industry long-run supply curve** shows how much is produced by the industry at every possible price. Because it is a long-run supply curve, at every point on the curve it must be the case that all firms earn zero profit. Why? Suppose that there is a point on the supply curve at which total industry output is Q when the price is p, and some firms earn positive profit. That would lead other firms to enter, raising output above Q, so such a point cannot possibly be on the supply curve. When the price is p, output is above Q. A similar argument establishes that profit cannot be negative, because then firms would exit the industry, reducing total industry output.

The fact that every firm's profit is zero at every point on the supply curve helps us construct the curve. But, we're going to construct it backwards. A supply curve shows the industry output for given prices. What we are going to do is find the price that corresponds to a given amount of output. To begin the construction, suppose that market demand is given by the curve DD_1, and that the point (Q_1, p_1) in Figure 7-9(a) is the long-run equilibrium. This means that (Q_1, p_1) is on the long-run industry supply curve. Let's find another point on the industry supply curve. Suppose that market demand increases to DD_2, and that the new equilibrium output is $Q_2 > Q_1$. How can the industry produce this extra output? One possibility is that the number of firms stays the same, but each one produces more. A second possibility is that each firm produces the same amount as before, but more firms enter the industry. Or, there could be some combination of these possibilities.

We must determine which of these possibilities makes firms earn zero profit. Before doing so, we must make a crucial assumption about what happens to input prices when the demand for inputs rises. The reason we must consider this is because when the industry's output rises from Q_1 to Q_2, it must use more inputs. This causes the demand for inputs to increase, which may cause the prices of inputs to increase. Or it may not. Whether or not input prices increase depends on how big an impact this industry has on total demand for the inputs. In some cases the increase in input demand is very small. For example, consider the case of hairstylists in a particular city who must use more shampoo when they serve more customers. If the city

Figure 7-9   An Increasing-Cost Competitive Industry

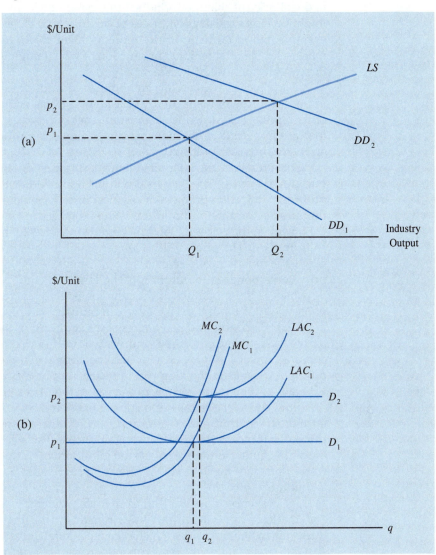

In an increasing-cost industry, input prices rise and the firm's cost curves shift up when industry output rises. So, when a demand increase causes industry output to rise from Q_1 to Q_2 in panel (a), the firm's long-run average cost curve shifts upward from LAC_1 to LAC_2 in panel (b). The new long-run equilibrium price is p_2, at the minimum point of LAC_2. Note that in panel (a), the price p_2, which is higher than p_1, is the equilibrium price corresponding to industry output of Q_2. So, we get a new point on the industry long-run supply curve, which is upward sloping, as shown.

is small enough, this increased demand would not have much impact on the national price of shampoo. On the other hand, the increase in input demand might be large, causing the prices of the inputs to change significantly. For example, wheat farmers require more fertilizer to produce more wheat. An increase in the total national production of wheat might lead to a significant increase in the price of fertilizer.

The preceding discussion highlights two cases. In one case, an increase in output in the industry under consideration has no impact on the prices of its inputs. This describes a **constant-cost industry.** In the other case, an increase in output in the industry causes input prices to rise. This is called an **increasing-cost industry.**

Consider first the case of an increasing-cost industry. Industry output grows from Q_1 to Q_2, as shown in Figure 7-9(a). Panel (b) shows the profit-maximization problem of a typical firm. When the price is p_1, the firm produces q_1, and its profit is zero. When total industry output increases to Q_2, however, the prices of the firm's inputs increase, so the firm's cost curves shift upward. The price p_1 is no longer equal to the minimum of the firm's new long-run average cost curve, so p_1 cannot be the long-run equilibrium price corresponding to output Q_2. The long-run equilibrium price must be p_2, which is the minimum of the new long-run average cost curve. So, the point (Q_2, p_2) is a point on the long-run industry supply curve, as shown in panel (a). By continuing this analysis, we could fill in the rest of the points on the industry supply curve, and we would find that the industry supply curve is upward sloping. It will become clear when we consider the next case that the reason the long-run industry supply curve is upward sloping is because when industry output increases, the prices of inputs rise.

Now consider the case of a constant-cost industry. This time when total industry output increases from Q_1 to Q_2, there is no increase in input prices. That means that there is no shift in the firm's cost curves. Since the long-run equilibrium price equals the minimum of the long-run average cost curve, and since the long-run average cost curve does not shift, the long-run equilibrium price does not change. In panel (b) of Figure 7-10, the long-run average cost curve does not shift from LAC_1 when industry output increases, and the long-run equilibrium price remains at p_1. For a constant-cost industry, then, the price does not change when total industry output increases, so (Q_2, p_1) is a point on the long-run industry supply curve, as shown in panel (a). The supply curve is horizontal, and, since every incumbent firm produces exactly what it did before, the increase in output comes entirely from new firms entering the industry.

There is one more possibility—a **decreasing-cost industry.** In this case, when industry output rises, costs for the individual firms decline. For example, consider a fishing industry in a small town, with each firm consisting of only one boat. When demand is low, there are not enough firms in the town to support a boat-repair firm. But, when demand gets high enough and the number of firms in the area increases, a boat-repair industry can

Figure 7-10   A Constant-Cost Competitive Industry

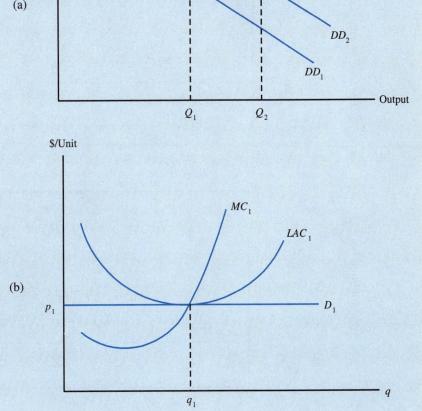
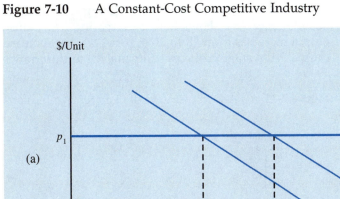

In a constant-cost industry, input prices remain unchanged when industry output rises. So, when industry output rises from Q_1 to Q_2 in panel (a), the firm's long-run average cost curve does not shift in panel (b). The new long-run equilibrium price is the same as the old long-run equilibrium price, p_1. The industry supply curve is horizontal, as shown in panel (a).

arise in the town. This lowers the fishing firms' cost of maintaining their boats. Figure 7-11 shows how a decreasing-cost industry works. Industry output increases from Q_1 to Q_2 in panel (a). The increase in industry output causes the average cost curve in panel (b) to shift downward from LAC_1 to

Figure 7-11   A Decreasing-Cost Competitive Industry

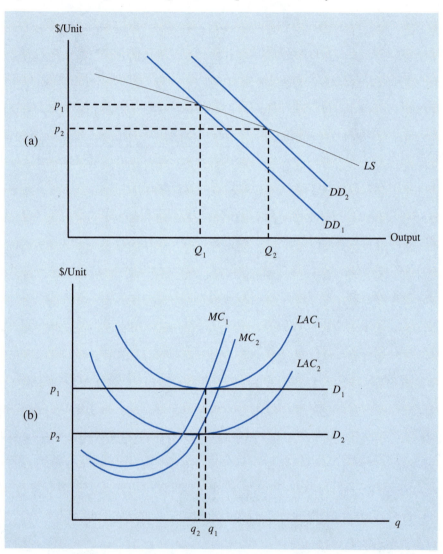

In a decreasing-cost industry, input prices decline and the firm's cost curves shift down when industry output rises. So, when industry output rises from Q_1 to Q_2 in panel (a), the firm's long-run average cost curve shifts downward from LAC_1 to LAC_2 in panel (b). The new long-run equilibrium price is p_2, which is lower than p_1. The industry supply curve is downward sloping, as shown in panel (a).

APPLICATION
An Increase in the Demand for Lobster

Suppose that demand for lobster in the United States were to increase permanently. What would happen to the price of lobster in the long run? Most lobsters are caught by fishermen with very small shares of the total industry output, so we can use the competitive model to answer this question. We have found that there are three possibilities for what happens to the price of lobster when demand increases. If it is an increasing-cost industry, the price of lobster rises. If it is a constant-cost industry, the price of lobster does not change. If it is a decreasing-cost industry, the price falls. Which type is the lobster industry? To answer this question, we must think about whether it becomes more costly or less costly to catch lobsters when the total number of lobsters being caught rises. If more lobsters are being harvested, it makes lobsters more scarce, and thus more difficult to catch. Each fishing trip yields a smaller number of lobsters, which makes the cost of producing one lobster rise. So, the lobster industry is an increasing-cost industry. The long-run supply curve is upward sloping, as in Figure 7-9, and when demand increases, the price rises.

LAC_2. The new long-run equilibrium price is p_2, which is below p_1. Panel (a) then shows that the long-run industry supply curve is downward sloping. This is a somewhat strange result (that a supply curve is downward sloping), and decreasing-cost industries are rarely, if ever, observed.

To summarize, we have found that the slope of the long-run industry supply curve depends on how input prices react to a change in industry output. In an increasing-cost industry, input prices rise when industry output rises, and the long-run supply curve is upward sloping. In a constant-cost industry, input prices do not change when industry output changes, and the long-run supply curve is horizontal. In a decreasing-cost industry, the long-run industry supply curve is downward-sloping.

7.3 PRICE UNCERTAINTY

The most frequently used example of a competitive industry is the agricultural industry. An individual farmer produces only a small fraction of the total industry output, and all farmers grow virtually identical produce. Farming has one feature that has not been captured in the standard competitive model, though. When farmers plant their crops, they do not know for sure what the price of the produce will be when it is harvested. If the weather is good in the rest of the country, so that the quantity supplied is large, the market price is low. Conversely, if the weather is bad in the rest of the country, the market price is high. Therefore, the farmer faces risk.

In Chapter 4 we learned that individuals tend to dislike risk. That is, they tend not to like it when their wealth is random. They would prefer to have the average amount of wealth with certainty. If, as viewed from the beginning of the season, the price a farmer receives for her crop is random, then so is her wealth at the end of the growing season. In this section we investigate what steps the farmer can take to reduce this risk.

Short-Run Output with Price Uncertainty

Suppose that the price of apples can take two possible values, $10 per bushel and $20 per bushel. Each of these prices is equally likely, so the expected, or average, price is $15 per bushel. Let's ask the following question: Is the firm's optimal output any different when the price is random compared to when it is certain to be $15? The answer, as we shall see, depends on whether or not the firm is risk averse.

To begin, let's find the firm's optimal output if the price is certain to be $15. This is shown in Figure 7-12. The firm's cost curves are shown, and optimal output is where the marginal cost curve crosses the price line, or at 500 bushels. When this quantity is produced, average total cost is $5 per bushel, so the firm earns a total profit of $5,000. Obviously, this is not a long-run equilibrium, because the firm is earning a positive profit.

What we really want to know is whether a risk-averse firm would choose to produce 500 bushels when prices are random. To figure this out, first find the firm's profit if the firm produces 500 bushels of apples and the random price turns out to be $20. In that case the firm would earn a $15 profit per unit and sell 500 units, so total profit would be $\pi_H = \$7,500$. What if the random price turned out to be $10? The firm would earn a $5 profit per unit, for a total profit of $\pi_L = \$2,500$. The firm's expected profit would be $(0.5)(\$7,500) + (0.5)(\$2,500) = \$5,000$.

Now we need to remember some things about risk aversion from Chapter 4. Risk-averse individuals, and firms owned by risk-averse individuals, dislike having different payoffs in different states. More explicitly, if two payoff combinations have the same expected value, risk-averse individuals would prefer the combination whose payoffs are closer together. So, let's see whether there is a way to keep the firm's expected profit at $5,000, but with the profit levels in the two states closer together. Let's try reducing output by one unit. We want to calculate the new profit when the price is $20 and when the price is $10. We can do this using marginal revenue and marginal cost. Marginal revenue is the extra revenue generated when output is increased by one unit. Or, it is the decrease in revenue when output is decreased by one unit. For a competitive firm, marginal revenue equals price,

Figure 7-12   Price Uncertainty and a Risk-Averse Farmer

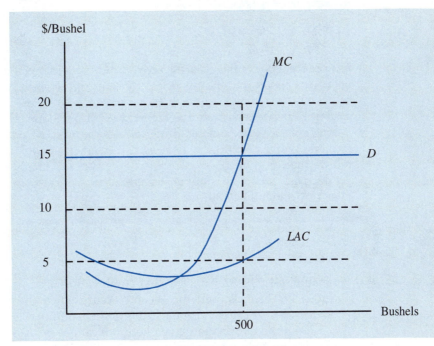

A risk-averse farmer with the cost curves shown faces price uncertainty. With probability 0.5 the price is $20, and with probability 0.5 the price is $10. The expected price is $15. If the $15 price were certain, the farmer would produce 500 bushels, average cost would be $5, and profit would be $5,000. If the farmer produces 500 bushels and the price is uncertain, though, the farmer earns $7,500 with probability 0.5 and $2,500 with probability 0.5. If the farmer is risk averse, he wishes to reduce his output and earn more profit when the price is low and less profit when the price is high.

so when output is decreased by one unit, revenue falls by the amount equal to the market price. Marginal cost is the extra cost incurred by producing one additional unit of output. Or, put another way, it is the decrease in cost when output is decreased by one unit. In Figure 7-12, when output is 500 bushels, marginal cost is $15.

If the market price is high at $20, reducing the firm's output by one bushel results in a $20 reduction in revenue and a $15 reduction in cost. Profit, then, falls by $5. So if the firm produces 499 units and the price is $20, profit is $\pi_H = \$7{,}495$. If the market price is low at $10, reducing the firm's output by one bushel results in a $10 reduction in revenue and a $15 reduction in cost. In this case profit actually *rises* by $5. So, when the firm produces 499 bushels of apples and the price is $10 per bushel, profit is $\pi_L = \$2{,}505$. Expected profit is $(0.5)(\$7{,}495) + (0.5)(\$2{,}505) = \$5{,}000$. So, the expected profit is the same, but the two possible profit levels are closer together. The firm prefers the (π_H, π_L) combination ($7,495, $2,505) to the com-

APPLICATION
Farm Price Supports

The federal government places price supports on many agricultural industries. This means that the government sets a support price, and farmers can sell as much as they want to the government at this price. Essentially, this system guarantees farmers that the market price will not fall below the support price. The effect of this program is to reduce the price risk faced by farmers. We just saw that when prices become riskier, risk-averse farmers reduce their output. Equivalently, when prices become less risky, farmers produce more. So, one result of the agricultural price support program is to raise U.S. agricultural output.

bination ($7,500, $2,500). The first combination occurs when the firm produces 499 bushels, and the second occurs when the firm produces 500 bushels. So, we can say that the firm's optimal output is less than 500 bushels.

From the information given here, we cannot say exactly how much less than 500 bushels, but we can say that it is less. But this is an important point, because, as we have shown, reducing output also reduces risk. This argument leads to a relatively simple statement about how risk-averse firms behave. When the market price becomes less certain, keeping the expected price the same, risk-averse firms reduce their output.

Long-Run Equilibrium Profits

One of the features of the standard long-run competitive model is that, in equilibrium, firms earn zero profit. More specifically, if the market price is not random, competitive firms earn zero profit in long-run equilibrium. Is there an analogous condition when prices are random? The answer to this question turns out to be yes.

To find the counterpart of the zero profit condition when prices are random, let's begin by reviewing why profits are zero in the standard case. Positive profits attract other firms to enter the industry, increasing industry supply and driving the price down. When the price goes down, profits fall. If profits are negative, some firms leave the industry, decreasing industry supply and driving the price up. When the price rises, the profits of the remaining firms rise. For the industry to be in equilibrium, there must be no incentive for firms to enter or exit the industry. Therefore, we need to find the condition that rules out entry or exit when prices are random.

Since profits are random when prices are random, we can no longer say that the firm maximizes profit. Instead, we say that it maximizes the *expected utility* of profits. Expected utility was introduced in Chapter 4 as a method of describing individuals' preferences in risky situations. Here, though, we are analyzing a firm, not a person. Why does it make sense to use expected utility in this case? Remember that in this particular example, we are talking about an apple farm. Typically the owner of a farm also runs it, and the owner's decisions about profits are also decisions about her income. If the owner is risk averse, this risk aversion will spread to the production decisions of the farm. So, when firms are small and operated by their owners, it makes sense to consider them as risk-averse firms that choose output to maximize the expected utility of profits.

A firm will enter the industry if its expected utility is higher when it enters than if it stays out. Similarly, a firm will exit the industry if its expected utility is lower in the industry than elsewhere. So, to find the long-run competitive equilibrium, we must calculate the expected utility of profits outside the industry and compare it to the expected utility of profits inside the industry. How much profit do firms earn in other industries? In Section 7.2 we said that firms earn zero profit in other industries, and that's why firms want to enter an industry with positive profit and exit an industry with negative profit. We can retain this assumption in the new setting. If other industries do not have price uncertainty, we can assume that firms earn zero profit in other industries.

A firm wants to enter the industry if it is better off entering than staying out. In expected utility terms, a firm wants to enter the industry if the expected utility of profits is higher when it enters than when it stays out. When a firm stays out of the industry, its profit is zero for sure. If it enters the industry, it earns some random amount of profit, because the amount of profit depends on the market price, which is itself random. So, the entry decision takes the following form. A firm should enter the industry if the expected utility of the random profit is greater than the expected utility of receiving zero profit for sure. Similarly, a firm should exit the industry if the expected utility of the random profit is less than the expected utility of receiving zero profit for sure.

This is different from saying that a firm should enter the industry if the *expected profit* from entering the industry is positive. In fact, the expected profit has to be positive just to keep risk-averse firms from exiting the industry. Let's see why. We can predict the choice of a risk-averse individual in one specific type of situation. Suppose that the individual has a choice between receiving a random payoff and receiving a fixed payoff for sure. If the expected value of the random payoff is the same as the fixed payoff, a risk-averse individual will choose the fixed payoff. This is just the definition of risk aversion. Now consider the decision of a risk-averse firm. If the firm stays in the industry it receives a random amount of profit. If the firm exits the industry it receives zero profit for sure. If the firm is risk averse and the expected profit from staying in the industry is zero, the firm will exit the industry. So, for risk-averse firms to stay in the industry, expected profit must be positive.

We have found in this section that random prices and risk-averse firms make some important changes to the standard model. Risk-averse firms produce less when the price is random than they would if the price were fixed at the expected price. Instead of leaving the industry when the expected profit is negative, risk-averse firms leave the industry when the expected utility of the random profit is less than the expected utility of zero profit. Similarly, risk-averse firms enter if the expected utility of the random profit is greater than the expected utility of zero profit. In long-run equilibrium, the expected utility of the random profit is equal to the expected utility of zero profit. Even so, long-run expected profit is positive. Expected profit has to be positive in order to entice risk-averse firms to stay in the industry and bear the risk.

It is clear that risk aversion makes a big difference. Is there any reason to believe that competitive firms might be risk averse? Individuals tend to be risk averse, but what about firms? Competitive firms tend to be small. In agricultural industries, firms are often just family businesses. If individual farmers are risk averse when buying insurance or investing their savings, it makes sense that they would be risk averse when running their firms. So, for competitive firms at least, there are good reasons to believe that firms might be risk averse.

7.4 GAINS FROM TRADE AND SOCIAL WELFARE

Several years ago, a local newspaper reporter in Texas wrote an article on the changing eating habits of grade-school children. He interviewed many children to find out what snacks their parents had packed in their lunches. Many children had healthy snacks, such as fruit. Other children had junk food snacks, such as candy bars. The interviewer asked the children with the healthy snacks whether they traded their snacks for the unhealthy ones. Almost unanimously, the answer he received was no. He concluded that these children were being health conscious. Good for them! An economist can offer a different interpretation of what was happening. If a child with an apple doesn't trade his apple for a candy bar, it may not be because he is being health conscious. The problem is: What child would want to trade his candy bar for an apple? Would you? Whenever trade occurs, *both* parties involved in the transaction must benefit from that transaction. If not, why would trade occur? In this section, we will examine what consumers and producers gain from transacting with each other and how these gains can be used to analyze the welfare effects of social policies.

APPLICATION
The Efficient Market Hypothesis

The field of finance has a concept very similar to the idea that the expected utility of profit must be zero in long-run competitive equilibrium. This concept is the *efficient market hypothesis*. The hypothesis states, basically, that any new information about an asset, such as a stock or bond, is instantly incorporated into the price of that asset. We can put this concept into the framework of the competitive model. Suppose that some new information becomes available suggesting that Walmart stock will be worth more in the future. This makes investors want to buy more Walmart stock, because the new information suggests that they will make above-average profit by doing so. According to standard supply and demand analysis, the price of Walmart stock rises. The efficient market hypothesis goes one step further, saying that the price adjusts instantly.

Continuing the analogy between the stock market and the competitive market, what does the efficient market hypothesis say about the ability of an investor to make above-average profit on the stock? Since stock prices adjust instantly to their long-run equilibrium levels, some sort of zero profit condition holds right away. Remember that we are talking about economic profit, which takes into account the use of the investor's money in the next best alternative investment. Zero profit means that the investor can do no better with this stock than with any other stock.

Since investments are inherently risky, the zero profit condition means that the expected utility the investor receives from investing in Walmart stock is the same as the expected utility he receives from investing in other stocks. What about expected profit? As we saw with the risk-averse competitive firm, if investors are risk averse they will need additional expected profit to compensate them for bearing additional risk. In other words, there is a way to earn above-average *expected* profit by investing in the stock market: Bear more risk than the market average.

Consumer Surplus

Figure 7-13 shows a market demand curve for some representative good. Every demand curve is a *marginal willingness to pay* schedule. At point *E*, for example, there is some consumer who is exactly willing to pay price P_D for the last unit at Q_D. No consumer is willing to pay more than P_D for that last unit. Thus, each point along a demand curve represents some consumer's

Figure 7-13   Willingness to Pay and Consumer Surplus

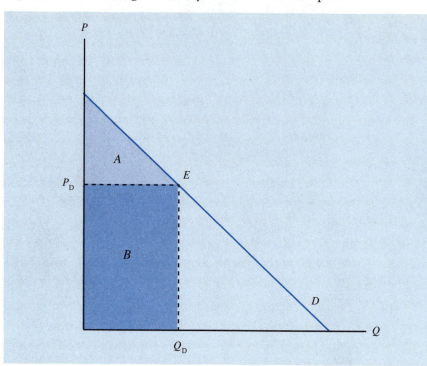

A demand curve is a marginal willingness to pay schedule. At point E, there is some consumer who is willing to pay no more than price P_D for the last unit at Q_D. The area under the demand curve, $A+B$, represents consumers' total willingness to pay for all Q_D units. Area B is the total expenditure, $P_D Q_D$. Area A is the consumer surplus, which represents the difference between total willingness to pay and total expenditure.

willingness to pay for the last unit shown at that point. A downward-sloping demand curve suggests that as consumers have more of a good, they are willing to pay less and less for each successive unit.

Because the demand curve is a marginal willingness to pay schedule, the area under the demand curve represents the *total willingness to pay*. Basically, as we add up the marginal willingnesses to pay for each level of output, the marginals add up to the total. If you are willing to pay $2 for the first unit of a good, $1 for the second unit, 50 cents for the third unit, and 0 for any more units, your total willingness to pay for three units is $3.50. Thus, for *all* Q_D units, consumers are willing to pay a total equal to area $A+B$.

Area $A+B$ can be broken down into two separate components. If the market price is P_D, area B represents the *total expenditure* on the good, $P_D Q_D$. Since $A+B$ is the *total* willingness to pay, and B is the *actual* amount paid, area A represents the amount that consumers are willing to pay for Q_D units, but don't have to. Area A is known as **consumer surplus.** Consumer surplus is an *implicit* gain to consumers. Every consumer who pays P_D for a unit of the good, except the marginal consumer at point E, is willing to pay more than P_D for that unit. If you are willing to pay $15 for a compact disc, but the price at the store is $12, you have implicitly saved $3. You will never pay more than $15, and every cent you pay less than $15 is consumer surplus. The lower the price, the greater your consumer surplus, and the more you benefit from buying the compact disc.

Producer Surplus

As with consumers, producers also receive surplus. Figure 7-14 shows a market supply curve for a representative good. A supply curve is a *marginal willingness to accept* schedule. At point F, for example, at price P_S some producer

Figure 7-14   Willingness to Accept and Producer Surplus

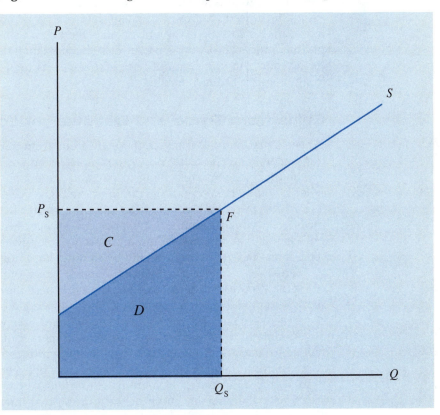

A supply curve is a marginal willingness to accept schedule. At point F, there is some producer who is willing to supply the last unit at Q_S for price P_S. The area under the supply curve, D, represents the total (minimum) willingness to accept. Area $C+D$ represents total revenue when the price is P_S. Area C is producer surplus, which represents the difference between total revenue and total (minimum) willingness to accept.

is, at a minimum, willing to accept that price to supply the last unit at Q_S. No producer is willing to supply that last unit at a price less than P_S. The area under the supply curve, area D, represents the *total (minimum) willingness to accept*. This means that for producers as a whole to be willing to supply Q_S units of the good, they must receive, at a minimum, area D. If the price in the market is P_S, however, the total revenue producers receive for producing Q_S is area $C+D$, or $P_S Q_S$. Thus, area C represents the amount producers receive above what they need at a minimum to produce Q_S. Area C is known as **producer surplus.**

It is common to confuse producer surplus with profit, but the two are not necessarily the same. Recall from Section 7.1 the short-run production decision of a competitive firm. If the price is greater than the firm's average variable cost, the firm is better off producing than shutting down. Because of this, a competitive firm may earn zero (or even negative) profit, yet still receive positive producer surplus. Profit is explicitly defined as total revenue minus total cost, but producer surplus is the amount above the *minimum* a firm needs to produce. This minimum for a competitive firm is its total variable cost. So if the price equals the firm's average cost, for example, its profit is zero, but its producer surplus is equal to its total fixed cost. In the short run, the firm only needs to cover its total variable cost. Anything more is producer surplus.

Gains from Trade and Deadweight Loss

Whenever individuals transact, there are **gains from trade.** *Both* parties to a transaction are made better off. For example, when you buy a car there is a maximum price you are willing to pay and there is a minimum price the seller is willing to accept. If the minimum selling price is less than the maximum offer price, both you and the seller can benefit from trade. Any price lower than your maximum offer price gives you consumer surplus. Any price higher than the seller's minimum asking price gives him producer surplus. If one individual cannot gain by trading, he simply won't trade.

Figure 7-15 combines a market demand curve with a market supply curve for a representative good. At the point where the supply curve intersects the demand curve, at quantity Q^*, not only is it a competitive equilibrium, there are no gains from trade to exploit. Let's see why this is the case.

Assume that, for some reason, the initial market quantity is Q'. To be willing to increase production from Q' to Q^*, producers (as a group) need at a minimum the area under the supply curve between these two quantities—area H. Consumers (as a group) are willing to pay at a maximum the area under the demand curve between these two quantities—area $G+H$. Thus, consumers are willing to pay up to G more than what producers need at a minimum to increase production. Area G represents the gains from trade that can be exploited by consumers and producers. Once at the intersection of the supply and demand curves, however, there are no more gains from

Figure 7-15   Gains from Trade

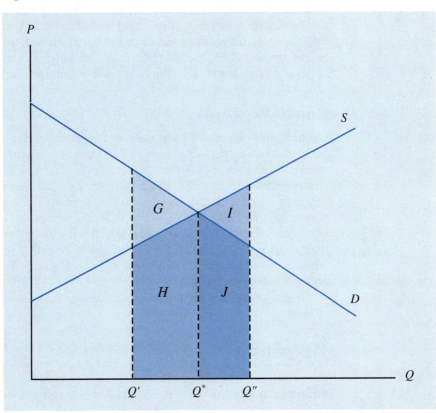

At output level Q', producers need a minimum of area H to increase production to Q^*. Consumers are willing to pay a maximum of $G+H$ for that increased production. Consumers are willing to pay area G more than what producers need. Area G represents the gains from trade available from increasing production from Q' to Q^*. Once at Q^*, there are no more gains from trade to exploit. Producers need area $I+J$ to increase production to Q'', but consumers are only willing to pay at most area J.

trade to exploit. To increase production from Q^* to Q'', for example, producers need at a minimum area $I+J$. Consumers are willing to pay at a maximum only area J. Producers will have no incentive to increase production beyond Q^*, the competitive quantity where supply intersects demand.

In Figure 7-15, when looking at an increase in production from Q' to Q^*, area G represents the gains from trade that can be exploited by consumers and producers. If that additional amount is not produced, however, area G becomes an *unexploited* gain from trade. Another term for an unexploited gain from trade is **deadweight loss.** Consumers value an increase in production from Q' to Q^* by area $G+H$. Area H on its own represents how much producers need at a minimum to draw resources into the production of the additional units. If we think of these consumers and producers as the only individuals in society, we can say that society values the increased production by an amount greater than the cost to society of producing the additional units. If the additional units are not produced, society is made poorer by the amount G, the deadweight loss. Thinking of consumers and producers as a society leads us to the next topic—social welfare.

Social Welfare

Up until this point, we have only put consumers and producers together when discussing perfectly competitive market equilibrium. By definition, a market must consist of two sides—buyers and sellers. Consumers gain consumer surplus from trade, and producers gain producer surplus. Taken together, we can define a **social welfare function** to be the sum of the two surpluses, that is, $W = CS + PS$, where W is social welfare. The advantage of a social welfare function is that it provides us with an objective to analyze social policies. Specifically, if the social objective is to maximize social welfare, does the policy in question achieve this objective? To illustrate this point, it is best to use an example.

In Chapter 1 we discussed price gouging, using as an example the price of bottled water in Los Angeles after an earthquake. Figure 7-16 (similar to Figure 1-6) shows the market supply and demand curves for bottled water. Prior to the earthquake, the market price of bottled water is P_0 and the quantity is Q_0. The earthquake shifts the demand for bottled water to D_1, and the price rises to P_1 and the quantity increases to Q_1. (The initial demand curve through the point (Q_0, P_0) is not drawn to avoid additional clutter.) If the task force on price gouging interprets the price increase to be an act of gouging, they enforce a price restriction of P_0 on producers. What are the social welfare effects of the anti-price-gouging law?

Prior to the law, the market price and quantity are P_1 and Q_1. Consumer surplus is the area above the price and below the demand curve—area $A+B$. Producer surplus is the area below the price and above the supply curve—area $C+D+E$. Social welfare, then, is $CS + PS = A+B+C+D+E$. After the law is in effect, the original price P_0 restricts supply back down to Q_0. Producers simply will not bring more resources into the production of bottled water at the legally maintained lower price. At the price P_0, consumer surplus is now $A+C$. Producer surplus at the enforced price is area E. Social welfare after the law is, therefore, $A+C+E$, which is obviously less than the prelaw amount of $A+B+C+D+E$. Area $B+D$ is the deadweight loss created by the anti-price-gouging law.

From a social point of view, the law reduces welfare, but consumers and producers are affected differently. If area C is greater than area B, consumers as a whole gain from the policy. Note, however, that not all consumers gain. Those who continue to buy water at the low price reap additional surplus equal to area C, but those who no longer can get water lose surplus equal

Figure 7-16   Anti-Price-Gouging Laws and Deadweight Loss

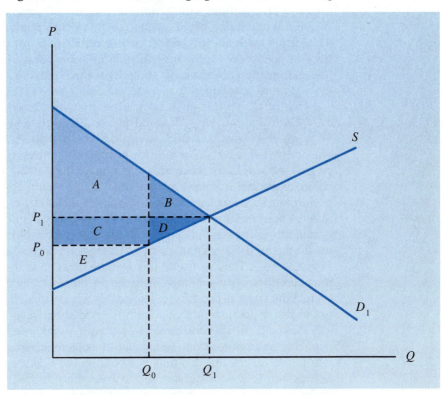

Before the anti-price-gouging law, the price is P_1 and the quantity is Q_1. Consumer surplus is area $A+B$, and producer surplus is area $C+D+E$. Social welfare, then, is $W = CS + PS = A + B+C+D+E$. With the anti-price-gouging law in effect, the price is held at P_0 and only Q_0 units are supplied. Consumer surplus is now area $A+C$, and producer surplus is area E. Social welfare is $W = A+C+E$. The anti-price-gouging law has reduced social welfare by area $B+D$, the deadweight loss due to unexploited gains from trade.

to area B. While area C is a gain to consumers, it is part of the loss to producers. Producers unambiguously lose $C+D$ in surplus, but C is simply transferred to consumers, so it is not part of a social welfare loss of $B+D$. Consumers may gain from the anti-price-gouging law, but producers lose. Overall, a deadweight loss is created. As long as there are unexploited gains from trade, social welfare is not maximized. What this means is that at the perfectly competitive outcome, where supply equals demand, social welfare is maximized.

If the anti-price-gouging law reduces social welfare, why do politicians consider imposing it? This question raises controversial issues in social welfare analysis that are usually not raised in consumer or producer theory. In consumer theory, economists assume that a consumer's objective is to maximize utility. This is far from controversial, since utility is an abstract measure of consumer satisfaction. In producer theory, economists assume that firms maximize profit. Although this assumption can be challenged, since firms are made up of real people with utility functions that may not depend solely on profit, most economists are comfortable with the profit-maximization objective. The objective of maximizing social welfare, however, is more problematic.

First of all, what is a social welfare function? Above, we defined it as $W = CS + PS$, but why? It could just as easily be defined as $W = CS$, or $W = PS$, or $W = \alpha CS + \beta PS$, where α and β are different weights. If social welfare is defined as $W = CS$, for example, the anti-price-gouging law increases social welfare when area C is greater than area B in Figure 7-16. The choice of a social welfare function, then, is important. There are two steps in performing social welfare analysis: Choose a social welfare function, and then observe how social welfare is affected by the policy in question. The first step is subjective. The second step, *given* the first step, is objective. Many economists who do social welfare analysis use the standard social welfare function $W = CS + PS$. The defense of this welfare function is that it includes all the members of society who are included in our analysis, and consumers are treated the same as producers. The goal is to maximize the wealth of society, not to worry about how that wealth is divided between the two groups.

This leads to a second problem with our social welfare function. We are explicitly assuming that a dollar gain to consumers exactly offsets a dollar loss to producers. But this may not be true. If a dollar is transferred from a rich person to a poor person, the loss in utility to the rich person may be more than offset by the gain in utility to the poor person. In other words, if we are concerned with the *utility* of income, and not just income itself, it becomes difficult to make interpersonal comparisons. A dollar-for-dollar transfer will no longer have a neutral social welfare effect.

As a final word, the best way to think of our social welfare function is as a tool that provides an easy-to-understand dollar measure of the potential gains and losses of social policies. It may not be a perfect measure, but at least we are aware of its shortcomings.

Summary

- Some important characteristics of a **competitive industry** are: All firms produce exactly the same product; consumers know the prices charged by every firm in the industry; each firm's output is small relative to the total output of the industry; and firms may enter and exit the industry freely.

- A competitive firm's demand curve is horizontal at the **market price.** Thus, competitive firms are said to be **price-takers.** Price is determined by the market, not by any individual firm.

- Because a competitive firm's demand curve is horizontal, its **marginal revenue curve** is also horizontal and equal to the market price. To maximize profit, a competitive firm produces its output at the point where its marginal revenue equals its marginal cost. Because its marginal revenue is the price, the profit-maximizing condition is to produce where price equals marginal cost.

- In the short run, a competitive firm produces as long as price exceeds the firm's average variable cost. In this case, the firm can cover all of its total variable costs and at least a part of its total fixed costs. If price falls below the average variable cost, it is in the firm's best interest to shut down. In this case, the firm cannot even cover all of its total variable costs. By shutting down, *losses* are minimized and equal to the total fixed costs that must always be incurred.

- The competitive firm's short-run **supply curve** is the portion of its marginal cost curve that lies above the average variable cost curve. The **industry supply curve** is the horizontal summation of all the individual firms' supply curves.

- In a **long-run competitive equilibrium:** Each firm produces where price equals its marginal cost; short-run supply equals demand; because of free entry and exit, each firm earns zero (economic) profit; and, long-run supply equals demand.

- A **constant-cost industry** has a long-run supply curve that is horizontal. In this case, as firms enter the industry, input prices do not change for all firms.

- An **increasing-cost industry** has a long-run supply curve that is upward sloping. In this case, as firms enter the industry, input prices increase for all firms.

- A **decreasing-cost industry** has a long-run supply curve that is downward sloping. In this case, as firms enter the industry, input prices decrease for all firms.

Problems

1. A perfectly competitive firm can sell all it wants to at a price of $12 or less per unit. If it produces 4,000 units its short-run marginal cost is $10 and its average variable cost is $8. If it produces 5,000 units its short-run

marginal cost is $15 and its average variable cost is $9. Should the firm produce less than 4,000, more than 5,000, or something in between 4,000 and 5,000? Explain your answer.

2. Suppose that because of an increase in the minimum wage, labor costs rise for all firms in a competitive industry.
   a. If the market price does not adjust in the short run, what happens to a typical firm's output?
   b. What happens to the short-run industry supply curve?
   c. What happens to the long-run equilibrium price of the industry's output?
   d. What happens to the industry's total output in the long run?
   e. What happens to the number of firms in the industry in the long run?

3. Retail stores often have clearance sales. Does this suggest that retail stores are perfectly competitive or not? Explain your answer.

4. A competitive firm's long-run marginal cost curve is given by $MC(q) = 3q^2 - 60q + 120$, and its long-run average cost curve is given by $LAC(q) = q^2 - 20q + 120$.
   a. Find the firm's long-run equilibrium output and the long-run equilibrium price.
   b. If the market price is $25, do firms enter or exit the industry?

5. Suppose that the U.S. timber industry is a perfectly competitive, increasing-cost industry.
   a. If Japanese construction companies start buying U.S. lumber for use in Japan, what happens to the long-run equilibrium price of timber? Can you say anything about what happens to the number of firms in equilibrium?
   b. If, instead, the demand for paper products falls because people and firms use computers and telephone lines to transmit information, what happens to the long-run equilibrium price of timber? Can you say anything about what happens to the number of firms in equilibrium?

6. Suppose that the profit-maximizing level of output for a firm is 1,000 units when the market price is $15 and the corresponding average cost is $10. But prices are random. With probability 0.5 that the price is $25, and with probability 0.5 that the price is $5, show that if the firm is risk-averse, the firm is better off producing less than 1,000 units of output.

7. In the example in Section 7.3, an apple farmer thinks there is a 50 percent probability that the market price will be $10 and a 50 percent chance that the market price will be $20. If, at the beginning of the season, the farmer could sign a contract to sell all of his apples at $15 per bushel and avoid the price risk, would it be in her best interest to do so? Why or why not?

8

MONOPOLY POWER

Overview

There are many types of powers in the world. In baseball, a power hitter can hit home runs on a fairly regular basis. The United States is known around the world as a superpower, and Superman is known around the universe for his super powers. But if Superman wants to subscribe to the HBO cable channel, the last son of Krypton must confront a still more powerful opponent—his local cable company. Most cable companies do not face competitive pressure from many other firms. They generally have the ability to be price setters (unless they are regulated by the government), unlike competitive firms, which must be price takers. They also have the ability to control which cable channels customers may access. In the extreme, when there is only a single firm in an industry, that firm is said to be a **monopolist.** More generally, even if there are many firms in an industry, **monopoly power** is said to exist when at least one firm can set its price above its marginal cost. Monopolists may be rare in the real world, but monopoly power is more common. This is one reason to study monopoly behavior: If we understand pure monopoly (that is, a single firm in the industry), we can have a much better understanding of the more general concept of monopoly power. A second reason is that, along with the competitive model, monopoly pricing provides an important benchmark for comparing other models of price determination, such as the oligopoly models we will study in Chapter 10. This chapter introduces the following aspects of monopoly behavior:

- How to find the monopolist's profit-maximizing price and output.
- How the monopoly outcome differs from the competitive outcome.
- How to measure monopoly power.
- How monopoly power is maintained.
- How the monopolist can use different pricing strategies to increase its profit.
- How the monopoly outcome is affected by goods that last for more than one period.

8.1 MONOPOLY PROFIT MAXIMIZATION

A monopolist wants to maximize profit, just as a competitive firm does. That is, the monopolist wants to set its marginal revenue equal to its marginal cost. In Chapter 7, we saw that a competitive firm faces a horizontal demand curve at the market price, and therefore its marginal revenue equals the market price at every level of output. A monopolist, on the other hand, does not face a horizontal demand curve. Because it is the only firm in the industry, the monopolist's demand curve is the industry's downward-sloping demand curve; and therefore, the monopolist's marginal revenue curve lies *below* its demand curve. This relationship between demand and marginal revenue will now be explained in more detail.

The Marginal Revenue Curve

Suppose the monopolist is trying to compare the total revenue it will receive from two output levels, Q_1 versus Q_2 units. In Figure 8-1, output level Q_2 is chosen so that it is just one unit more than Q_1. That is, $Q_2 = Q_1 + 1$. If the monopolist sells Q_1 units, its market price will be P_1. To sell an additional unit, the monopolist must set a slightly lower price of P_2. What happens to total revenue if the monopolist increases its output by one unit? Another way to phrase this question is: What is the firm's marginal revenue of producing one more unit? Because it sells one more unit, the monopolist receives some additional revenue from the increase in quantity. Specifically, the last unit adds $P_2(Q_2 - Q_1) = P_2$ in revenue, or area A. But, to sell the last unit, the monopolist must set a lower price that also applies to *each* of the previous Q_1 units. By lowering its price, the monopolist loses $(P_1 - P_2)Q_1$, or area B, in revenue. Relative to Q_1, then, by selling Q_2 units the monopolist gains P_2 in revenue but loses $(P_1 - P_2)Q_1$. Therefore, marginal revenue from the last unit sold is $MR = P_2 - (P_1 - P_2)Q_1$. How does MR compare to P_2? Because $P_1 > P_2$, it is clear that $P_2 - (P_1 - P_2)Q_1 < P_2$. In other words, we have just shown that the monopolist's marginal revenue is less than its price. This holds true at every level of output.

As an example, consider the only automobile dealership in a small town. Its demand curve for automobiles is the following:

$$P = 16{,}000 - 20Q,$$

where P is the price of an automobile and Q is the quantity sold in a year. Figure 8-2 shows this demand curve and the marginal revenue curve that lies below the demand curve. How do we derive the MR curve? In general, when drawing a marginal revenue curve for any *linear* demand curve, you only have to remember two things: Have it intersect the vertical axis at the same point as the demand curve, and have it intersect the horizontal axis

Figure 8-1   Monopoly Pricing and Marginal Revenue

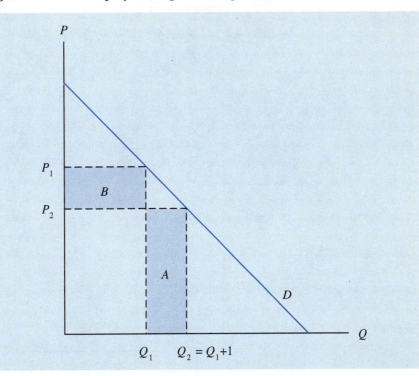

The monopolist is comparing the total revenues it receives from two output levels. As the monopolist increases its output by one unit from Q_1 to Q_2, its increase in total revenue is the price it gets for the last unit, P_2, or area A. However, to sell the additional unit, the monopolist must lower its price for each of the previous Q_1 units, thus losing $(P_1 - P_2)Q_1$ in revenue, or area B. The *marginal revenue*, then, of selling the additional unit is $P_2 - (P_1 - P_2)Q_1$, which is less than the price P_2.

halfway between the origin and the horizontal intercept of the demand curve. Thus, as can be seen in the figure, the marginal revenue curve has the same vertical intercept, 16,000, as does the demand curve, but twice the slope, -40, of the demand curve (which has slope -20).

Maximizing Profit

Now that we understand how to derive the marginal revenue curve, we need to know the monopolist's marginal cost curve in order to find its profit-maximizing price and output. Assume that the automobile dealership has a constant marginal cost of $MC = 10,000$ per automobile and that there are no fixed costs. (Thus, marginal cost is equal to average cost.) In Figure 8-3, we now have all the information we need to find the monopolist's profit-maximizing outcome. Since profit is maximized at the point where $MR =$

Figure 8-2   The Relationship Between Demand and Marginal
Revenue for a Monopolist

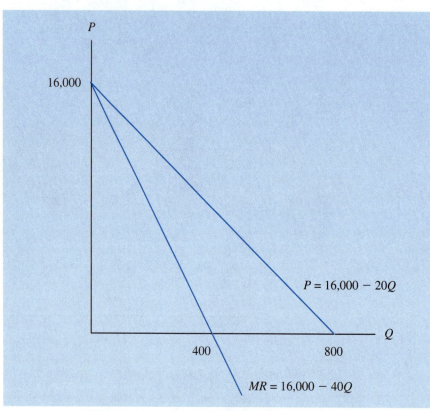

For any linear demand curve, the monopolist's marginal revenue curve has the same vertical
intercept as the demand curve and twice the slope.

MC, we have $16,000 - 40Q = 10,000$. Therefore, to reap the greatest profit,
the monopolist must set its output level at 150 automobiles and sell each at
a price determined by the demand curve: $P = 16,000 - 20(150) = \$13,000$.
In this case, total revenue is equal to $(150)(13,000) = \$1.95$ million, and to-
tal cost is equal to $(150)(10,000) = \$1.5$ million. The monopolist's profit is
$TR - TC = \$450,000$. (As an exercise, you should convince yourself that if
the monopolist were to produce any other level of output, its profit would
be less than $450,000.)

Figure 8-4 shows the profit-maximizing outcome under more general
cost conditions. Specifically, it uses U-shaped marginal and average cost
curves. The monopolist's profit-maximizing price and output, *P** and *Q**, are
still found by setting marginal revenue equal to marginal cost. To determine
the monopoly profit, recall from Chapter 6 that total cost is equal to aver-

Figure 8-3   Monopoly Profit Maximization

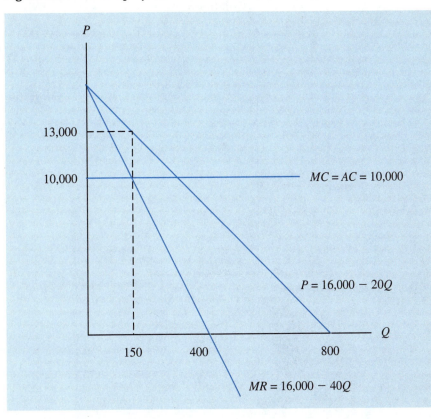

To maximize profit, the monopolist produces its output at the point where its marginal revenue equals its marginal cost. In this example, the profit-maximizing price and output are 13,000 and 150, respectively.

age cost times quantity. In Figure 8-4 the average cost of producing Q^* units is equal to AC^*. Therefore, the monopolist's profit is equal to $TR - TC = P^*Q^* - AC^*Q^*$, or area $A+B+C+E$.

8.2 MONOPOLY VERSUS COMPETITION

There are some obvious differences between the monopoly model we discussed in the previous section and the competitive model we examined in Chapter 7. The most obvious difference is that in a monopoly model there is only a single firm, while in a competitive model there are many. We also saw in the previous section that a monopolist faces a downward-sloping demand curve, but a competitive firm faces a horizontal demand curve at the market price. Finally, we have seen that a monopolist can earn positive eco-

Figure 8-4   Monopoly Profit Maximization Under General Cost
Conditions

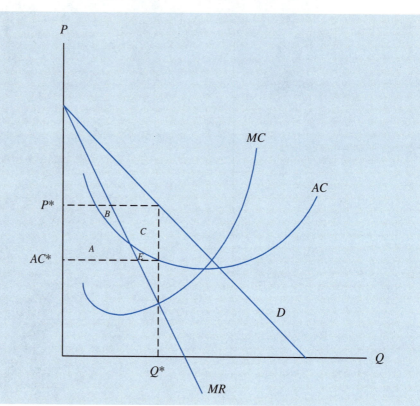

Even under general cost conditions, the monopolist maximizes profit by setting marginal
revenue equal to marginal cost. Total revenue is price times quantity, P^*Q^*. Total cost is average
cost times quantity, AC^*Q^*. Therefore, profit is area $A+B+C+E$.

nomic profit, while in a long-run competitive equilibrium all firms must earn
zero profits. None of these differences, however, addresses an important
question economists and others are concerned with: What are the social welfare differences between pure competition and pure monopoly?

Monopoly and Deadweight Loss

We've seen in Chapter 7 that the competitive outcome, where demand equals
supply, maximizes social welfare. What about the monopoly outcome? Let's
return to the automobile dealership example from the previous section, but
now we'll consider two cases, both shown in Figure 8-5. The first case is the
monopoly outcome, which we'll denote $(Q_M, P_M) = (150, 13,000)$. In the sec-

APPLICATION
A Rock 'n Roll Monopoly

If there is one example of monopoly behavior that hits close to home, it's that of Ticketmaster, the nation's largest distributor of live-event tickets. Ticketmaster controls tickets sold at 3,000 venues, including Madison Square Garden and the Hollywood Bowl.* For premiere events, a Ticketmaster surcharge can be more than $6 per ticket. (Do you think that this is greater than the marginal cost of selling a ticket?) With monopoly pricing, however, comes complications. Ticketmaster is facing investigation for monopolistic practices from the Justice Department and the New York State Attorney General. Furthermore, customers are forming class action lawsuits against the company. Finally, some of the most popular rock 'n roll bands of the decade—Pearl Jam, Stone Temple Pilots, R.E.M.—are also fighting Ticketmaster.

*Business Week, June 26, 1995.

ond case, we have the same industry demand curve, but now we assume that there are many automobile dealerships in the town. (By "many" we mean that each dealership is a price taker.) Also, we assume that each competitive firm has the same marginal cost curve as the monopolist does, so that when all the individual marginal cost curves are summed we have the industry marginal cost curve $MC = \$10,000$. The competitive outcome in Figure 8-5 is denoted $(Q_C, P_C) = (300, 10,000)$. Clearly, the monopolist's price-setting behavior allows it to restrict output and set a higher price than the competitive price.

In Figure 8-5, we have identified five areas. Recall from Chapter 7 that in long-run competitive equilibrium there is no profit and there is no deadweight loss. The area $A+B+C+F+E$ is all consumer surplus. Under the monopoly outcome, however, only area $A+B$ is consumer surplus, because the price is now P_M. What happened to the rest of the consumer surplus? Area $C+F$ is now monopoly profit equal to $(P_M - AC)Q_M$, and area E is now a deadweight loss. That is, by setting price above marginal cost, the monopolist does not sell the last $(Q_C - Q_M)$ units, even though the marginal willingness to pay for each of those units is greater than the marginal cost. Because of this, the monopoly outcome does not maximize social welfare. Does this mean that monopolists must be eliminated from the face of the earth? Although this idea would make a great movie, there may be benefits of monopoly power that we have yet to consider.

Figure 8-5   Monopoly Pricing and Deadweight Loss

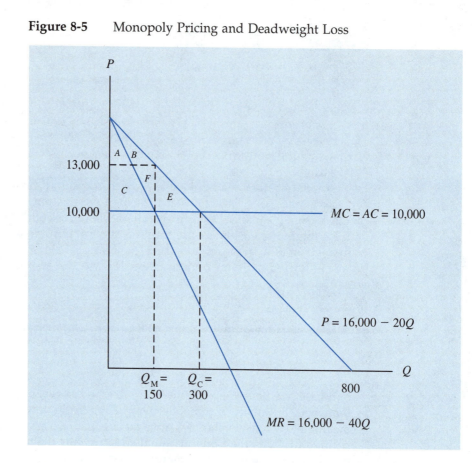

Under the competitive outcome, $Q_C = 300$ and area $A+B+C+F+E$ is the consumer surplus. Under the monopoly outcome, $Q_M = 150$, area $A+B$ is still consumer surplus, area $C+F$ is now monopoly profit, and area E is a deadweight loss. Area E is a "loss" to society because the marginal willingness to pay for each of the $(Q_C - Q_M)$ units is greater than the marginal cost.

Monopoly and Cost Savings

It is possible that a monopolist, because it is the only firm in the industry, can produce each unit of output at a lower marginal cost than can a competitive industry made up of many small firms. In Figure 8-6, we once again compare a monopoly outcome (Q_M, P_M) with a competitive outcome (Q_C, P_C), but it is not exactly the same comparison we made in Figure 8-5. In Figure 8-6, the monopolist has a lower marginal cost curve (MC_M) than the competitive industry (MC_C), and so its profit-maximizing outcome is found by equating $MR = MC_M$. The competitive industry, on the other hand, finds its profit-maximizing outcome at the point where the demand curve intersects MC_C. A quick glance at Figure 8-6 reveals that the monopolist still sets a higher price and a lower output than the competitive outcome, and there is

Figure 8-6   The Williamson Trade-Off Model

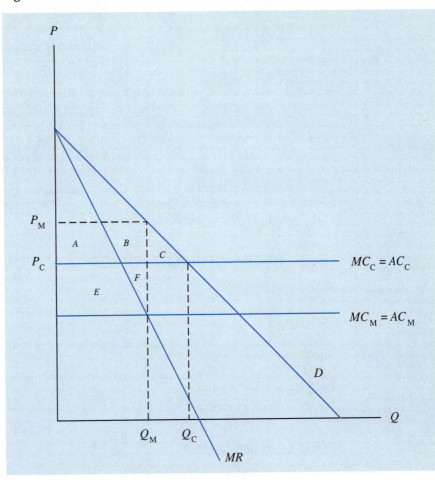

The **Williamson trade-off model** compares the competitive outcome with marginal cost curve MC_C to the monopoly outcome with the lower marginal cost curve MC_M. Area $A+B$ represents a transfer from consumers to the firm, area C is a deadweight loss, and area $E+F$ is a cost savings associated with the more efficient production of the first Q_M units. Monopolization, then, creates a social loss of area C, but a social gain of area $E+F$.

still a deadweight loss represented by area C. Now, however, there is an additional area, $E+F$, that must be taken into account. What does $E+F$ represent? With the competitive industry, $E+F$ is a part of the total cost of producing the first Q_M units of the total Q_C units produced.[1] With the monopoly

---

1 In general, the area under a marginal cost curve represents the total *variable* cost of production. In this example, with $MC = AC$, there is no fixed cost and the area under the marginal cost curve represents the *total* cost.

industry and its lower marginal cost curve, $E+F$ is no longer part of the total cost of producing the first Q_M units. Instead, $E+F$ is the part of the monopoly profit that is made up of the cost savings associated with MC_M. The rest of the monopoly profit, $A+B$, is due to the higher price associated with monopoly power.

Figure 8-6 demonstrates that there can be a social welfare trade-off between a monopolist and a competitive industry. Relative to the competitive outcome, the monopolist creates a deadweight loss equal to area C, but it may also create a cost savings like area $E+F$. Thus, if C is larger than $E+F$, there is a net welfare loss associated with the monopoly, but if C is smaller than $E+F$, there is a net welfare gain. Professor Oliver Williamson was the first to formally identify this welfare trade-off. It should be noted that Williamson's intention was not to defend monopoly power, but simply to point out that before condemning the monopolist, we must consider both the possible costs *and* benefits of monopoly power.

8.3 MEASURING MONOPOLY POWER

From what we've seen so far in this chapter, it would be fun to be a monopolist. More often than not, a monopolist can earn positive economic profits, while a competitive firm is constrained to earning zero profits (in long-run equilibrium). But how does a firm become a monopolist? Or, more generally, where does monopoly power come from? While it is rare that we observe firms that are pure monopolists, monopoly power is relatively common. Before we examine how firms maintain monopoly power, we must develop a way to measure it.

The Lerner Index

What exactly is monopoly power? It usually refers to the ability of at least one firm to set its profit-maximizing price above its marginal cost. When a firm maximizes profit, it must set its marginal revenue equal to its marginal cost. This condition allows us to measure monopoly power in a very convenient way. Recall from Chapter 6 that we can express marginal revenue as $MR = (P^* - P^*/e_f)$, where P^* is the profit-maximizing price, MC is marginal cost, and e_f is the *firm's* price elasticity of demand. When setting $MR = MC$, we can rearrange terms to show that the following condition holds at a profit maximum:

$$(P^* - MC)/P^* = 1/e_f.$$

The term on the left is known as the **Lerner index** of monopoly power, named after the late Professor Abba Lerner. The Lerner index is very simple to interpret: It measures the proportion of P^* that is *not* attributable to marginal cost, and this proportion is equal to the inverse of the firm's price elasticity of demand.

What does all this mean? For a constant marginal cost, the larger the elasticity of demand, the smaller the Lerner index. For a competitive firm, $e_f = \infty$; therefore, all of its price is attributed to marginal cost (that is, $P^* = MC$) and the Lerner index is zero. For a pure monopolist, e_f equals the market price elasticity of demand, since there is only one firm in the industry. For any firm, as long as e_f is less than ∞ but not less than 1, $(1 \le e_f < \infty)$, the firm's profit-maximizing price is greater than its marginal cost. Therefore, for the Lerner index to be greater than zero, it must be the case that the firm sets its price along a *downward-sloping* demand curve, since a horizontal demand curve is infinitely elastic.

Lerner Indices of Representative Industries

Many empirical studies have measured monopoly power in various industries. An industry Lerner index is similar to a firm's Lerner index:

$$(P^* - MC)/P^* = 1/e,$$

where e is the *industry* price elasticity of demand (as opposed to e_f, the firm's elasticity of demand). Professor Timothy Bresnahan has summarized many of these studies, and Table 8-1 is adopted from his work.[2]

Monopoly power, as measured by the Lerner index, provides an indication of how well an industry performs relative to the competitive outcome of price equal to marginal cost. From a social welfare point of view, the larger the Lerner index, the *poorer* the performance, because price is farther away from marginal cost. Of the six industries in Table 8-1, tobacco exhibits the worst performance, while rubber exhibits the best. We know that the larger

Table 8-1   Representative Lerner Indices

Industry	Lerner Index
Tobacco	0.65
Food processing	0.50
Electrical machinery	0.20
Retail gasoline	0.10
Textile	0.07
Rubber	0.05

---

2 Timothy Bresnahan. "Empirical Studies of Industries with Market Power." In R. Schmalensee and R. Willig, eds., *Handbook of Industrial Organization*, Vol. 2. Amsterdam: North Holland, 1989.

the Lerner index, the smaller the elasticity of demand. One important determinant of the elasticity of demand is the number of substitutes available to consumers. The fewer substitutes there are, the smaller the elasticity of demand and, therefore, the larger the Lerner index. Thus, large Lerner indices are generally associated with industries that have a small number of firms. The tobacco industry certainly fits this description.

8.4 MAINTAINING MONOPOLY POWER

In the competitive model, a firm can maintain a positive profit only in the short run. In the long run, the entry of new firms leads to a zero-profit equilibrium. We have not discussed the monopoly problem in terms of the short run or long run. By assumption, the pure monopoly model does not allow entry to occur, so there is no reason to worry about long-run adjustments. In general, however, economists believe that positive profits will attract entry and, unless the monopolist can prevent the entry of new firms, monopoly power will be weakened over time.

Barriers to Entry

In the 1950s, Professor Joe Bain pioneered in examining ways in which **incumbent firms**—that is, firms that already exist in a market—can maintain their monopoly power over time. When entry into a profitable industry is deterred, it is said that **barriers to entry** exist in that industry. Bain identified three broad categories of barriers to entry.[3]

1. *Product Differentiation:* A firm can lower its price elasticity of demand (and, therefore, increase its Lerner index) if it can differentiate its product from other products. In the competitive model, all firms produce an identical good. If there is room for product differentiation, however, some firms may face a downward-sloping demand curve for their product. For example, even though there are many brands of cola, Coke and Pepsi enjoy some degree of market power because of their continual efforts to differentiate their products from the rest. Bain considered advertising and other promotional expenses to be key aspects of product differentiation.

2. *Absolute Cost Advantage:* If an incumbent firm's average cost curve lies completely below an entrant's average cost curve, the incumbent has an absolute cost advantage at every level of output. For an entrant to at least break even after entry, it must set its price no lower than its average cost. If an incumbent can price above its own average cost

---

3 Joe Bain. *Barriers to New Competition.* Cambridge: Harvard University Press, 1956.

but below its rival's average cost, the rival cannot compete against the incumbent. Bain identified many sources of absolute cost advantage, including superior managerial skill, patents and copyrights, control of scarce inputs, and lower cost of capital for established firms.

3. *Economies of Scale:* Recall from Chapter 6 that economies of scale exist when a firm's average cost curve slopes downward as output increases. If an incumbent firm is producing along the downward-sloping portion of the average cost curve, and an entrant can only enter at a smaller level of output than the incumbent's output level, the incumbent has a cost advantage. This cost advantage could discourage entry. Note that with this form of barrier to entry the incumbent and the entrant can have *identical* average cost curves. The incumbent does not need an absolute cost advantage at every level of output if it has a cost advantage by producing more than the entrant can.

Since Bain's pioneering work, economists have spent a great deal of time looking closely at many of the activities that have been considered barriers to entry. It is well beyond the scope of this book to discuss these issues in detail. If you are interested, you should take an elective course in industrial organization or antitrust economics. For now, just as we demonstrated that there can be costs and benefits associated with monopoly power, we will mention that there can be costs and benefits associated with many of the barriers to entry. For example, while advertising may make it difficult for new firms to enter a market, it may also make it easier for new firms to enter, since advertising facilitates the announcement of a new product. Furthermore, advertising may benefit consumers by providing them with important information. Economies of scale may also provide a situation in which it is in society's best interest to allow only one firm in an industry. Let's explore this last point.

Regulating a Natural Monopolist

In Chapter 6 we saw that when a firm's average cost function exhibits *economies of scale,* as the firm increases its production its average cost falls. Thus, with a downward-sloping industry average cost curve, one firm can produce any given level of output at a lower cost than can any combination of two or more firms. Figure 8-7 shows a downward-sloping average cost curve and a demand curve that intersects the AC curve at output level Q_R. When a demand curve intersects the average cost curve along the downward-sloping portion, we have a situation known as **natural monopoly;** that is, all the profitable levels of output can be produced most efficiently by just one firm.

The benefit to society of a natural monopolist is that it can produce its output at a lower total cost than can any combination of two or more firms. But what level of output does a natural monopolist produce? In Figure 8-7,

Figure 8-7   Regulating a Natural Monopolist

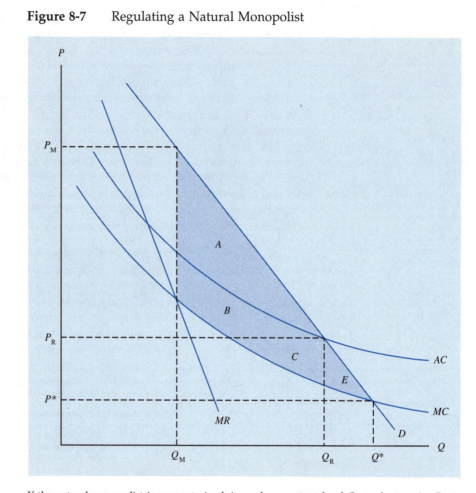

If the natural monopolist is unconstrained, it produces output level Q_M and sets price P_M to maximize profit. In this case, the deadweight loss of monopoly power is area $A+B+C+E$. Because the industry is a natural monopoly, this is the classic setting for price regulation. **First-best pricing** has price set equal to marginal cost at P^* and eliminates deadweight loss. At output level Q^*, however, price is less than average cost and the natural monopolist does not break even. **Second-best pricing** minimizes deadweight loss while allowing the firm to break even. This occurs where price equals average cost at P_R and the output level is Q_R. The deadweight loss from second-best pricing is area E.

if the monopolist is unhampered, it would find its profit-maximizing price and output by setting marginal revenue equal to marginal cost. These are shown as levels P_M and Q_M. Now, however, we have a cost to society—the deadweight loss of setting price greater than marginal cost (equal to area $A+B+C+E$). Once again, we have found a trade-off. If more firms are allowed to enter the industry, the deadweight loss can be reduced as competition drives the price down. But with more firms, the total costs of production will increase. Can we simultaneously enjoy the benefits of a natural monopolist without incurring the costs of monopoly power? Possibly, with price regulation.

Figure 8-7 demonstrates the classic setting for price regulation. Because of the natural monopoly setting, society benefits by having only one firm in the industry, but society loses if that firm sets the monopoly price. To enjoy the benefits of natural monopoly but not the costs, government regulation can allow only one firm in the industry but control its price. To completely eliminate the deadweight loss, price must be set at marginal cost. The price and output combination P^* and Q^* eliminates deadweight loss. The price P^*, then, is the **first-best price,** because it is the price that minimizes deadweight loss. At output level Q^*, however, price is *less* than average cost, and the monopolist earns a negative profit. In Figure 8-7, first-best pricing *and* (at least) zero profit are not compatible.

When first-best pricing is not a viable option, the regulator can adopt **second-best pricing.** With second-best pricing, the regulator's objective is to minimize deadweight loss subject to a break-even constraint. What this means is that price must be set in such a way as to give the firm at least zero profit, while trying to keep the deadweight loss as small as possible. In Figure 8-7, the price and output combination P_R and Q_R achieve the second-best outcome. With P_R, price is equal to average cost and the firm earns zero profit. With $P_R > MC$, there is a deadweight loss equal to area E associated with second-best pricing. At any higher price, however, the deadweight loss would be greater, and at any lower price the firm would not break even.

Patents, Monopoly Power, and Innovation

In addition to natural monopoly, another source of monopoly power is the patent system. A patent provides an inventor exclusive rights over an invention for a period of 17 years. In theory, when a patent is granted, the patented product (or process) cannot be reproduced without permission of the patent holder. In effect, then, the most obvious cost of the patent system is that it legally creates and protects monopoly power. And with monopoly power, society may have to bear the burden of any deadweight loss that is created.

There is, however, an important benefit of the patent system: It encourages research and development. For example, suppose a firm is deciding to develop a new audio format that greatly improves on the compact disc format. Research and development for this project will take at least two years and cost approximately $2 million. If, after the product is developed and introduced, any other firm can simply copy the technology without having to incur the R&D expenses, the original producer of the product may not recoup its expenses. If this is the case, the original producer has little incentive to invest in the development of the new product in the first place. With patent protection, however, the holder of the patent can enjoy monopoly power and expect to recoup its R&D expenses and then some. A perfect patent system, then, should grant the patent holder enough protection to encourage innovation, but not enough protection to abuse its monopoly position. In practice, this is a difficult trade-off to measure.

Professor Edwin Mansfield has studied the patent system, and Table 8-2 is a small sample of some of his findings.[4] For a group of eight industries, Table 8-2 shows the percentage of products that would *not* have been introduced without patent protection, because the firms did not believe they could recoup their R&D expenses. This evidence suggests that in some industries, (the bottom four), new products would be introduced even without the patent system. In these cases, there appears to be no benefit to patents.

Do patents create and protect monopoly power? If the patent system does not encourage innovation in an industry, this does not mean that it enhances monopoly power in that industry. For example, recall from Table 8-1 that both the textile and rubber industries have low Lerner indices and, therefore, little monopoly power. In these cases, patent protection is not very effective, because it is easy to "get around" a patent by slightly differentiating the product.

On the other hand, the pharmaceutical industry requires patent protection as an incentive to introduce new products. In this case, patent protection is valuable because it is effective. It is difficult for rival firms to slightly differentiate a drug and circumvent the patent system, because even a slight deviation can dramatically change the product. Without patent protection, producers of new drugs might not recoup their R&D expenses. For this increased incentive to innovate, society must bear the cost of enhanced monopoly power.

Table 8-2   Representative Industries and the Patent System

Industry	Percentage of Products That Would Not Have Been Introduced
Pharmaceuticals	65
Chemicals	30
Petroleum	18
Machinery	15
Office equipment	0
Motor vehicles	0
Rubber	0
Textiles	0

---

4 Edwin Mansfield. "Patents and Innovation: An Empirical Study." *Management Science*, Vol. 32, 1986, pp. 173–181.

APPLICATION
Patents and Surgical Techniques

In January 1992, the U.S. Patent and Trademark Office issued a patent to Dr. Samuel Pallin for his new technique for performing stitchless cataract surgery.* This technique is used during cataract surgery an estimated 500,000 times a year, and Dr. Pallin wants to enforce his patent and collect a royalty each time the technique is used. Recently, patents for surgical techniques have become quite common and extremely controversial. As reported in *Business Week,* doctors who favor patents argue that they provide incentives to doctors to fund research efforts, enable physicians to benefit financially from medical discoveries, and broaden channels for professional recognition. Medical groups opposed to patents argue that they inhibit access to new medical innovations and reduce quality of care, drive up health-care costs by imposing licensing fees on physicians, and invite abuse by physicians making spurious claims for protection. Taken together, the opposing groups have done a good job identifying many of the costs and benefits of patents.

* *Business Week*, July 24, 1995.

In conclusion, in many industries in which patent protection is not necessary to encourage innovation, it generally does not enhance monopoly power. In the industries in which patent protection is necessary for innovation, there generally is a monopoly power trade-off. What all this means is that the patent system does not appear to enhance monopoly power often without at least some benefits of increased innovation.

8.5   EXTRACTING CONSUMER SURPLUS

While a monopolist (like the one in Figure 8-3) that sets a single price can earn a positive profit, the single- price selling strategy has its shortcomings from the monopolist's point of view. For example, let us return to our car dealership monopoly, but now we will consider the demand for cars by only a single consumer—the owner of a taxi company. Table 8-3 shows the consumer's total and marginal willingness to pay for each output level. (Recall that the marginal willingness to pay schedule is the consumer's demand curve.) Assume, as before, that the marginal cost (and the average cost) of producing one car is $10,000.

Table 8-3   Extracting Consumer Surplus

Quantity	Total Willingness to Pay	Marginal Willingness to Pay
1	20,000	20,000
2	38,000	18,000
3	54,000	16,000
4	68,000	14,000
5	80,000	12,000
6	90,000	10,000
7	98,000	8,000
8	104,000	6,000
9	108,000	4,000
10	110,000	2,000
>10	110,000	0

If the monopolist can set just one price for its cars, what is its profit-maximizing price? If the price is set at $20,000, the taxi company will purchase just one car, since the marginal willingness to pay for a second car is only $18,000. Therefore, at $P = \$20,000$, the monopolist's total revenue is $TR = \$20,000$, its total cost is $TC = \$10,000$, and its profit is $TR - TC = \$10,000$. If the monopolist sets a lower price of $P = \$18,000$, the consumer will purchase two cars. In this case, $TR = \$36,000$, $TC = \$20,000$, and profit is $16,000. If we continue in this fashion, we find that at $P = \$16,000$, the consumer purchases three cars and the monopolist's profit is maximized at $18,000. (You should verify that when $P < \$16,000$, the monopolist's profit is less than $18,000.)

By setting a single price, the monopolist cannot exploit two additional sources of potential profit. First, while the consumer is willing to pay a total of $54,000 for three cars, he only spends $3P = \$48,000$. Thus, the consumer surplus is equal to $6,000. Second, there is a deadweight loss of $6,000. (Can you explain why?) It will never be in the monopolist's best interest to sell this consumer more than six cars, since the consumer's marginal willingness to pay is less than the monopolist's marginal cost for the seventh unit. But if the monopolist could sell six units and extract the consumer's total willingness to pay of $90,000, it could earn a profit of $TR - TC = \$90,000 - \$60,000 = \$30,000$. This $30,000 is made up of the monopolist's single-price profit of $18,000, the consumer surplus of $6,000, and the deadweight loss of $6,000. Alternatively, the $30,000 represents the consumer surplus that would exist if the good was priced competitively. Clearly, the single-price strategy cannot extract all of this surplus. An alternative strategy is needed.

Perfect Price Discrimination

Let's return to Table 8-3 and consider the following price schedule: The first unit is priced at $20,000; the second at $18,000; the third at $16,000; the fourth at $14,000; the fifth at $12,000; and the sixth unit and up at $10,000. As you can see, the monopolist is pricing each successive unit (up to six units) exactly at the consumer's marginal willingness to pay. This form of pricing is known as **perfect price discrimination.** With this price schedule, the consumer purchases six units (because the price for the seventh unit is greater than the marginal willingness to pay for that unit). Total revenue is the sum of the six prices—that is, $90,000. Total cost is $60,000. Therefore, profit is $30,000. Perfect price discrimination allows the monopolist to earn the greatest amount of profit available in this example—$30,000.

Figure 8-8 demonstrates the perfect price discrimination outcome for the general case. The monopolist does not find it profitable to sell more than q^* units. (We use a *lower case q* to represent the purchase of a single consumer.) The consumer's total willingness to pay for q^* units is area $A+B$. To extract all of $A+B$, the monopolist begins at a high price, P_{MAX}, and sets a very slightly lower price for each successive unit until price P_{MIN} is reached. In effect, the monopolist extracts as revenue all of the area under the demand curve up to q^*. With total revenue equal to area $A+B$, and total cost equal to area B, area A represents the monopolist's profit from practicing perfect price discrimination. Thus, perfect price discrimination allows the monopolist to earn the greatest amount of profit available in a market.

All-or-Nothing Pricing

Perfect price discrimination, since it allows a monopolist to extract the maximum amount of profit a market can yield, provides a benchmark for every other pricing scheme. One such scheme, **all-or-nothing pricing,** can exactly mimic perfect price discrimination. With all-or-nothing pricing, the monopolist sets a price for a specific quantity of its good and allows the consumer to buy *only* that quantity or nothing at all. An example of this pricing practice involves the De Beers diamond company, by far the largest diamond company in the world. When De Beers sells diamonds to manufacturers and dealers, it presents each buyer with a quantity of stones at an all-or-nothing price. There is no negotiation over price, and individual buyers cannot sort through the set of stones to eliminate certain pieces. Even more severely, a buyer who refuses the all-or-nothing offer may not ever be invited back to purchase from De Beers again!

In Figure 8-9, curve D represents the monopolist's ordinary demand curve. Consider output level q^*. The consumer's total willingness to pay for q^* is area $A+C$. If the monopolist could perfectly price discriminate up to level q^*, $A+C$ would be its total revenue. Now consider the curve labeled $A–N$. This is the monopolist's **all-or-nothing demand curve.** An all-or-nothing demand curve represents a consumer's *average* willingness to pay for each output level. For output level q^*, the consumer's average willingness to pay is P^*. That is, if the monopolist sets its price at P^* and allows the consumer to purchase only the amount q^*, the monopolist's total revenue would be P^*q^*, or area $B+C$.

Figure 8-8   Perfect Price Discrimination

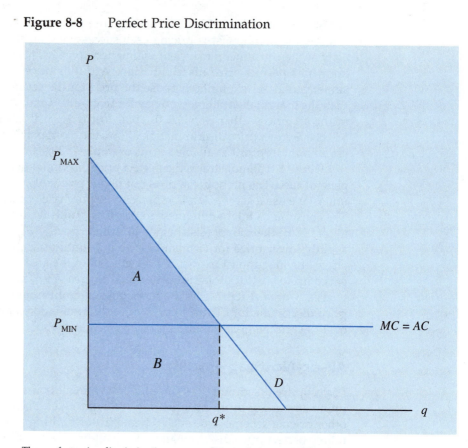

The perfect price discriminating monopolist produces output level q^*, and sells each unit at a successively lower price between P_{MAX} and P_{MIN}. Total revenue is area $A+B$, and this also represents the consumer's total willingness to pay for q^* units. Profit is area A, and this is the greatest amount of profit available in the market.

Would the consumer purchase q^* at the all-or-nothing price P^*? Because he is willing to pay $A+C$ for q^* units, the amount he must spend, P^*q^*, must be no greater than $A+C$. But if P^* represents the consumer's average willingness to pay for q^*, then P^*q^* must be the consumer's *total* willingness to pay for q^*, area $A+C$. In other words, since $P^*q^* = B+C$, it must also be the case that area $B+C = A+C$, or $A = B$. Thus, the all-or-nothing demand curve is constructed by setting $A = B$ for output level q^*. The consumer would pay exactly P^* for an all-or-nothing choice of q^* units.

Returning to Table 8-3, we already know that the monopolist can maximize profit by selling six cars and earning a profit of $30,000. With an all-or-nothing pricing scheme, the monopolist can set a price of $15,000 and allow the consumer to purchase exactly six cars. In this case, the consumer would have to spend $90,000 for the six cars. This is exactly what he is will-

Figure 8-9   All-or-Nothing Pricing

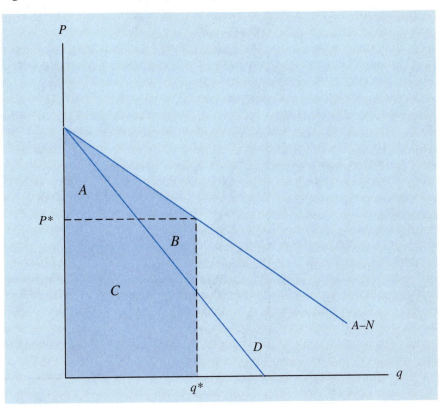

The **all-or-nothing demand curve,** *A–N*, represents the consumer's average willingness to pay for each output level. At output level *q**, the total willingness to pay is area *A+C*. If the monopolist can set the price at the average willingness to pay for *q** units, *P**, and allow the consumer to purchase the amount *q** or nothing at all, the consumer will make the purchase since *P*q** = *B+C* = *A+C*, or *B* = *A*. When **all-or-nothing pricing** is practiced, the monopolist's total revenue equals the consumer's total willingness to pay for *q** units.

ing to spend for six cars. The monopolist earns a total revenue of $90,000, incurs a total cost of $60,000, and makes a profit of $30,000.

Two-Part Pricing

Using Figure 8-10, we know that a perfect price discriminating monopolist would set a declining price schedule and sell output level *q**. Total revenue would be area *A+B*, and profit would be area *A*. Now consider an alternative pricing scheme. The monopolist sets the price at *P** per unit for any number of units the consumer wishes to purchase, but first the consumer must pay a fixed fee equal to area *A* to gain access to the monopolist's product. What does the consumer do? At price *P**, he would purchase *q** units.

Figure 8-10   Two-Part Pricing

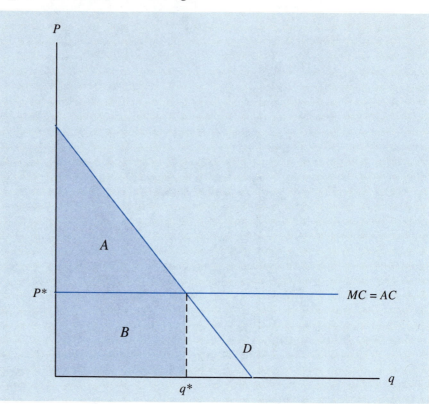

With **two-part pricing,** the monopolist sets a fixed entry fee equal to area A and a per-unit price of P^* and allows the consumer to purchase any number of units at that price. In this case, the monopolist's total revenue is area $A+B$, and this also represents the consumer's total willingness to pay for q^* units. Profit is area A, and this is the greatest amount of profit available in the market.

If this was the only price, there would be a consumer surplus equal to A. Thus, area A represents the consumer's additional willingness to pay for q^* units. As long as the monopolist charges an **entry fee** that is no greater than the amount A, the consumer is willing to pay the fee to purchase q^* units. By setting the entry fee equal to A and the per-unit price equal to P^*, the monopolist extracts the consumer's total willingness to pay for q^*, area $A+B$, and earns a profit equal to area A.

By setting two prices, a per-unit price and a fixed fee, the monopolist is practicing **two-part pricing.** Many amusement parks use this form of pricing. To enter the park, consumers must pay a fixed charge at the gate. Once inside the park, they must pay per-unit prices to take the rides or play the games.

If we return to our example in Table 8-3, we can find the optimal two-part pricing scheme. If the monopolist sets a per-unit price equal to marginal cost—that is $10,000—the consumer will purchase six cars and have a consumer surplus of $30,000. Thus, the profit-maximizing two-part pricing scheme is to set a fixed fee of $30,000 and a variable fee of $10,000. As before, this would lead to a monopoly profit of $30,000.

Although pricing strategies that allow extraction of all the consumer surplus in a market are ideal from the monopolist's point of view, in practice they are virtually impossible to accomplish. In the example just given, for complete surplus extraction the monopolist needs to know the consumer's total willingness to pay for six cars. In practice, this information is difficult to get. And of course, there can be many consumers with many different willingnesses to pay. To be able to perfectly price discriminate, the monopolist would need to set a unique declining price schedule for *every* single consumer. Even if the monopolist could acquire all the necessary information to perfectly price discriminate, there is another impediment: Many forms of price discrimination are illegal. In the next section, we examine a form of price discrimination that is often observed in practice.

8.6   MARKET DISCRIMINATION

While it is virtually impossible to identify each consumer's total willingness to pay for a good, it is quite common for firms with monopoly power to divide consumers into different market groups and charge different prices to each group. There are many examples of this pricing practice, referred to as **market price discrimination.** Students often pay discounted subscription rates for magazines; senior citizens often get discounts on a variety of goods and services; and matinee movie customers pay discounted prices.

Profit Maximization in Two Markets

Figure 8-11 demonstrates how to find the profit-maximizing prices and outputs for a monopolist that discriminates between two markets. Unlike an ordinary monopolist, a market-discriminating monopolist faces two demand and marginal revenue curves. These curves are represented in panels (a) and (b). Like an ordinary monopolist, however, a market-discriminating monopolist must still equate marginal revenue to marginal cost for profit maximization. Panel (c) shows the marginal cost curve and the *horizontal sum* of the marginal revenue curves from markets 1 and 2. Where the sum of the marginal revenue curves (ΣMR) intersects the marginal cost curve, the monopolist finds its profit-maximizing total output. Why is this so?

Figure 8-11   Market Price Discrimination

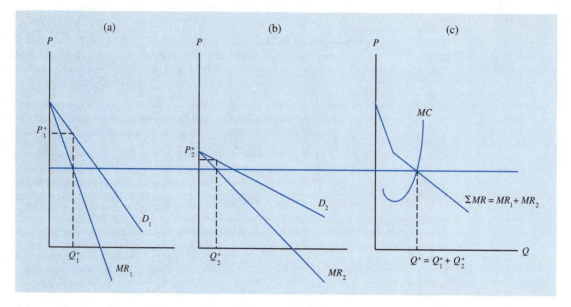

A monopolist that practices market price discrimination between two markets maximizes profit by setting the marginal revenue in each market equal to the marginal cost, that is, $MR_1 = MR_2 = MC$. This occurs in panel (c) at the output level Q^*, where the horizontal sum of the marginal revenue curves, ΣMR, equals marginal cost. By drawing a horizontal line from this intersection across panels (a) and (b), we find the profit maximizing output levels Q_1^* and Q_2^* and the corresponding prices P_1^* and P_2^*. The monopolist sets the higher price in the market with the lower price elasticity of demand.

With each additional unit of output, profit maximization requires that the monopolist sell that unit in the market in which the marginal revenue is the greater. For example, if $MR_1 > MR_2$, the next unit produced can earn a greater revenue in market 1 than in market 2. As the monopolist continues to sell in market 1, MR_1 decreases. At the point where $MR_1 = MR_2$, the monopolist is indifferent between selling the next unit in market 1 or market 2. If at that point we also have each marginal revenue equal to marginal cost, the monopolist cannot increase its profit by producing additional output. Thus, a price-discriminating monopolist produces its total output at the point where $MR_1 = MR_2 = MC$.

Using panel (c), we can draw a horizontal line from the intersection of the ΣMR curve and the MC curve across to panels (a) and (b). Where this line intersects the MR_1 curve in panel (a) and the MR_2 curve in panel (b), we find the profit-maximizing output levels Q_1^* and Q_2^* and the corresponding prices P_1^* and P_2^*. If we add together Q_1^* and Q_2^*, we have the total profit maximizing output level Q^* in panel (c). At Q^*, then, the monopolist satisfies the profit-maximizing condition $MR_1 = MR_2 = MC$.

APPLICATION
Pricing Economics Journals

There are many scholarly journals in which economists publish their research. In setting the subscription rates for most of these journals, market price discrimination is practiced. In general, the subscription markets are divided into three groups: institutions (for example, libraries), individuals, and students. Table 8-4 presents the different 1993 subscription rates for four of the leading journals.

Table 8-4   Economics Journals' Subscription Rates

Journal	Institution Rate	Individual Rate	Student Rate
Journal of Political Economy	$91	$41	$27
Quarterly Journal of Economics	95	34	20
International Economic Review	150	45	20
Economic Inquiry	135	50	25

The prices shown in the table suggest that institutions have the lowest price elasticity of demand of the three groups and students have the highest. On average, libraries have the greatest willingness to pay for journal subscriptions because the role of a library is to have a complete collection of scholarly books and journals. Professors, however, are less willing to pay for a subscription, especially since they can simply go to the library. Finally, students have the lowest willingness to pay for a subscription, probably because they are relatively poor.

In addition to the three main group distinctions, some journals further separate their subscription markets. For example, *The American Economic Review* individual subscription rate is $49 for individuals with annual incomes less than $37,000, $59 for those with incomes between $37,000 and $50,000, and $69 for those with incomes greater than $50,000. The journal *Econometrica*, on the other hand, has an individual subscription rate of $69 for the United States, but only $25 for individuals living in countries with a per-capita income of less than $500.

As drawn in Figure 8-11, it is the case that $P_1^* > P_2^*$. Why is P_1^* the greater price? Recall from Section 8.3 that by setting $MR = MC$, we can derive the Lerner index for the monopolist. With price discrimination, by setting $MR_1 = MR_2 = MC$, we can derive a Lerner index for each market; that is:

$$\text{Lerner index for market 1: } (P_1^* - MC)/P_1^* = 1/e_1$$

$$\text{Lerner index for market 2: } (P_2^* - MC)/P_2^* = 1/e_2,$$

where e_1 and e_2 are the price elasticities of demand for markets one and two, respectively. For P_1^* to be greater than P_2^*, it must be the case that $e_1 < e_2$. In other words, the price-discriminating monopolist sets the higher price in the market with the lower price elasticity of demand.

Compared to charging an identical monopoly price in each market, the price-discriminating monopolist can increase its profit by separating out its markets based on different price elasticities of demand. A lower price elasticity of demand implies, *on average,* a higher willingness to pay for the good. Thus, while market price discrimination is far from perfect price discrimination, whenever the monopolist can make some distinction between consumers' willingness to pay, there is a profit gain from price discrimination.

8.7 DURABLE GOOD MONOPOLY

So far in this chapter we have ignored the concept of time. Implicitly, we have assumed that the monopolist's pricing decision is for a single period only. An alternative way to think about what we have done is to assume that the good in question is **perishable.** If the good perishes after a single period, in the next period the monopolist can start all over again facing the *same* demand curve it did in the first period (assuming that demand is stable over time). Thus, with a completely perishable good, the monopolist's pricing decision in a single period is independent of its price in any other period.

In reality, however, many goods last for several periods. These are said to be **durable goods.** Consider the automobile example in Figure 8-3. The monopolist's profit-maximizing output is 150 cars in the single period. What would happen if we added a second period? Because cars are durable, many of the consumers who purchased a car in the first period would not purchase one in the second period. In other words, the monopolist's demand curve in the second period would depend on how many cars it sold in the first period. Other examples of durable goods include air conditioners, computers, stereos, and boats, among many others. We will see in this section that a monopoly producer of a durable good faces a surprising problem.

Pricing a Durable Good

Nobel Laureate Ronald Coase of the University of Chicago is given credit for identifying the pricing problem of a durable-good monopolist.[5] Using Coase's example, in Figure 8-12 there is a fixed stock of land, Q_C, that never depreciates. To get the main point across, we will make two simplifying assumptions: The marginal cost of production is zero (that is, the marginal cost curve is the horizontal axis); and, once a consumer purchases land, that consumer will not purchase any more land. To maximize profit the monopolist sets marginal revenue equal to marginal cost. The profit-maximizing levels of price and output are P_M and Q_M. If land was not a durable good, the story would be over now: The good would perish after the first period, and the monopolist would face the same demand curve again in the next period. With stable demand, the perishable-good monopolist continues to set its profit-maximizing price in every period. In our example, however, once consumers purchase the durable good, they no longer have a demand for it in future periods. Thus, with Q_M units sold, the monopolist still has an amount of land left unsold. This amount is $Q_C - Q_M$.

What can the monopolist do with the remaining land? Figure 8-13 shows the unsold land as the new stock of land, $Q_C - Q_M$, in the next period. The demand curve D' in Figure 8-13, referred to as a **residual demand curve,** is simply the portion of the demand curve in Figure 8-12 that lies below the price P_M. The residual demand curve is the demand curve for the individuals who did not purchase land at the initial monopoly price. To maximize profit, the monopolist once again sets marginal revenue equal to marginal cost and sets its new price at P'_M. Thus, the first period consumers pay P_M for the good, but the second period consumers pay only P'_M. If this continues throughout many periods, from Figure 8-12 price will eventually fall to P_C and the total amount of land sold will be Q_C.

The monopolist appears to be in good shape. It makes its initial monopoly profit in the first period, and then it makes additional profit in every subsequent period. But there is a problem here. If the consumers in the first period know that the price will eventually fall, why don't they wait to buy the good in a later period? If consumers are willing to wait to buy the durable good, the monopolist cannot make sales at the initial high price of P_M. Moreover, if consumers are infinitely patient, the monopolist will *never* be able to set a price greater than P_C. Therefore, a durable-good monopolist has less market power than an ordinary monopolist. In the extreme, a durable-good monopolist has no market power at all! The inability of a durable-good mo-

5 Ronald Coase. "Durability and Monopoly." *Journal of Law and Economics,* Vol. 15, 1972, pp. 143–149.

Figure 8-12   Durable Good Monopolist

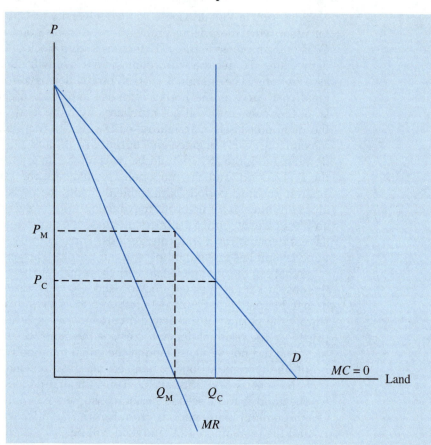

The durable good monopolist has a stock of land, Q_C. If the monopolist was selling for a single period only, it would set marginal revenue equal to marginal cost (assumed to be zero in this example) and sell Q_M units at price P_M. The stock of land left unsold is $Q_C - Q_M$. This unsold stock of land provides an incentive for the monopolist to sell more land, at a lower price, in the next period. (See Figure 8-13.)

nopolist to set its price above the competitive price is often referred to as the **Coase conjecture.**

In the example just given, the monopolist did not produce the good; there was simply a stock of land that the monopolist owned. Even if the monopolist does decide how much to produce, the Coase conjecture can still apply. Once a certain amount of the good is produced and completely sold in the first period, in the next period the durable-good monopolist has an incentive to produce more and sell at a lower price to consumers

Figure 8-13   Residual Demand for a Durable Good Monopolist

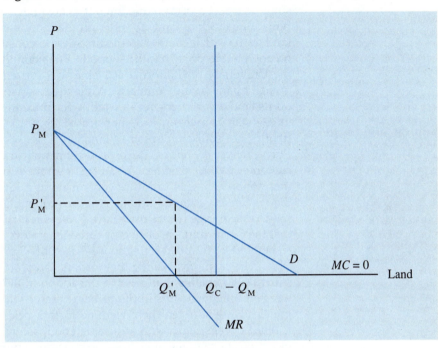

Curve D is a **residual demand curve;** that is, it represents the portion of the demand curve from Figure 8-12 that lies below the price P_M. The residual demand curve represents the demand of consumers who did not purchase land in the previous period. Once again, the monopolist sets $MR = MC$ to find its profit maximizing price, P'_M. Because the good is durable, the monopolist's price falls over time. If patient consumers do not buy at the high initial price, the durable good monopolist is unable to sustain price P_M in the first period. In the extreme, a durable good monopolist cannot set price above marginal cost.

who did not purchase in the first period. Whenever the monopolist has an incentive to lower price in future periods, the Coase conjecture can apply.

Circumventing the Coase Conjecture

When patient consumers expect a durable-good monopolist to lower its price in the future, the monopolist is unable to set a high price in the present, since consumers would just wait for the price to fall. There are several ways in which the durable-good monopolist may be able to eliminate the problem of consumers' expectations of a lower price.

1. *Destroying Remaining Quantities:* In the land example, first-period consumers expect a price reduction in the next period because there is a remaining stock of land, $Q_C - Q_M$. If the monopolist can destroy this land to the satisfaction of all the first-period consumers, there will be no good left to price in future periods. For example, legend has it that the University of California at Irvine was started with gifts of land owned by the Irvine Company. While the company was trying to sell off its land, consumers began waiting for price to fall. By giving land to the state, however, it demonstrated its willingness to "destroy" (that is, not sell) many plots of land.

2. *Price Protection Policies:* Price protection policies, or **most-favored-customer (MFC) pricing,** guarantees current consumers a rebate if the monopolist sells to future consumers at a lower price. In effect, the rebate acts as an additional cost the monopolist imposes upon itself to discourage future price cuts. Professor David Butz has argued that the two producers of electric turbogenerators in the early 1960s—General Electric and Westinghouse—used MFC pricing to discourage customers from postponing their orders and waiting for future price cuts.[6] Butz explains that prior to the adoption of MFC pricing, there were chronic price cuts in the turbogenerator industry, but after the policies were adopted there were no further price cuts.[7]

3. *Planned Obsolescence:* With a durable good, as we have seen, the demand curve changes over time, as consumers who purchase in the first period already have the durable good in the second period and do not need to purchase it again. If a good is perishable and lasts only one period, however, then with stable demand the monopolist can face the same demand curve in successive periods. Thus, if a durable good monopolist has the ability to make the good perishable, it can circumvent the Coase conjecture. An example of this behavior involves the textbook industry. For many texts, publishers require authors to write new editions every three years, thereby making the previous edition obsolete.

4. *Renting:* If a monopolist does not sell its good, but rents it instead, there is no longer a problem of consumers waiting for future price cuts. In each period, the monopolist can rent the good to the same group of customers as in the previous period.

---

6 David Butz. "Durable-Good Monopoly and Best-Price Provisions." *American Economic Review,* Vol. 80, 1990, pp. 1062–1076.

7 The other main explanation for MFC pricing is that it facilitates collusion. This topic will be explored in Chapter 11.

SUPPLEMENT
Choosing the Durability of a Watch Battery

Firms have control over how durable some products can be. For example, light bulb manufacturers can produce bulbs that last for varying amounts of time. How does a firm decide how durable to make its product? Much of the academic research on durable goods has been concerned with this question, especially with respect to the durability choice of a competitive firm versus a monopolist. Compared to a competitive firm, we know that a monopolist tends to restrict output. But how do the durability choices of the two types of firms compare? While the answer to this question can be very complicated and depend on many factors, we will offer a simple example that demonstrates that a competitive firm and a monopolist may choose the same level of durability.

Consider a firm that produces watch batteries. These batteries have the characteristic that they work perfectly until they fail, and then they must be replaced. We will assume that when a consumer buys a watch, it comes with a lifetime guarantee that when the battery fails, it will immediately be replaced for free. The consumer does not really care about the battery in and of itself. Instead, the consumer cares about the *service* the battery provides, and this service is guaranteed for the life of the watch. The consumer, then, is not interested in how long the battery lasts, since there is a guarantee that the watch will *always* have a working battery. We also assume that the consumer does not bear a replacement cost when the battery is replaced.

The firm has three choices of how durable to make the battery: It can last for 4 years, 8 years, or 12 years. The more durable the battery, the greater the marginal cost of production. Assume that there is a constant marginal cost of $1.00 to produce a 4-year battery, $1.50 for an 8-year battery, and $2.00 for a 12-year battery. These marginal costs are assumed to be constant not only in a given period, but also over time. That is, when the firm produces the replacement for the 8-year battery in the future, the marginal cost of production will still be $1.50. Of course, $1.50 eight years from now is not worth $1.50 today. Instead, it is worth $\delta^8(\$1.50)$ today. (Recall from Chapter 2 that δ is the discount factor, and $\delta^8(1.50)$ represents the present value of $1.50 eight years from now.) Therefore, the longer the battery life, the less often replacement batteries have to be produced and the greater the discounting of the future cost. The more durable the battery, however, the greater is the marginal cost of production. How does the firm resolve this trade-off?

Table 8-5 shows the present values of marginal costs for the three types of batteries. We assume that the interest rate, r, is 10 percent. This implies that $\delta = 1/(1+r) \approx 0.909$. So, for example, the present value of marginal cost in period 24 for the 4-year battery is $(0.909)^{24}(1.00) \approx 0.102$; for the 8-year battery it is $(0.909)^{24}(1.50) \approx 0.152$; and for the 12-year battery it is $(0.909)^{24}(2.00) \approx 0.203$. When we sum up these per-period present value costs across all periods, we find that the marginal cost of providing a lifetime of service for the 4-year battery is $3.15; for the 8-year battery it is $2.81; and for the 12-year battery it is $2.94. If the firm is a profit maximizer, whether it is a competitive firm or a monopolist, we know that it will minimize the cost of whatever level of output it produces. In this example, the 8-year battery is the cheapest to produce.

Table 8-5   Durability of Watch Batteries

Years	4-Year Battery	8-Year Battery	12-Year Battery
0	$1.000	$1.500	$2.000
4	0.683	0	0
8	0.467	0.700	0
12	0.319	0	0.637
16	0.218	0.326	0
20	0.149	0	0
24	0.102	0.152	0.203
28	0.069	0	0
32	0.047	0.071	0
36	0.032	0	0.065
40	0.022	0.033	0
44	0.015	0	0
48	0.010	0.015	0.021
52	0.007	0	0
56	0.005	0.007	0
60	0.003	0	0.007
64	0.002	0.003	0
68	0.002	0	0
72	0.001	0.002	0.002
Lifetime Present Value	≈ $3.15	≈ $2.81	≈ $2.94

Summary

- When there is only a single firm in an industry, that firm is said to be a **monopolist.** The monopolist's demand curve is the industry's downward-sloping demand curve. The monopolist's marginal revenue curve lies *below* its demand curve.

- A profit-maximizing monopolist produces its output at the point where its marginal revenue equals its marginal cost. Because its marginal revenue curve is below its demand curve, the profit-maximizing price is greater than marginal cost. A monopolist, then, creates a deadweight loss by not producing at the point where its price equals its marginal cost.

- **Monopoly power** refers to the ability of at least one firm to set its profit-maximizing price above its marginal cost. The **Lerner index,** expressed as $(P* - MC)/P*$, measures the proportion of the profit-maximizing price, $P*$, that is *not* attributable to marginal cost. The Lerner index is used to measure monopoly power.

- When entry into a profitable industry is deterred, it is said that **barriers to entry** exist in that industry. Three broad categories of barriers to entry are *product differentiation, absolute cost advantages,* and *economies of scale.*

- A **natural monopoly** can produce a level of output at a lower total cost than can any combination of two or more firms.

- A perfect price discriminating monopolist extracts as revenue the

- A **perfect price discriminating** monopolist extracts as revenue the consumers' *total* willingness to pay for a good. Perfect price discrimination allows the monopolist to earn the greatest amount of profit available in a market.

- **Market price discrimination** occurs when a firm divides consumers into different market groups and charges different prices to each group. With two market groups, for example, a monopolist produces its total output at the point where the marginal revenue in the first market is equal to the marginal revenue in the second market, and both marginal revenues are equal to the marginal cost. The monopolist sets the higher price in the market with the *lower* price elasticity of demand.

- A **durable good** is one that lasts for more than a single period. To the extent that consumers are patient and continue to wait for a durable-good monopolist to lower its price over time, the durable-good monopolist will have less market power than an ordinary monopolist.

Problems

1. A monopolist faces a demand curve $P = 80 - 5Q$, where P is the product price and Q is the output. The marginal cost of production is a constant $MC = 10$. There are no fixed costs. What are the monopolist's profit-maximizing price, output, and profit? What are the consumer surplus and deadweight loss?

2. Unlike a competitive firm, a monopolist does not have a supply curve. Explain why not.

3. A monopolist always produces its output in the elastic portion of the demand curve. Explain why.

4. From a social welfare standpoint, we know that monopoly power creates a deadweight loss. In trying to develop public policies to alleviate the monopoly problem, what are the advantages and disadvantages of using Professor Williamson's trade-off model?

5. Consider a consumer with the following total willingness to pay, and corresponding marginal willingness to pay, for different output levels:

Quantity	Total Willingness to Pay	Marginal Willingness to Pay
1	50	50
2	90	40
3	115	25
4	125	10
5	130	5
> 5	130	0

The marginal cost of production is a constant $MC = 15$.

a. What are the single-price monopolist's profit-maximizing price, output, and profit?

b. What are the perfect price discriminating monopolist's price, output, and profit?

c. What are the profit-maximizing all-or-nothing price, output, and profit?

d. What are the profit-maximizing two-part prices, output, and profit?

6. How can the pricing schemes discussed in Section 8.5 be used to regulate a natural monopoly? How do these pricing schemes compare to first-best and second-best pricing?

7. Movie theaters generally charge different prices for different groups. Assume that movie theaters charge $3.00 a ticket for children and senior citizens and $6.00 a ticket for all others. If a law is passed that does not allow theaters to price discriminate so that they must set a single price, would this law increase or decrease social welfare? (*Hint:* Think about how the theaters would determine their new profit-maximizing price and how each consumer group would be affected.)

8. What other examples of market price discrimination can you think of? Explain, in these examples, why the different consumer groups have different elasticities of demand.

9. One important condition for a monopolist to be successful at price discrimination is that it must prevent its customers from *reselling* the product between themselves. Explain why preventing resale is important. In the examples you identified in problem 8, how is resell prevented?

10. If consumers are not infinitely patient, and they have varying discount factors, discuss how a durable-good monopolist can use price discrimination to circumvent the Coase conjecture.

11. If a durable-good monopolist rents its product, rather than sells it, the firm could circumvent the Coase conjecture. But what are the possible disadvantages of renting instead of selling?

12. Refer to the watch battery example of Table 8-5. Is the 8-year battery still the monopolist's best choice if we lower the discount factor to $\delta = 0.8$? Explain. What happens if we raise the discount factor to $\delta = 1$? Explain.

9

GAME THEORY

Overview

So far, throughout most of this book, we have considered situations in which a decision maker's behavior is largely independent of anyone else's. Consider firms in each of the two types of market structures we have examined in previous chapters—perfect competition and monopoly. In a competitive market, each firm is too small to have any effect on any other firm. In a monopoly market, by definition, there is only one firm, and therefore there is no interaction with competitors. When there are just a few firms in a market, however, each firm's behavior may depend on what other firms do. For example, how much advertising Coca-Cola decides to undertake will depend on how much advertising Pepsi is going to undertake. More specifically, Coke's actions may depend on what it *believes* Pepsi will do. The decision to open a fast-food restaurant in a certain city may depend on what another restaurant chain is planning to do. Other examples of industries in which a firm's behavior may depend directly on its rivals' behavior are the airline and automobile industries.

Economists analyze situations like these by using **game theory.** Game theory is the study of behavior in situations in which each party's payoff directly depends on what another party does. Game theory has most often been applied to market structures in which there are just a few firms, but there are many other economic applications for game theory. Examples include trade wars between two countries, economic policy debates between the Federal Reserve and the Congress, and wage negotiations between employers and employees.

In this chapter, you will be introduced to some of the basic tools of game theory.

- How to represent games in which players move simultaneously.
- How to find the equilibrium outcomes in games of varying degrees of complexity.
- How to analyze games in which players choose their actions at random.
- How to represent games in which players move one at a time.
- How to distinguish between credible and incredible threats.

This chapter is primarily a *tools* chapter, but we do provide several applications to help you understand the basics of game theory. In the chapters that follow, we will often use game theory to analyze a wide variety of economic examples.

9.1 REPRESENTING GAMES IN NORMAL FORM

Games are best analyzed in two steps. The first is to find a useful way to represent games, and the second is to find a way to predict outcomes. Of course, the second step is easier if we do a good job with the first. We begin with an example. Coke and Pepsi, the **players** of the game, are trying to decide how much advertising to purchase during the televising of the Super Bowl. Both firms know that while advertising is costly, it can also increase the demand for each of their products. Let's say that each firm can choose one of two actions or **strategies:** purchase a moderate or an extravagant amount of advertising.[1] They must pick their strategy without knowing what the other firm is going to do. For each combination of strategies that the two firms can choose, each firm receives a **payoff** in terms of profit. If both firms choose a moderate amount of advertising, each earns $100 of profit. If both firms choose an extravagant amount of advertising, each earns $50 (because each firm's extravagant advertising begins to cancel out the benefit of advertising to its rival). Finally, if one firm chooses to advertise extravagantly while it's rival chooses to advertise moderately, the firm that advertises extravagantly earns $125 and the firm that advertises moderately earns $35 (because it is "out-advertised"). Keeping track of the details of this game can be difficult. It would be even more confusing if each firm had more than two strategies to choose from. A simple way to summarize this lengthy description is to present the game in **normal form,** as shown in Figure 9-1.

Figure 9-1   A Normal-Form Game

		Pepsi	
		Moderate	Extravagant
Coke	Moderate	100, 100	35, 125
	Extravagant	125, 35	50, 50

---

1 In a game in which the players choose their actions simultaneously, the terms *action* and *strategy* can be used interchangeably. Later in the chapter, there will be an important distinction between the two terms.

The normal-form representation of a game consists of three components: (1) a list of the players of the game; (2) a list of the strategies each player can choose; and (3) a list of the payoffs each player receives for each combination of strategies he chooses. In Figure 9-1, there are two players—Coke and Pepsi. Each of Coke's two strategies makes up a row of the matrix, and each of Pepsi's two strategies makes up a column of the matrix. Because each firm has two strategies, there are four possible payoff combinations, or four **outcomes** (one for each cell of the matrix). For each possible outcome, the payoff on the left of the cell is for the row player (Coke), and the payoff on the right of the cell is for the column player (Pepsi). For example, if Coke decides to advertise moderately and Pepsi decides to advertise extravagantly, their payoffs are found in the upper-right cell. Coke receives $35 and Pepsi receives $125. Finally, we assume that both players know exactly what the normal form of the game looks like.

We will use the normal-form representation often in this chapter. If we use a specific example, the players have names, such as Coke and Pepsi. If we use a generic example, one player is referred to as Row, and the other player is referred to as Column, corresponding to where their strategies are depicted in matrix form. Now that we have a simple way to depict a game, we can begin to examine ways to predict its equilibrium outcome.

9.2   SOLVING GAMES

The second step in analyzing a game is to **solve** it, that is, to figure out what strategies the players choose. Once the chosen strategies are known, it is a simple matter to figure out the payoff each player receives from the game. How do we solve for the strategies the players choose? We begin by eliminating combinations of strategies that will not be chosen. In a game in which the players choose their strategies simultaneously, a strategy combination lists one strategy for each player. In general, we eliminate a strategy combination if one player would like to change his strategy given the other player's strategy specified by the combination. We keep a strategy combination if no player wants to change his strategy from the proposed combination. This is simply an equilibrium concept, just like the equilibrium concept used to show that profit must be zero in long-run competitive equilibrium (Chapter 7). In earlier chapters, we stated that a system is in equilibrium if there is no pressure for any participant to change his action. We use this same definition to solve games.

Dominant Strategy Equilibrium

In the Coke/Pepsi advertising game, how can we determine the amount of advertising each firm chooses in equilibrium? Let's consider Coke's perspective on this game. If it believes that Pepsi is going to pick Moderate,

Coke would pick Extravagant and receive $125 rather than pick Moderate and receive only $100. If Coke believes that Pepsi is going to pick Extravagant, Coke would again pick Extravagant and receive $50 rather than pick Moderate and receive $35. In other words, regardless of what Pepsi chooses, Coke's best response is to pick Extravagant. Thus, Extravagant is a **dominant strategy** for Coke. It can easily be demonstrated that Extravagant is also a dominant strategy for Pepsi. When a player has a dominant strategy, that player's best response to *all* of its rival's strategies is the one dominant strategy. Because each firm has a dominant strategy, we have already answered the question that began this paragraph: The equilibrium outcome of this game is for both firms to advertise extravagantly; each firm receives a payoff of $50.

The Coke/Pepsi advertising game has a peculiar equilibrium outcome from the perspective of each of the players. As a short-hand convenience, refer to the equilibrium outcome of this game as (Extravagant, Extravagant), with the row player's strategy on the left and the column player's strategy on the right. Similarly, we can depict the payoffs received as (50, 50), again with the row player's payoff on the left and the column player's payoff on the right.

Now consider the outcome (Moderate, Moderate) with the corresponding payoffs (100, 100). If the two firms could somehow agree to each choose Moderate, they would *both* increase their payoffs from $50 to $100. If both firms can be made better off by changing strategies, why don't they? Again, consider Coke's thought process. Coke and Pepsi "agree" to purchase a moderate amount of advertising during the Super Bowl, but if Coke believes that Pepsi will adhere to the agreement, Coke would prefer to cheat on the agreement and receive $125 rather than only $100. Of course, Pepsi would have the same incentive to cheat, and they would end up at the dominant-strategy equilibrium (Extravagant, Extravagant). This is an example of the classic game theoretic problem called the **prisoner's dilemma,** which refers to games where the equilibrium of the game is not the outcome the players would choose if they could perfectly cooperate. (Homework problem 6 asks you to consider the prisoner's dilemma problem in more detail.) Prisoner's dilemma demonstrates the conflict between *group* interest and *individual* interest in strategic situations; it is one of the most common applications of game theory analysis.

Iterated Dominance

We have seen that when each player has a dominant strategy, it is easy to find the equilibrium outcome of a game: Each player chooses the dominant strategy. Most games, however, do not have a dominant-strategy equilibrium. Nevertheless, there still may be a way to apply the concept of dominance when solving for equilibrium. Consider the normal form game depicted in Figure 9-2. In this game, player Row has two strategies, R_1 and R_2.

APPLICATION
Prisoner's Dilemma Examples

Each prisoner's dilemma example has the same basic set-up. There is always a cooperative outcome in which *all* players do better when compared to the noncooperative outcome. The problem with the cooperative outcome, however, is that each player has an incentive to deviate from it. There are many real-world examples of this conflict between group and individual interest, such as the following:

1. In the cruise-ship industry, aggressive competition for passengers has led to "glorious excess."* Royal Caribbean Cruises is building a new ship that includes an 18-hole miniature golf course. Princess Cruises' new ship will include three show lounges, a wedding chapel, a virtual reality theater, and a wine and caviar bar.

2. In many group-work situations, some workers reduce their effort while relying on the rest of the group to successfully complete the project. If enough workers are lazy, the quality of the completed project is often reduced.

3. Owners of professional sports teams often get into vicious bidding wars over talented athletes.

4. Politicians spend millions of dollars on advertising campaigns to get elected.

5. In the newspaper industry, there has long been a debate as to whether one local newspaper can provide the same quality of news reporting as can two (or more) local newspapers. One early study found that competitive papers carried more news about accidents and disasters than did noncompetitive papers.**

In each of these examples, the players could do better in a cooperative group setting if they could eliminate the incentives for individual deviations. Keep in mind, however, that it is only the players who benefit from cooperation. For example, while the owners of sports teams may want to prevent runaway bidding for athletes, the athletes themselves benefit from the prisoner's dilemma problem. In Chapter 11, we examine ways in which players can credibly resolve the prisoner's dilemma problem. For now, can you think of ways the players in the examples just given can successfully achieve cooperation?

* *Business Week*, May 1, 1995, p. 140.
** Raymond B. Nixon and Robert L. Jones. "The Content of Non-Competitive vs. Competitive Newspapers." *Journalism Quarterly*, Vol. 33, 1956, pp. 299–314.

Figure 9-2   A Normal-Form Game

Column

		C_1	C_2	C_3
Row	R_1	3, 1	3, 3	2, 2
	R_2	2, 4	1, 2	4, 1

Player Column has three strategies, C_1, C_2, and C_3. Does either player have a dominant strategy? If Column were to choose C_1, Row would choose R_1, but if Column were to choose C_3, Row would choose R_2. Thus, Row does not have a strategy he would always choose regardless of what Column chose. Similarly, Column does not have a dominant strategy, since he would choose C_2 if Row were to choose R_1, and he would choose C_1 if Row were to choose R_2. Since neither player has a dominant strategy, there obviously can be no dominant-strategy equilibrium. Alternatively, we may be able to find an equilibrium by a process of elimination. This is done by eliminating strategies that are **strictly dominated.** That is, if there is a strategy that a player *never chooses,* regardless of what the other player does, we can, in effect, eliminate that strategy from the game.

In Figure 9-2, compare the payoffs Column receives between strategies C_2 and C_3. Regardless of what strategy Row chooses, Column's payoff is always greater with C_2 than it is with C_3. Therefore, as long as C_2 is an available strategy, Column will never choose strategy C_3, and we can say that C_3 is strictly dominated by C_2. If C_3 is never chosen by Column, we can eliminate that strategy from the game and be left with the new normal form game shown in Figure 9-3. As we eliminate strategies from the game, we are applying the concept of **iterated dominance.** If we can keep eliminating strategies until we are left with a unique outcome, we have found the equilibrium of the original game.

When the game is reduced to the one shown in Figure 9-3, Row now has a dominant strategy, since Row's best choice is R_1 whether Column picks C_1 or C_2. Column, however, still does not have a dominant strategy. (Can you verify this?) Since Column knows that it is not rational for Row to ever choose R_2, the strategy R_2 is now strictly dominated and can be eliminated, leaving us with the game shown in Figure 9-4. This game has a very simple

Figure 9-3   Revising the Game in Figure 9-2

Column

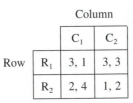

		C_1	C_2
Row	R_1	3, 1	3, 3
	R_2	2, 4	1, 2

Figure 9-4   Revising the Game in Figure 9-3

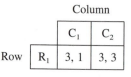

dominant-strategy equilibrium: Row chooses R_1 since it is his only choice, and Column chooses the now dominant strategy C_2. Thus, by using iterated dominance, we have found the equilibrium outcome of the original game to be (R_1, C_2). Unfortunately, iterated dominance does not always work, since many games do not have any strictly dominated strategies that can be eliminated. Is there a way to find the equilibrium outcome of a game that has no dominant or dominated strategies? Yes, with a solution concept known as *Nash equilibrium.*

Nash Equilibrium

A **Nash equilibrium** is a strategy combination in which no player has an incentive to change his strategy, holding constant the strategies of the other players. We do not need the concept of dominance to find a Nash equilibrium. Consider the normal-form game shown in Figure 9-5. Let's take a close look at this game to determine whether there are any dominant or dominated strategies for either of the players. Each player has three strategies to choose from, and we can determine each player's best response to each of the other player's strategies. First, we determine Column's best response to each of Row's strategies:

> If Row chooses R_1, Column's best response is C_3;
> If Row chooses R_2, Column's best response is C_2;
> If Row chooses R_3, Column's best response is C_1.

Column clearly has no dominant strategy, since no single strategy is a best response to all of Row's strategies. Column also has no dominated strategy, since no single strategy is strictly dominated by any other strategy.

Figure 9-5   A Normal-Form Game

Column

	C_1	C_2	C_3
R_1	7, 1	3, 6	2, 8
R_2	4, 1	6, 5	3, 3
R_3	2, 5	4, 4	4, 1

Row (to the left of R_2)

Moreover, in this example *each* of Column's strategies is a potential best response to one of Row's strategies. Now, we turn to Row's best response to each of Column's strategies:

If Column chooses C_1, Row's best response is R_1;
If Column chooses C_2, Row's best response if R_2;
If Column chooses C_3, Row's best response is R_3.

As with Column, Row has no dominant or dominated strategies. How can we predict the equilibrium of this game? If we can find an outcome such that neither player has an incentive to change his strategy, given the strategy of his rival, we have found a Nash equilibrium. For example, consider the outcome (R_1, C_1). Can this be a Nash equilibrium? Given Column's choice of C_1, Row's best response is R_1, and Row has no incentive to change his strategy. Given Row's choice of R_1, however, Column's best response is C_3, *not* C_1. Therefore, the outcome (R_1, C_1) cannot be a Nash equilibrium. Probably the surest way to find a Nash equilibrium is to repeat this exercise for each of the nine possible outcomes. When we do this for the combination (R_2, C_2), we find that neither player wants to deviate given the strategy of the other player.

There is another way of thinking about a Nash equilibrium. We know that with a Nash equilibrium, the players must simultaneously be choosing a best response, or else at least one of the players will have an incentive to deviate. If we look at the best response choices shown above, we can see that C_2 is a best response when Row chooses R_2, and R_2 is a best response when Column chooses C_2. Thus, (R_2, C_2) is a Nash equilibrium outcome for this game because it is a strategy combination in which both players are simultaneously best responding to each other. As we will discuss later in this chapter, there can be more than one Nash equilibrium in a game. We leave it as an exercise to demonstrate that (R_2, C_2) is the only Nash equilibrium in the game shown in Figure 9-5.

If you look back at Figures 9-1 and 9-2, you can immediately find the Nash equilibrium for each of those games without looking for dominant or dominated strategies. Every dominant-strategy equilibrium and every iterated dominant-strategy equilibrium must be a Nash equilibrium. (Can you explain why?) The concepts of dominance and iterated dominance, however, are very useful in familiarizing you with the technique of solving for equilibrium in normal-form games. A slightly more complicated game is now presented to provide further practice in finding Nash equilibria.

Supplemental Example: The Good, the Bad, and the Ugly

In the classic western movie *The Good, the Bad, and the Ugly*, Clint Eastwood (the Good), Lee Van Cleef (the Bad), and Eli Wallach (the Ugly, perhaps unjustly), end up in a three-man gunfight to determine who gets to keep the stolen gold. Can the concept of Nash equilibrium help us predict the outcome of this duel, or do we have to watch the movie? To answer this question, we need to add more structure to this example.

There are many ways to model a three-person gunfight, but our purpose here is to provide just enough structure to allow us to solve the game. Assume that each gunfighter can draw a gun at a different speed, with Good being the fastest, Bad second, and Ugly slowest. If a faster gunfighter shoots a slower gunfighter, the slower one is killed before he gets to shoot. Also, we assume that each gunfighter gets *at most* one shot if he is not killed by a faster man, and all shots are perfectly accurate. If only one man survives the fight, he gets all the gold, worth V dollars. If more than one man survives, the gold is split equally between them. Finally, all three gunfighters have perfect knowledge of the structure of this game; that is, each one knows who is the fastest draw, the second fastest, and the third fastest.

In this game, each player has two strategies. Good can aim at Bad or Ugly; Bad can aim at Good or Ugly; and Ugly can aim at Good or Bad. Because each player has two strategies, there are eight ($2 \times 2 \times 2$) possible outcomes in this game. Presenting this game in normal form is a little more difficult than in the two-player case, but it can still be done as shown in Figure 9-6. In Figure 9-6, Bad chooses his strategy along the rows, Ugly chooses his strategy along the columns, and Good chooses his strategy by choosing a matrix. The cell of each matrix lists the payoffs for the players, with the payoff on the left for Good, the payoff in the middle for Bad, and the payoff on the right for Ugly. As an example, let's say Good aims at Bad, Bad aims at Good, and Ugly aims at Bad. With Good's strategy on the left, Bad's strategy in the middle, and Ugly's strategy on the right, this strategy combination can be summarized as (Bad, Good, Bad). What are the payoffs in this case? Because Good is the fastest, he kills whoever he aims at, which in this case is Bad. Since Bad is killed, he doesn't get a shot off at Good. Finally, Ugly's shot doesn't matter because he aims at Bad, who is killed by Good. Thus, only Bad dies with this strategy combination, and Good and Ugly get to split V. This outcome is shown in the upper-right corner of the top matrix.

Now let's consider the strategy combination (Ugly, Good, Bad) to further familiarize ourselves with Figure 9-6. In this case, Good aims at Ugly, and so Ugly dies. Ugly aims at Bad, but Ugly is killed before he can shoot. Finally, Bad aims at Good, and so Good dies. Therefore, with the strategy combination (Ugly, Good, Bad), only Bad survives and gets the total V. This outcome can be found in the upper-right corner of the bottom matrix.

If we look closely at the top matrix, we can see that Ugly has a dominant strategy. If Ugly aims at Good, Ugly always receives V as opposed to $V/2$. Also in the top matrix, Bad is indifferent between his two choices, since he is killed by Good. Similarly, if we look at the bottom matrix, Bad has a dominant strategy. If Bad aims at Good, Bad receives V as opposed to $V/2$.

Figure 9-6   The Good, the Bad, and the Ugly Game

Good Aims at Bad:

Ugly

		Aim at Good	Aim at Bad
Bad	Aim at Good	0, 0, V	½V, 0, ½V
	Aim at Ugly	0, 0, V	½V, 0, ½V

Good Aims at Ugly:

Ugly

		Aim at Good	Aim at Bad
Bad	Aim at Good	0, V, 0	0, V, 0
	Aim at Ugly	½V, ½V, 0	½V, ½V, 0

Also in the bottom matrix, Ugly is indifferent between his two choices, because he is always killed by Good. What does all this mean? For both Bad and Ugly, aiming at Good is a dominant strategy, which means that we end up in the upper-left corner of either the top or bottom matrix. Since Good receives zero in both of these cases, he is indifferent between his two choices. Therefore, there are two Nash equilibria in this game: (Ugly, Good, Good) and (Bad, Good, Good). With both of these outcomes, the fastest gunfighter, Good, is killed. Which of the other two survives the gunfight depends on who Good decides to kill. In this case, game theory allows us to predict that the fastest draw always gets killed.

Now that we know the Nash equilibria of this game, how well do we predict the end of the movie? Does Clint Eastwood get killed? If you don't want the end of the movie spoiled for you, turn to the next section.

As you probably guessed, Clint doesn't die in the movie. But before you abandon game theory, it turns out that Clint was actually an excellent game theorist. He must have known that the dominant strategy for his two opponents was to aim at him, because the night before the gunfight, Clint removed the bullets from Ugly's gun, thus turning the three-man gunfight into a two-man gunfight. In a two-man gunfight, there is only one possible outcome—the fastest man wins. Congratulations Clint![2]

---

2 Because of his firm grasp of game theory, Clint Eastwood went on to become a big star, an Academy Award winning director, and a mayor. Of course, results do vary among users.

9.3 MIXED STRATEGIES

Many of the situations usually referred to as "games" do not have the type of equilibrium discussed in the previous section. Often, a player's best strategy is to choose an action at random. For example, a baseball pitcher who has several pitches to choose from can always keep the batter guessing about which pitch is coming next. If the pitcher throws the same pitch all the time, the batter can be well prepared to hit the ball. In football, a team on the offense can choose between passing and running. Again, a team that always passes or always runs will not fare as well as a team that can keep its rivals guessing. Even in a war, if an army can randomly choose to attack one of several of its enemy's positions, the enemy may have a difficult time defending itself. We can even apply this thinking to one of the all-time great children's games—hide-and-seek. When you played this game as a child, did you hide in the same place every time? (If you did, did you ever win?) We will use the hide-and-seek example to further explain the concept of choosing actions randomly.

Two children, Rita and Carl, are playing hide-and-seek. Rita is "It" and must count to ten. While Rita is counting, Carl must find someplace to hide. To keep things simple, let's restrict our attention to the case where there are only two places to hide, behind the curtains or in the closet. Rita gets one chance to find Carl. If she finds him, she wins; but if she doesn't, she loses. The winner receives a utility level equal to 1, and the loser receives a utility level equal to 0. The normal form of this game is shown in Figure 9-7.

The next step is to look for a Nash equilibrium. Consider the strategy combination (Curtains, Curtains). If Rita were to look behind the curtains, Carl would rather hide in the closet; therefore, (Curtains, Curtains) is not a Nash equilibrium. If Carl were hiding in the closet, Rita would rather look in the closet, so (Curtains, Closet) is not a Nash equilibrium. But if Rita were to look in the closet, Carl would rather hide behind the curtains, so (Closet, Closet) is not a Nash equilibrium. Finally, if Carl were behind the curtains, that is where Rita would rather look, so (Closet, Curtains) is not a Nash equilibrium. Thus, we have established that there is no Nash equilibrium in which Rita always looks behind the curtains, nor is there a Nash equilibrium in which Rita always looks in the closet. Does this mean that there is no Nash equilibrium to this game? The answer is no, but the Nash equilibrium in this game is different from the Nash equilibria in the games we have

Figure 9-7   Hide-and-Seek Game

		Carl	
		Curtains	Closet
Rita	Curtains	1, 0	0, 1
	Closet	0, 1	1, 0

considered up to this point. The difference is that in this game there is a
mixed-strategy Nash equilibrium, and in the previous games there have
been **pure-strategy** Nash equilibria.

Mixed-Strategy Nash Equilibrium

When a player plays a mixed strategy, she selects an action randomly. If she
plays a pure strategy, she selects a particular action with probability equal
to one (that is, she plays it *for sure*). Rita has only two pure strategies to
choose from in Figure 9-7, and we have seen that neither of them is consistent with Nash equilibrium. In addition to her pure strategies, Rita has many
possible mixed strategies. For example, Rita can look behind the curtains
with probability equal to 0.5, or look behind the curtains with probability
equal to 0.3, or look behind the curtains with probability equal to 0.75, and
so on.

How does she select among all these mixed strategies? The answer comes
from remembering the definition of a Nash equilibrium strategy. For a particular mixed strategy to be a Nash equilibrium, it must be a best response
to the equilibrium strategy of the other player. Let's see what this means for
Rita. Suppose she chooses to look behind the curtains with probability equal
to p. What is Carl's best response? If p is close to 0, it is more likely that Rita
will look in the closet, and Carl's best response is to hide behind the curtains. If Carl hides behind the curtains, Rita's best response is to look behind the curtains, so this is not an equilibrium. If p is close to 1, it is more
likely that Rita will look behind the curtains, and Carl's best response is to
hide in the closet. But if Carl is in the closet, Rita's best response is to look
there, so once again we do not have a Nash equilibrium. The problem with
these examples is that Carl's best response is always a pure strategy, and in
this game there is no equilibrium with pure strategies. For her strategy to
be part of a Nash equilibrium, then, Rita must select p so that Carl is *indifferent* between his two actions. Otherwise, he wants to respond with a pure
strategy.

The way to calculate p for Rita's equilibrium mixed strategy is to find
the value of p that makes Carl indifferent between the curtains and the closet.
He is indifferent if his expected utility from hiding behind the curtains is
equal to his expected utility from hiding in the closet. If he hides behind the
curtains, then with probability p Rita looks there and finds him, in which
case he receives 0, and with probability $(1 - p)$ she looks in the closet and
doesn't find him, and he receives 1. Carl's expected utility from hiding behind the curtains is

$$EU_C(\text{Curtains}) = 0p + 1(1-p) = 1 - p.$$

Similarly, his expected utility from hiding in the closet is

$$EU_C(\text{Closet}) = 1p + 0(1-p) = p.$$

The two expected utilities are equal if

$$p = 1-p,$$

that is, when $p = 0.5$. Thus, Rita's equilibrium mixed strategy entails looking behind the curtains with probability $p = 0.5$, and looking in the closet with probability $(1-p) = 0.5$. If $p > 0.5$, Carl gets greater utility from hiding in the closet, and if $p < 0.5$, he gets greater utility from hiding behind the curtains.

Rita chooses her equilibrium mixed strategy to make Carl indifferent between his two actions. Similarly, Carl chooses his equilibrium mixed strategy to make Rita indifferent between looking behind the curtains and looking in the closet. Suppose that Carl hides behind the curtains with probability q. Rita's expected utility from looking behind the curtains is

$$EU_R(\text{Curtains}) = 1q + 0(1-q) = q.$$

Her expected utility from looking in the closet is

$$EU_C(\text{Closet}) = 0q + 1(1-q) = 1 - q.$$

She is indifferent if

$$q = 1-q,$$

that is, if $q = 0.5$. Carl's equilibrium mixed strategy entails hiding behind the curtains with probability $q = 0.5$, and hiding in the closet with probability $(1-q) = 0.5$. If $q > 0.5$ Rita prefers to look behind the curtains, and if $q < 0.5$ she would rather look in the closet.

We have done something rather strange here. We found Rita's equilibrium mixed strategy by looking at Carl's payoffs, and we found Carl's equilibrium mixed strategy by looking at Rita's payoffs. This works because the trick to finding a mixed-strategy Nash equilibrium is to make both players indifferent between their possible actions. If one player prefers one of his own actions, he will choose that action. If either player plays a pure strategy, the mixed-strategy equilibrium breaks down and, as we saw above, the game has no pure-strategy Nash equilibrium. The payoff an individual player gets from choosing a particular action depends on the strategy chosen by the other player. The only way for one player to become indifferent between his actions, then, is for the other player to select a strategy that makes him indifferent. This is what we have done in calculating the equilibrium mixed strategies, and we can say that the strategy combination ($p = 0.5, q = 0.5$) is a **mixed-strategy Nash equilibrium.** In the next example, we will provide you with more practice in finding a mixed-strategy Nash equilibrium.

APPLICATION
Monitoring Workers

Mixed strategies are used not only in games like hide-and-seek, but also in economic situations. Consider the case of an employee who gets paid $200 a day, but must exert effort in order to actually produce anything. If he does the work he's supposed to, he generates $300 per day in revenue for the firm, but because of the nature of his job, the firm cannot directly observe his contribution to revenue unless it exerts some effort of its own. For example, the firm can pay someone else to monitor the employee, and the monitor can accurately determine whether or not the employee is working. If the monitor finds that the employee is not working—that is, the employee is *shirking*—the employee is fired and gets paid nothing. Monitors are expensive, though, costing $60 per day, and the firm would rather not spend the money on monitoring workers if it is at all possible.

Before setting up the normal form of this game, we will assume that payoffs in games are utility values. The simplest utility function is the risk-neutral utility function, so we will use it. Consequently, the employee obtains utility of 200 if he gets paid $200, and he gets utility of 0 if he gets paid $0. Before we can enter the payoffs, however, we must state how costly it is for the employee to exert effort. Assume that the employee expends 150 units of utility when he works. Therefore, if the employee works, he receives 50 units of utility regardless of whether or not the firm monitors his effort. (He gets paid $200, which gives him 200 units of utility, but he expends 150 units of utility in effort). If he shirks and the firm monitors his effort, he gets fired and receives utility of 0. If he shirks but the firm does not monitor, he receives $200 but exerts no effort, so his payoff is 200 utility units.

Now for the firm's payoffs. For simplicity, assume that the firm is also risk neutral, so that it simply attempts to maximize expected profit. If the employee works, the firm gets $300 in extra revenue, but it must spend $200 on the employee's wage. If the firm does not monitor, then it keeps the remaining $100 as profit, but if it does monitor, its profit falls to $40. If the employee shirks and the firm monitors, the employee generates no revenue, the firm pays no wage, but the firm still bears the $60 monitoring cost, so it suffers a $60 loss. Finally, if the employee shirks and the firm does not monitor, the firm pays the employee $200 and receives nothing in return, a $200 loss. These payoffs are summarized in Figure 9-8.

This game has no pure-strategy Nash equilibrium. If the worker works, the firm does not wish to monitor, but if the firm doesn't monitor, the worker won't work. This means that there is no equilibrium in which the worker always works. If the worker shirks, the firm wants to monitor, but then the

Figure 9-8   Monitoring Workers Game

Firm

		Monitor	Not Monitor
Employee	Work	50, 40	50, 100
	Shirk	0, −60	200, −200

worker wants to work. This means that there is no equilibrium in which the worker always shirks, either.

To find the employee's equilibrium mixed strategy, assume that he works with probability p, and make the firm indifferent between monitoring and not monitoring him. The firm's expected payoff from monitoring is

$$EU_F(\text{Monitor}) = 40p + (-60)(1-p) = 100p - 60.$$

The firm's expected payoff from not monitoring is

$$EU_F(\text{Not Monitor}) = 100p + (-200)(1-p) = 300p - 200.$$

The two expected payoffs are equal when

$$300p - 200 = 100p - 60,$$

that is, when $p = 0.7$. The employee's equilibrium mixed strategy entails working with probability $p = 0.7$, and goofing off with probability $(1-p) = 0.3$.

Now turn to the firm's equilibrium mixed strategy. If the firm monitors with probability q, the employee's expected payoff from working is

$$EU_E(\text{Work}) = 50q + 50(1-q) = 50.$$

The employee's expected payoff from goofing off is

$$EU_E(\text{Goof Off}) = 0q + 200(1-q) = 200 - 200q.$$

The employee is indifferent between the two actions if $q = 0.75$. The firm's mixed strategy entails monitoring with probability $q = 0.75$, and not monitoring with probability $(1-q) = 0.25$.

Games with Both Pure- and Mixed-Strategy Equilibria

Suppose that two electronics companies invent the VCR at the same time. What they must do, however, is decide what size videotape to use. One company, Alpha, bases its design on a large-format tape. The other company, Beta, bases its design on a small-format tape. It is unlikely that both sizes of tape will succeed in the marketplace. If the two companies must decide on tape sizes independently and at the same time, what should they do?

The normal form of this game is shown in Figure 9-9. Alpha gets a higher payoff when both companies choose the large format, because Alpha has already developed the large format technology. Similarly, Beta gets a higher payoff when both companies choose the small format. If they each choose their own favorite formats, they each get an expected payoff of 5, but if they each choose their less favored formats, they each get an expected payoff of 0. Choosing different formats is more costly than choosing the same format, because the different formats must compete for prominence, and competition drives down profits.

There are two pure-strategy Nash equilibria in this game. One occurs when they both choose the small format. If Alpha chooses the small format, Beta can either choose the small format and receive 20 or the large format and receive 0. Since 20 is better, Beta would choose the small format. If Beta chooses the small format, Alpha can either choose the small format and receive 10 or the large format and receive 5, so Alpha would choose the small format. Since both firms choose their best responses to the other's equilibrium strategies, this is a Nash equilibrium. Similarly, there is another pure-strategy equilibrium in which both firms choose the large format.

The mixed-strategy equilibrium can be found in the usual way. Assume that Alpha chooses Small with probability p. Beta's expected payoff from choosing the small format is

$$EU_B(\text{Small}) = 20p + 5(1-p) = 15p + 5.$$

Beta's expected payoff from choosing the large format is

$$EU_B(\text{Large}) = 0p + 10(1-p) = 10 - 10p.$$

Figure 9-9   Videotape-Format Game

		Beta	
		Small	Large
Alpha	Small	10, 20	0, 0
	Large	5, 5	20, 10

Beta is indifferent between the two when $EU_B(\text{Small}) = EU_A(\text{Large})$, that is, when $p = 0.2$. Next, assume that Beta chooses the small format with probability q. Alpha's expected payoff from choosing the small format is

$$EU_A(\text{Small}) = 10q + 0(1-q) = 10q,$$

and its expected payoff from choosing the large format is

$$EU_B(\text{Large}) = 5q + 20(1-q) = 20 - 15q.$$

Alpha is indifferent between the two formats when $q = 0.8$. The mixed-strategy equilibrium, then, has Alpha choosing its favorite format with probability 0.8 and Beta choosing its favorite format with probability 0.8. Therefore, the probability that we observe the outcome (Large, Small) is $pq = .64$. Both firms receive an expected payoff of 8. (Can you verify this?)

The three Nash equilibria we have found can be compared on the basis of expected payoff. Alpha prefers the pure-strategy equilibrium in which both firms choose the large format, since then it receives a payoff of 20. Beta, on the other hand, prefers the pure-strategy equilibrium in which both firms choose the small format and it receives 20. If they play the mixed-strategy equilibrium, the most likely outcome is that Alpha uses the large format and Beta uses the small format, so both receive 8. This game may help explain why we had both the beta and VHS formats when VCRs became common in the 1980s.

In many games, as in the example just given, there is more than one Nash equilibrium. In the next section, we introduce a technique that allows us to choose between the different equilibria that may be found. For now, however, we will leave you with the general result that (in most cases) every normal-form game has at least one Nash equilibrium, and if there are multiple equilibria, there are an odd number of them.

9.4 SEQUENTIAL-MOVE GAMES

All of the games we have discussed so far have had one common feature: All players made their moves simultaneously. While this framework fits a large number of economic situations, it by no means fits them all. For example, after a firm introduces a new product, its competitors get to observe its price and quantity decisions before developing their own variations on the product. If one movie theater in town decides to increase its price, all the other theaters in town get to observe this action before making their own pricing decisions. Even in poker, after one player bets, all the other players get to respond. Situations like these require a change in the way we represent and solve games.

Extensive-Form Games

Let's return to the Coke/Pepsi advertising game of Figure 9-1. In that game, Coke and Pepsi simultaneously chose their advertising levels during the Super Bowl, and we found the Nash equilibrium to be (Extravagant, Extravagant). In this section, we slightly modify the rules of the game. Assume that Coke gets to advertise during the first half of the Super Bowl and Pepsi gets to advertise during the second half. In addition, Pepsi gets to make a last-minute advertising decision during halftime. In this version of the game, Coke chooses to advertise moderately or extravagantly, and then, after observing Coke's decision, Pepsi chooses to advertise moderately or extravagantly.

The normal form of this new game is more complicated than the one shown in Figure 9-1. Although Coke still has two strategies, Moderate and Extravagant, Pepsi now has *four* strategies. To see why this is the case, consider Pepsi's thought process. During the first half of the Super Bowl, Pepsi gets to observe how often Coke advertises. By halftime, Pepsi must be prepared to make a quick decision, and so it must be ready to respond to each of Coke's choices. For example, Pepsi can adopt the following strategy: If Coke chooses Moderate, Pepsi will choose Moderate, but if Coke chooses Extravagant, Pepsi will choose Extravagant. Thus, each strategy choice of Pepsi must consist of two **actions**—what to do if Coke chooses Moderate, and what to do if Coke chooses Extravagant.[3] Because Coke has two strategies, and Pepsi has two actions, Pepsi has four (2 × 2) strategies, and they are the following:

1. Choose Moderate if Coke chooses Moderate, and choose Moderate if Coke chooses Extravagant.
2. Choose Moderate if Coke chooses Moderate, and choose Extravagant if Coke chooses Extravagant.
3. Choose Extravagant if Coke chooses Moderate, and choose Moderate if Coke chooses Extravagant.
4. Choose Extravagant if Coke chooses Moderate, and choose Extravagant if Coke chooses Extravagant.

Probably the easiest way to think of Pepsi's strategies is to think of them as *contingent* strategies—that is, Pepsi must be prepared to respond to either of Coke's choices, and each strategy combination gives Pepsi a complete plan, regardless of Coke's choice. For notational convenience, Pepsi's strategies 1–4 above can be written more concisely as:

---

3 Because Pepsi chooses second in a sequential game, there is a difference between its *actions* and its *strategies*. Each of Pepsi's strategies consists of two actions. For Coke, on the other hand, we can still use the terms *action* and *strategy* interchangeably.

1. {Moderate, Moderate}
2. {Moderate, Extravagant}
3. {Extravagant, Moderate}
4. {Extravagant, Extravagant},

where the term on the left refers to Pepsi's action if Coke chooses Moderate, and the term on the right refers to Pepsi's action if Coke chooses Extravagant.

Figure 9-10 presents this sequential-move game in normal form. In this case, the Nash equilibrium outcome is (Extravagant, {Extravagant, Extravagant}), with Coke's strategy on the left and Pepsi's strategy on the right. Let's examine why this is a Nash equilibrium. If Coke chooses Extravagant, the best Pepsi can do is to receive a payoff of 50, and so Pepsi has no incentive to deviate from {Extravagant, Extravagant}.[4] If Pepsi chooses {Extravagant, Extravagant}, Coke receives 50 with Extravagant and only 35 with Moderate, and so Coke has no incentive to deviate from Extravagant. It is left as an exercise to verify that there is only one Nash equilibrium in Figure 9-10.

The normal-form representation in Figure 9-10 obscures the fact that the players are choosing their strategies sequentially. A more convenient way to display a sequential-move game is to use the **extensive form,** as shown in Figure 9-11. This form of a game allows us to present the moves of the players in the order in which they are taken. At the top of the figure, or the **initial node,** Coke has two actions it can choose. If Coke chooses Moderate we move to the P_1 node, and Pepsi can choose Moderate or Extravagant. If at P_1 Pepsi chooses Extravagant, for example, the payoffs at the **terminal node** are 35 for Coke and 125 for Pepsi. (At each terminal node, the top payoff is for the player who moves first, and the bottom payoff is for the player who moves second.) If Coke chooses Extravagant we move to the P_2 node, and again Pepsi can choose Moderate or Extravagant.

To solve for the equilibrium outcome of this game, we introduce a concept known as **backward induction.** With backward induction, we start at the end of the game and work backward to the beginning of the game. Con-

Figure 9-10   Sequential Game in Normal Form

		Pepsi			
		(Mod, Mod)	(Mod, Ex)	(Ex, Mod)	(Ex, Ex)
Coke	Moderate	100, 100	100, 100	35, 125	35, 125
	Extravagant	125, 35	50, 50	125, 35	50, 50

---

4 When Coke chooses Extravagant, Pepsi is indifferent between {Extravagant, Extravagant} and {Moderate, Extravagant}. Because Pepsi does not strictly prefer {Extravagant, Extravagant}, we say that the outcome (Extravagant, {Extravagant, Extravagant}) is a **weak Nash equilibrium.**

Figure 9-11   An Extensive-Form Game

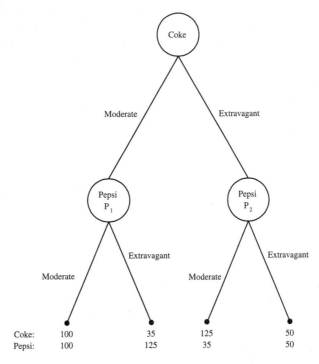

sider Figure 9-11 again, and let's start at the P_1 node. If Pepsi is choosing at P_1, it receives 100 with Moderate and 125 with Extravagant, and, therefore, will pick Extravagant. If Pepsi is at the P_2 node, it receives 35 with Moderate and 50 with Extravagant, and again will pick Extravagant. We now know what Pepsi will do in the second stage of the game: at P_1 or P_2, Pepsi will pick Extravagant. Using backward induction, we can now move back to the beginning of the game to predict Coke's strategy. Coke knows that if it chooses Moderate, the game moves to P_1, Pepsi will choose Extravagant, and Coke's final payoff will be 35. If Coke chooses Extravagant, the game moves to P_2, Pepsi chooses Extravagant, and Coke's final payoff will be 50, which is greater than 35. Therefore, Coke decides to choose Extravagant in the first stage and Pepsi chooses Extravagant in the second stage, and the final payoffs are (50, 50). This is the same result we found in Figure 9-10.

Subgame-Perfect Equilibrium

In the Coke/Pepsi sequential advertising game, there is only one Nash equilibrium (as we learned from Figure 9-10). We now set up an example of a sequential game in which there are two Nash equilibria, and we discuss a way of choosing between the two equilibria. Consider the extensive-form game shown in Figure 9-12. Player A chooses first from two actions—a_1 and a_2. Player B chooses between two actions—b_1 and b_2—after observing A's choice. It is easy to find the backward induction outcome of this game. If player B ends up at the B_1 node, he will choose b_2. If he ends up at the B_2 node, he will choose b_1. Since Player A knows how B will respond, A will receive 3 with a_1, but only 2 with a_2. Therefore, the equilibrium outcome of this game is for Player A to pick a_1 in the first stage, and player B to pick b_2 in the second stage. In this case, the equilibrium payoffs are (3, 2).

Figure 9-13 presents the normal form of the game shown in Figure 9-12. As we saw in the previous section, the player that chooses second has four strategies. In this case, Player B's strategies are:

1. Choose b_1 if A chooses a_1, and choose b_2 if A chooses a_2—denoted by $\{b_1, b_2\}$.
2. Choose b_1 if A chooses a_1, and choose b_1 if A chooses a_2—denoted by $\{b_1, b_1\}$.
3. Choose b_2 if A chooses a_1, and choose b_1 if A chooses a_2—denoted by $\{b_2, b_1\}$.
4. Choose b_2 if A chooses a_1, and choose b_2 if A chooses a_2—denoted by $\{b_2, b_2\}$.

From Figure 9-13, you should be able to verify that there are two Nash equilibria: $(a_1, \{b_2, b_1\})$ and $(a_2, \{b_1, b_1\})$. What is the difference between these two equilibria?

Figure 9-12   An Extensive-Form Game

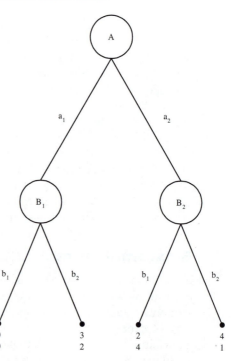

| a: | 0 | 3 | 2 | 4 |
| b: | 0 | 2 | 4 | 1 |

Figure 9-13   Sequential Game in Normal Form

B

		(b_1, b_2)	(b_1, b_1)	(b_2, b_1)	(b_2, b_2)
A	a_1	0, 0	0, 0	3, 2	3, 2
	a_2	4, 1	2, 4	2, 4	4, 1

Consider the first Nash equilibrium—$(a_1, \{b_2, b_1\})$. Player B's equilibrium strategy is $\{b_2, b_1\}$, which means that if Player A chooses a_1, B chooses b_2, and if A chooses a_2, B chooses b_1. This is exactly what we predict B will do when we use backward induction. As for Player A's equilibrium strategy, we also know from backward induction that a_1 is better for A than a_2. Thus, the equilibrium $(a_1, \{b_2, b_1\})$ perfectly corresponds to the backward induction outcome, except instead of just saying that Player A picks a_1 in the first stage and Player B picks b_2 in the second stage, we say that A's equilibrium strategy is a_1 and B's equilibrium strategy is $\{b_2, b_1\}$. In other words, we are now taking into account Player B's *strategy*, $\{b_2, b_1\}$, instead of just his *action*, b_2.

Now consider the second Nash equilibrium—$(a_2, \{b_1, b_1\})$. To demonstrate that this is a Nash equilibrium, we must verify that neither player has an incentive to deviate, given the strategy of his rival. B's strategy of $\{b_1, b_1\}$ means that he chooses b_1 regardless of what A chooses. In that case, Player A receives 0 if he chooses a_1 and 2 if he chooses a_2; therefore, A has no incentive to deviate from strategy a_2. Given A's strategy of a_2, B has no incentive to deviate from $\{b_1, b_1\}$ since b_1 is his best response to a_2. The problem with B's equilibrium strategy $\{b_1, b_1\}$, however, is that it specifies that Player B should choose b_1 even if A chooses a_1—but this makes no sense! If Player B ended up at the B_1 node, his best response would be b_2, not b_1. This is the key difference between the two Nash equilibria. When B's equilibrium strategy is $\{b_2, b_1\}$, Player B is responding rationally to both of Player A's strategies. When B's equilibrium strategy is $\{b_1, b_1\}$, Player B is only responding rationally when A chooses a_2.

To formally distinguish between the two Nash equilibria, we can use the concept of **subgame-perfect Nash equilibrium.** A **subgame** is a part of an extensive-form game that begins at a node (but not the initial node) and continues to the terminal nodes.[5] In Figure 9-12, there are two subgames—the one beginning at the B_1 node, and the one beginning at the B_2 node. These two subgames are reproduced in Figure 9-14. A subgame-perfect Nash equilibrium is a Nash equilibrium not only for the complete game, but also

---

5 An alternative definition of a subgame can include the initial node, which makes the complete game also an additional subgame. We will continue not to refer to the complete game as a subgame.

Figure 9-14   Subgames

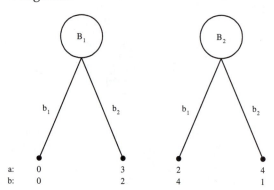

a:	0	3	2	4
b:	0	2	4	1

for *every* subgame. For example, we have already seen that the strategy combination (a_1, {b_2, b_1}) is a Nash equilibrium for the complete game, and it is also a subgame-perfect Nash equilibrium. Player B's strategy {b_2, b_1} specifies that he chooses b_2 at the B_1 node and b_1 at the B_2 node, and he has no incentive to deviate from these choices. Thus, the strategy combination (a_1, {b_2, b_1}) involves rational behavior *at every node of the game.* In contrast, the strategy combination (a_2, {b_1, b_1}) is not a subgame-perfect Nash equilibrium since it specifies that at the subgame beginning at the B_1 node, Player B chooses b_1, and this is not a Nash equilibrium for that subgame.

The attentive reader may ask at this point: With the Nash equilibrium (a_2, {b_1, b_1}), who cares what Player B chooses at the B_1 node if Player A is choosing a_2 as his equilibrium strategy? What happens at a subgame, however, even if that subgame is never reached during the course of play, can determine the final outcome of a game. With the Nash equilibrium (a_2, {b_1, b_1}), let's carefully examine why Player A has no incentive to deviate from a_2. If Player A decides to choose a_1, *given Player B's strategy of {b_1, b_1},* A expects to end up with a payoff of 0. Therefore, A prefers to choose a_2 and end up with a payoff of 2. But why should Player A believe that B will stick to his equilibrium strategy? Player A knows that if he were to choose a_1, the game would be at the B_1 node and Player B would rationally choose b_2. The important point here is that B's strategy {b_1, b_1} is not **credible;** that is, the only way the Nash equilibrium (a_2, {b_1, b_1}) can be maintained is if Player A believes that B will choose b_1 if the game progresses to the B_1 node. A subgame-perfect Nash equilibrium, such as (a_1, {b_2, b_1}), does not require that any incredible threat be believed. In the final section of this chapter, we will examine an economic application of the importance of making threats credible.

9.5 ENTRY DETERRENCE

Let us once again return to the Coke/Pepsi advertising example, but now we tell a different story. Assume that Coke is a monopolist in a market, and

Pepsi is deciding whether or not to enter the market. In this case, we refer to Coke as the **incumbent,** and to Pepsi as the **entrant.** Figure 9-15 presents the extensive form of this entry deterrence game. At the initial node P_1, Pepsi has two actions to choose from—stay out of the market or enter the market at an entry cost of 10. If Pepsi stays out, it earns zero profit, and Coke, the incumbent, earns monopoly profit equal to 100. If Pepsi enters the market, we are at the C_1 node, and we assume that Coke can then choose between two actions—collude with Pepsi and share the monopoly profit, or fight Pepsi by undertaking a malicious advertising campaign at a cost of $k = 25$. If Coke decides to collude with Pepsi, Coke's payoff is 50 and Pepsi's pay-off is 50 minus the entry fee, that is, 40. If Coke decides to fight Pepsi, Coke's payoff is $70 - k$ and Pepsi's payoff is -10 (that is, Pepsi loses the entry fee).

   In this game, can Coke deter Pepsi from entering the market? If Coke's strategy is to fight Pepsi upon entry, Pepsi will not enter, since it prefers a profit of 0 to a profit of -10. Thus, the strategy combination (Stay Out, Fight) is a Nash equilibrium.[6] But is Coke's threat credible? Using backward induc-

Figure 9-15   Entry Deterrence Game

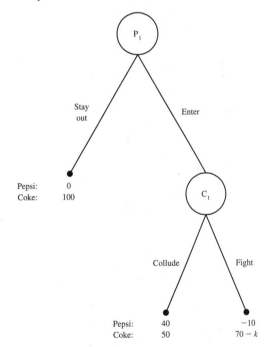

Pepsi: 0   40   −10
Coke: 100   50   70 − k

_____

6 When Pepsi's strategy is Stay Out, Coke does not get to move in this game; therefore, Coke is indifferent between its two actions.

tion and starting at the C_1 node, Coke would prefer to collude with Pepsi, since $50 > 70 - k = 45$. Moving up to the P_1 node, if Pepsi chooses to stay out its profit will be 0, but if it enters it will earn a profit of 40, since it is not in Coke's best interest to fight if the C_1 node is reached. In this version of the game, then, Coke can threaten to fight Pepsi, but the threat is not credible, since the outcome (Stay Out, Fight) is not subgame perfect. The outcome (Enter, Collude), however, is a subgame-perfect Nash equilibrium. Intuitively, when an incumbent threatens an entrant *prior* to entry, but the threat will only be carried out *after* entry, the threat must be credible or it will be ignored.

Can we modify the game in a way that allows Coke to deter entry? Consider a second version of the entry deterrence game shown in Figure 9-16. In this case, we assume that k is made up of two parts: the cost of making the commercial, c, and the cost of purchasing the advertising space, v, (that is, $k = c + v$). This game has three stages. First, Coke must decide whether or not to make the commercial, so that if Pepsi enters and Coke decides to fight, Coke only needs to incur the cost of purchasing the advertising space.

Figure 9-16   Entry Deterrence Game

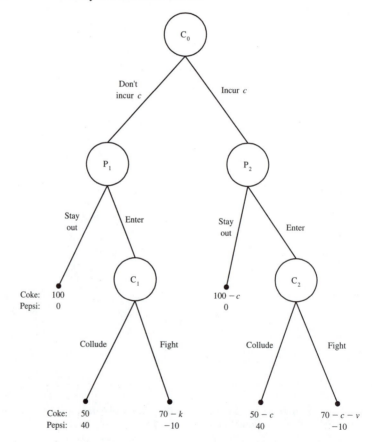

After Coke's initial action, Pepsi must decide whether or not to enter the industry. In the final stage, as in the previous version of the game, Coke must decide whether to collude with Pepsi or to fight Pepsi. If you look closely at the terminal nodes, you will see that the subgame beginning at the P_1 node is exactly the game shown in Figure 9-15 (except the order of the payoffs are reversed, since Coke now moves first). The subgame beginning at the P_2 node is similar to the subgame beginning at the P_1 node, except for a slight adjustment to Coke's payoffs. Since Coke incurs the cost of making the commercial up front, its payoff if Pepsi does not enter is $100 - c$, and if Pepsi does enter Coke's payoffs are $50 - c$ if it colludes, and $70 - c - v$ if it fights. Notice that $70 - k = 70 - c - v$; that is, if Coke ends up fighting Pepsi, its total cost of fighting is the same whether or not it incurred the cost c up front.

The backward induction outcome of this game depends on the values of c and v. We will still assume that $k = 25$, but it is now made up of $c = 10$ and $v = 15$. Let's work through the subgames to find the equilibrium outcome. From the earlier version of the game, we know that if the game progresses to the P_1 node, Pepsi will enter and Coke will collude. Thus, if Coke chooses not to incur c up front, its final payoff will be 50. To find Coke's final payoff if it decides to incur c, we can begin at the C_2 node. If Coke colludes at that node, its payoff is $50 - c = 40$; if it fights, its payoff is $70 - 25 = 45$. Therefore, Cokes decides to fight if Pepsi chooses to enter at the P_2 node, but Pepsi will not enter, because it prefers the payoff of 0 to the payoff of -10. If Pepsi doesn't enter, Coke's payoff from incurring c up front will be $100 - 10 = 90$, which is greater than its payoff of 50 if it doesn't incur c. In all, the backward induction outcome is for Coke to incur c and for Pepsi to stay out of the market.

Why is the outcome of the second version of the game different from the outcome of the first version? In the first version, Coke can carry out its threat only after Pepsi enters the market, but by then it is too late—Coke's bluff will be called! In the second version of the game, Coke *precommits;* that is, Coke incurs enough of a cost up front to prove to Pepsi that it will credibly incur the rest of the cost if the game reaches the C_2 node. Even though the commercial ends up being wasted (since Coke will never purchase the advertising space), the small cost up front affects Coke's future payoffs in a way that makes fighting a credible threat.

Summary

- **Game theory** is the study of behavior in situations in which each party's payoff directly depends on what another party does.

- The **normal-form** representation of a game, presented in matrix form, consists of three components: (1) a list of the players of the game; (2) a list of the strategies each player can choose; and, (3) a list of the payoffs each player receives for each combination of strategies they choose.

- When a player has a **dominant strategy,** that player's best response to *all* its rival's strategies is the one dominant strategy. When both players have a dominant strategy, the outcome of the game is called a **dominant strategy equilibrium.**

- **Prisoner's dilemma** refers to games where the equilibrium of the game is not the outcome the players would choose if they could perfectly cooperate.

- A **Nash equilibrium** is a strategy combination in which no player has an incentive to change his strategy, holding constant the strategies of the other players. With a Nash equilibrium, the players must simultaneously be choosing a best response, or else at least one of the players will have an incentive to deviate.

- If a player plays a **pure strategy,** he selects a particular action with probability equal to one. If a player plays a **mixed strategy,** he selects an action randomly. With a mixed strategy, the probabilities assigned to each action must sum to one.

- A **mixed-strategy Nash equilibrium** is an equilibrium in which both players play mixed strategies.

- A convenient way to display a sequential move game is to use the **extensive form.** This form of game allows us to present the moves of the players in the order in which they are taken.

- To solve for the equilibrium of an extensive-form game, **backward induction** can be used. With backward induction, we start at the end of the game and work backward to the beginning of the game. At every point in the game, the players choose their best response.

- A **subgame** is a part of an extensive-form game that begins at a decision node (but not the initial node) and continues to the terminal nodes. A **subgame-perfect Nash equilibrium** is a Nash equilibrium not only for the complete game, but also for *every* subgame. A subgame-perfect Nash equilibrium does not allow any incredible threat to be believed.

Problems

1. Find the dominant-strategy equilibria for the following games:

a.

Column

		L	R
Row	T	0, 5	2, 4
	B	6, 2	4, 1

b.

Column

		X	Y	Z
	A	0, 18	3, 4	1, 20
Row	B	5, 11	20, 11	7, 12
	C	4, 4	12, 1	3, 5

2. Find the equilibria of the following games using iterated dominance:

a.

Column

		L	R
	T	2, 11	4, 9
Row	M	3, 1	6, 2
	B	5, 3	1, 4

b.

Column

		X	Y	Z
	A	4, 11	1, 15	6, 20
Row	B	12, 12	3, 3	7, 2
	C	15, 4	9, 10	8, 8

3. Find the Nash equilibria of the following games:

a.

Column

		X	Y	Z
	A	4, 6	6, 1	1, 3
Row	B	1, 8	1, 5	4, 10
	C	15, 3	2, 9	2, 7

b.

	Column		
	X	Y	Z
A	0, 8	4, 7	10, 10
Row B	3, 0	2, 5	8, 0
C	4, 2	0, 1	12, 1

4. Find the mixed-strategy equilibria of the following games:

a.

	Column	
	L	R
Row T	8, 5	2, 4
B	9, 3	1, 6

b.

	Column	
	L	R
Row T	5, −1	−1, 2
B	-1, 2	5, 1

5. Find the subgame-perfect equilibria of the following games:

a. **Figure 9-17**

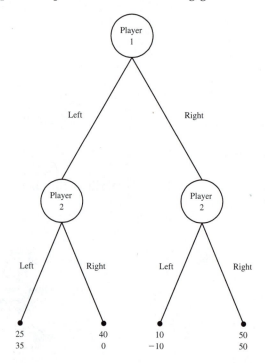

Player 1:	25	40	10	50
Player 2:	35	0	−10	50

b. **Figure 9-18**

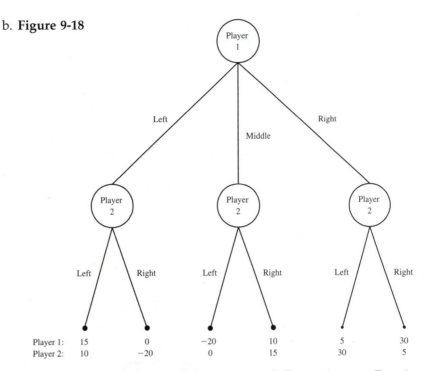

| Player 1: | 15 | 0 | −20 | 10 | 5 | 30 |
| Player 2: | 10 | −20 | 0 | 15 | 30 | 5 |

6. (This is the classic Prisoner's Dilemma game.) Two prisoners, Bonnie and Clyde, are accused of committing armed robbery together. They are being kept in separate cells (of course), and the warden comes into Bonnie's cell and tells her the following: The state has a pretty good case against them, even if neither of them confesses and testifies against the other. If neither confesses, they both get 3 years in jail. If Bonnie confesses but Clyde does not, Bonnie gets 1 year but Clyde gets 10. If they both confess, they both get 5 years. After leaving her cell, the warden goes to visit Clyde, and tells him the same story, but this time Clyde is given the opportunity to confess. Draw the payoff matrix for the two prisoners, and tell what they do in equilibrium.

7. (This is the classic game known as the Battle of the Sexes.) Harry and Sally have been dating for a long time, and like most couples who have been dating for a long time, they no longer talk to each other. It's Friday night, though, and they would both like to spend it together. The problem is that they have not discussed their plans. There are two events going on in town that night. There is a ballet, and Sally loves the ballet, and there is a hockey game, and Harry loves violence. If Harry goes to the game and Sally shows up, too, then Harry gets utility of 10, but he gets utility of 5 even if Sally doesn't show up. If Harry goes to the ballet and Sally is there, his utility is 7, but if he is stuck at the ballet all by himself his utility is 0. If Sally goes to the ballet and Harry is there her utility is 10, but her utility is only 5 if Harry doesn't join her. If she goes

to the hockey game and finds Harry there her utility is 7, but if she is there alone her utility is 0.

Draw a payoff matrix for this game, and find all three equilibria.

8. Three people have scheduled a meeting together for 11 o'clock, and no business can be discussed until all three are present. The three are experienced meeting-goers and know that they should either show up exactly on time or they should show up exactly ten minutes late. By showing up late each person knows that the meeting will start right when he gets there, and he can guarantee himself utility of 10 regardless of what the other people do. If everyone shows up on time, however, they each get utility of 20. If someone shows up on time but the meeting is delayed for ten minutes, that person gets no utility. Assuming that no person knows what anyone else is doing until he gets into the meeting room, draw a payoff matrix for the game, and find the pure-strategy Nash equilibria.

9. Bill and Harold are walking down a street filled with restaurants, wondering where to stop for lunch. They have decided that as they come to restaurants, they will alternate who decides whether or not to go in, with Harold making the first choice. They cannot choose to go back to a restaurant they have already passed. The first restaurant is a fast-food hamburger place. The second restaurant is a Mexican restaurant. The third restaurant makes great pizza. The fourth restaurant has an all-you-can-eat Chinese buffet, and the fifth and final restaurant has an all-you-can-eat beef bar. Harold's order of preference is the beef bar, then the pizza place, then the Chinese buffet, then the hamburger place, then the Mexican restaurant. Bill's order of preference is the Chinese buffet, then the beef bar, followed by the Mexican place, then the pizza place, then the hamburger place. Draw a game tree, and tell what Bill and Harold end up having for lunch.

10. A firm employs a worker who likes to use drugs, and must decide whether or not to test the employee for drug use. When straight, the worker generates $60 in revenue for the firm, but after using drugs the worker is only worth $30 to the firm. The worker's wage is $40. Drug testing costs the firm $5, while staying straight costs the worker an equivalent of $15. Drug testing is perfectly reliable, and if the worker is caught, he gets fired, generates no revenue, and receives no wage.

Show the game in normal form, and find the Nash equilibrium of the game.

10

OLIGOPOLY

Overview

In Chapter 7, we examined competitive markets, in which there are very many small price-taking firms. In Chapter 8, we examined pure monopoly, in which a single firm is a price setter. Obviously, these are two extreme market structures with very many firms at one extreme and a single firm at the other. In between these extremes, there are many other possible types of market structures. One type is **duopoly,** in which there are exactly two firms. This market structure lies close to the single firm extreme. Another type is **monopolistic competition,** in which there are many firms, but each firm is a price setter. This market structure lies close to the very many firms extreme.

In general, the term **oligopoly** refers to market structures that include duopoly and monopolistic competition and many other market structures that lie between perfect competition and pure monopoly. For example, many towns have several automobile dealerships that compete against each other. Although there are usually not enough dealerships to consider the market perfectly competitive, there is more than one, which rules out the pure monopoly model. The airline industry is another example of a market structure that is oligopolistic. Primarily, when you see a market structure with more than one firm but less than "very many" firms, some form of oligopoly model is best suited to examine behavior in that industry.

In some oligopoly models, the firms interact strategically. In these cases, the tools of game theory can be used to examine market outcomes. In fact, we've already seen some simple duopoly games in Chapter 9: the Coke and Pepsi advertising game and the entry deterrence game. Other oligopoly models combine aspects of perfect competition and pure monopoly and, therefore, do not use game theoretic techniques to examine market outcomes. In the first half of this chapter, we use duopoly models to examine different types of strategic interaction between firms. In the second half, we examine oligopoly models that involve many firms. You will learn:

- How to find the equilibrium outcome in a simultaneous-move game between two firms.
- How to find the equilibrium outcome in a sequential-move game

between two firms, with one firm in the role of a leader and the other firm a follower.

- How to find the equilibrium outcome in a market structure in which one firm is dominant over many smaller firms.

- How to find the equilibrium outcome in a market structure in which many firms compete against each other by producing slightly differentiated products.

10.1   COURNOT DUOPOLY

The first duopoly model we examine was developed by French economist Augustin Cournot. To examine this model, let's return to the car dealership example we used in discussing monopoly pricing. Assume we have the following demand function: $P = 16,000 - 20Q$, where P is the product price and Q is the industry output. In the monopoly example, a single firm produced the total industry output. With a duopoly, however, total industry output is divided between two (identical) firms such that $Q = q_1 + q_2$, where q_1 is Firm 1's output and q_2 is Firm 2's output. As can easily be seen, by replacing Q with $q_1 + q_2$, the demand function can be rewritten as $P = 16,000 - 20q_1 - 20q_2$. This makes it clear that neither firm has complete power to set the price. The price each firm can get for its output depends on the amount *the other firm* produces. Because the firms are interdependent, it is important to specify exactly how they compete against each other. In a Cournot duopoly, each firm uses output as its **strategic variable,** and both firms choose their output levels simultaneously. As before, we will also assume that each firm has a constant marginal cost of production equal to $10,000 per unit.

It is difficult to set up the normal form of the Cournot game because there are many possible values for output.[1] Instead, we can derive a **best response curve** that, for each firm, shows the most profitable output choice for *each* of its rival's output choices. Let's begin by deriving Firm 1's best response curve. For a given level of Firm 2's output, q_2, Firm 1's demand function can be written as $P = (16,000 - 20q_2) - 20q_1$. What is Firm 1's marginal revenue? If Firm 1 were a monopolist, we already know from Chapter 8 that its marginal revenue curve would have twice the slope of the demand curve, but in this case Firm 1 is not a monopolist and must take into account the level of q_2. For any *constant level* of q_2, however, Firm 1's marginal revenue is still twice the slope of the demand curve, that is, $MR_1 = (16,000 - 20q_2) - 40q_1$, since $(16,000 - 20q_2)$ is a constant for any fixed level of q_2. To maximize its profit, Firm 1 sets its marginal revenue equal to its marginal

---

1 Formally, output is a continuous variable in this example.

cost. This yields $(16,000 - 20q_2) - 40q_1 = 10,000$, or after dividing each side by 20 and rearranging, $q_1 = (300 - q_2)/2$. This relationship between q_1 and q_2 is linear, as shown in Figure 10-1.

How do we interpret Figure 10-1? For any level of q_2 Firm 2 chooses, we can use the relationship in Figure 10-1 to find Firm 1's profit-maximizing response. For example, when $q_2 = 0$, Firm 1 can act as if it has no competitor, and, therefore, its profit-maximizing output is identical to the monopoly output we found in the earlier chapter—$q_1 = 150$. If we look at the other extreme, when $q_2 = 300$, Firm 2 produces the perfectly competitive output, and, therefore, Firm 1's profit-maximizing response is to produce $q_1 = 0$ (because price must be less than marginal cost to sell one more unit). Thus, for any level of q_2 between (and including) 0 and 300, Firm 1's profit-

Figure 10-1   Cournot Best Response Function

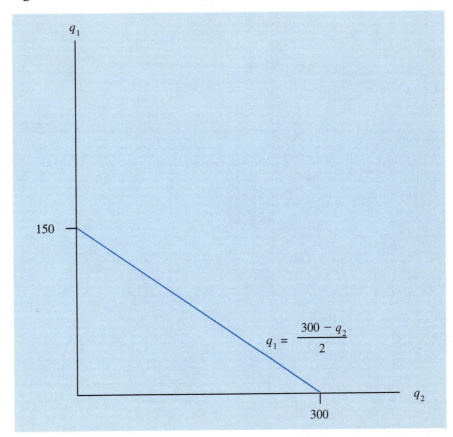

In a Cournot duopoly, each firm chooses its own output level by assuming that its rival's output is fixed. In this example, the function $q_1 = (300 - q_2)/2$ represents Firm 1's profit-maximizing choice of output for each of Firm 2's possible output levels.

maximizing response is found by the relationship $q_1 = (300 - q_2)/2$. Another way of saying the same thing is that Firm 1's **best response function** is $R_1(q_2) = (300 - q_2)/2$. Because we are assuming that the firms are identical, by symmetry we can see that Firm 2's best response function is $R_2(q_1) = (300 - q_1)/2$. Both firms' best response functions are shown in Figure 10-2. To put both firms' best response functions in the same graph, Firm 1's best response function from Figure 10-1 is inverted in Figure 10-2.

To find the Nash equilibrium of the Cournot game, we must find an output combination (q_1^*, q_2^*) such that neither firm has an incentive to deviate, given the output of its rival. As we already know from Chapter 9, each player must be best responding to its rival, or at least one of the players has an incentive to deviate. In Figure 10-2, therefore, the Nash (or Cournot) equilib-

Figure 10-2   Nash Equilibrium in the Cournot Model

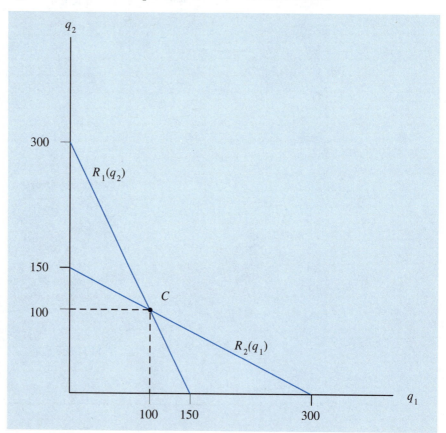

Each Cournot duopolist has a best response function—$R_1(q_2)$ for Firm 1 and $R_2(q_1)$ for Firm 2—that represents the profit-maximizing level of output for each firm, assuming its rival's output is constant. Where the two best response functions intersect, a Nash equilibrium is found. The Nash equilibrium in this Cournot example is at point C, where each firm produces an output level of 100.

rium must be at the intersection of the two best response functions—that is, point C at output levels $q_1^* = q_2^* = 100$.[2] At the combined level of output $q_1^* + q_2^*$, the industry price is $P = 16{,}000 - 20(q_1^* + q_2^*) = \$12{,}000$, and each firm's profit equals \$200,000 (i.e., total revenue = (100)(\$12,000) = \$1.2 million and total cost = (100)(\$10,000) = \$1 million).

If you refer back to Section 9.2, we introduced the concept of *prisoner's dilemma*, which identified the case in which the Nash equilibrium of a game is not the outcome the players would choose if they could cooperate perfectly. The Cournot equilibrium in Figure 10-2 is an example of the prisoner's dilemma. From Chapter 9, we already know that the maximum profit that can be found with the demand relationship $P = 16{,}000 - 20Q$ is the monopoly profit of \$450,000 (with monopoly output equal to 150). If each firm in our duopoly model agreed to produce half of the monopoly output, they would split the monopoly profit and each would receive a profit equal to \$225,000, which is greater than the Cournot profit of \$200,000. Why don't these firms play nice and increase their profits? Figure 10-3 answers this question.

In Figure 10-3, point M refers to the output combination (75, 75) where each firm produces half of the monopoly output. Remember, both firms choose their output levels simultaneously, so there is no way to see whether one firm is cheating before the other firm produces. Also, we will assume (as is the case under the antitrust laws) that it is illegal for the two firms to enforce cooperation by signing contracts. Why can't the firms sustain the outcome at point M? Consider Firm 1's choice of $q_1 = 75$. If Firm 1 believes that Firm 2's choice of $q_2 = 75$ is fixed, $q_1 = 75$ *is not a best response* for Firm 1. We know from Firm 1's best response function that when $q_2 = 75$, the profit-maximizing level of $q_1 = (300 - 75)/2 = 112.5$, which is shown at point B. Similarly, when Firm 1's output of $q_1 = 75$ is held constant, Firm 2's best response is $q_2 = 112.5$, as shown at point A. Quite simply put, the combination (75, 75) is not a Nash equilibrium, because each firm has an incentive to deviate from the cooperative outcome given that its rival's output is held constant. But for you future businessmen and businesswomen, don't worry. In the next chapter, we'll examine ways in which firms credibly overcome the prisoner's dilemma problem.

10.2   STACKELBERG DUOPOLY

With the Cournot duopoly model, both firms choose their output levels simultaneously. In the Stackelberg model, developed by German economist

---

2 Because we have two equations, $R_1(q_2)$ and $R_2(q_1)$, and two unknowns, q_1 and q_2, it is easy to find the equilibrium quantities. In Firm 1's best response function, replace q_2 on the left-hand side with $R_2(q_1)$, and then solve for q_1^*. Once you have q_1^*, plug it into $R_2(q_1)$ to find q_2^*. It is left as an exercise to verify that $q_1^* = q_2^* = 100$.

Figure 10-3   Comparing the Cournot Outcome to the Cooperative Outcome

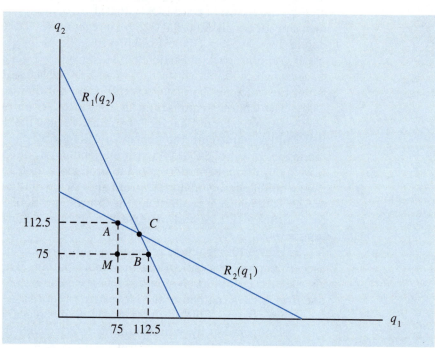

Point C represents the Cournot equilibrium. Point M represents the cooperative outcome in which each firm produces half of the monopoly output. Although *each* firm has a greater profit at point M than at point C, point M is not a Nash equilibrium, because if one firm produces 75, the other firm's best response is to produce 112.5.

Heinrich von Stackelberg, the firms choose their output levels *sequentially:* One firm is the **Stackelberg leader** and the other firm is the **Stackelberg follower.** In this example, Firm 1 will be the leader and Firm 2 will be the follower. The sequence of a Stackelberg game is as follows. Firm 1 chooses its output level, q_1. Firm 2 observes Firm 1's choice and then chooses q_2. With both output levels chosen, the market price is determined and each firm earns its profit.

To compare the Stackelberg and Cournot outcomes, we will use the previous demand function, $P = 16{,}000 - 20(q_1 + q_2)$. As with the sequential games we solved in Chapter 9, we will use backward induction and begin with Firm 2's output decision. Because Firm 2 observes q_1, for any level of q_1 Firm 2's demand is $P = (16{,}000 - 20q_1) - 20q_2$, and, therefore, its marginal revenue is $MR_2 = (16{,}000 - 20q_1) - 40q_2$. Setting $MR_2 = MC$, we have $(16{,}000 - 20q_1) - 40q_2 = 10{,}000$, which yields $q_2 = (300 - q_1)/2$. Thus, Firm 2's profit-maximizing response to any q_1 is found along Firm 2's best response function $R_2(q_1) = (300 - q_1)/2$. This is the same best response function that a Cournot firm faces. Why is this so? For a Cournot firm, the best response function is found by holding the rival's output choice constant. For a Stackelberg follower, the leader's output choice *is* a constant, since q_1 is chosen first. Thus, a Stackelberg follower always chooses its output level along its Cournot best response function.

Moving back up to the beginning of the game, Firm 1 must decide what output to produce, knowing exactly what Firm 2 will do in its role as the follower. Firm 1, then, cannot assume that Firm 2's output is a constant. On the contrary, Firm 2's output is found with the best response function $R_2(q_1) = (300 - q_1)/2$, which clearly depends on the level of output Firm 1 chooses. Given this, we have to find Firm 1's marginal revenue. We know that Firm 1's demand curve is $P = 16{,}000 - 20q_1 - 20q_2$. Because Firm 1 knows that Firm 2 will set $q_2 = (300 - q_1)/2$, Firm 1's demand curve can be rewritten as $P = 16{,}000 - 20q_1 - 20[(300 - q_1)/2] = 13{,}000 - 10q_1$. Thus, Firm 1's marginal revenue is $MR = 13{,}000 - 20q_1$. By setting marginal revenue equal to marginal cost, we have $13{,}000 - 20q_1 = 10{,}000$, which yields $q_1 = 150$. Plugging $q_1 = 150$ into Firm 2's best response function, we find $R_2(q_1) = (300 - 75)/2 = 75$.

Let's catalog what we have found so far. In this example, the Stackelberg leader (Firm 1) produces 150 units. The Stackelberg follower (Firm 2) produces 75 units. The price in the market is, therefore, $P = 16{,}000 - 20(150) - 20(75) = \$11{,}500$. The leader's total revenue is $(\$11{,}500)(150) = \$1{,}725{,}000$, its total cost is $(\$10{,}000)(150) = \$1{,}500{,}000$, and its profit is $TR - TC = \$225{,}000$. Along the same line, the follower's total revenue is $\$862{,}500$, its total cost is $\$750{,}000$, and its profit is $\$112{,}500$. Thus, by choosing its output level first, the Stackelberg leader has an advantage and earns a greater profit than the follower.

In looking at the market as a whole, we can compare the Cournot outcome to the Stackelberg outcome. Total output in the Cournot model is 200, and in the Stackelberg model it is 225. In the Cournot model, each firm earns a profit of $\$200{,}000$, for a total profit of $\$400{,}000$. With the Stackelberg model, the leader's profit is $\$225{,}000$ and the follower's profit is $\$112{,}500$, for a total profit of $\$337{,}500$. Thus, a Stackelberg leader does better than a Cournot firm, but a Stackelberg follower does worse. This raises an important question concerning the Stackelberg model: How is it decided which firm is the leader?

In choosing to model industry behavior with the Cournot or Stackelberg model, the key element is the type of firms competing against each other. If a duopoly is made up of similar firms, with no firm having an obvious advantage over the other, the Cournot model may be better. If, on the other hand, it appears that one of the firms is in the position of a leader, either because it is larger than its rival, or it generally announces its production decisions earlier than its rival, the Stackelberg model may be better. Thus, it generally isn't best to think of Stackelberg firms *choosing* to be the leader or the follower. It is more appropriate to apply the Stackelberg model to an industry setting in which one of the firms has already established itself in the leadership position.

APPLICATION
Hot Dog Vendor Duopoly

In both the Cournot and Stackelberg models, the firms use output as their strategic variable. Firms have many other strategic variables they can use, such as advertising, plant size, and product quality, among others. One obvious strategic variable that we have ignored so far is the product price. By simply switching output with price as a firm's strategic variable, we find a surprising result: Even with only two firms in the market, neither firm will set price greater than marginal cost.

As an example, consider a busy street corner in which two hot dog vendors—Tony and Barbara—set up their stands right next to each other. Each vendor sells identical hot dogs, buns, and fixings. The constant marginal cost of a hot dog is assumed to be \$1, and there are no fixed costs. The daily demand for hot dogs at this street corner is given by $Q = 250 - 50P$. Finally, we assume that consumers buy all their hot dogs from the vendor with the lower price, but if each vendor sets the same price, they exactly split the market and sell the same number of hot dogs.

If Tony and Barbara set their prices simultaneously, what is the Nash equilibrium? We know that to at least break even, neither will set a price less than marginal cost, so \$1 is our bottom-line price. What if each sets a price of \$3? With $P = 3$, $Q = 100$, and each vendor sells 50 hot dogs and earns a profit of \$100. But if Tony believes Barbara is going to maintain

10.3 OLIGOPOLY WITH MANY FIRMS

In the previous sections of this chapter, we have assumed that there are only two firms in the industry—a duopoly setting. Duopoly, however, is only a special case of oligopoly that is easy to deal with, especially graphically. Many industries have more than two firms competing against each other but are not perfectly competitive. The Cournot and Stackelberg models can be applied to industries consisting of many firms.

In the Cournot model, the Nash equilibrium will consist of all the firms simultaneously best responding to each other. Although we will not show this numerically or graphically, the more firms there are in a Cournot model, the more total output is produced. As the number of firms becomes *very large*, the Cournot outcome approaches the perfectly competitive outcome. In the Stackelberg model, with many firms, you may have one firm acting as a leader and many smaller firms acting as followers. The leader will choose its output level first, and each of the followers will best re-her price at \$3, Tony's best response is not \$3, but slightly less, say \$2.98. If Tony sets the lower price, he gets all the customers and sells $Q = 250 - 50(2.98) = 101$, for a profit of $(101)(1.98) = \$199.98$. Obviously, \$199.98 is greater than \$100, so each setting a price of \$3 is not a Nash equilibrium. But if Tony sets a price of \$2.98, Barbara's best response is to slightly undercut Tony and get all the customers for herself.

If we continue with this reasoning, the only Nash equilibrium is for each vendor to set price equal to marginal cost, \$1. If either vendor were to set a price above \$1, the other vendor's best response would be to slightly undercut it. If each vendor sets $P = \$1$, they each sell 100 hot dogs and earn zero profit. Thus, when price is the strategic variable used by firms, the Nash equilibrium consists of price being set equal to marginal cost—the competitive outcome.

Recall that price is greater than marginal cost in both the Cournot and Stackelberg models. Thus, the choice of the strategic variable is critical in determining the outcome of the model. Using price as a strategic variable is generally referred to as a **Bertrand assumption,** named after the French economist Joseph Bertrand, who first demonstrated how sensitive the Cournot model is to its assumptions. So, in deciding how to model duopoly behavior, not only must we be concerned with whether firms are making decisions simultaneously or sequentially, but also with what strategic variables firms appear to be using.

spond not only to the leader's output, but also to each other follower's output level.

Although the *quantitative* results change as you go from two firms to many firms in the Cournot and Stackelberg models, the *qualitative* results do not change. That is, the same game theoretic techniques that are used to examine a Cournot or Stackelberg duopoly may be used to examine a Cournot or Stackelberg oligopoly. In this section, we are going to examine two other models of oligopoly behavior that specifically account for industries with many firms—the **dominant firm model** and the **monopolistic competition model.**

Dominant Firm Model

In previous chapters, we examined two extreme market structures, perfect competition and monopoly. In a perfectly competitive industry, firms are price takers. As a monopolist, a firm is a price setter. In a dominant firm model, these two extremes are cleverly combined. There are two key elements to a dominant firm model. First, and no surprise, there is a **dominant**

firm that acts as the industry price setter. Second, there is a **competitive fringe** made up of many firms, each acting as a price taker. Unlike a competitive model, however, the competitive fringe firms do not simply accept the price that is found by the intersection of an industry demand curve with an industry supply curve. In a dominant firm model, the dominant firm sets the price that the competitive fringe takes as given. How the dominant firm chooses its profit-maximizing price is the topic of this section.

As a monopolist, a firm has the industry demand curve all to itself. As a dominant firm, this is no longer the case. In Figure 10-4, the upward-sloping curve, labeled S_F, is the supply curve of the competitive fringe. This supply curve is derived in the same way a competitive industry's supply curve is derived: It is the horizontal sum of the individual price-taking firms' supply curves. The downward-sloping curve, labeled D_I, is the usual industry demand curve. Ordinarily, a monopolist prices along the industry demand curve. But in a dominant firm model, at any price set by the dominant firm, some output will be supplied by the competitive fringe.

In Figure 10-4, three prices are shown along the vertical axis. If the dominant firm sets the high price, P_H, what happens? The competitive fringe, acting as price-taking firms, produces the output level Q_2 along the supply curve S_F. By producing Q_2, however, the fringe is able to satisfy the whole demand at P_H, which is also Q_2. This leaves nothing for the dominant firm to produce. Therefore, point A represents one point along the dominant firm's demand curve.

If the dominant firm sets the middle price, P_M, the fringe produces the amount Q_1. What is left for the dominant firm to produce? At price P_M, the total quantity demanded in the market is Q_4. Because the fringe produces Q_1 of the Q_4 units, what is left for the dominant firm to produce is $(Q_4 - Q_1) = Q_3$. Point B, therefore, is another point on the dominant firm's demand curve.

Finally, if the dominant firm sets the low price, P_L, the fringe will not be willing to supply any amount. The dominant firm, at this price, can produce the total amount demanded in the market, Q_5. In this case, point C is another point on the dominant firm's demand curve. At any price below P_L, the competitive fringe will not supply any amount, and the dominant firm's demand curve exactly corresponds with the industry demand curve.

By connecting the points A, B, and C, and by following the original demand curve below price P_L, we have traced out the dominant firm's demand curve. This curve is referred to as a **residual demand curve.** It is a residual demand curve because it represents the market demand that is left for the dominant firm to produce *after* the competitive fringe has supplied all they can at a given price. Now that we have derived the dominant firm's demand curve, we can turn to the issue of what price the dominant firm sets to maximize its profit.

In Figure 10-5, several curves are depicted. Along with the supply curve for the competitive fringe, S_F, the industry demand curve, D_I, and the resid-

Figure 10-4   Dominant Firm Model

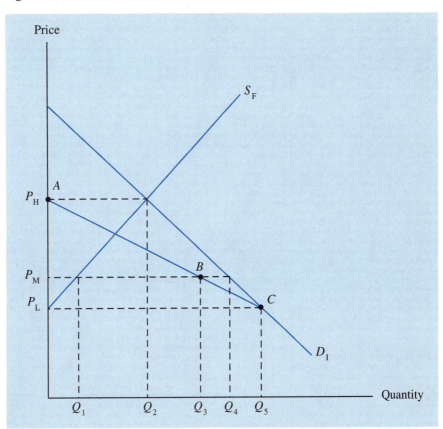

In a dominant firm model, the dominant firm sets the price and the competitive fringe produces along its supply curve, S_F, at that price. The difference between what the fringe produces and quantity demanded along the industry demand curve, D_I, represents what is left for the dominant firm to produce. At price P_M, for example, the fringe supplies Q_1, the quantity demanded in the industry is Q_4, and what is left for the dominant firm is $Q_4 - Q_1 = Q_3$. By repeating this for each price, the dominant firm's residual demand curve is found to be made up of two parts: the line connecting points A, B, and C above the price P_L and the industry demand curve, D_I, below the price P_L.

ual demand curve for the dominant firm, D_R, there are two other curves: the marginal revenue curve to the residual demand curve, MR_R, and the dominant firm's marginal cost curve, MC_D. Exactly like a monopolist, the dominant firm sets marginal revenue equal to marginal cost to find its profit-maximizing price and output. In Figure 10-5, with $MR_R = MC_D$, the profit-maximizing price is P^*, and the dominant firm's output is Q_D. Unlike a monopolist, however, at the price P^* the competitive fringe supplies Q_F, for a total amount produced of $Q_D + Q_F = Q_T$.

Figure 10-5   The Dominant Firm's Profit-Maximizing Price

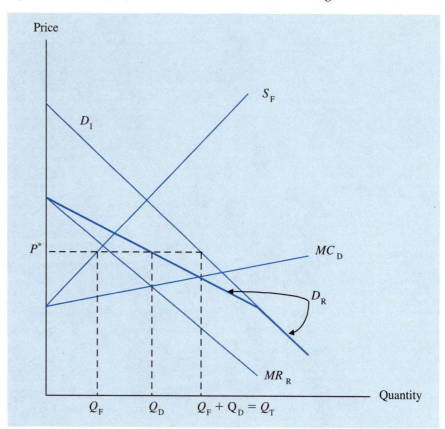

To find its profit-maximizing price, P^*, the dominant firm sets its marginal revenue, MR_R, equal to its marginal cost, MC_D. At price P^*, the dominant firm produces Q_D, the competitive fringe produces Q_F, and the total output produced is Q_T.

Dominant Firms in Representative Industries

Professor William Shepherd has long been interested in identifying markets with dominant firms. Table 10-1 provides examples of some of these industries for the year 1976.[3] The market share that is provided is the share of the dominant firm only.

---

3 William G. Shepherd. *The Treatment of Market Power.* (New York: Columbia University Press, 1975). Updated in W.G. Shepherd. *The Economics of Industrial Organization.* (Englewood Cliffs, N.J.: Prentice-Hall, 1979).

Table 10-1   Dominant Firms in Representative Industries

Market	Dominant Firm	% Market Share
Heavy electrical equipment	General Electric	50
Photographic supplies	Eastman Kodak	65
Copying equipment	Xerox	75
Aircraft	Boeing	45
Flavoring syrups	Coca-Cola	50
Canned soup	Campbell Soup	80
Razors/toiletries	Gillette	65
Dry cereals	Kellogg	45

Monopolistic Competition

Another oligopoly model that combines aspects of monopoly pricing and perfect competition is monopolistic competition. In monopolistic competition, each firm faces a downward-sloping demand curve, and, therefore, each firm is a price setter. Unlike a monopolist, however, each firm faces competition from its rivals. The competition comes from firms that produce similar, but not identical, products. Thus, a monopolistically competitive market is characterized by some degree of **product differentiation**—that is, product differences that give firms some power over price, but not complete monopoly power.

For example, there are many fast-food restaurants. Anyone who regularly eats at these restaurants can easily tell the difference between a "Whopper" and a "Big Mac." Even though each fast-food chain produces a somewhat unique product, it is not so unique as to give the chain full monopoly power. Another example involves shoe stores. A quick walk through any large shopping mall usually reveals an astounding number of shoe stores. Each store may have unique brands of shoes, but clearly each of these stores is in competition with the others. When firms compete against each other, even if the goods they produce are not perfect substitutes, it is difficult to sustain a positive profit without attracting entry of new firms in the long run.

Figure 10-6 demonstrates the short-run and long-run equilibria for a monopolistically competitive firm. With the short-run demand curve, D_{SR}, and its marginal revenue curve, MR_{SR}, the firm simply sets marginal revenue equal to marginal cost and produces output level Q_{SR} at price P_{SR}. At that price, however, the firm earns positive profit, because P_{SR} is greater than average cost. If the firm were a pure monopolist, the story could end here. But because it is a monopolistically competitive firm, its positive profit attracts entry of firms that produce similar, but not identical, products. As entry occurs and these new products are made available to customers, the firm's demand curve begins to shift inward. This happens because the firm loses some

Figure 10-6   Monopolistic Competition

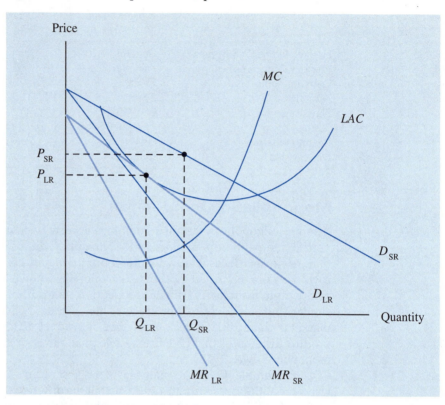

In the short run, a monopolistically competitive firm produces where $MR_{SR} = MC$, at a price of P_{SR}. Because this price is greater than average cost, the firm earns positive profit. In the long run, firms that produce similar, but not identical, products are attracted into the market, causing the firm's long-run demand curve to shift. Long-run equilibrium occurs where $MR_{LR} = MC$, and where D_{LR} is tangent to the average cost curve so that no profits are earned.

customers to the new entrants. In Figure 10-6, the firm's demand curve continues to shift inward until the new long-run demand curve, D_{LR}, is just tangent to the average cost curve. This occurs at output level Q_{LR}, at price P_{LR}. Notice at Q_{LR}, the firm still sets marginal revenue equal to marginal cost, except now it is the long-run marginal revenue, MR_{LR}. Because P_{LR} is exactly equal to average cost, the long-run equilibrium for the monopolistically competitive firm has it earning zero profit, just like a perfectly competitive firm. So even though a monopolistically competitive firm has the power to set price, it is constrained to earn zero profit in the long run because of the potential entry of firms that produce slightly differentiated products.

Summary

- **Oligopoly** refers to a market structure with more than one firm but less than "very many" firms. Examples of oligopolies include **duopoly**—exactly two firms in the market; **dominant firm model**—one price-setting firm and many price-taking firms in the market; and **monopolistic competition**—many price-setting firms in the market.

- In a **Cournot duopoly,** each firm uses output as its *strategic variable,* and both firms choose their output levels simultaneously. The output level in a Cournot duopoly is greater than the monopoly output level but less than the perfectly competitive output level.

- In a **Stackelberg duopoly,** the firms choose their output levels *sequentially.* One firm acts as a **Stackelberg leader,** and the other firm acts as a **Stackelberg follower.** Compared to the Cournot model, a Stackelberg leader makes more profit than does a Cournot firm, but a Stackelberg follower makes less profit than does a Cournot firm.

- In a **dominant firm** model, one firm acts as the industry price setter, and many firms act as price takers. The dominant firm's demand curve is a **residual demand curve**—that is, at every price level the price-taking firms supply as much as they can of the total demand, and the rest is left over for the dominant firm. The dominant firm maximizes profit by producing at the point where its marginal cost equals the marginal revenue of the residual demand curve.

- A **monopolistically competitive market** is characterized by some degree of *product differentiation*—that is, product differences that give firms some power over price, but not complete monopoly power. Even though a monopolistically competitive firm has the power to set price, it is constrained to earn zero profit in the long run because of the potential entry of firms that produce slightly differentiated products.

Problems

1. Assume the demand function for a good is given by $P = 70 - Q$, where P is the product price and Q is the industry output. There are only two firms in the industry, and the total industry output is the sum of the firms' individual outputs—that is, $Q = q_1 + q_2$. Each firm has a constant marginal cost of production $MC = 10$, and there are no fixed costs.

    a. Find the Cournot equilibrium levels of output for each firm. How much profit does each firm make?

    b. If the two firms could perfectly cooperate, what level of output would each produce? How much profit would each firm make? Explain why perfect cooperation is not a Nash equilibrium in this case.

    c. If Firm 1 is a Stackelberg leader and Firm 2 is a Stackelberg follower, what level of output would each firm produce? How much profit would each firm make?

2. In Chapter 8, we compared the monopoly model to the perfectly competitive model with respect to social welfare. How do the Cournot and Stackelberg models compare to the other two models in this respect? (*Hint:* It may help you to use a numerical example like the one used earlier in this chapter.)

3. Is the Stackelberg equilibrium a subgame-perfect Nash equilibrium? Explain.

4. In the Stackelberg model, what would happen if both firms tried to be the leader? What would happen if both firms tried to be the follower? Could the firms use a mixed strategy to determine who leads and who follows? Explain.

5. In industries that have a dominant firm, such as those shown in Table 10-1, what factors do you think can be responsible for allowing one firm to be dominant?

6. How does the follower in a Stackelberg model compare to a fringe firm in a dominant firm model?

7. Does the outcome in the dominant firm model create a deadweight loss? What about the outcome in a monopolistic competition model? Explain.

8. Compare the short-run equilibrium of a perfectly competitive firm with that of a monopolistically competitive firm. What about the long-run equilibrium?

9. Product differentiation is a key element of the monopolistic competition model. Provide some real-world examples of how firms differentiate their products. Do you think that consumers always benefit from product differentiation?

11

COLLUSION

Overview

In the chapter on monopoly power, we saw that a monopolist earns a greater profit than do all the firms in a competitive industry. If all the competitive firms could band together and produce as one firm, they could perfectly mimic a monopolist. Firms that explicitly collude to act in unison are known as a **cartel.** A cartel's objective is to maximize the joint profit of all its member firms. In any industry, then, there is some advantage to cartelization. While probably the most famous cartel in the world is the Organization of Petroleum Exporting Countries (OPEC), the lure of increased profit has led to attempted cartelization in such diverse industries as the electrical equipment, concrete, railroad, and swimsuit industries. When an industry is not at its joint profit-maximizing level of profit, there is *always* an incentive to cartelize. Whether or not the goal of cartelization can be achieved successfully is the topic of this chapter.

In this chapter, we will examine two types of collusion, explicit and tacit. **Explicit collusion** is when firms formally agree to act as a cartel. **Tacit collusion** is when firms do not formally agree to act in unison, but still implicitly act interdependently to improve their profit level relative to the competitive outcome. For example, in Chapter 10 we saw that in the Cournot duopoly model, the two firms did not explicitly collude. In the Cournot outcome, however, each firm earns a positive profit. Had the firms credibly been able to maximize their joint profits, they would have been a cartel.

The difference between explicit and tacit collusion is important for how we choose to model collusion. In our cartel model, the objective will be to maximize the joint profit of the member firms. In the tacit collusion models we will examine, the objectives will be to find subgame-perfect Nash equilibria that improve on the noncooperative outcomes. In this chapter, you will learn:

- How to find a cartel's profit-maximizing price and level of production for each member firm.
- How a cartel can achieve and maintain its outcome.
- How players can credibly sustain cooperation in games in which they play against each other repeatedly.
- How infinitely repeated games differ from finitely repeated games.

11.1 JOINT PROFIT MAXIMIZATION

Consider a duopoly industry in which the two firms act as a cartel. If the firms explicitly collude, the profit-maximizing outcome is to produce the monopoly output. In panel (c) of Figure 11-1, the monopoly output, Q_M, is found where the industry marginal revenue curve intersects the industry marginal cost curve. (The industry marginal cost curve is the horizontal sum of the individual firms' marginal cost curves.) The joint profit-maximizing cartel price is P_M.

How do the individual firms decide how much of Q_M each should produce? Recall that to maximize profit, the monopolist must minimize its total cost. For however much total output the cartel produces, cost minimization requires the individual firms' marginal costs to be equal, that is, $MC_1 = MC_2$. To see why this is so, if at the last unit produced by Firm 1 we have $MC_1 > MC_2$, the cartel could gain by having that last unit produced by Firm 2 instead. For each successive unit that the cartel wants to produce, profit maximization requires that the more efficient firm produce that unit. When the marginal costs are equal, there is no way to redistribute production between the two firms to lower costs. For profit maximization, then, not

Figure 11-1   Cartel Profit Maximization

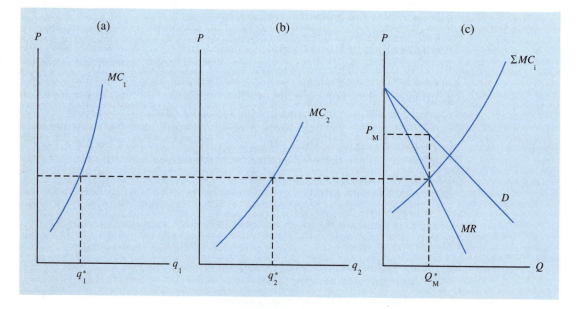

To maximize profit, the cartel sets the industry marginal revenue equal to the industry marginal cost, ΣMC_i. In panel (c), the profit-maximizing price and output are P_M and Q_M^*. In dividing production between the two firms, the cartel equates the two firms' marginal costs. Thus, cartel profit maximization requires $MC_1 = MC_2 = MR$. This occurs in panels (a) and (b) at output levels q_1^* and q_2^*, respectively, and at price P_M.

only must $MC_1 = MC_2$, but marginal revenue must equal industry marginal cost so that the cartel cannot gain by producing one more or one less unit. Looking at all three panels in Figure 11-1, all this occurs when Firm 1 produces q_1^*, firm 2 produces q_2^*, and the industry price is P_M.

If a cartel can maximize industry profit, it seems that firms should prefer cartelization to any form of competition. Why, then, don't we observe more cartels in the real world? Cartels are inherently unstable. Recall from Chapter 10 the Cournot duopoly example. We argued that if the two firms could cooperate perfectly, they would both increase their profits. However, the cooperative outcome was not a Nash equilibrium, because, given the strategy of its rival, each firm had an incentive to increase its output. In the Cournot model, the firms are not joint profit maximizers; that is, it is a *non-cooperative* model. But even if we assume that the firms explicitly cooperate to maximize industry profit, successful cartelization is difficult to achieve and even more difficult to maintain.

Conditions Favorable for Cartelization

A group of firms attempting to form a cartel has many obstacles to overcome. Not the least of their worries is that cartelization, often referred to as *price fixing*, is against the law. Price fixing violates the antitrust laws—statutes that prohibit many types of monopolistic practices. Of course, just because price fixing is against the law does not mean that firms don't attempt to fix prices. The firms must weigh the benefits of cartelization against the *expected punishment* they face from violating the law. The expected punishment depends upon two factors: the probability of being caught and found guilty, multiplied by whatever fine is eventually imposed. The expected punishment can be low, then, either because it is not likely the cartel will be caught or because the fine will be small. Breaking the law, however, can be just a minor obstacle. Even if it were perfectly legal for firms to cartelize, it could still be an extremely difficult task.

Consider some of the difficulties in achieving the cartel outcome. Firms wishing to cartelize must agree on the cartel price and each firm's level of production. The more firms there are, the greater the negotiation costs are. If the firms do not have similar marginal costs of production, the cartel must allocate more production to efficient firms and less production to the inefficient firms. There is bound to be some disagreement over the allocation of production. Also, the nature of the product is important. If a product has many *dimensions*, such as an automobile's size, engine power, interior comfort, gas mileage, stereo quality, and so forth, an agreement on price is not enough. If these other dimensions are not agreed upon, individual firms could cheat on the cartel by offering more quality, for example, without undercutting the cartel price. More product dimensions, then, also imply greater negotiation costs.

If the cartel can successfully achieve its desired outcome, it then must be able to maintain that outcome. Threats to the cartel can come from two sources—member firms and nonmember firms. If there are firms in the industry that are not part of the cartel, they may be able to undercut the cartel price and not be restricted by any rules the cartel attempts to enforce on its members. Also, a successful cartel will earn positive profits. Positive profits attract entry of new firms into the industry. With entry, the cartel now has to worry about either bringing more firms into the cartel or facing competition from firms that do not abide by the cartel's rules. The longer it takes for entry to occur, however, the more gains there can be from cartelization.

Even without the problem of nonmember firms threatening the cartel, each member firm will have an incentive to cheat on the cartel. As we have already discussed, cooperative outcomes tend to be unstable. A successful cartel must be able not only to detect cheating, but also to reduce each firm's incentive to cheat. Practices that aid a cartel in these goals are referred to as **facilitating practices.**

One type of facilitating practice is **most-favored-customer (MFC) pricing.** An MFC pricing policy guarantees the customer a rebate if the firm lowers its price in the future. In Chapter 8, we saw that this policy allows a durable good monopolist to prevent its price from falling over time. In a cartel, a firm that adopts MFC pricing can credibly discourage itself from cheating in the future. If the firm tries to undercut the cartel price, it must pay rebates to previous customers. These rebates act as a punishment that reduce the incentive to cheat on the cartel.

In Chapter 8, we discussed the use of MFC pricing in the electric turbogenerator industry to sustain the price of a durable good. An alternative explanation for the behavior of the two firms—General Electric and Westinghouse—is that they used MFC pricing to sustain a cartel price and facilitate cartelization. The two explanations, however, need not conflict. It is possible that the firms were attempting to cartelize a *durable* good. If this is the case, MFC pricing protected price erosion from two possible sources—the durable good problem *and* cheating on the cartel.

An example of a facilitating practice that can aid the cartel in detecting cheating is a **meeting competition clause (MCC).** If a firm adopts an MCC (in a long-term sales contract, for example) it guarantees its customers that it will match the lowest price available or it will release its customers and allow them to buy from another firm at the lower price. This type of pricing policy aids the firm in detecting cheating from other firms. If a firm's customers return to the firm and demand a lower price because they found a lower price elsewhere, the firm knows for a fact that some other firm was not adhering to the cartel price. Basically, this MCC policy allows the firm to use its customers as information gatherers.

An MCC also has the ability to reduce the gains from cheating. If rival firms adopt meeting competition clauses, a cheater has less to gain if it lowers its price. When a firm undercuts the cartel price, it sells more units of output to two groups—its original customers and new customers. If rival firms have the opportunity to match price cuts, the cheating firm will not gain as many new customers, and thus the gains from price cutting will be reduced.

An example of an industry in which firms used an MCC to possibly facilitate cartelization is the lead-based antiknock compounds industry. These compounds are added to gasoline to prevent engine "knock." Throughout the mid to late 1970s, there were only four domestic manufacturers of antiknock compounds in the United States, led by the two largest—Ethyl and DuPont. The MCC guaranteed a buyer the lowest possible price as long as the best price was reported to the company the buyer had the original contract with. In this way, the firms could monitor each others' price fluctuations.

One other facilitating practice is a **trigger price.** After agreeing on a cartel price, the members of a cartel can use that price as a *punishment trigger.* What this means is that if any firm lowers its price below the trigger, all the other firms immediately respond by lowering their prices to some predetermined punishment level for some amount of time. If all the firms respond to one firm's price cut, the gains from cheating are much smaller and the incentive to cheat is reduced.

Throughout the 1880s, the Joint Executive Committee railroad cartel apparently used trigger pricing to facilitate cartelization. Professor Robert Porter studied that cartel's pricing practices.[1] He concluded that there were three main periods of reversion to the noncooperative (or punishment) price level, one each in 1881, 1884, and 1885. Each punishment period lasted for about 10 weeks, and then price returned to the higher cartel level. This pricing pattern demonstrated the willingness of the cartel to punish cheating, but to then forgive and forget—until the next time.

As can be seen in Table 11-1, successful cartels have a longer length of agreement. Also, successful cartels are found in industries in which the concentration of production is high. Short-term substitutes are more of a problem for unsuccessful cartels, but long-term substitutes are more of a problem for successful cartels. This isn't surprising, since successful cartels will eventually attract substitutes in the long run. Finally, we argued earlier that cost differences among firms make it more difficult to cartelize. Table 11-1 confirms this point, as successful cartels have fewer cost differences than unsuccessful cartels.

11.2 INFINITELY REPEATED GAMES

The first class of games in which we will examine tacit collusion is **infinitely repeated games.** In these games, it is assumed that the players know that

---

1 Robert Porter. "A Study of Cartel Stability: The Joint Executive Committee, 1880–1886." *Bell Journal of Economics,* Vol. 14, 1983, pp. 301–314.

APPLICATION
The Experience of International Commodity Cartels

In a 1976 book, Paul Eckbo studied the performance of several international commodity cartels. Table 11-1 provides some characteristics of 23 incidents of cartelization between the years 1901 and 1964. The specific industries include rubber, mercury, aluminum, tin, sugar, steel, tea, and copper. A successful cartel was defined by Eckbo to be one that could raise its price to at least three times the marginal cost of production and distribution. An unsuccessful cartel would not be able to raise its price that high. Of the 23 incidents, 9 were successful and 14 were not. The five characteristics presented in Table 11-1 are defined by Eckbo* to be:

1. Average Length of Agreement—The length of survival of the formal agreement, in years.
2. Concentration of Production—The concentration of production in the industry is regarded as being high if the four largest producers produce more than 50 percent of the total output of the industry; if this is the case, the industry gets a score of 1; otherwise, a score of 0 is assigned.
3. Short-Term Substitutes—If short-term substitutes for the commodity exist, the value of 1 is assigned; if no substitutes exist, 0 is assigned.
4. Long-Term Substitutes—Scored the same as (3).
5. Cost Differences Among Cartel Members—A score of 1 is given if the high-cost producers produce at a cost no larger than 50 percent above the low-cost producers; otherwise, a score of 0 is given.

* Paul Eckbo. *The Future of World Oil.* (Cambridge, MA: Ballinger Publishing Co., 1976), pp. 27–28.

the game has no specific end period. This may seem like an extreme assumption, but it really isn't. An infinitely repeated game can be shown to be perfectly analogous to a finite game in which there is a positive probability that the game will continue for one more period. In any given period, then, the players believe that there is some probability that the game will continue. Thus, at the start of the game, no player can be certain as to when the game will end. This is exactly the key characteristic of an infinitely repeated game. In contrast, in a **finitely repeated game,** each player knows the specific end date of the game. As we will see in Section 11.3, a known end period can prevent credible cooperation. In an infinitely repeated game, credible cooperation is quite possible.

Table 11-1   Cartel Characteristics

	Successful	*Unsuccessful*
Number of Cartels	9.0	14.0
Average length of agreement (years)	5.0	3.1
Average concentration of production (High = 1; Low = 0)	0.90	0.36
Average short-term substitutes (Yes = 1; No = 0)	0.22	0.43
Average long-term substitutes (Yes = 1; No = 0)	0.77	0.43
Average cost differences (Low = 1; High = 0)	0.90	0.58

Consider the simple game shown in Figure 11-2. Each player has a dominant strategy—NC for Row and NC for Column. (The NC represents *noncooperation*.) At the (dominant strategy) Nash equilibrium, each player's payoff is 2. If the players could perfectly cooperate, however, the outcome would be (C, C) and each player's payoff would be 4. (The C represents *cooperation*.) At the cooperative outcome, *both players* are better off than at the Nash equilibrium. We already know from Chapter 9 that (C, C) is not a Nash equilibrium if the game is played a single time. But what if the players could play the game over and over again forever? For example, the players could be two firms that compete with each other every day. If the game is repeated infinitely often, the players have an incentive to always cooperate with each other. In other words, there may be a strategy combination that allows each player to receive a payoff of 4 in every stage. What we must be very careful about is that the strategy combination we propose be credible; that is, it must be a subgame-perfect Nash equilibrium strategy combination.

The Grim (Trigger) Strategy

As in the case with a sequential game, any strategy we propose in an infinitely repeated game must specify a player's action for every possible con-

Figure 11-2   A Normal-Form Game

Column

		C	NC
Row	C	4, 4	1, 5
	NC	5, 1	2, 2

tingency. In other words, our strategy must specify an action for each stage of the game. Consider the following proposed strategy for Row:

> Choose C in stage 1. Continue to choose C as long as the outcome is (C, C) in the previous period. If (C, C) is not observed in the previous period, choose NC forevermore.

This strategy is called a **grim (trigger) strategy.** It is a trigger strategy because a single case of noncooperation by *either player* triggers a punishment by Row. It is a grim strategy because the punishment *lasts forever.* We can also propose the identical grim (trigger) strategy for Column:

> Choose C in stage 1. Continue to choose C as long as the outcome is (C, C) in the previous period. If (C, C) is not observed in the previous period, choose NC forevermore.

Now that we have proposed our strategies, we can check to see whether they make up a Nash equilibrium; that is, is each player's strategy a best response to the other player's strategy? Before we answer this question, we must assume that each player has a discount factor $\delta < 1$. In an infinitely repeated game, if we do not discount future payoffs, the present value of any positive payoff stream is infinite. This would make it impossible to distinguish between any two streams. With $\delta < 1$, the payoff streams from different strategies will differ. As we will see, the size of δ will determine whether the grim trigger strategies make up a Nash equilibrium.[2]

We begin by considering Row's best response to Column's grim strategy. When we hold constant Column's grim strategy, Column plays C in stage 1. If Row chooses its grim strategy, it will play C in stage 1 and receive a payoff of 4. Because the stage 1 outcome is (C, C) and we are holding constant Column's strategy, Column will pick C in stage 2. If Row continues to respond to Column's grim strategy by playing its own grim strategy, it will choose C in stage 2 and again receive a payoff of 4. Thus, given Column's grim strategy, if Row responds with its own grim strategy, Row will receive a payoff of 4 in *every stage.* In terms of present value, Row's payoff is $4/(1-\delta)$. (Recall from Chapter 2 that a constant payoff k received over an infinite number of periods has a present value of $k/(1-\delta)$.)

If Row's grim strategy is the best response to Column's grim strategy, $4/(1-\delta)$ must be the greatest present-value payoff that Row can receive. What is the best payoff Row can get if it deviates from its grim strategy? Remember, we must hold constant Column's grim strategy, which means that Column plays C in stage 1. In stage 1 alone, then, Row's best response to C is NC. This gives Row a payoff of 5 (instead of 4) in stage 1. But beginning

---

2 If, instead of assuming the game is infinitely repeated, we assume it is a finite game with an unknown end period, δ can be interpreted as the probability in each period that the game will continue for one more period.

in stage 2, given Column's grim strategy, Column plays NC forevermore because the outcome (C, C) was not observed in stage 1. If Column plays NC
forevermore, Row's best response is NC forevermore. Thus, if Row deviates
from its grim strategy in stage 1, it receives a payoff of 5 in stage 1 and a
payoff of 2 in every other stage. The present value of this payoff stream is
$5 + 2\delta/(1-\delta)$. (The present value *in stage 2* of receiving a constant k forever
more is $k/(1-\delta)$, and that value in terms of a stage 1 present value is
$\delta[k/(1-\delta)]$.)

For Row's grim strategy to be a best response to Column's grim strategy, it must be the case that

$$4/(1-\delta) > 5 + 2\delta/(1-\delta).$$

By multiplying each side by $(1-\delta)$, we get

$$4 > 5(1-\delta) + 2\delta.$$

By collecting terms and rearranging, the inequality holds if $\delta > 1/3$. Thus,
if $\delta > 1/3$, Row's best response to Column's grim strategy is its own grim
strategy. Because the game is symmetric (i.e., Column faces the same possible payoffs that Row faces), $\delta > 1/3$ is also the condition needed to prevent
Column from deviating from its grim strategy.

What we have found so far is that the discount factor must be *sufficiently
large* for the grim strategies to constitute a Nash equilibrium. The intuition
behind this result is that for the players to not deviate from the cooperative
outcome, they must care enough about the future so that the punishment is
effective. For example, if $\delta = 0$, the players do not care about the future at
all. If this is the case, the gain from deviating in stage 1 (a payoff of 5 instead of 4) cannot be offset by the loss beginning in stage 2 (a payoff of 2
instead of 4 forevermore). In our example, for any $\delta < 1/3$, the players do
not care enough about the future to make the punishment effective. But even
for $\delta > 1/3$, we still must check to see whether the punishment is *credible*.
That is, while the strategies make up a Nash equilibrium, is it a subgame-
perfect Nash equilibrium?

Subgame Perfection and the Grim Strategy

For the grim strategies to make up a subgame-perfect Nash equilibrium,
they must make up a Nash equilibrium in every subgame. In an infinitely
repeated game, however, there are an infinite number of subgames. Figure
11-3 helps explain what the subgames look like for the infinitely repeated
game shown in Figure 11-2.

In Figure 11-3, the game itself begins in stage 1. After the game is played
in stage 1, there are four possible outcomes: (C, C), (C, NC), (NC, C), and

Figure 11-3   An Infinitely Repeated Game

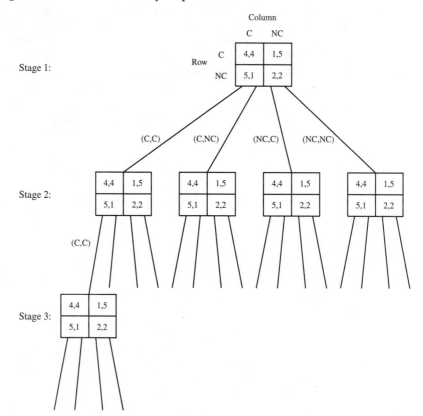

(NC, NC).[3] After each of these possible outcomes, the game is repeated in stage 2. Therefore, in stage 2, four subgames begin. Each subgame that begins in stage 2 looks exactly like the whole game that begins in stage 1, since the game is played infinitely often. The only distinguishing factor between the four subgames is each subgame's *past history*. In stage 3, sixteen subgames begin, since there are sixteen possible past histories. Once again, each subgame looks like the whole game. While it is obviously impossible to represent the whole game, Figure 11-3 conveys the general idea. In this infinitely repeated game, each subgame is identical to the whole game, and each subgame is distinguished by its past history of play.

With an infinite number of subgames, it appears to be a frightening task to check whether the grim strategies make up a Nash equilibrium in every

---

3 In this game, we are considering pure strategies only. If we were to allow for mixed strategies, there would be an infinite number of outcomes in stage 1.

subgame. Fortunately, we only have to worry about two classes of subgames: One class begins after the cooperative outcome is chosen, and the other class begins after a noncooperative outcome is chosen. Consider the four sub-games that begin at stage 2 in Figure 11-3. Of these subgames, one begins after the players choose the cooperative outcome (C, C). The other three begin after at least one of the players chooses a noncooperative outcome. For the grim strategies to make up a subgame-perfect Nash equilibrium, they must make up a Nash equilibrium in each of the four cases. Let's see if they do.

In the subgame that begins after the cooperative outcome (C, C), if we hold constant Column's grim strategy, Column will choose C in stage 2 since (C, C) was previously observed. If Row adheres to its grim strategy in stage 2, it will also cooperate and choose C. Thus, beginning in stage 2, when the past history has been cooperation, and if Row responds with its grim strat-egy to Column's grim strategy, then Row will receive a payoff of 4 forever-more, for a present value of $4/(1-\delta)$. What if Row deviates from its grim strategy? Exactly as we argued in the previous section, given Column's grim strategy, if Row deviates in stage 2 it will receive a payoff of 5 immediately but then be punished with a payoff of 2 forevermore, for a present value of $5 + 2\delta/(1-\delta)$. As long as $\delta > 1/3$, then, neither player will deviate from the grim strategy in the subgame that begins in stage 2 after cooperation in stage 1.

What about the other three subgames in stage 2 that begin after a non-cooperative outcome in stage 1? In each of these subgames, if we hold con-stant Column's grim strategy, Column will choose NC in stage 2 and forever-more, since (C, C) was not previously observed. If Column chooses NC forevermore, Row's best response is NC forevermore. Likewise, if Row chooses NC forevermore, Column's best response is NC forevermore. Be-cause both players are best responding to each other, (NC, NC) forevermore is Nash equilibrium for the subgame that begins in stage 2 after noncoop-eration in stage 1. More generally, any Nash equilibrium for a *single stage* of the game, such as (NC, NC), can be a Nash equilibrium for *every stage* of the game.

What can we conclude from this discussion? Regardless of which stage we begin with, in the infinitely repeated game shown in Figure 11-3, there are two classes of subgames: those that have a past history of cooperation in every previous stage and those that have at least one instance of nonco-operation. In the first class of subgames, adherence to the grim strategy leads to cooperation forevermore. Cooperation forevermore is a Nash equilibrium in the first class of subgames if the discount factor is sufficiently large. In the second class of subgames, adherence to the grim strategy leads to the noncooperative outcome (NC, NC) forevermore. This noncooperative out-come is a Nash equilibrium in the second class of subgames if it is a Nash equilibrium in a single stage of the game. In this example, (NC, NC) is a credible punishment outcome since it is a Nash equilibrium in a single stage.

Therefore, as long as $\delta > 1/3$, the grim strategies make up a subgame-perfect Nash equilibrium.

Infinitely Repeated Cournot Duopoly

In Chapter 10, we discussed in detail a Cournot duopoly example for the demand function $P = 16{,}000 - 20(q_1 + q_2)$, where q_1 and q_2 are Firm 1's and Firm 2's output, respectively. We also assumed that each firm's marginal cost and average cost are constant, with $MC = AC = \$10{,}000$. We found the Cournot output to be $q_c = 100$ and the Cournot profit to be $\pi_c = \$200{,}000$ for each firm. We also found that at the joint profit-maximizing level of output, each firm would produce half the monopoly output, $q_m = 75$, and each firm would increase its profit to $\pi_m = \$225{,}000$. In a single playing of the game, however, the joint profit-maximizing outcome is not a Nash equilibrium. Recall that if one firm's output of $q_m = 75$ is held constant, the other firm's best response would not be $q_m = 75$, but would be $q_d = (300 - q_m)/2 = 112.5$. If the game is infinitely repeated, however, the firms may be able to sustain the joint profit-maximizing outcome. Let's propose a grim strategy for each firm.

> Choose the joint profit-maximizing output q_m in stage 1. Continue to choose q_m as long as the outcome is (q_m, q_m) in the previous period. If (q_m, q_m) is not observed in the previous period, choose the Cournot outcome q_c forevermore.

This grim strategy is analogous to the one we proposed earlier. With the Cournot game, the grim strategy specifies that as long as both firms choose the joint profit-maximizing outcome, there will be no punishment. But if either firm deviates, the punishment will be the Cournot outcome forevermore. We already know that if we are in the class of subgames in which there has been a deviation from q_m in its past history, the punishment outcome (q_c, q_c) is credible since the Cournot outcome is a Nash equilibrium in a single stage of the game. All that is left to do to demonstrate that the grim strategies make up a subgame-perfect Nash equilibrium is to find how large the discount factor must be to prevent each firm from deviating from the joint profit-maximizing outcome.

We already have most of the information we need to find the threshold discount factor. When both firms adhere to the grim strategy, they each earn the joint profit-maximizing profit $\pi_m = \$225{,}000$ forevermore. If in stage 1 one firm deviates from q_m, holding constant the other firm's output level at q_m, the most profitable deviation is $q_d = 112.5$. What profit does the firm earn from deviating? With one firm producing $q_m = 75$ and the other firm producing $q_d = 112.5$, the industry price is $P = 16{,}000 - 20(75 + 112.5) = \$12{,}250$. Therefore, the firm that deviates has $TR = (\$12{,}250)(112.5) = \$1{,}378{,}125$ and $TC = (\$10{,}000)(112.5) = \$1{,}125{,}000$. The profit from deviating is $\pi_d = TR - TC = \$253{,}125$. Once the firm deviates, however, the other firm, by adhering to its grim strategy, chooses the Cournot output q_c forever-more. The deviating firm's best response to q_c forevermore is also to produce q_c forevermore and earn a profit of $\pi_c = \$200,000$ in every stage.

Is it profitable for one firm to deviate from its grim strategy in stage 1? No it isn't, if the following inequality holds:

$$\pi_m/(1-\delta) > \pi_d + \pi_c\delta/(1-\delta).$$

The term on the left-hand side is the present-value profit of adhering to the grim strategy. The term on the right-hand side represents the immediate gain from deviating, π_d, plus the present value of the punishment profit forevermore, $\pi_c\delta/(1-\delta)$. When we plug in all the numbers, we find the inequality holds if

$$225,000/(1-\delta) > 253,125 + 200,000\delta/(1-\delta), \text{ or}$$

$$225,000 > 253,125(1-\delta) + 200,000\delta, \text{ or}$$

$$53,125\delta > 28,125, \text{ or}$$

$$\delta > 0.529.$$

For the symmetric Cournot firms in this example, then, the grim strategies make up a subgame-perfect Nash equilibrium if $\delta > 0.529$. Again we have shown that in an infinitely repeated game, the cooperative outcome can credibly be sustained if the discount factor is sufficiently large.

11.3   FINITELY REPEATED GAMES

Consider the game shown in Figure 11-4. If the game is played just once, the Nash equilibrium is (R_2, C_2). The cooperative outcome, however, is (R_1, C_1), where each player is better off than at the Nash equilibrium. The cooperative outcome is not a Nash equilibrium, because given Column's strategy C_1, Row has an incentive to deviate to R_2. If this game is infinitely repeated, we can propose a grim strategy that will sustain the cooperative outcome throughout the whole game. But what if the game is repeated a fi-

Figure 11-4   A Normal-Form Game

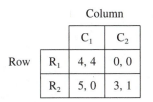

		Column	
		C_1	C_2
Row	R_1	4, 4	0, 0
	R_2	5, 0	3, 1

nite number of times? Can we still propose a credible strategy combination that will sustain the cooperative outcome?

Let's begin to answer this question with a simple two-stage playing of the game in Figure 11-4. In stage 1, the players will choose one of the four possible outcomes, and then they'll play the game one last time in stage 2. As in Figure 11-3, there are four possible subgames to consider beginning in stage 2. But unlike Figure 11-3, there are no other subgames to consider. Subgame perfection requires that the players' strategies make up a Nash equilibrium in every subgame. In this example, there is only one Nash equilibrium for the game played in stage 2—(R_2, C_2). Because the players never meet again after stage 2, it is impossible to propose any further punishment strategies to make them play cooperatively in stage 2. Therefore, the only credible outcome in stage 2 is the single-stage Nash equilibrium (R_2, C_2). Whatever strategies we propose, then, must have Row choose R_2 and Column choose C_2 in stage 2.

What we have done so far is to use backward induction to solve the game, just as in Chapter 9. We have shown that *regardless* of what the players do in stage 1, the only credible outcome in stage 2 is (R_2, C_2), and Row receives a payoff of 3 and Column receives a payoff of 1. If we now move to the beginning of the game at stage 1, the players can look ahead and know what their payoffs must be in stage 2. Whatever payoff the players get in stage 1, Row knows that it gets 3 more and Column knows that it gets 1 more in stage 2. Therefore, we can alter Figure 11-4 in a way that incorporates the second-stage payoff of (3, 1) into the first-stage game. Figure 11-5 presents such an alteration.

In Figure 11-5, a payoff of 3 is added to all of Row's payoffs from Figure 11-4, and a payoff of 1 is added to all of Column's payoffs. For example, if the stage 1 outcome is (R_1, C_1), then because the stage 2 outcome must be (R_2, C_2), Row gets a *total payoff* of $4 + 3 = 7$, and Column gets a total payoff of $4 + 1 = 5$. In Figure 11-5, each player's actions are for stage 1 only, but the payoffs are summed over *both stages*, given that the stage 2 outcome will be (R_2, C_2). In Figure 11-5, there is only one Nash equilibrium—(R_2, C_2). Therefore, the cooperative outcome (R_1, C_1) cannot be sustained if the game is repeated for two stages.

Before we continue with this discussion, we want to point out something about discounting future payoffs. You may have already noticed that

Figure 11-5   The Revised Normal-Form Game

		Column	
		C_1	C_2
Row	R_1	7, 5	3, 1
	R_2	8, 1	6, 2

in this section we do not discount the players' second-stage payoffs. In other words, we are implicitly assuming that $\delta = 1$. In the infinitely repeated games of the previous section, we needed to use discounting (i.e., $\delta < 1$) so that all the present-value payoffs would not equal infinity. In this finite game, discounting would only affect the *quantitative* results (the payoffs would change), but it would not affect the *qualitative* results (cooperation cannot be sustained in the first period). When an assumption cannot affect the qualitative results we are showing, but can make the example easier to present, it is a useful assumption to adopt.

Backward Unraveling

What if we repeat the game in Figure 11-4 for a larger but still *finite* number of stages? For example, if the game is repeated for 10 stages, can the players credibly sustain the cooperative outcome for any amount of time? Although we will not use a figure to represent the 10-stage game, we can use our intuition to answer this question. Let's use backward induction and begin with the 10th stage. In stage 10, the players play the game for the last time. Because they never meet again, there is no credible future punishment that allows them to sustain the cooperative outcome in stage 10. In fact, there is only one credible outcome in stage 10—the Nash equilibrium (R_2, C_2).

Now let's move back to stage 9. The only way to sustain cooperation in stage 9 is to be able to punish in stage 10. But we already know that no matter what the players do in stage 9, the stage 10 outcome will be (R_2, C_2). In stage 9, then, each player has an incentive to deviate from the cooperative outcome (R_1, C_1) because what happens in stage 10 is independent of the stage 9 outcome. The only credible outcome in stage 9 is also the single-stage Nash equilibrium (R_2, C_2).

If you continue with this line of reasoning back through stages 8, 7, 6, and so on, you will find that the only credible outcome in *every stage* is the outcome (R_2, C_2). No matter how many times we repeat this game, as long as it is a finite number of times, the only credible outcome is (R_2, C_2) in every stage. The players' failure to sustain the cooperative outcome in a finitely repeated game, even for a single stage, is known as **backward unraveling.**

Backward unraveling implies that in any finite game in which there is only *one* single-stage Nash equilibrium outcome, it becomes the only credible outcome in every stage. If the Nash equilibrium is not the cooperative outcome, there is no credible way to sustain the cooperative outcome in any stage. In a finite game, there is a definite last stage. In the last stage, cooperation is not possible, because there is no future punishment mechanism. In the second-to-last stage, the only way to sustain the cooperative outcome is to reward cooperative behavior and punish noncooperative behavior in the next stage. But the next stage is the last stage, and cooperative behavior in the second-to-last stage cannot credibly be rewarded with cooperative behavior in the last stage. The last stage of the game dictates the behavior of all the previous stages, right back until stage 1.

In an infinitely repeated game, *there is no last stage*. Thus, there can be a credible punishment (such as the grim strategy) that sustains the cooperative outcome in every stage. Is it possible to have a finitely repeated game that does not fall victim to backward unraveling? The answer is yes, as we will now demonstrate.

Credible Cooperation in Finitely Repeated Games

In Figure 11-6, we have added another action for each player of the game shown in Figure 11-4. In this game, there are two (pure strategy) Nash equilibria—(R_2, C_2) and (R_3, C_3). Neither of these outcomes, however, would be preferred by either player to the cooperative outcome (R_1, C_1). We know that if the game is played a single time, the cooperative outcome is not a Nash equilibrium, because Row would deviate to R_2 given Column's choice of C_1. But in this case, if we repeat the game, it is now possible to propose a strategy combination that will allow the players to credibly sustain the cooperative outcome for some amount of time.

Let's repeat the game for two stages. Consider the following strategy for Row:

> Choose R_1 in stage 1. In stage 2, choose R_2 if (R_1, C_1) was observed in stage 1. If any outcome other than (R_1, C_1) was observed in stage 1, choose R_3 in stage 2.

And now we propose a strategy for Column:

> Choose C_1 in stage 1. In stage 2, choose C_2 if (R_1, C_1) was observed in stage 1. If any outcome other than (R_1, C_1) was observed in stage 1, choose C_3 in stage 2.

Do these strategies make up a subgame-perfect Nash equilibrium strategy combination?

As usual, we will use backward induction to answer this question. The proposed strategies allow for two possible outcomes in stage 2. If (R_1, C_1) was observed in stage 1 and the players adhere to the above strategies, Row

Figure 11-6   A Normal-Form Game

Column

		C_1	C_2	C_3
	R_1	4, 4	0, 0	0, 0
Row	R_2	5, 0	3, 1	0, 0
	R_3	0, 0	0, 0	1, 2

chooses R_2 and Column chooses C_2 in stage 2. Is (R_2, C_2) a credible outcome in stage 2? Yes, because it is a single-stage Nash equilibrium. If (R_1, C_1) was not observed in stage 1 and the players adhere to the above strategies, Row chooses R_3 and Column chooses C_3 in stage 2. Is (R_3, C_3) a credible outcome in stage 2? Yes again, because it also is a single-stage Nash equilibrium. By backward induction, then, the proposed strategies can lead to two possible credible outcomes in stage 2. All that is left to check is whether the proposed stage 1 actions of R_1 and C_1 are also credible.

As we did with Figures 11-4 and 11-5, we can alter Figure 11-6 in a way that shows the total two-stage payoffs for the players' stage 1 actions. We already know the only two possible outcomes in stage 2—(R_2, C_2) and (R_3, C_3). If we match the credible stage 2 outcomes with each of the possible stage 1 outcomes and sum the payoffs from each stage, we can create Figure 11-7. For example, if the stage 1 outcome is (R_1, C_1), the proposed strategies lead to a stage 2 outcome of (R_2, C_2). In this case, Row receives a total of $4 + 3 = 7$, and Column receives a total of $4 + 1 = 5$. Thus, the payoff in Figure 11-7 for the stage 1 outcome of (R_1, C_1) is (7, 5).

For any stage 1 outcome *other than* (R_1, C_1), the proposed strategies lead to a stage 2 outcome of (R_3, C_3) and payoffs of 1 for Row and 2 for Column. If we add 1 to each of Row's payoffs and 2 to each of Column's payoffs for every stage 1 outcome other than (R_1, C_1), we can fill in the rest of Figure 11-7. For example, if the stage 1 outcome is (R_2, C_1), the stage 2 outcome will be (R_3, C_3) and Row will receive a total of $5 + 1 = 6$ and Column will receive a total of $0 + 2 = 2$. Figure 11-7 shows the total payoffs the players will receive over both stages based on their stage 1 actions and their proposed stage 2 actions.

In Figure 11-7 there are three Nash equilibria—(R_1, C_1), (R_2, C_2), and (R_3, C_3). The first of these outcomes, however, is the cooperative outcome, since both players prefer it to the other two outcomes. What we have demonstrated is that with the strategies just given, the players can credibly choose (R_1, C_1) in stage 1 and (R_2, C_2) in stage 2. Cooperation can be sustained in stage 1.

Intuitively, the problem with the cooperative outcome is that Row would deviate from it. In a repeated game, to prevent Row from deviating, Col-

Figure 11-7   The Revised Normal-Form Game

Column

		C_1	C_2	C_3
	R_1	7, 5	1, 2	1, 2
Row	R_2	6, 2	4, 3	1, 2
	R_3	1, 2	1, 2	2, 4

umn must have a credible strategy that rewards Row in stage 2 if there was cooperation and punishes Row in stage 2 if there was a deviation. For the punishment to be credible, it must be part of a Nash equilibrium outcome in stage 2. Unlike the previous 2 by 2 game, there are now two credible outcomes in stage 2. The first outcome, (R_2, C_2) yields a payoff of 3 to Row, while the second, (R_3, C_3), yields a payoff of only 1 to Row. The first outcome, then, can act as a reward. The second outcome can act as a punishment. The difference between the reward payoff and the punishment payoff to Row is 2. The gain to Row from deviating in stage 1 from the cooperative outcome is only 1 (a payoff of 5 instead of 4). As long as the reward and punishment outcomes are credible, Row prefers the stage 2 reward over the stage 1 deviation *plus* the stage 2 punishment.

Experimental Evidence on Backward Unraveling

Although there have been many experiments on repeated games, we will spotlight just one by Selten and Stoecker on the existence of backward unraveling.[4] Using a game similar to the one illustrated in Figure 11-2, Selten and Stoecker had subjects repeat the game for 10 stages. At the end of the 10th stage the game was over. Then, the players would start the 10-stage game over again. In all, subjects played the 10-stage game a total of 25 times.

The theoretical prediction of backward unraveling is that, in a finitely repeated game, the players will not be able to sustain the cooperative outcome in any single stage. Selten and Stoecker found that the players were able to sustain cooperation for several of the 10 stages, but then there would be a defection. After the defection, the noncooperative outcome would be sustained for the rest of the game. As subjects played this 10-stage game over and over, however, they eventually learned to defect from the cooperative outcome *earlier* in the game. This behavior provides some experimental confirmation of backward unraveling.

Summary

- Firms that *explicitly* collude to act in unison are known as a **cartel.** *Tacit* collusion is when firms do not formally agree to act in unison, but still

---

4 Selten and Stoecker. "End Behavior in Sequences of Finite Prisoner's Dilemma Supergames: A Learning Theory Approach." *Journal of Economic Behavior and Organization*, Vol. 7, 1986, pp. 47–70.

implicitly act interdependently to improve their profit level relative to the competitive outcome.

- To maximize profit, a cartel must have each member firm produce its output at the point where all the firms' marginal costs are equal to each other and also equal to the industry's marginal revenue.

- Threats to the success of a cartel can come from two sources—nonmember firms and member firms. In general, cartel outcomes are unstable.

- Practices that aid a cartel in achieving and maintaining the cartel outcome are referred to as **facilitating practices.**

- In an **infinitely repeated game,** it is assumed that the players know the game has no specific end period. In contrast, in a **finitely repeated game,** each player knows the specific end date of the game.

- In an infinitely repeated game, strategies can be proposed that allow players to credibly support a cooperative outcome if the players are sufficiently patient. An example of such a strategy is a **grim trigger strategy.** With a grim trigger strategy, a player cooperates forevermore unless there is a single case of noncooperation by *any* player. If there is a case of noncooperation, the player doesn't cooperate forevermore.

- In any finite game, because there is a definite last period, **backward unraveling** implies that if there is only one single-stage Nash equilibrium outcome, it becomes the *only* credible outcome in every stage. If the Nash equilibrium is not the cooperative outcome, there is no credible way to sustain the cooperative outcome in any stage.

- If a finite game has more than one single-stage Nash equilibrium, it may be possible to propose strategies that allow the players to credibly sustain a cooperative outcome, even if the cooperative outcome is *not* a single-stage Nash equilibrium itself.

Problems

1. When most-favored-customer pricing is used to facilitate collusion, it can be detrimental to consumers. Are there possible benefits that MFC pricing can have for consumers? In answering this question, consider two types of consumers—those who buy a final good for personal consumption and those who buy an intermediate good to use as an input in the production of a final good.

2. The meeting competition clause we discussed in Section 11.1 had the firm meet *or* release its customer if a lower price was found elsewhere. Another type of MCC is a meet *no* release clause, which guarantees the cus-

tomer that the original firm will match any lower price but not allow the customer to buy elsewhere. Which type of MCC would more effectively facilitate collusion? Which type would consumers prefer? Which type would individual firms prefer?

3. In each of the following infinitely repeated games, each player has a discount factor δ and plays the following grim trigger strategy:

> Choose C in stage 1. Continue to choose C as long as the outcome (C, C) is observed in the previous period. If (C, C) is not observed in the previous period, choose NC forevermore.

In each game, under what conditions do the grim trigger strategy combinations make up a subgame-perfect Nash equilibrium? (*Hint:* The first game is symmetric, the last two are not.)

a.

		Column	
		C	NC
Row	C	5, 5	1, 7
	NC	7, 1	3, 3

b.

		Column	
		C	NC
Row	C	6, 5	1, 6
	NC	8, 2	5, 3

c.

		Column	
		C	NC
Row	C	4, 4	3, 5
	NC	5, 1	2, 2

4. In the infinitely repeated Cournot example discussed in Section 11.2, we found that the firms could credibly sustain the monopoly outcome of $q_M = 75$ as part of a grim trigger strategy if $\delta > 0.529$. If $\delta < 0.529$, it is still possible to do better than the Cournot outcome, but not as well as the monopoly outcome. Use the same example to demonstrate that this is true for the following grim trigger strategy, used by each firm:

> Choose the cooperative output $q_i = 90$ in stage 1. Continue to choose $q_i = 90$ as long as the outcome (q_i, q_i) is observed in the previous period. If (q_i, q_i) is not observed in the previous period, choose the Cournot outcome $q_c = 100$ forevermore.

5. For each of the two period games below, can you propose a subgame-perfect strategy combination that will sustain the outcome (R_3, C_3) in the first period?

a.

Column

		C_1	C_2	C_3
	R_1	2, 2	1, 3	5, 1
Row	R_2	0, 2	3, 3	1, 1
	R_3	1, 5	2, 1	4, 4

b.

Column

		C_1	C_2	C_3
	R_1	1, 3	1, 2	2, 1
Row	R_2	0, 0	2, 1	1, 0
	R_3	0, 5	1, 3	4, 4

12

LABOR MARKETS

Overview

There are several reasons for devoting an entire chapter to labor markets. First, the supply of labor is different from standard notions of supply. Usually, supply curves are derived from the behavior of firms, but labor is supplied by individual workers, and so labor supply is derived from a utility-maximization problem. Second, the demand for labor is different from standard notions of demand. Usually, demand curves are derived from the behavior of consumers, but labor is demanded by firms, and so labor demand is derived from a profit-maximization problem. Third, labor market issues are interesting in their own right. So, for example, we can discuss issues such as why some people earn such high salaries and how government programs affect earnings and employment.

The study of labor markets also leads to discussion of some topics related to getting a job. In many cases, when a firm identifies a potential employee, the firm and the employee negotiate a contract. The tools of game theory can be used to analyze bargaining processes and to identify ways in which the two parties can strengthen their bargaining power, thereby getting a better deal. Before any of this can occur, however, a job applicant must get a job offer, and the employer must find a suitable applicant to make the offer to. In this chapter we formalize the job search process, transforming it into a comparison of the benefits and costs of further search. Studying the search process uses some of the tools introduced in Chapter 4.

All of this can be made more concrete by using an example. Consider the case of a college student who is considering whether or not to get a part-time job. One issue the student must face is how much she wants to work. This depends on the wage she can earn, of course, but it also depends on how she values her time. It might be that her time is better spent studying, sleeping, or relaxing. We will analyze this decision formally using budget lines and indifference curves. On the other side of the market, the firm must determine how much labor it wants to employ at a given wage rate. For the firm to demand some additional labor, it must be able to sell the output at a price high enough to cover the additional labor cost. Again, we can analyze this decision formally using the tools of producer theory. The wage that the student will receive, and that the firm must pay, is determined by the market as a whole. So it is worthwhile to identify some of the factors that affect the supply and demand for labor and thereby affect the market wage.

Before the student can work she has to find a job. It takes time to apply for a job, so she does not want to apply for too many of them. How does she know when to stop searching? Put another way, which jobs are good enough to take even though there might be some higher-paying jobs that she hasn't applied for yet? Finally, once she finds a job, she might be able to negotiate her salary. This is not likely for part-time jobs, but it might occur if she gets a job caring for children, for example. Does it help to have another offer when trying to negotiate a higher salary?

We address all of these issues in this chapter. In particular, you will learn:

- How workers determine how much labor to supply at a given wage.

- How firms determine how much labor to demand at a given wage.

- How to use supply and demand analysis to investigate issues regarding equilibrium wages and levels of employment.

- How workers and firms behave in the bargaining process and what can be done to increase bargaining power.

- How workers optimally search for a job.

12.1 LABOR SUPPLY

To analyze the labor market, it is helpful to analyze the supply side and the demand side of the market separately, just as we did with other types of goods. Labor is supplied by workers, so in this section we look at the behavior of individual workers. The tools we use are identical to those introduced in Chapters 2 and 3, the chapters on preferences and consumer choice. In this section, however, the questions are slightly different. Specifically, given the choice between working, which earns money, and not working, how much does an individual work? If the wage rate rises, do individuals work more or less? If the income tax rate rises, do people work more or less? These are the questions to be answered in this section.

The Choice of How Much to Work

Rose is deciding how much to work in a week. She doesn't particularly like to work and derives no enjoyment from it. But if she works she earns income, which can be used to purchase consumption goods. If she doesn't work, she forgoes this income, but she can then enjoy some leisure activities, such as reading, watching movies, playing volleyball, or sleeping. Suppose that her job pays $7 per hour and she can choose how many hours to work. There are 168 hours in a week. How many of them does she work?

Figure 12-1   The Decision to Work

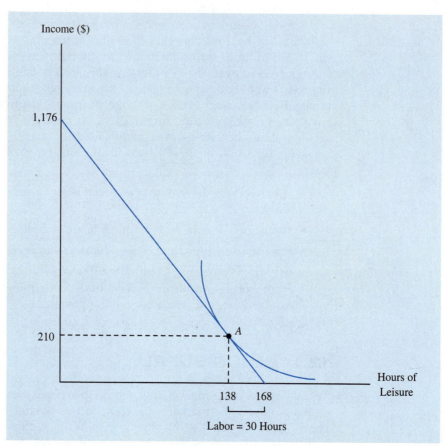

The decision of how much to work in a week can be modeled using budget lines and indifference curves. The budget line shows how working can transform leisure time into income. If Rose works one more hour, she consumes one less hour of leisure but receives one hour's wages. In the case shown, the wage rate is $7 per hour, so the slope of the budget line is −7. The optimal combination of leisure and income is given by point A, the point on the budget line that is on the highest indifference curve. In the case shown here, she consumes 138 hours of leisure. She works for 30 hours, and earns $210.

This question can be answered using budget lines and indifference curves. Figure 12-1 shows one of Rose's indifference curves over income and leisure. Rose gets utility from income because she can purchase consumption goods with it, and leisure is a catch-all category of all the activities she can do if she is not at work. The indifference curve has the standard shape discussed in Chapter 2. The figure also shows a budget line. If Rose consumes only leisure and no income, the most leisure she can consume in a week is the entire week, or 168 hours. So, the point (168, 0) is on the budget line. If she consumes only income and no leisure, she earns 168 · 7 = $1,176 during the week. So, the point (0, 1,176) is also on the budget line. To find a general equation for the budget line, note that if Rose consumes L hours of leisure, she works 168 − L hours, and earns 7(168 − L). Her income, then, is

$$I = 7(168 - L) = 1176 - 7L,$$

and this is the equation of the budget line. Its vertical intercept is 1,176, and its slope is −7, or the negative of the wage.

Rose's optimal combination of income and leisure is shown by point A, where the indifference curve is tangent to the budget line. At this point, Rose consumes 138 hours of leisure, so she works 168 − 138 = 30 hours and earns 7 · 30 = $210 per week. As in Chapter 3, it is possible to interpret the tangency condition. The slope of the indifference curve is the marginal rate of substitution, which is the most income Rose is willing to give up for an additional hour of leisure. The slope of the budget line is the amount of income Rose has to give up to consume an additional hour of leisure. If she consumes one more hour of leisure, she gives up one hour of work, which translates into $7 of income. At point A, the most income she is willing to give up for more leisure is exactly equal to the amount she has to give up to get the extra leisure.

The slope of the budget line can also be interpreted as the *opportunity cost* of leisure—that is, the value of time in its best alternative use. If Rose gives up one hour of leisure, she can work for an extra hour and earn an extra $7. So Rose's opportunity cost of time, or, equivalently, her **value of time,** is $7 per hour, or the wage she earns.

Wage Increases and Labor Supply

What happens if Rose's wage rate increases to $10 per hour? In Figure 12-2, her budget line rotates upward from the dark blue line to the light blue line. When the wage is $10 per hour, if she works all 168 hours her income is 168 · 10 = $1,680, which is the vertical intercept of the new budget line. If she consumes only leisure, then the most she can consume is still 168 hours, so the horizontal intercept does not change. The budget line becomes steeper when the wage rises.

In panel (a) of Figure 12-2, the new tangency point is B. Rose now consumes only 132 hours of leisure, which means that she works 168 − 132 = 36 hours during the week, and earns 36 · 10 = $360 during the week. How can we explain this? When the wage rate rises from $7 to $10 per hour, the opportunity cost of leisure rises from $7 to $10. Since leisure becomes more expensive, Rose consumes less of it, which means that she works more. Her income rises for two reasons. First, she is working six more hours than before. Second, she gets paid more per hour. The important point, though, is

Figure 12-2   The Effect of a Wage Increase

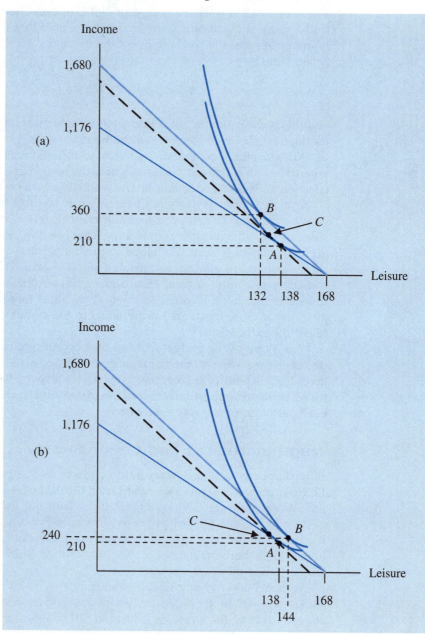

that in the case depicted in panel (a), when the wage rises, Rose supplies more labor.

Panel (b) of Figure 12-2 tells a different story. In this panel, when the wage rises the new tangency point is again labeled *B*, and at this point Rose consumes *more* leisure than before. She consumes 144 hours of leisure, which means that she works for only 24 hours, and earns $240 during the week. This time when the wage rises Rose supplies *less* labor. How do we explain this? When the wage rises, Rose gets more income to spend. One of the things she can spend it on is leisure, which now costs $10 per hour. Because of the extra income, the extra leisure is worth the price, so she consumes more leisure.

To get a clearer picture of what is going on, it is helpful to separate Rose's choice into income and substitution effects, as in Section 3.5. To do this, return to panel (a) of Figure 12-2. First draw an imaginary budget line parallel to the new budget line and tangent to the original indifference curve. This is the dashed budget line in panel (a), and point *C* is the tangency point. The *substitution effect* is the movement from point *A* to point *C*, and it is caused by the change in the opportunity cost of leisure. Since leisure becomes more expensive, Rose consumes less of it, and the substitution effect is negative. The *income effect* is the movement from point *C* to point *B*, which looks like the effect of a standard income increase from Chapter 3. If leisure is a normal good, when Rose earns more income she consumes more leisure, so the income effect is positive. In panel (a), the positive income effect only partially offsets the negative substitution effect, and consumption of leisure declines. In panel (b), however, the income effect more than offsets the substitution effect, and consumption of leisure increases. Rose still earns more income, even though she works less, as can be seen in the fact that the thick budget line is positioned farther from the origin than the dashed budget line. So whether the amount of labor supply increases or decreases when the wage rate rises depends on the relative sizes of the income and substitution effects.

It is possible to make some general statements about how labor supply responds to the wage rate. If someone is currently earning a low wage, other

---

What happens when the wage rises from $7 to $10? Because the slope of the budget line is the negative of the wage, the budget line rotates upward, as shown in both panels. The optimal combination of leisure and income moves from point *A* to point *B* in both panels. In panel (a) the worker consumes less leisure as a result of the wage increase, but in panel (b) the worker consumes more leisure.

We can gain some insight into why leisure increases for some preferences but decreases for others by looking at income and substitution effects. Draw an imaginary budget line parallel to the new, steeper budget line and tangent to the original indifference curve. This yields point *C*. The change in leisure in the movement from *A* to *C* is the substitution effect, which says that workers consume less leisure when its opportunity cost rises. The change in leisure in the movement from *C* to *B* is the income effect, which shows whether leisure is a normal or inferior good. In panel (a) leisure is inferior, but in panel (b) it is normal.

consumption goods are likely to be more important to that individual than leisure. Consequently, when income rises, most of the extra income is devoted to other consumption goods, and the income effect on leisure is small. In this case, the increase in the wage rate would lead to a decrease in consumption of leisure and an increase in the quantity of labor supplied. In contrast, if someone is earning a very high wage, when the wage increases the individual might prefer to consume more leisure rather than more consumption goods. In this case, a wage increase leads to an increase in consumption of leisure and a decrease in the quantity of labor supplied. Figure 12-3 summarizes this by showing what is thought to be a typical individual

Figure 12-3   Labor Supply Curve

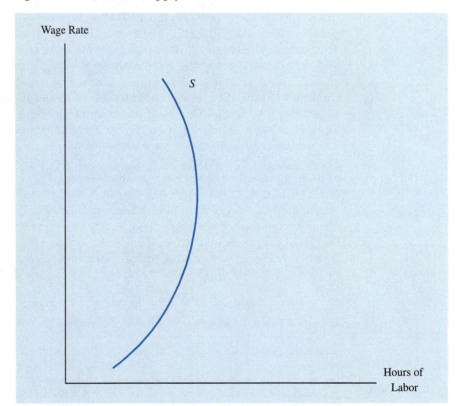

This figure shows what a typical individual's labor supply curve is thought to look like. When wages are low, an increase in the wage leads to an increase in the quantity of labor supplied and, therefore, a decrease in the consumption of leisure. This occurs because when wages are low, leisure is an inferior good. When the wage rate gets high enough, however, further increases in the wage lead to decreases in the quantity of labor supplied, and the labor supply curve becomes backward bending. This occurs because when income is high enough, leisure is a normal good and increases in the wage are used to pay for increases in leisure. The upward-sloping portion of the supply curve is consistent with the preferences shown in Figure 12-2(a), and the backward-bending portion is consistent with Figure 12-2(b).

APPLICATION
Income Taxes and the Labor–Leisure Trade-Off

When individuals must pay income taxes, it affects their labor–leisure decisions by changing the opportunity cost of leisure. Suppose that someone earns $10 per hour and that the individual pays 15 percent of her income to the government. This means that if the individual works one hour less, she only gives up $8.50 in income, which is the opportunity cost of an hour of leisure. Now suppose that the income tax rate rises to 20 percent. Then the after-tax wage, and hence the opportunity cost of leisure, falls to $8.00 per hour. The effect of this change on the individual's labor supply decision depends on which portion of the labor supply curve the individual is on. If she is on the upward-sloping portion of the labor supply curve, the increase in the tax rate reduces the after-tax wage, and she works less than before. Thus, an increase in income tax rates causes this type of person to work less. If, on the other hand, the individual is on the backward-bending portion of the labor supply curve, an income tax increase causes the individual to work more. Either way, income tax changes have an effect on the labor–leisure trade-off, and because of this income taxes are **distortionary.** Distortionary taxes alter individuals' decisions at the margin.

labor supply curve. The wage rate is shown on the vertical axis, and the number of hours worked is shown on the horizontal axis. When the wage rate is low, an increase in it leads to an increase in the number of hours worked, and the labor supply curve slopes upward. At some point the wage rate gets high enough that a further increase in it leads to a decline in the number of hours worked, and the labor supply curve bends backward.

12.2 LABOR DEMAND

We now turn our attention to the demand curve for labor. Labor is used by firms, so the demand for labor is derived from the behavior of firms. Firms choose the amount of labor that maximizes profit. For example, grocery stores must decide how many cashiers to have on duty at a given time. In making this decision, the grocery store manager weighs the benefit of having one more cashier against the cost of having one more cashier. If the benefit outweighs the cost, the manager brings in one more cashier. If, instead, the cost is greater than the benefit, the manager does not bring in the extra cashier. This is the same type of marginal analysis used by a profit-maximizing firm in Chapter 6, and it does not just apply to the use of labor, but to the use of other inputs as well.

Short-Run Labor Demand

Let's begin with the case of a strawberry farmer who is deciding how many migrant workers to hire to pick strawberries on a given day. The strawberries can be sold for $4 per bushel, and one additional worker can pick 20 bushels of strawberries in a day. The worker is paid $40 for the day. Should the farmer hire the worker or not? If she hires the worker, she can sell an additional 20 bushels of strawberries for a total of $80, so her revenue increases by $80. She must pay the worker $40, so her cost increases by $40. Her profit increases by $80 − 40 = $40. By hiring the additional worker, the farmer's profit rises, so she should hire the additional worker.

We can state all of this more formally. If the farmer hires an additional unit of labor, output rises by the marginal product of labor, MP_L. In this example, $MP_L = 20$. This additional output is sold at the market price p, which, in this case, is $p = 4$. The additional revenue from one more unit of labor, then, is $p \cdot MP_L = 80$. The additional cost of one more unit of labor is the wage rate, denoted w. The rule is to hire the additional unit of labor if $p \cdot MP_L > w$ and to reduce labor by one unit if $p \cdot MP_L < w$. From this we can see that the farmer hires labor until $p \cdot MP_L = w$, that is, until the additional revenue generated by the last unit of labor is exactly equal to the cost of the last unit of labor.

One thing is special about the strawberry farming industry: It is competitive. In a competitive industry, the market price does not depend on how much is produced by a single firm. This means that if the farmer hires an additional unit of labor and produces more strawberries, the extra revenue is still $4 per bushel. If the industry is not competitive, the extra output has the effect of lowering the market price, which makes a difference to our analysis. So consider instead the case of a firm with some monopoly power hiring an additional unit of labor. The additional unit of labor increases output by MP_L units, as before. This time, however, the increased output has an effect on the price the firm receives, so instead of multiplying MP_L by p, as we did with a competitive firm, we multiply MP_L by MR, the firm's marginal revenue. Marginal revenue is the extra revenue generated by an additional unit of output, so

$$MR \cdot MP_L = \left(\frac{\text{extra revenue}}{\text{unit of output}}\right)\left(\frac{\text{extra output}}{\text{unit of labor}}\right) = \frac{\text{extra revenue}}{\text{unit of labor}}.$$

The expression $MR \cdot MP_L$ is called the **marginal revenue product of labor,** or MRP_L. The firm hires labor until the additional revenue generated by the last unit of labor exactly equals the additional cost incurred—that is, until $MRP_L = w$.

This can be shown graphically. Recall from Chapter 5 that the marginal product curve is downward sloping in the range in which the firm produces, and recall from Chapter 6 that the marginal revenue curve is also downward sloping. The marginal revenue product curve is the product of these two curves, so it is also downward sloping, as shown in Figure 12-4. The figure also has a horizontal line labeled w, which corresponds to the wage rate. The firm hires the amount of labor that equates marginal revenue product and the wage rate. In the figure, the firm's optimal amount of labor can be found where the two curves cross, or at L^* units of labor. Notice, though, that the marginal revenue product curve shows how much labor the firm hires at each wage rate, so the marginal revenue product curve is also the firm's **short-run labor demand curve.**

When the wage rate rises, the firm demands less labor. Suppose that the wage rises from w to w' in Figure 12-4. At wage w, the firm is using L^* units

Figure 12-4   Demand for Labor

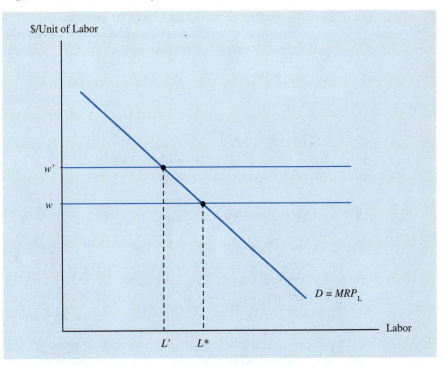

An individual firm's demand curve is given by its marginal revenue product of labor, which is defined as the marginal revenue of the firm's output times the marginal product of labor. The demand curve is downward sloping because both the marginal revenue curve and the marginal product curve are downward sloping. When the wage rate is w, the firm chooses the amount of labor that makes $MRP_L = w$, which is L^* in the figure. When the wage rises to w', the firm uses less labor, L'.

of labor, and the last unit of labor generates $MRP_L = w$ revenue for the firm. When the wage rises to w', if the firm still uses L^* units of labor, the last unit of labor generates only $w < w'$ in revenue. So the last unit of labor generates less revenue than it costs to hire that unit of labor. The firm should decrease its usage of labor, to L'. Because $L' < L^*$, the labor demand curve is downward sloping.

The short-run labor demand curve can shift for a number of reasons. Since the labor demand curve has two components, the marginal product of labor curve and the marginal revenue curve, anything that shifts one of these two component curves shifts the labor demand curve. For example, if the demand for the firm's output increases, the marginal revenue curve shifts to the right, causing the labor demand curve to shift to the right. If one firm in the industry has more capital than another, workers at the more capitalized firm are more productive than workers at the less capitalized firm. The marginal product of labor curve is higher (farther to the right) at the more capitalized firm, so the labor demand curve is also farther to the right. This makes sense, because if one firm's workers are more productive than another's, the first firm should hire more labor than the other. These shifts will be used in the next section when we put labor demand and labor supply together to determine the market wage.

APPLICATION

Increased Foreign Competition and U.S. Labor Demand

Two factors have led to increased competition in U.S. markets. First, other countries—especially Pacific Rim countries such as Korea, Taiwan, and China—have become more industrialized, allowing them to produce goods that are closer substitutes for goods manufactured in the United States. Second, there has been a global reduction in trade restrictions, reducing the costs of selling foreign goods in the United States. What does this do to labor demand in the United States?

Consider a firm producing some good that competes with foreign-made goods. As imports become more available, demand for the domestic firm's output decreases. This reduces the marginal revenue of the firm's output. (Can you explain why?) Since short-run labor demand coincides with the marginal revenue product curve, which is given by marginal revenue times marginal product, the decrease in marginal revenue shifts the short-run demand curve downward. At any given wage, the firm demands fewer workers.

Long-Run Labor Demand

The difference between the short run and the long run is that in the short run one of the inputs—usually capital—is fixed, while in the long run all inputs can be varied. We have seen that when capital is held fixed, increases in the wage cause the firm to use less labor. In the long run this effect is magnified. Suppose that there is a long-run increase in the wage. This makes labor more expensive relative to capital, so the firm substitutes capital for labor, and labor usage declines by even more than in the short-run case. Consequently, long-run labor demand curves are flatter than short-run labor demand curves, as shown in Figure 12-5. The long-run labor demand curve is labeled LD, and the short-run labor demand curve is labeled D.

To see why the long-run labor demand curve is flatter, suppose that the wage rate is w_0 initially. The firm employs L_0 units of labor. Now see what

Figure 12-5   Short-Run Versus Long-Run Labor Demand Curve

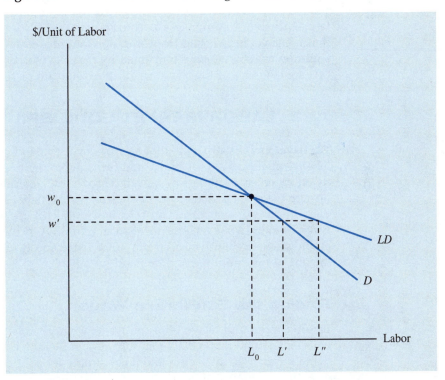

The curve D is the firm's short-run labor demand curve, and the curve LD is the firm's long-run labor demand curve. The long-run labor demand curve is flatter than the short-run labor demand curve. To see why, suppose that the wage falls from w_0 to w'. In the short run the firm increases its use of labor from L_0 to L' because the firm chooses the amount of labor that makes $MRP_L = w$, as in Figure 12-4. In the long run the firm increases its labor use even more (to L'') because when the wage rate falls, labor becomes less expensive relative to capital, and the firm replaces some capital with labor.

happens if the wage rate falls to w'. In the short run the firm cannot change its capital stock, but it can change the amount of labor it employs. Since labor is less expensive, the firm uses more labor, and the quantity of labor demanded in the short run is L'. This is consistent with Figure 12-4. In the long run, the firm can change its capital as well as its labor. In addition to using more labor because it is relatively less expensive, as it did in the short run, the firm also replaces some of its capital with the less-expensive labor. This further increases the quantity of labor demanded to L''. To summarize, when the wage rate falls from w_0 to w', the quantity of labor demanded increases to L' in the short run and to L'' in the long run. Consequently, the long-run labor demand curve is flatter than the short-run labor demand curve.

This can be clarified with an example. An automobile union wins wage concessions from Chrysler, causing the wage rate of auto workers to rise. In the short run, Chrysler responds by using fewer workers. In the long run, Chrysler replaces some of its workers with machines, since machines are now relatively less expensive. Evidence of this can be found easily. Over the past 20 years, labor has become more expensive and machinery has become less expensive. Auto makers have responded to this by shutting down labor-intensive factories and opening new automated factories. The factory shut-downs have been accompanied by massive worker layoffs. These layoffs are evidence of the changing relative long-run price of labor.

12.3 LABOR MARKET EQUILIBRIUM

We have now constructed labor supply curves for individual workers and labor demand curves for individual firms. It is time to put supply and demand together. In doing so, we can discover the determinants of the equilibrium wage and discuss some issues relevant to labor markets. For example, why do some actors and professional athletes get so much? Why are wages higher in some countries than in others? And why is European unemployment so high? Insight into all of these questions can be gained by looking at the supply of and demand for labor.

Finding the Equilibrium Wage

Before we can find the equilibrium wage, we must construct the market labor demand and market labor supply curves. So far we only have labor demand for an individual firm and labor supply for an individual worker. By now the technique for constructing market curves from individual curves should be familiar. An individual labor supply curve shows how much an individual worker desires to work at a given wage. The **market labor supply curve** shows how much all of the workers desire to work at a given wage. So to get quantity of labor supplied by the market at a given wage, just add up how much every worker desires to work at that wage. Doing this for every wage gives us the market labor supply curve, which is usually drawn as being upward sloping, as in Figure 12-6. This convention of drawing upward-sloping market labor supply curves deserves some explanation, especially since individual labor supply curves have backward-bending portions, as in Figure 12-3. Market labor supply curves are derived by adding individual labor supply curves horizontally. As long as more people are on the upward-sloping portions of their individual curves than on the backward-bending portions, the resulting market labor supply curve is upward sloping.

We can get the market labor demand curve in much the same way. The individual labor demand curve shows how much labor an individual firm wishes to employ at a given wage. The **market labor demand curve** shows

Figure 12-6   The Equilibrium Wage Rate

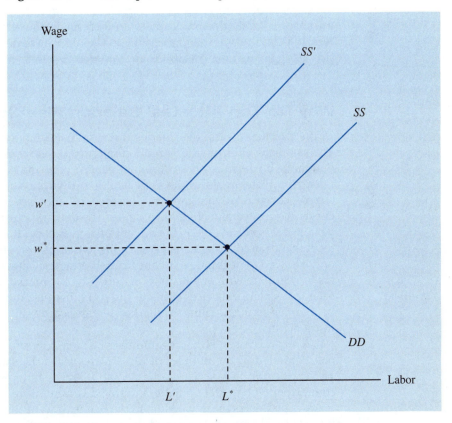

The equilibrium wage, w^* is determined by the intersection of the market labor supply curve, SS, and the market labor demand curve, DD. If market labor supply decreases from SS to SS', the equilibrium wage rises from w^* to w' and the equilibrium amount of labor falls from L^* to L'.

the total amount of labor desired by all firms at the given wage. To get the quantity of labor demanded by the market at a given wage, add up how much labor every firm wants to employ at that wage. Doing this for every wage gives us the market labor demand curve, which is downward sloping, as in Figure 12-6. The intersection of the market labor demand curve and the market labor supply curve determines the equilibrium wage, as shown in the figure. We can use standard supply and demand analysis to look at some particular issues facing labor markets.

For example, as more and more doctors specialize, the supply of family doctors and general practitioners falls. The labor supply curve shows the number of hours of labor provided in family practice medicine at different wage levels, and the labor demand curve shows the number of hours of family practice labor desired by hospitals, health maintenance organizations, and other employers of doctors. In Figure 12-6, the market labor supply curve shifts to the left. The equilibrium wage rate rises from w to w', and the number of hours of labor employed falls from L to L'. The decline in the number of family doctors leads to an increase in the wages of family doctors, which in turn leads to a decline in the number of hours of family practice medicine desired by HMOs and other employers.

Why Do Top Athletes' Salaries Rise So Fast?

In the past few years, the salaries of top athletes have risen dramatically. Top salaries went from the $1 million range in the early 1980s to the $20 million range by the mid-1990s. What happened? First, the number of extremely talented athletes is about the same as it has always been, making the labor supply curve relatively inelastic. Figure 12-7 shows a steep labor supply curve. Also, several factors have caused the demand curve to shift over the past 20 years or so. One is the advent of free agency. It used to be that the team that drafted a player had sole rights to that player, and so players were only allowed to negotiate with one team. Free agency, however, allows players to negotiate with any team. Consequently, the market demand curve for each top athlete's services shifts to the right, because more teams can compete for his services. Thus, the market demand curve shifts from DD_0 to DD_1 in the figure.

A second reason is that the number of teams in most professional leagues has expanded. If the number of top athletes stays the same, but more employers desire their services, the demand curve shifts even farther to the right, from DD_1 to DD_2. Finally, improved communications technology has made top athletes more valuable to the teams. It used to be that most of the interest in a team was local, and the only way to watch games was to go to the stadium or arena. Now, with the proliferation of cable television, games are much more widely watched. Furthermore, cable sports networks show highlights of all the games, so it is easier for teams to build loyalty through-

Figure 12-7   Salaries of Top Athletes

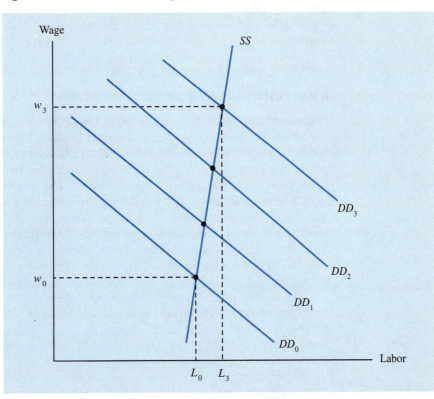

This figure shows why the salaries of top professional athletes have risen so much in the past 15 years. The supply curve is steep because the number of top athletes in any single sport is fairly fixed, regardless of the wage. The market labor demand curve DD_0 corresponds to 1980. Free agency allowed more teams to bid on top athletes than before, shifting the demand curve to DD_1. The increase in the number of teams shifted the demand curve to DD_2. Increased exposure caused by increased cable TV coverage shifted the demand curve to DD_3. The result was a huge increase in the wages of top athletes, from w_0 to w_3, and only a small increase in the number of top athletes.

out the country. Winning teams with superstars are able to make more money selling licensed team merchandise than losing teams without super-stars. All of this makes superstars more valuable to the teams, again mak-ing the labor demand curve shift to the right to DD_3. The total effect on wages is a large increase, from w_0 to w_3 in Figure 12-7. Also notice that the number of top athletes rises from L_0 to L_3. Most of these new top athletes, especially in baseball and basketball, came from other countries.

The same upward wage pressure happens outside of sports, too. For example, movie stars are getting much higher salaries than they did before. At the time of this writing, Sylvester Stallone and Jim Carrey each receive

$20 million per movie. The demand for top movie stars has increased because the demand for movies has become much larger, both because of video sales and because top American movies are now shown all over the world.

International Wage Differences

It is common that workers performing the same job in two different countries earn different wages. For example, high-tech jobs in Chicago pay $13 per hour after taxes, while high-tech jobs in Budapest, Hungary, pay $1.20 per hour after taxes.[1] Why the difference? There are two potential explanations, both having to do with labor demand. The first possible explanation is that firms in Budapest do not have as much capital as firms in Chicago. Since an increase in capital raises the worker's marginal product, and since the wage is equal to marginal revenue times marginal product, more capital means higher wages. Consequently, high-tech workers in Chicago get higher wages because firms in Chicago have more capital than firms in Budapest.

The second potential explanation is that there are not as many high-tech firms per worker in Budapest as there are in Chicago. This would mean that for the same market labor supply curve, the labor demand curve for Chicago would be to the right of the labor demand curve for Budapest. The result is lower wages in Budapest.

Expectations are that these wage differences will not last forever. For example, Chicago firms might discover that they can make more profit by moving their production operations to Budapest. If they move their capital to Budapest, the workers there will be just as productive as the workers in Chicago. Also, as more and more American firms set up operations in other countries, competition for the workers will increase, further driving up the wages.

Some firms are already taking advantage of the wage discrepancies. For example, it is estimated that there are more than 350,000 information-technology engineers in China earning about $105 per month. Northern Telecom opened a lab employing 250 engineers near Beijing University, and Motorola opened a plant in Tianjin where 3,000 workers will make semiconductors and telecommunications equipment. And high-tech jobs are not the only ones being affected. American Airlines and Citicorp have been shipping work to low-paid keypunch operators in the Dominican Republic and the Philippines.

---

1 *Business Week,* November 18, 1994, p. 112.

Government Social Policies and Unemployment

European unemployment has grown dramatically over the last two decades. For example, the unemployment rate was under 5 percent in France and Germany in the late 1970s, but now it is closer to 12 percent. It is about 20 percent in Spain, and it is even higher for workers under 25 years of age. In contrast, the U.S. unemployment rate is under 6 percent, and has not grown appreciably during the last 15 years.

Nobel Laureate Gary Becker blames European government social programs for these high unemployment rates.[2] European governments have caused labor costs to increase by raising the amount employers must pay for such benefits as social security, health insurance, unemployment compensation, and disability insurance. The government even mandates the amount of vacation time employees receive. In fact, about half of a firm's average labor cost in France or Germany goes to paying for these government-mandated benefits.

To see what effect this has on employment and the equilibrium wage, look at Figure 12-8. Before the government mandates, the market labor demand curve is DD_0, the market labor supply curve is SS_0, the equilibrium wage is w_0, and the equilibrium level of employment is L_0. If the government mandates double the cost of labor, the labor demand curve shifts downward by half of its previous height, to DD_1. Because of all the new benefits, workers are more willing to work, shifting the labor supply curve to the right to SS_1. The new equilibrium wage (representing the worker's monetary wage) is w_1, and it is lower than before. This does not mean that firms are paying less for labor, however. Firms must pay mandated benefits equal to the monetary wage, so firms' labor costs are twice the wage rate. In the figure, the w_1 is more than half of w_0, so firms' labor costs are higher under the government mandates than they would be without. Also, employment is lower than before.

Notice that if the labor supply curve had shifted farther to the right, such as to SS_2, employment would have increased from its original level. For this to happen, workers would have had to find the mandated benefits so appealing that they would have been much more willing to work than before. But, as it turned out, the mandates did not have as much of an effect on labor supply as they did on labor demand, and employment fell. What can European governments do to increase employment? They can undo some of the mandates that caused the problem in the first place. This would move the labor demand curve back up toward its original position, and it would move the labor supply curve back toward its original position, thereby increasing employment.

---

2 Gary S. Becker, "Why Europe Is Drowning in Joblessness," *Business Week*, April 8, 1996, p. 22.

Figure 12-8   Government Social Policies and Unemployment

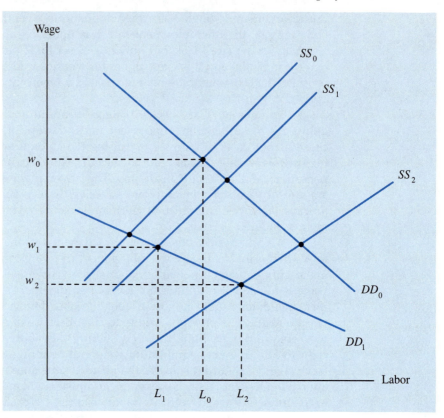

Government mandates forcing firms to pay for excessive health insurance and retirement benefits caused the labor demand curves in most European countries to shift downward dramatically, from DD_0 to DD_1. They also caused the labor supply curve to shift slightly to the right, from SS_0 to SS_1. The result was a big drop in wages and a big drop in employment. If workers had found the mandated benefit packages more attractive, they would have been willing to work more at lower wages to get the benefits, and the labor supply curve would have shifted farther to SS_2. This would have led to lower wages but higher employment. But, since workers did not find the mandated benefits sufficiently attractive, employment in Europe has fallen because of the large fall in demand.

12.4   BARGAINING

In the usual labor market equilibrium setting, wages are set to equate quantity supplied and quantity demanded. Sometimes, though, the usual supply and demand analysis does not work for finding the wage. When a college basketball player is drafted by a team in the National Basketball Association, he is only allowed to negotiate with that one team. If he fails to reach an agreement with that team, he is barred from the league for some set amount of time. Even though other teams would like to hire the player, only the team that drafted him is allowed to.

Suppose that the player requires $4 million to play for one year, and the team is willing to pay $5 million to get him to play. At any salary between $4 million and $5 million, then, quantity supplied equals quantity demanded. According to standard supply and demand analysis, any salary between $4 million and $5 million is an equilibrium salary. This is quite a wide range of possible solutions. What we would like is a model describing exactly how an agreement is reached when one party bargains with another.

The Alternating-Offers Model

Suppose that a worker and a firm meet to negotiate the worker's salary. If the firm values the worker's time and effort more than the worker values his leisure time, there is surplus to be shared, and the efficient outcome has the firm paying the worker for labor. But efficiency just states that the salary should be somewhere in between the firm's valuation and the worker's valuation. A bargaining process could take any number of forms, but we will restrict our attention to just one. In our model of the process, the firm makes the first offer. This is sensible, because when a firm hires a worker the firm usually offers the worker both a job and a salary level. The offer consists of a share of the surplus for the firm and a share for the worker. The worker has the option of either accepting the offer or rejecting it. If he accepts it, the game ends and the players take their agreed-upon shares. If he rejects it, the game may go on to the next stage, in which case the worker makes an offer (sometimes called a *counteroffer*). The firm can respond to the worker's offer by either accepting it or rejecting it. Accepting it means that the game ends and the players take their assigned shares, and rejecting it means that the game may continue with the firm making the next offer.

A strategy in this game is a complete contingent plan covering every possible sequence of events. For example, the firm's strategy must specify what to offer in the first period, what responses to make to all the different offers the worker could make in the second period, what offer to make in the third period if the game progresses that far, and so on. Similarly, the worker's strategy must specify how to react to all the different offers the firm can make in the first period, what offer to make in the second period if the game progresses that far, how to respond in the third period if the game gets that far, and so on.

Before we can find the equilibrium strategies for the players, though, we must first specify the payoffs in the different periods. To give the two parties some pressure to reach an agreement soon, assume that there is some probability that the game ends after any period. For example, there is some chance that a more attractive applicant comes along, and the firm chooses to negotiate with that applicant instead. Or, it could be that if the process takes too long, the firm's upper-level management cuts the position. Let p

denote the continuation probability, that is, the probability that the game continues for one more period. If a player is to receive x one period in the future if the game continues, the expected future payoff is px. Similarly, the expected value of x received t periods in the future is $p^t x$. Since p is a probability, $p < 1$, so that $p^t x < x$ for any t, that is, players prefer to receive x now as opposed to sometime in the future. The reason is simple: The game might not last long enough for the player to receive the future payment, so the player would prefer to have the payment now.[3]

Single-Period Bargaining

If there is only one period of bargaining, the game does not look much like what we would call a negotiation process. Still, it is a useful starting point for the analysis. The firm makes an offer to the worker, who can either take it or leave it. If he takes it the two players get their agreed-upon shares, but if he rejects it the game ends and both players get nothing.

To examine equilibrium behavior in this game, let's begin by giving the players a specific amount to split, $1. The firm offers to give x to the worker, keeping $1 - x$ for itself. The worker can either accept or reject the offer. The game tree is shown in Figure 12-9. As is usual with extensive-form games, we begin solving the game at the end. Suppose that the firm has already made an offer of x. What is the worker's optimal response? If the worker accepts the offer he gets x, but if he rejects the offer he gets 0. Obviously, the worker should accept any offer with $x > 0$.

Now consider what happens at the beginning of the game. We have already figured out that the worker will accept any offer that gives him a positive amount of money. The optimal action for firm, then, is to give the worker the smallest amount of money that the worker will accept, which is $.01. The subgame-perfect outcome of the game, then, is for the firm to get $.99, and the worker to get $.01. The reason that the firm gets almost all of the surplus in this game is because the firm has all of the bargaining power and the worker has none. The worker could threaten to reject any offers that are too low, but these threats would not be credible and the firm would ignore them. The only thing the worker can do is take whatever the firm gives him.

Two-Period Bargaining

One way to increase the worker's bargaining power is to increase the number of periods, so that the worker gets to make some offers. The game tree for a two-period game is shown in Figure 12-10. In the first period the firm

---

3 If we had wanted to, we could have replaced the continuation probability, p, with a discount factor, δ, which would reflect the impatience of the players. All of our results would still hold.

Figure 12-9   Single-Period Bargaining

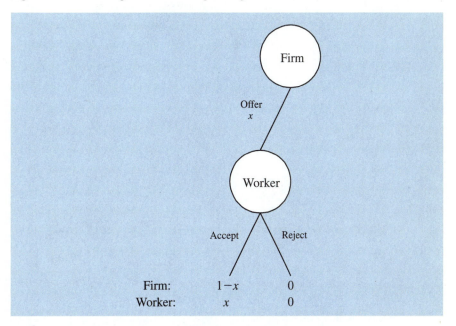

A firm and a worker bargain over a $1 surplus. In a one-period bargaining game, the firm makes an offer and the worker either accepts it or rejects it. If the worker accepts, he gets x and the firm gets the rest of the dollar. If the worker rejects, they both get 0. The firm's payoffs are on top because the firm makes the first move.

offers to give x_1 to the worker, keeping $1 - x_1$ for itself. If the worker rejects the first offer, and if the game continues, he offers to give x_2 to the firm in the second period, and the worker's share is $1 - x_2$. Since the second period may not be reached even if there is no agreement in the first period, second-period payoffs must be multiplied by the continuation probability $p < 1$ to turn them into expected payoffs.

To solve this game by backward induction, begin with the firm's decision of whether to accept or reject the worker's offer in the second period. If the firm accepts the offer it gets x_2 in the second period, and if it rejects the offer it gets nothing. If $x_2 > 0$ the firm is better off accepting the offer. Given this behavior by the firm, the optimal action for the worker in the second period is to keep .99 for himself, and give the firm only .01.

Now go to the first period, and consider the worker's decision of whether to accept or reject the firm's initial offer. If the worker accepts the offer, he gets x_1 in the first period, and if he rejects the offer the second period is reached with probability p, in which case he gets .99 in the second period. If he rejects the first-period offer, then, the worker's expected second-period payoff is .99p. So the worker accepts the firm's initial offer if

$$x_1 > .99p.$$

Figure 12-10   Two-Period Bargaining

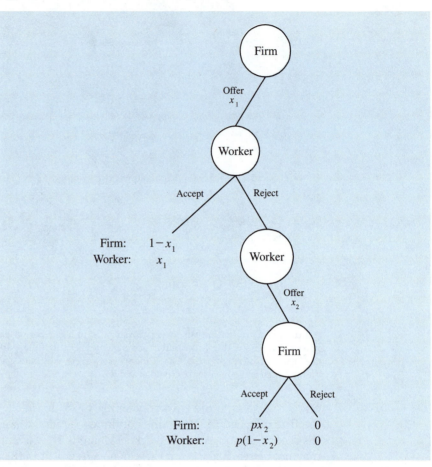

In a two-period bargaining model, the firm makes the first offer and the worker either accepts or rejects it. If he accepts, he gets x_1 and the firm gets the rest of the dollar. If he rejects the initial offer, the game moves to the second period with the probability p, and the worker makes an offer to the firm, who either accepts or rejects it. If the firm accepts the offer, the firm gets x_2 and the worker keeps the rest of the dollar. The final payoffs in period 2 are multiplied by p because this yields the expected value of the payoffs from the point of view at the beginning of the game.

Given this behavior by the worker, the firm's optimal action is to offer the worker the amount $.99p$ rounded up to the nearest penny. This gives the worker enough to accept the firm's offer, so an agreement is reached in the first period.

Let's do a numerical example, supposing that the continuation probability is $p = 0.95$. The worker's share is $(.99)(.95) = 0.95$, and the firm's share is 0.05. Letting the worker make an offer in the last period of the two-period bargaining game gives him most of the bargaining power.

Bargaining with No Set Endpoint

Suppose now that the game has no fixed last period. There is still probability $1 - p$ that the game ends after a disagreement, but there is no point at which the players know for sure that they are in the last period whether an agreement is reached or not. This essentially makes the game an infinite-period game, because players never know whether they are in the last period. Even though the idea of an infinite-period bargaining problem may seem unreasonable at first glance, the assumption of an infinite number of periods is not terribly unrealistic. Usually when two people get together to negotiate, there is not a strict limit on how many rounds of offers can be made. Instead, negotiations continue either until an agreement is reached or until one party decides to go negotiate with someone else. All we are doing is assuming that there is a probability $1 - p$ that someone else shows up to stop the bargaining process.

In the infinite-period bargaining game, the firm offers to give x_1 of the $1 surplus to the worker in period 1, keeping $1 - x_1$ for itself. If the worker rejects this offer, the game continues with probability p, and he makes a counteroffer in period 2. If the worker offers to give x_2 to the firm in period 2, he keeps $1 - x_2$ for himself. If the firm rejects the worker's offer, with probability p the game continues into a third round. The firm offers x_3 to the worker in the third round. If the worker rejects this offer, with probability p play continues into a fourth round with the worker making an offer. The game continues like this until either the game ends randomly or an offer is accepted. Figure 12-11 shows the game tree for this game. Note that the way we have set up this game, x_t denotes the amount the proposer offers to give away in period t, regardless of which player is making the offer.

The usual method for finding a subgame-perfect equilibrium is to begin at the end of the game and work backward. When the game has an infinite number of periods, though, there is no end of the game, so backward induction cannot be used. This does not mean that we cannot find a subgame-perfect equilibrium, however. It just means that we have to find it some other way.

Let's begin by looking at the worker's decision in period 1. If he accepts the offer he gets x_1, and if he rejects it he offers x_2 to the firm in period 2. If offering x_2 is part of an equilibrium strategy, the worker must expect the firm to accept it. Otherwise, the worker would be better off by making an acceptable offer and not having to face some probability that the game ends. For the worker to accept the firm's offer in the first period, it must be that $x_1 \geq p(1 - x_2)$, since $p(1 - x_2)$ is the expected value of receiving $(1 - x_2)$ in the second period. The optimal action for the firm in the first period is to make x_1 as low as possible and still acceptable to the worker, so

Figure 12-11   Infinite-Period Bargaining

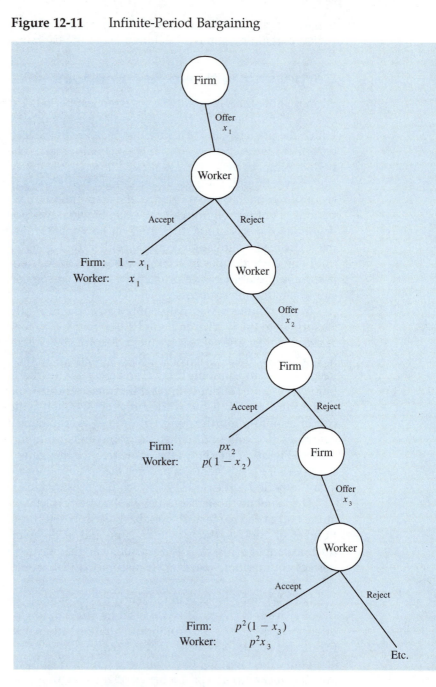

In the infinite-period bargaining problem, the game has no set endpoint. Instead, every time an offer is rejected the game continues with probability p. The firm makes the first offer, and the worker either accepts or rejects. If he rejects, the worker makes the next offer, and the firm either accepts or rejects. If it rejects, the firm makes the next offer, and so on.

(1) $$x_1 = p(1 - x_2).$$

Now look at the firm's decision in period 2. If it accepts the offer, it gets x_2 in period 2; and if it rejects the offer, the firm offers x_3 to the worker in period 3. If offering x_3 in period 3 is an equilibrium strategy for the firm, it must anticipate that the offer will be accepted in period 3. Otherwise it would be better off making a higher offer that would be accepted. For the firm to accept the offer in period 2 it must prefer receiving x_2 in period 2 to the chance of receiving $1 - x_3$ in period 3. Thus, it accepts the offer if $x_2 \geq p(1 - x_3)$. For the worker's offer of x_2 to be optimal, it must be the smallest offer that the firm will find acceptable; that is, x_2 must be set so that

(2) $$x_2 = p(1 - x_3).$$

Now consider the firm's decision in period 3. At this point the firm is making an offer to the worker that he can either accept or reject. The number of periods remaining is infinite. To the firm, this looks exactly the same as the situation in period 1 did. In period 1 the firm was making the offer, and the number of periods remaining was infinite. Since the firm faces the same problem in period 3 as it did in period 1, it must come up with the same solution. That is, if x_1 is the equilibrium offer in period 1, then x_1 must also be the equilibrium offer in period 3. This gives us one more equation:

(3) $$x_3 = x_1.$$

We now have three equations in three unknowns. To solve the equations, first substitute x_1 in for x_3 in equation (2), so that $x_2 = p(1 - x_1)$. Now substitute this expression for x_2 into equation (1) to get

$$x_1 = p(1 - p(1 - x_1)),$$

which simplifies to

$$x_1(1 - p^2) = p(1 - p).$$

Remembering that $(1 - p^2)$ can be factored as $(1 - p)(1 + p)$, we get that

$$x_1 = \frac{p}{1 + p}.$$

The subgame-perfect equilibrium of the infinite-period bargaining game has the firm offering $p/(1 + p)$ in the first period and the worker accepting the offer. Even though the game could, theoretically, go on forever, it only lasts one period.

Notice that since $p < 1$, $p/(1 + p) < .50$. This means that the firm gets more than half of the surplus and the worker gets less than half. How much more than half depends on the continuation probability. For example, if $p = 0.95$, in equilibrium the firm's payoff is \$0.51 and the worker's payoff is \$0.49. There is a **first-mover advantage** in the infinite-period bargaining game. The player who gets to make the first offer gets to keep more than half of the surplus. In the single- and two-period bargaining games analyzed earlier, there was no first-mover advantage. Instead, in those games there was a **last-mover advantage,** with the player proposing in the final period getting more than half of the surplus.

Strengthening Bargaining Power

We have now learned that when the bargaining process has a finite number of periods, the individual making the last offer has most of the bargaining power, and when the process can go on forever, the individual making the first offer has most of the bargaining power. There are other determinants of bargaining power, though, and sometimes there are actions a person can take to improve his bargaining position.

One potential source of bargaining power is an outside option. Labor markets are full of examples of one party trying to get outside options while eliminating the possibility of the other party getting outside options. In sports, for example, teams draft players, which means that the players cannot negotiate with any other teams. This eliminates the outside options for the players. In most sports, however, after a certain amount of time the players can become free agents, which opens up many outside options. Players who oppose the institution of the draft oppose it because it eliminates outside options. When firms negotiate labor contracts with unions, firms are better off if there is a nonunion work force that can take over in the case of a strike. Either management can fill in and do the union jobs during the strike or the firms can hire nonunion workers to fill the positions. The labor unions would like to eliminate these outside options, which is why picket lines outside of the workplace sometimes get violent. The unions want to keep the nonunion workers from entering the plant. Finally, in the extremely competitive Japanese market for new college graduates, a custom has arisen in which all hiring takes place during a specified narrow time period. Some firms take top prospects on outings, such as trips to amusement parks, to make them unavailable to other firms during the hiring period. This practice both strengthens the firm's bargaining position by eliminating the prospect's outside options and enhances the firm's ability to hire the employee in the first place.

Outside offers are a good way for a worker to improve his bargaining position. One way that a firm can improve its bargaining position is by somehow committing to not going above some prespecified wage. For example, the federal government and many large firms set salary ranges for specific positions. Suppose that new employees are hired by division managers, but that salary limits are dictated by the firm's top-level managers. The managers doing the hiring have no way to get around the salary limits. If the company declares that all accountants must be paid between $35,000 and $37,000 per year, this reduces the surplus that a new applicant and the firm can share.

This idea is similar to the salary caps used in many professional sports leagues. A salary cap states that a team's total salary will not exceed a specific figure, and if it does exceed the cap the league can nullify one or more of the players' contracts. When the owner of the team bargains with the players, then, the owner cannot let the players' salaries get too high. The salary cap commits the owner to keeping a certain amount of the surplus, and a low salary cap guarantees the owner a large share of the team revenue. Because salary caps can benefit the team owners and hurt the players, the players are, naturally, opposed to the imposition of a cap. Disagreements over salary caps were one of the main causes of the major league baseball strike of 1994.

12.5   JOB SEARCH

So far in this chapter we have considered only cases in which workers and firms have complete information: Workers know everything there is to know about every firm, and firms know everything there is to know about every worker. In particular, workers know exactly where to go to find a job at a given wage, and firms know exactly whom to hire to fill those jobs. While these are useful assumptions, they are somewhat unrealistic and hide an important facet of the labor market: Workers must search for jobs, and employers must search for the right workers. The search problem is interesting in its own right, and here we analyze one of the two labor search problems—the problem of a worker searching for a job. The central question is this: When should a worker stop searching and take the best offer to date?

The Costs and Benefits of the Search

Isabel is in her junior year of college and is searching for a summer job that will last for three months. She spends the summer in a city with a large number of potential employers with the type of job she wants, but she does not know which employers will offer her a job, nor does she know how much the different employers will offer her. She does know two important facts. First, the probability that a given employer offers her a job is 0.5. Second, if she is offered a job, there are only five possible salaries for the summer— $2,600, $2,700, $2,800, $2,900, and $3,000—and that all these salaries are equally likely. There are many employers offering each of these salaries, but

Isabel does not know which ones are which. This means that each salary is equally likely at every place Isabel applies. The probability that any given employer offers a particular salary is the probability that she gets an offer (0.5) times the probability that an offer takes a given value (0.2), so the probability of receiving a particular salary offer from a given employer is (0.5) (0.2) = 0.1.

For simplicity, let's assume that the only feature of the job that Isabel cares about in making her decision is the amount of money that she makes during the summer. One might object to this assumption because the location of the job and the work environment both matter. It might be the case, though, that all of the employers offering this particular type of job are located very close together, so that location does not matter. As for work environment, Isabel is a typical summer applicant who knows very little about the environment inside the firms to which she applies and has no way of finding out about the work environment, so she has no way to distinguish which firms have good work environments and which have bad ones. Because of this, the only feature left that differentiates between the firms is the salary offered.

Isabel applies for a job and either gets an offer or does not. If she gets an offer, she can either accept it or hold onto the offer. If she does not accept the offer, or if she is turned down for the job, she applies for another job, and the same things can happen. She continues applying for jobs until she finally accepts one. Let's assume that she gets unlucky with her first application and is offered $2,700 for the summer. Should she accept the offer, or should she apply somewhere else? One step in determining the answer to this question is figuring out how costly it is for Isabel to submit another application. One cost of searching is the actual travel expense of going to another employer. A more significant expense, in most cases, is the opportunity cost of the time spent applying for the job. It may be that if Isabel was not applying for another job, she could have been working and earning wages, so her income is reduced because of the extra search. Even if she searches during nonwork hours, there is still an opportunity cost of her time. If she was not searching she could have been studying, or sleeping, or undertaking some other activity that provides enjoyment or utility, so she is worse off when she searches. How should we quantify the opportunity cost of search time? It is most convenient for our analysis if we quantify it as a monetary cost. If she loses utility instead of money when she searches, we can quantify the opportunity cost of the search as the monetary loss that would lead to the same decrease in utility as one more search. We denote the total cost of an additional search, including both travel expenses and opportunity costs, by c. This is the **marginal cost of search.**

The other consideration in determining whether or not Isabel should continue searching is the benefit she expects to receive from applying to another employer. The same five offers are possible at the next employer, and they occur with the same probabilities as before. With probability 0.1 the offer at the second employer is $3,000, which provides Isabel with a benefit of $300. With probability 0.1 the offer is $2,900, which provides her with a benefit of only $200. There is also probability 0.1 that the offer is $2,800, in which case her benefit is a mere $100. If the offer is $2,700, which occurs with probability 0.1, Isabel receives no benefit from the extra search. Finally, if the offer is $2,600, or if she is not offered a job, Isabel is better off going back to the first employer and accepting that job, so again her benefit is zero. What is the expected benefit from searching one more time? It is 0.1(300) + 0.1(200) + 0.1(100) + 0.7(0) = 60.

The **marginal benefit of search** is $60 in this case; that is, the expected benefit of one more search is $60. Notice that the marginal benefit depends on the first offer that Isabel receives. For example, if the first offer is $3,000, there is no benefit to a further search because she cannot possibly find a higher offer. The marginal benefit of search for each possible initial price is shown in Table 12-1. Notice that the marginal benefit decreases with the highest existing offer, as we would expect, because the higher the existing offer the lower the probability that Isabel will get a better offer with her next application.

Optimal Search

Let's go back to the case where Isabel's first offer is $2,700 and suppose that the marginal cost of search is $c = \$30$. Should Isabel continue searching or not? From Table 12-1 we know that the marginal benefit of search is $60, and, as we have just said, the marginal cost of search is only $30. If Isabel searches one more time, her net increase in expected salary is $60 − 30 = $30, so she is made better off by searching one more time. What if Isabel's first offer had been $2,900, not $2,700? When the initial offer is $2,900, the marginal benefit of search is only $10, which is less than the marginal cost of $30. So Isabel chooses not to search any more and accepts the offer of $2,900. If the first offer is $2,800, Isabel is indifferent between searching and not searching, so she might as well accept the offer. Isabel's decision process can be described by the following rule: If the offer is at least $2,800 for the summer, accept it, but if the offer is less than $2,800, continue searching. Ac-

Table 12-1   Marginal Benefit of Search

Highest Existing Offer	Marginal Benefit of Search
$0	$1,400
$2,600	$100
$2,700	$60
$2,800	$30
$2,900	$10
$3,000	$0

cording to this rule, then, Isabel accepts the first offer that is at least as high as $2,800, and because of this, Isabel never returns to an employer that she has already visited. Since Isabel accepts any offer of $2,800 or more, the salary $2,800 is her **reservation offer;** that is, it is the least Isabel is willing to accept for a summer job. The **optimal search rule** is to accept the first offer at or above the reservation offer.

This example used a case in which employers were restricted to five possible salary offers. It is also possible to find reservation offers when employers can offer a range of salaries. Figure 12-12 shows the case in which

Figure 12-12   Optimal Search

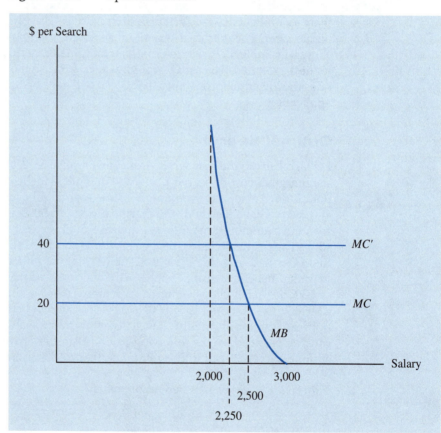

When any offer between $2,000 and $3,000 is equally likely, the marginal benefit of search curve, *MB*, has the shape shown. It is downward sloping and bowed toward the origin. The reservation offer is found where the marginal benefit of search equals the marginal cost of search. When an additional search costs $20, *MB* and *MC* intersect at a salary of $2,500. The applicant is willing to accept any offer with a salary of $2,500 or more. If search is more costly, the reservation offer is lower. For example, when the marginal cost of search is $40, as with *MC'*, the applicant accepts any offer of $2,250 or more.

APPLICATION
Job Search When Jobs Become More Scarce

When jobs become more scarce, it means it is less likely that any one application will result in an offer. Intuition tells us that when jobs become more scarce, people should lower their standards and become less picky about the jobs they accept. In the terminology of this section, their reservation offers should decline when it is harder to find a job.

To check that this is true, let's reconsider the example used to construct Table 12-1, but let's increase the probability of getting no offer to 0.75 from 0.5. This means that the probability of getting an offer with one of the five positive salary levels is 0.25, and the probability of getting an offer of $2,600 is 0.05, the probability of getting an offer of $2,700 is 0.05, and so on. Using these numbers, it is possible to fill in the new marginal benefit of search table, yielding Table 12-2.

Table 12-2   Marginal Benefit of Search

Highest Existing Offer	Marginal Benefit of Search
$0	$700
$2,600	$50
$2,700	$30
$2,800	$15
$2,900	$5
$3,000	$0

According to Table 12-2, if the marginal cost of search is $30, the reservation offer is $2,700. She accepts any offer paying at least $2,700. Compare this with the reservation offer from Table 12-1, where the probability of not getting an offer was 0.5 instead of 0.75. From Table 12-1, when the marginal cost of search is $30, the reservation offer is $2,800. So, when it becomes less likely that Isabel will find a job, she searches less and is willing to accept lower-paying jobs than before.

offers lie between $2,000 and $3,000, with salaries measured along the horizontal axis. The vertical axis measures the marginal benefit and marginal cost of search. For this example, Isabel's marginal cost of search is $20, so the marginal cost line is the horizontal line that crosses the axis at 20, and it is labeled *MC*. The marginal benefit curve, labeled *MB*, is downward sloping and becomes flatter as offers get larger. The reservation offer is found where the marginal benefit of search just offsets the marginal cost—that is, where the marginal cost line intersects the marginal benefit curve, which in this case is at a salary of $2,500. The reservation offer is $2,500, and the optimal search rule is to search until an offer no lower than $2,500 is found and then accept that offer.

What happens if the search becomes more expensive, say, to $40? Intuitively, we would expect Isabel to search less. In the graph, the marginal search cost line shifts upward to MC'. The intersection of the marginal cost line and the marginal benefit curve is farther to the left, at $2,250, so Isabel's reservation offer falls. This also means that she searches less, because she is willing to accept lower offers than she would before.

Summary

- A worker's labor supply decision can be analyzed using budget lines and indifference curves over income and leisure.

- A workers' labor supply curve might be **backward bending.** Specifically, when wages are low, a wage increase induces the worker to decrease his consumption of leisure (by working more) and increase his income, but when wages are already high, a further wage increase induces the worker to consume more leisure (and work less).

- A firm's **marginal revenue product of labor** is the additional revenue generated by the last unit of labor.

- A firm demands labor up to the point where the marginal revenue product of labor exactly equals the wage rate.

- A firm's short-run labor demand curve is given by the firm's marginal revenue product curve. Its long-run labor demand curve is flatter than the short-run labor demand curve because when the wage rate rises, in the long run the firm can substitute capital for labor, thereby further reducing its employment of labor.

- The **equilibrium wage** equates the quantity of labor supplied by workers in the market and the quantity of labor demanded by firms in the market.

- The tools of supply and demand can be used to analyze labor markets, as illustrated by the examples in Section 12.3 covering athletes' salaries, international wage differences, and government social policies.

- The tools of game theory can be used to analyze situations in which a worker and employer bargain over wages. In an alternating-offers model, the employer makes the first offer and the worker either accepts or rejects it. If he rejects the initial offer, the worker makes a counteroffer and the firm either accepts or rejects it. If it rejects the offer, the firm makes the next offer, and so on.

- In a game with a finite number of periods, the last mover has an advantage. In a game with an infinite number of periods, the first mover has an advantage. Bargaining power can be strengthened by obtaining an outside option or by committing not to exceed a certain limit.

- A worker searches for a job until the marginal benefit of search equals the marginal cost of search. The **optimal search rule** specifies a **reservation offer:** The worker accepts the first offer greater than or equal to the reservation offer and rejects any offer less than the reservation offer.

Problems

1. Al is a workaholic, and Ben is lazy. Draw indifference curves corresponding to these two behavioral patterns.
2. Suppose that a firm employs only unskilled labor and pays workers the minimum wage.
   a. Show that if the government raises the minimum wage, the firm demands less labor.
   b. Show that the increased minimum wage results in unemployment for unskilled workers.
3. Some firms have child-care facilities that employees can send their children to during work hours.
   a. Show how establishing a child-care facility affects the supply of labor to a firm.
   b. Show the effect on the equilibrium wage paid by the firm.
   c. Does the firm pay the entire cost of caring for the children? Justify your answer.
4. In the early 1990s, sport-utility vehicles became very popular. Automobile manufacturers had to increase the amount of labor used in their sport-utility vehicle plants. Show the steps that led to this increase in equilibrium.
5. Suppose that two parties participate in the standard alternating-offers bargaining game, the surplus being shared is $1, and both parties have a continuation probability of $p = 0.7$.
   a. In a single-period game with player A making the offer, what is the final allocation?
   b. In a two-period game with player A making the offer in the first period, what is the final allocation?

    c. In an infinite-period game with player *A* making the offer in the first period, what is the final allocation?

    d. Compare these results to the results in the text when the continuation probability was 0.95. Who benefits when the game is more likely to end?

6. Suppose that two players are bargaining over $1 and they have three periods in which to reach an agreement. The players alternate making offers, with player *A* making the first offer. The continuation probability is *p*.

    a. Draw a game tree showing the three-period bargaining game.

    b. If the third period is reached, what offer is made by player *A* in that period?

    c. If the second period is reached, what offer is made by player *B* in that period?

    d. What equilibrium offer is made by player *A* in the first period?

7. Modify the standard alternating-offers bargaining game in the following way. In the last period, one player makes an offer, but the other player does *not* have the choice of accepting or rejecting the offer. In essence, the player making the offer in the last period is a dictator and gets to impose an allocation on the other player.

    a. Draw a game tree showing this game when there are two bargaining periods, assuming that player *A* makes the offer in the first period and player *B* makes the offer in the second period.

    b. If no agreement is reached in the first period, what is player *B*'s optimal action in the second period?

    c. What offer does A make in the first period in equilibrium? Does B accept or reject?

    d. Compare this result to the result of the standard two-period alternating-offers bargaining game. Which player benefits from the modification?

8. Jeremy is assured of getting a job if he applies for one, but the salary is random. Four possible salaries are equally likely: $22,000, $23,000, $24,000, and $25,000.

    a. Determine the marginal benefit of searching when the highest existing offer is equal to $22,000, $23,000, $24,000, and $25,000.

    b. If the marginal cost of search is $100, what is his reservation offer? What if his marginal cost is $250?

9. Margaret is searching for a job. With probability 0.5 she does not get a job. With probability 0.4 she gets a good job paying $30,000. With probability 0.1 she gets a great job paying $50,000. How low must her marginal cost of search be for her to hold out for a great job?

13

INFORMATION ECONOMICS

Overview

When a person applies for a job, he wants the employer to think that he is extremely qualified for the job. If he truly is qualified, he just has to be truthful about his qualifications. But if he is not so qualified, he must find some other way to convince the employer that he is qualified. Employers know this, and they react by discounting, or even dismissing outright, some claims made by employees. Employers are more concerned with what they can verify than with what they cannot. You would think that this process would only hurt unqualified applicants, but it might hurt qualified applicants, too, if their qualifications are difficult to verify.

In this chapter we study situations in which participants on one side of the market have more information than participants on the other side. In the example we just used, job applicants have information that employers do not: Applicants know whether or not they are qualified for the job. This sort of information asymmetry shows up in other places, as well. For example, sellers of used cars know more about the quality of their cars than potential buyers do. Also, independent contractors know more about how much effort they are putting into a construction job than the people who hired them do.

Information asymmetries can cause markets to fail. Up to this point in the book, we have always assumed that everyone knows everything. So, for example, in competitive markets we assumed that all consumers know the prices charged by every firm, and we also assumed that all goods are identical. We did not allow goods to differ in quality. In this chapter we allow quality to differ and to be unknown to the buyers. This small addition to the model is enough to cause a market to fail to exist. Therefore, we also study ways in which the problems stemming from information asymmetries can be avoided.

One setting with information asymmetries currently receives a lot of attention in the national political arena: health care and health insurance. Patients have two types of information that health insurance providers do not have. They know how likely they are to need medical care, and they know how hard they try to take care of themselves. If health insurance companies knew this information, they would be better able to price insurance policies correctly. But because health insurance companies do not know this information and individuals buying insurance do, all sorts of problems arise.

In this chapter you will learn:

- How markets fail when sellers of goods know more about the quality of the goods than buyers do.

- How in some cases sellers can successfully reveal information about quality, relieving the market failure.

- How markets fail when quality depends on the seller's effort and buyers cannot verify the seller's effort.

- How information asymmetries cause market failure in the health insurance industry.

13.1 ADVERSE SELECTION

There is a saying that if something appears too good to be true, it probably is. This is exactly what happens in the used car market. The seller of the used car knows more about the car than the buyer does. In particular, the seller knows why she is getting rid of the car. It could be that she just likes newer cars and so is replacing the used car because it is too old for her tastes. Or it could be that there is something wrong with the car, and she is selling it before the problem becomes readily apparent. The buyer cannot know the seller's motive, nor can he know what is wrong with the car. This situation in which the seller knows something that the buyer does not is prevalent throughout economics. For example, tobacco companies are being sued over what they knew about the harmful effects of tobacco use and when they knew it. In this section we study markets in which one side of the market has information that the other side of the market does not.

Used Car Markets

To illustrate what happens in the used car market, assume that there are two types of cars—good cars and bad cars—and that it is impossible for someone to tell whether a car is good or bad until he actually owns it. This means that a brand new car, fresh off the production line, is good with some probability and bad with some probability, and no one can tell whether it is good or bad before it is sold. Only after it is sold does the owner discover whether he got a good car or a bad car. Also assume that cars never lose their value. This means that a car that starts off as a good car is always a good car, and a car that starts off as a bad car is always bad. Assume, furthermore, that a 10-year-old car provides the same amount of service as it did 10 years ago, and its value to the owner does not change over time. Finally, assume that there are no used car dealers, so that all used car transactions take place between an individual owner and a buyer.

We need to state how much people value the two types of cars. Assume that a bad car is worth $10,000 to everyone, but that a good car is worth different amounts to different people. Half of the people value a good car at $21,000, and half value it at only $19,000. The average value of a good car, then, is $20,000. A brand new car is good with probability 0.8 and bad with probability 0.2. We want to find the equilibrium price of a used car. Before doing so, let's clarify what we mean by an equilibrium in this setting. As always, an equilibrium is a situation in which no one has any reason to change his actions. In this case an equilibrium has five components: (1) the actions of high-valuation owners of good cars—that is, people who value good cars at $21,000; (2) the actions of low-valuation owners of good cars; (3) the actions of owners of bad cars; (4) the beliefs of buyers about whether a used car is good or bad; and (5) the equilibrium price. Beliefs matter because they determine how much a buyer is willing to pay for a used car. For example, suppose that a high-valuation buyer believes that half of all used cars on the market are good and half are bad. Then his expected value of a used car is $(0.5)(\$21,000) + (0.5)(\$10,000) = \$15,500$, and this is the most he is willing to pay for a used car. If, instead, he believes that all used cars on the market are bad, his expected value is $(0)(\$21,000) + (1.0)(\$10,000) = \$10,000$. In this case he is only willing to pay $10,000 for a used car.

To be in equilibrium, buyers' beliefs must be consistent with the sellers' actions. If all owners of bad cars *and* all owners of good cars put their cars on the market, then in equilibrium buyers must believe that 80 percent of the used cars are good and 20 percent of them are bad. These are the same probabilities as for new cars. If, instead, only owners of bad cars put their cars on the market, in equilibrium buyers must believe that 100 percent of the used cars are bad. All we are saying is that buyers cannot be fooled in equilibrium. The other requirements of equilibrium are that owners of used cars sell them if the price is higher than the value, and that the equilibrium price makes the quantity of used cars supplied equal the quantity demanded.

We know that the price of used cars cannot be higher than $21,000, because no car is worth more than $21,000 to any buyer. Second, we know that the price cannot be lower than $10,000 because no one would be willing to sell a car for less than $10,000. Even if it's a bad car, it's still worth $10,000, and owners will not sell bad cars for less. Therefore, the only possible prices are between $10,000 and $21,000.

Let's consider what happens if the price is between $10,000 and $19,000. No owners of good cars will sell for less than $19,000, so no good cars are for sale. On the other hand, owners of bad cars would be happy to sell their $10,000 cars for a price between $10,000 and $19,000. So, only bad cars are for sale. In equilibrium buyers must believe that the probability of a used car being bad is 100 percent, so the highest price a buyer will pay is $10,000. Thus, the equilibrium price must be $10,000. Only bad used cars are for sale, and it is impossible for owners of bad used cars to make any profit by selling their cars. Sellers are indifferent about selling, and buyers are indifferent about buying. There are no gains from trade, and thus there is no reason for a market to exist.

Now let's consider prices between $19,000 and $21,000. At these prices low-valuation owners of good cars would be willing to sell them. Owners of bad cars would like to sell their cars, too. But will high-valuation people be willing to buy? To answer this question, we must first figure out buyers' beliefs. In the whole population, 20 percent of the cars are bad and 40 percent are good but valued at $19,000. The other 40 percent are good and valued at $21,000. If the whole population consists of 100 cars, 60 will be for sale, and 40 of those will be good. So, two-thirds of the cars for sale are good and one-third are bad. The expected value to a high-valuation buyer of a used car bought on the used-car market is then $(2/3)(\$21,000) + (1/3)(\$10,000) = \$17,333$. This is the most a high-valuation buyer would be willing to pay for a used car. So, when the price is between $19,000 and $21,000, there are plenty of sellers, but no buyers.

What we have found is that the only equilibrium has a price of $10,000. Owners of good cars are not willing to sell, and owners of bad cars are indifferent about selling since the selling price is the same as the value of a bad car. Buyers are indifferent about buying since the price is the same as the value of a bad car. Trade may take place, but there is no surplus to share, and therefore no gains from trade are realized, even though potential gains from trade exist. Low-valuation owners of good cars would like to sell their cars to high-valuation buyers, splitting a $2,000 surplus. But they can't, because buyers cannot tell whether cars are good or bad before they buy them. We have a situation of **market failure,** because the market is unable to exploit all gains from trade.

In this example, the very fact that someone wants to sell a car means that it is a bad car. There is no market for good cars. Why not? The only way buyers will pay a price high enough to entice owners of good cars to sell them is if only good cars are on the market. But if the price is high enough for owners of good cars to sell them, it must be high enough for owners of bad cars to sell theirs, too. Bad cars drive good cars out of the used car market, even though only a relatively small proportion of cars are bad to begin with. This is an example of **adverse selection,** a term used to describe a situation in which the market fails because one side of the market has different information about quality than the other side of the market.

Adverse selection is an important problem. It describes any situation in which one group of individuals has information about the quality of a good or service and the other group of individuals does not. Some information is hidden from one group, and this hidden information causes market forces to break down; that is, markets are not able to allocate goods efficiently. This occurs in places besides used car markets. For example, banks would like to loan money only to people who are likely to repay it, but borrowers have more information about whether or not they will repay loans than banks do.

This makes it expensive for people with no credit history to get loans, and so people who are likely to repay loans may find the interest rates too high to make borrowing worthwhile. Again, the adverse selection problem causes market failure.

A Role for Middlemen

A middleman is an individual or a firm that buys goods from a supplier and resells them to customers without changing the goods in any way in between. In the used car market, middlemen are used car dealers. Since middlemen do not change the good in any way, why would anyone pay for their services? One answer is that middlemen make it possible to avoid the adverse selection problem. Under certain circumstances a middleman can create a market for good used cars. First, the middleman must be able to tell whether a car is good or bad before she buys it. Second, all buyers must be able to find out if the middleman ever sold a bad car for the price of a good car and must refrain from buying from the middleman if that ever occurs. Then it is possible for the middleman to buy only good cars and sell them to high-valuation buyers, providing a more efficient allocation of good cars.

To see how this works, suppose that the middleman can buy good used cars for $19,500, and that she charges $20,500 for a used car. Also assume that she can get as many bad used cars as she wants for $10,000. She makes one transaction per period, and her discount factor is 0.95 (see Section 2.5 for a review of discount factors). We are interested in the game played between the middleman and high-valuation buyers. The game is very similar to the infinitely repeated prisoner's dilemma discussed in Section 11.2. To find an equilibrium of this game, we first propose some strategies for the middleman and the high-valuation buyers, and then show that they constitute an equilibrium. To do this, we must show that no one has an incentive to deviate from the proposed strategies.

Remember that buyers know whether or not the middleman has ever tricked a buyer by selling a bad car at the price of a good car. Therefore, the buyer's strategy can be based on this knowledge. Consider the following strategy for a high-valuation individual who does not already own a car:

> Buy a used car from the middleman as long as she has never sold a bad car for $20,500. Do not buy a used car from the middleman if she has ever sold a bad car for $20,500.

This is just a grim strategy, as discussed in Section 11.2. High-valuation buyers are willing to buy from the middleman as long as she is honest. But, if she ever cheats, all buyers punish her forever by never buying a car from her again. Now consider a strategy for the middleman:

> Buy only good cars to resell.

We need to check that the two strategies constitute an equilibrium. To do so, we must check that the buyers' strategy is a best response to the middleman's strategy, and that the middleman's strategy is a best response to the buyers' strategy.

Begin with the buyers' strategy. As long as the middleman is only selling good cars, high-valuation buyers can buy a good car for $20,500. Since they value good cars at $21,000, high-valuation buyers are better off buying than not buying. Also, since the middleman's strategy is to sell only good cars, the second part of the buyers' strategy is never used. The second part of the buyers' strategy is important, though, because it keeps the middleman from cheating. If she is honest, she buys good cars for $19,500 and sells them for $20,500, making $1,000 per transaction. When she makes one transaction per period, and when her discount factor is $\delta = 0.95$, her present value of future income is (see equation (2.1))

$$\frac{\$1,000}{1 - \delta} = \frac{\$1,000}{1 - .95} = \$20,000.$$

This is today's value of making $1,000 every period forever. If the middleman cheats, she buys a bad car for $10,000 and sells it for $20,500, but never sells another car. She earns $20,500 − $10,000 = $10,500 this period but nothing else, for a present value of future profit equal to $10,500. So, if she is honest, her present value of future income is $20,000, and if she is dishonest, her present value of future income is $10,500. She is better off being honest, so her strategy of selling only good cars is a best response to the buyers' strategy. We have an equilibrium, and there is no adverse selection problem in the equilibrium. Buyers now have a way to distinguish between good and bad cars before they buy them; they only buy from the middleman, who only sells good cars.

Middlemen provide a valuable service. They can tell the difference between good used cars and bad used cars, and people who value good cars highly are willing to pay for this service. And, the middlemen make a profit in the process. Two things enable the middleman to make a profit. One is her ability to distinguish between good and bad cars. The other is her reputation. As long as she has a reputation for selling only good cars, she can continue to earn a profit. Without the reputation, though, her ability to distinguish between good and bad cars is of no value on the market. As long as middlemen maintain their reputations, they are able to solve the problems caused by adverse selection.

13.2 SIGNALING

Adverse selection also occurs in labor markets. Workers differ in their productivity levels, but it is difficult for employers to tell which job applicants are high-productivity workers and which are low-productivity workers. If employers could distinguish between high- and low-productivity workers they would offer a high wage to high-productivity workers and a low wage to low-productivity workers. By now, though, you should see the problem. If employers cannot distinguish between the two types, low-productivity workers will claim to be high-productivity workers so they can get the higher wage. Therefore, employers cannot pay high-productivity workers what they are worth. What we want to show in this section is that, under the right conditions, a college degree can solve this problem.

Education As a Signal

Let's begin by explicitly stating the components of our model. A firm in a perfectly competitive industry sells its output for $2 per unit. Workers stay at this firm for four years.[1] There are two types of workers: High-productivity workers have a marginal product of 18,000 units of output per year, and low-productivity workers have a marginal product of 10,000 units of output per year. One-fourth of the workers are high-productivity workers, and the remaining three-fourths are low-productivity workers. Finally, both types of workers have the opportunity to work in a different industry for $25,000/year if they want to. This outside opportunity means that the firm cannot hire any workers for less than $25,000/year, because if the firm offers less than $25,000/year, both types of workers switch to the other industry.

If the firm can distinguish between the two types of workers, then using the analysis of Chapter 12, high-productivity workers should get paid their marginal revenue product, or

$$\left(\frac{\$2}{\text{unit of output}} \right) \left(\frac{18{,}000 \text{ units of output}}{\text{year}} \right) = \frac{\$36{,}000}{\text{year}}.$$

Similarly, the firm should only offer low-productivity workers $20,000/year. Since low-productivity workers can get $25,000/year in the other industry, if the firm can distinguish between the two types of workers, it only employs high-productivity workers. Finally, let's assume that labor markets are competitive. This means that if a firm is able to tell which workers have high productivity and which do not, the firm cannot hire any high-productivity workers for less than $36,000. Without this assumption, we would need to discuss how the firm bargains with high-productivity workers. With this assumption, we know that the equilibrium salary for high-productivity work-

---

1 This is a key assumption, and problem 6 at the end of the chapter asks what happens if it does not hold.

ers must be $36,000/year, and the equilibrium salary for low-productivity workers must be $25,000/year earned working at the outside industry.

What if the firm cannot tell how productive an individual worker is? Specifically, assume that the firm cannot tell a worker's productivity level either before or after the worker is hired. This assumption makes sense if you think about firms that are so large, and with sufficiently complicated production processes, that they cannot tell how much output a single individual produces. All they can determine is the average productivity of all their employees. If such a firm offers $36,000/year, both types of workers apply for jobs, since $36,000/year is more than they can get anywhere else. The average level of marginal product is 12,000 units per year, however, so on average the firm only gets $24,000/year in revenue from the workers. The firm cannot just fire the low-productivity employees, because it cannot tell which employees are which, even after they have been working for a while. The firm cannot hire anyone for $24,000/year, since workers can get paid $25,000/year elsewhere. The firm loses money if it pays more than $24,000/year, so it does not produce when it cannot distinguish between the two types of workers. This is an adverse selection problem.

We want to find a way for the firm to distinguish between the two types of workers, so that it can pay the high-productivity workers what they are worth and keep the low-productivity workers out. Education provides a way to do this. Suppose that in addition to being more productive employees, high-productivity workers are better students than low-productivity workers. There is a cost, in terms of effort, of getting a college degree, and high-productivity workers can earn a college degree at a lower cost than low-productivity workers can. Suppose that, in terms of monetary costs and effort costs, a high-productivity worker expends $30,000 earning a college degree, but a low-productivity worker expends $50,000 earning the same degree because of the increased effort required to earn a degree.

Now let's specify some beliefs and strategies for the firm and the two types of workers and see if we can get an equilibrium in which there is no adverse selection problem. We begin with the firm:

> The firm believes that everyone with a college degree is a high-productivity worker and everyone without a college degree is a low-productivity worker. It offers $36,000/year to workers it believes to have high productivity and nothing to workers it believes to have low productivity.

Now for the high-productivity workers:

> High-productivity workers earn college degrees.

Finally, for the low-productivity workers:

> Low-productivity workers do not earn college degrees.

Do these strategies and beliefs constitute an equilibrium? Let's begin with the firm. The firm believes that high-productivity workers have college degrees and low-productivity workers do not. These beliefs fit exactly with the behavior of the two types of workers, so the beliefs are consistent with an equilibrium. We also need to check that the firm's actions are best responses to its beliefs. Since the firm correctly believes that college graduates are high-productivity workers, the firm is correct in offering them $36,000.

The next step is to check whether the high-productivity workers are best-responding to the firm's beliefs and strategy. If a high-productivity worker does not earn a college degree, the best she can do is get a job with the outside industry for $25,000/year. If she works for four years, as we have assumed, this means that her total salary is $100,000. If, instead, she does earn a college degree, she can get a job at the firm for $36,000/year. Over four years, she earns $144,000. She must spend $30,000 to get the college degree, so her net earnings are $114,000 if she gets a college degree. Comparing this with the $100,000 she earns without a degree, we see that it is optimal for high-productivity workers to earn college degrees.

The final step is to check that the low-productivity workers' strategy is a best response to the firm's beliefs and strategy. If a low-productivity worker does not go to college, he earns $100,000 over four years working in the outside industry. If he does get a college degree, the firm will believe that he is a high-productivity worker and pay him $144,000 over four years. But, he must spend $50,000 to get the degree, so his net earnings are only $94,000 over four years. Low-productivity workers are better off not earning college degrees.

Since the firm's beliefs are consistent with the equilibrium actions of the workers, and since the firm's strategy is a best response to its beliefs, and since the workers' strategies are best responses to the firm's strategy, we have an equilibrium. In the equilibrium all high-productivity workers get college degrees and get paid $36,000/year. All low-productivity workers skip college and earn $25,000 per year. The firm successfully avoids hiring the low-productivity workers it does not want. So, we have avoided the adverse selection problem.

College education plays a very strange role here. It does not make anyone more productive. This means that students do not actually learn anything in college. Even so, college is still beneficial to high-productivity workers because it allows them to distinguish themselves from the low-productivity workers, enabling them to earn higher salaries. In this case we say that a college degree is a **signal.** It has no effect on productivity, but it signals the firm about whether or not a worker has high or low productivity. In general, a signal is an activity that has no productive value but conveys information. In our example, education does not increase students' productivity, but it does enable students to separate themselves from nonstudents on the job market.

13.3 MORAL HAZARD

Adverse selection occurs in situations in which information about quality is hidden from one group of individuals. We now turn our attention to situations in which information about *actions* is hidden from one group of individuals. For example, when a professor assigns a group project, it is difficult for her to award different grades to different members of the group. Because of that, individual members of the group have an incentive to reduce their effort, hoping that other members of the group will compensate for it so that the group's grade does not fall too much. If the professor could observe how much effort each member of the group contributed, she could use grades to ensure that some members don't shirk. But, because effort cannot be observed, members have an incentive to do less work, and the group project does not force students to learn as much as the professor might otherwise have hoped.

A Simple Contract

Consider the case of Nikki, who hires Acme Jewelers to make her a custom-designed ring. She and the people at Acme discuss what she has in mind, and the Acme people quote her a price of $750 for the ring. She agrees to the price, and they sign a contract stating that Acme will make a ring and Nikki will pay Acme $750 upon completion. This creates a problem, as we shall see. Once the contract is signed, Acme loses its incentive to put a lot of effort into Nikki's ring. In fact, Acme has no incentive to put in any more than the lowest possible amount of effort. Let's see why.

The value of the ring to Nikki depends on the amount of effort Acme puts into it. The more effort Acme puts into the ring, the closer it is to what Nikki had in mind, and the more she likes it. Nikki's benefit curve is labeled B in Figure 13-1. The amount of effort expended by Acme is measured on the horizontal axis, and the value of the ring to Nikki, measured in terms of dollars, is shown on the vertical axis. The benefit curve can be thought of as the most Nikki is willing to pay for a ring resulting from different levels of effort. The benefit curve is upward sloping, reflecting the fact that more effort results in a ring that Nikki likes more. It also gets flatter with movements to the right, reflecting the fact that each additional unit of effort yields less additional benefit than previous units of effort. Finally, notice that the benefit curve crosses the horizontal axis at a point where effort is equal to e_L. This is the smallest amount of effort consistent with there being a finished ring, no matter how bad. If Acme exerts less effort than e_L, they cannot possibly finish the ring, yielding no benefit to Nikki.

Effort is costly for Acme, since it must pay for workers and materials. There are a number of ways that Acme can increase its effort. It can use higher-quality materials, or it can devote more time to finishing and polishing the ring. It can also hire more talented jewelers, resulting in a better

Figure 13-1   A Simple Contract

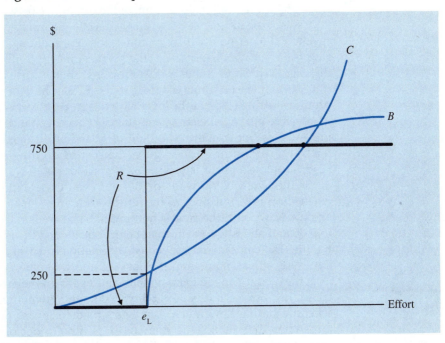

The amount of benefit Nikki receives from a ring depends on the amount of effort exerted by the jeweler. The harder the jeweler works, the more Nikki likes the ring, so her benefit increases with effort, as shown by Nikki's benefit curve, B. The jeweler must exert at least e_L units of effort to complete the ring, and this is the smallest amount of effort that leads to any benefit for Nikki. The more effort the jeweler exerts, the higher its cost, as shown by the jeweler's cost curve, C.

If the contract specifies that Nikki will pay the jeweler $750 upon completion of the ring, the jeweler earns $750 in revenue as long as it exerts at least the minimal amount of effort, e_L. If it exerts less revenue, it earns zero. The jeweler's revenue curve is R. The jeweler's optimal choice of effort maximizes the vertical distance between R and C, and the optimal level of effort is e_L. The jeweler earns $750 in revenue and pays $250 in costs, leaving it a profit of $500. Nikki pays $750 for a ring that generates a benefit of zero to her, so she loses $750. Nikki would be better off not agreeing to the contract.

ring. All of these require Acme to spend more on the ring. Acme's cost curve is labeled C in Figure 13-1. It is upward sloping, reflecting the fact that more effort costs more money. Also, it gets steeper as the level of effort increases, reflecting the fact that each additional unit of effort costs more than previous units of effort.

It is tempting to look at the point that maximizes the vertical distance between B and C, since this would maximize the difference between benefits and costs. But this is not exactly what Acme does. The benefit curve B measures the benefit to Nikki when Acme exerts effort, and the cost curve C measures the cost to Acme of increasing effort by one unit. The benefit goes to Nikki, but the cost goes to Acme. When Acme maximizes its profit, it sets the level of effort to maximize the difference between *its* revenue and *its* cost, not the difference between *Nikki's* benefit and *its* cost. What is Acme's revenue? To get paid, all Acme must do is exert enough effort to finish the ring. As we have already said, the smallest level of effort needed to finish the ring is e_L. So, if Acme exerts effort less than e_L, its revenue is zero, but if it exerts at least e_L units of effort, it gets \$750. Therefore, Acme maximizes profit by setting effort at the level with the greatest vertical distance between its revenue curve, labeled R, and its cost curve, C. Since C is upward sloping and R is horizontal to the right of e_L, the profit-maximizing level of effort is e_L. According to the figure, the cost of exerting e_L units of effort is \$250, so Acme's profit is \$750 − \$250 = \$500.

Is this what Nikki wanted? It's not even close. Nikki's benefit is zero when effort is e_L, but since Acme finished the ring, she has to pay \$750. From Nikki's viewpoint, the ring is nothing like she envisioned, but she still has to pay, and she is worse off than before she signed the contract. What went wrong? The contract only specified completion of a ring, so Acme gets paid if it exerts at least some minimal level of effort. Maybe things would be better if the contract made the payment contingent on the amount of effort provided. Let's explore this possibility. Nikki and Acme negotiate a payment schedule stating how much Acme gets paid for every possible level of effort. Acme then makes the ring, and it is time to decide how much Nikki should pay. But it's hard to verify effort. Acme can claim that it exerted more effort than Nikki thinks it did, and she would have no way to prove that she is right and Acme is wrong. It is impossible to prove in a court of law how much effort Acme used. Also, an independent observer might think that the finished ring is worth \$750, because of its materials and workmanship, so Nikki would not be able to establish in court that Acme did not produce a ring worth \$750. Her problem is that the ring is not worth \$750 to *her*. So, since Nikki cannot verify how much effort Acme puts into making the ring, she cannot make the payment contingent on effort.

Economists refer to this type of scenario as a situation of **moral hazard.** Moral hazard occurs when an agreement removes the incentive for one party to behave in the way intended when the other party signed the agreement. The contract removed the incentive for Acme to produce the ring Nikki wanted. For moral hazard to occur, one party's actions must be hidden, so that the agreement cannot be based directly on actions. It is usually enough that the actions are hidden from legal authorities—that is, they cannot be verified in a court of law.

A More Complicated Contract

In spite of moral hazard problems, people sign contracts all the time. There must be something about real-world contracts that allows them to avoid the extreme moral hazard problem encountered by our simple contract. So let's look at a more complicated contract. In this contract, Nikki has the right to accept or reject Acme's work. If she rejects it, Acme is stuck with the ring. If she accepts it, she pays Acme $750. The ability to reject Acme's work is called a *walk-away clause,* and it makes Nikki much better off. The walk-away clause changes Acme's benefit curve. Figure 13-2 shows the same B and C curves as in Figure 13-1. For Acme to get paid, Nikki must find the ring acceptable, which means that it must be worth at least $750 to her. So, Acme gets paid when effort is above the level e_W in the figure, where e_W is the amount of effort that makes Nikki's benefit equal to $750. Acme's revenue curve is R'. Its revenue is zero when effort is less than e_W and $750 when effort is e_W or more. Acme maximizes profit by setting effort at the level that maximizes the vertical distance between its R' and C. As shown in the figure, the profit-maximizing level of effort is e_w.

Figure 13-2   A Contract with a Walk-Away Clause

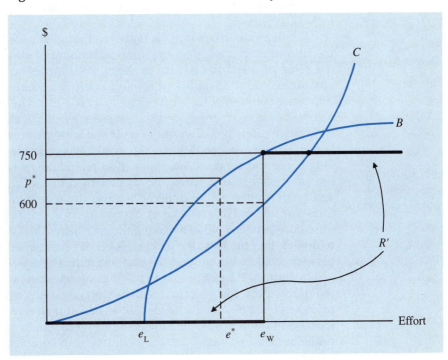

When the contract specifies a price of $750 but allows Nikki to reject the ring and pay nothing, the jeweler's revenue curve is R'. It earns no revenue if it exerts less effort than e_w, the level of effort where Nikki's benefit is equal to $750. It earns $750 if it exerts at least this much effort. When the jeweler chooses the amount of effort to maximize its profit, it chooses an effort level of e_w.

The efficient level of effort is e^*, where the vertical distance between Nikki's benefit curve, B, and the jeweler's cost curve, C, is greatest. When the contract price is $750, the jeweler exerts too much effort. If, instead, the contract price is p^*, the jeweler exerts the efficient level of effort.

Three important points can be made about this contract. First, Nikki is better off with this contract than with the simple contract analyzed in Figure 13-1, and Acme is worse off. With the simple contract, Nikki lost $750 and Acme gained $750 − $250 = $500. With the walk-away clause, Nikki breaks even and Acme only gets $750 − $600 = $150. The second important point to notice is that Nikki still gains nothing from the contract. She's not worse off with the contract, as she was with the simple contract, but she still has no incentive to sign the contract. One way to rectify this problem would be for Acme to hand her $75 when she signs the contract. The contract then provides Nikki with a net benefit of $75, and Acme still makes a profit of $75. This is rather strange, though, and you may not think that it occurs much in the real world. Firms don't often make cash payments to people who sign contracts with them, but they do sometimes provide up-front benefits. For example, Acme might provide Nikki with a design for a custom-made ring, and if things fall through Nikki could take the design to a different jeweler and try again. The design is worth something, and it is a benefit to Nikki.

The third important point is that even though the walk-away clause gets the firm to exert more than the minimal amount of effort, thereby alleviating some of the moral hazard problem, it still does not yield the efficient amount of effort. The efficient level of effort is the one that maximizes the difference between Nikki's benefit and Acme's cost. The efficient level of effort is shown as e^* in Figure 13-2. To see why this is efficient, think about how much effort Nikki would exert if she were making her own ring and her cost curve matched Acme's. She would maximize the difference between her benefit and her cost. Any more effort would not be worthwhile, because the additional benefit would be smaller than the additional cost, and any less effort would not be optimal because the reduction in benefits would outweigh the reduction in costs. From society's point of view, there is no difference between Nikki's making the ring herself and Acme's getting paid to do it. Either the way, the efficient level of effort maximizes the difference between Nikki's benefit and the cost of producing the ring.

In Figure 13-2, notice that the $750 contract actually makes Acme exert too much effort. The efficient level of effort could be attained if the contract price had been p^*. Nikki's net benefit would still be zero, but at least the allocation of effort would be efficient, and there would be no moral hazard problem. So, a properly designed contract can completely alleviate moral hazard.

13.4 HEALTH INSURANCE

Health insurance and health care have been major topics in both of the last two U.S. presidential races. In their speeches, candidates have often complained about people's inability to purchase health insurance, either because it is too expensive or because no insurance company will cover them. Some of the candidates have set "universal coverage" as a goal, so that every American has access to good, inexpensive health insurance. In this section we explore some of the reasons that the perceived problems with health insurance have arisen. It turns out that health insurance markets are subject to both adverse selection and moral hazard, and, as we have already seen, these problems can lead to market failure.

Adverse Selection and Group Coverage

People buy health insurance to cover their costs should they ever need medical care. Some people are more prone to need medical care than others. People know whether or not they are likely to need medical care, and, therefore, whether or not they are likely to file a claim with the health insurance company, but the insurer does not know how likely it is that any given individual will need medical care. Thus, we have a situation of hidden quality (of the health status of the person buying insurance), and adverse selection problems can arise.

To see what goes wrong, let's do a specific example. A large corporation arranges with an insurance company to provide health insurance for its employees. Every employee starts off healthy, and every employee begins with wealth of $100,000. Let's restrict attention to one particular type of health problem—a knee injury. When people suffer knee injuries, they must have corrective surgery accompanied by long hospital stays and rehabilitation, all at a total cost of $70,000. But not everyone faces the same probability of injuring his knees. High-risk individuals suffer a knee injury with probability $p_H = 0.2$, and low-risk individuals suffer a knee injury with probability $p_L = 0.1$. All individuals are risk averse, and they are identical in every way except for the probability of suffering an injury. In particular, everyone has the same utility function u. Finally, half of the people are high-risk and half are low-risk.

This information enables us to draw indifference curves for a high-risk individual and for a low-risk individual in the same way that we drew indifference curves in Chapter 4. To do this, we identify two states of the world. In state 1 the individual suffers a knee injury, and in state 2 the individual remains healthy. Since initial wealth is $100,000 and treating a knee injury costs $70,000, the individual's final wealth is $30,000 if state 1 occurs and $100,000 if state 2 occurs. We show this state-payoff combination as point E (for endowment) in Figure 13-3. Note that the endowment point is the same for both types of individuals. What differs for the two types of individuals is the probability of state 1 occurring—that is, the probability of suffering a knee injury. For a low-risk individual, the probability of suffering an injury is 0.1. Referring back to Section 4.2, a low-risk individual's marginal rate of substitution is given by

$$MRS_L = \frac{p_L}{1 - p_L} \cdot \frac{MU(w_1)}{MU(w_2)} = \frac{0.1}{0.9} \cdot \frac{MU(w_1)}{MU(w_2)} = \frac{1}{9} \cdot \frac{MU(w_1)}{MU(w_2)},$$

Figure 13-3   Adverse Selection in Health Insurance Markets

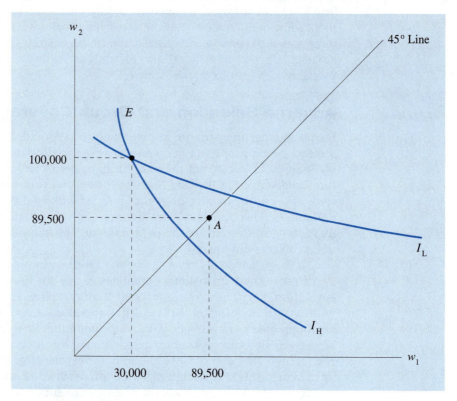

When an individual does not have health insurance, he suffers a knee injury in state 1 and must spend $70,000 on treatment. In state 2 he stays healthy and his wealth is $100,000. So, without health insurance, his wealth distribution is shown by point E. The indifference curve I_H is for high-risk individuals, and the indifference curve I_L is for low-risk individuals. The high-risk indifference curve is steeper because high-risk people suffer injuries with probability 0.2 and low-risk people suffer injuries with probability 0.1.

Suppose the insurance company offers a policy with full coverage and a $10,500 premium. This policy earns zero expected profit for the insurance company if everyone buys it. The wealth distribution resulting from the policy is shown by point A. Point A is on a higher indifference curve than E for high-risk individuals, but it is on a lower indifference curve than E for low-risk individuals. Consequently, only high-risk individuals buy the policy, and the insurance company can expect to lose money.

where $MU(w)$ denote the marginal utility of wealth when wealth is equal to w. Similarly, a high-risk individual's marginal rate of substitution at the endowment point is given by

$$MRS_H = \frac{p_H}{1 - p_H} \cdot \frac{MU(w_1)}{MU(w_2)} = \frac{0.2}{0.8} \cdot \frac{MU(w_1)}{MU(w_2)} = \frac{1}{4} \cdot \frac{MU(w_1)}{MU(w_2)}.$$

Comparing the two equations, we see that the high-risk individual has a higher marginal rate of substitution than the low-risk individual at any point in state-payoff space. This means that when they cross, the high-risk individual's indifference curve is steeper than the low-risk individual's indifference curve, as shown in Figure 13-3.

How the insurance company behaves depends in part on the agreement with the sponsoring corporation. Let's begin with the case in which the agreement states that employees are allowed to buy insurance if they want to, but the insurance company has to charge a specific price. The next step is to analyze the insurance company. We make two assumptions. First, let's assume that the company cannot distinguish between high- and low-risk individuals. Since the average probability of an accident for a randomly selected employee is 0.15, the sponsoring corporation and the insurance company agree that the price of insurance will be $0.15 for every $1 of coverage. So, if the company sells a policy paying $70,000 in case of an injury, it charges a premium of (0.15)($70,000) = $10,500. When an individual buys this policy, his loss is fully covered, and his wealth is equal to $100,000 minus the premium, or $89,500 in both states of the world. The wealth distribution of someone buying the insurance policy is shown as point A in Figure 13-3.

Notice that in the figure, high-risk individuals are better off buying the insurance policy, but low-risk individuals are worse off. For them, the endowment point E is on a higher indifference curve than point A is. So, high-risk individuals buy the insurance policy and low-risk individuals do not. But when a high-risk individual buys the policy, the insurance company pays out $70,000 with probability 0.2, for an expected benefit payment of (0.2)($70,000) = $14,000. The premium is only $10,500, so the company expects to lose $3,500 on every policy it sells. Clearly, the company is better off staying out of the insurance business.

There is a way, though, that the company would be willing to provide insurance. Suppose that instead of letting employees decide whether or not to buy insurance, the employer buys it for them. Then all employees are insured, not just the high-risk ones, and the insurance company breaks even. This is an example of **group insurance,** and it avoids the adverse selection problem by making sure that both types of individuals "demand" the same type of insurance.

These arguments also show why people who do not get health insurance at work have trouble buying it on their own. The reason is illustrated by Figure 13-3. Government regulations state that insurance companies must set premiums consistent with the average level of risk for the population. As the figure shows, if someone wants to buy insurance at this rate, it must be that they face higher risk than the average for the population, so the insurance company can expect to lose money on the policy.

Different Policies for Different People

We have seen that adverse selection prohibits the insurance company from agreeing to a program wherein the insurance company must charge the same premium to everybody and employees are allowed to choose whether or not to buy insurance. One remedy to this problem is to force everyone to purchase insurance, thereby avoiding the possibility of adverse selection. A different remedy is to allow the insurance company to offer different policies, with different premiums, to the two types of employees.

To do this, we must find a pair of insurance policies with two properties. First, only high-risk individuals buy one type of policy, and only low-risk individuals buy the other type. This allows the insurance company to charge different premiums to the two groups. Second, the company sets premiums that are fair for the group that buys the policy. So, if only low-risk individuals buy a particular policy, the insurance company sets the premium equal to the expected value of the loss faced by a low-risk individual.

We can construct the pair of insurance policies graphically in Figure 13-4. We begin with a high-risk individual, and the first step is to draw his budget line. If an insurance policy is fair, the premium is equal to the expected benefit payment. Consequently, if someone buys a fair insurance policy, his expected wealth does not change. It falls by the amount of the premium, but it rises by the amount of the expected benefit payment, resulting in no change in expected wealth. For a high-risk individual, expected wealth is $(0.2)(\$30,000) + (0.8)(\$100,000) = \$86,000$. The budget line (labeled H) passes through the point E, the endowment point, and point B, where wealth is $86,000 in both states.

We saw in Section 4.3 that when a risk-averse individual has the opportunity to buy fair insurance, he buys full insurance; that is, he buys the amount of insurance that fully covers any potential loss, making wealth the same in both states. Graphically, the high-risk individual chooses point B, and his indifference curve is tangent to the budget line at point B (refer back to Figure 4.7). Point B is reached when the individual buys an insurance policy with $70,000 of coverage and a $14,000 premium, and such a policy is the high-risk individual's favorite fair insurance policy.

The next step is to find the budget line for low-risk individuals. The expected wealth of a low-risk individual is $(0.1)(\$30,000) + (0.9)(\$100,000) = \$93,000$. So, the budget line (labeled L) passes through E and C. Just like the high-risk individuals, the low-risk individuals would like to purchase full insurance when premiums are fair. But if the insurance company offers a policy that allows low-risk individuals to reach point C, high-risk individuals would buy it, too, since point C is on a higher indifference curve than point B. This would generate the same adverse selection problem as before. To avoid adverse selection, the insurance company cannot offer any policy that high-risk individuals like better than point B. The only policies that can be offered to low-risk individuals are policies yielding points between E and

Figure 13-4   Solving the Adverse Selection Problem

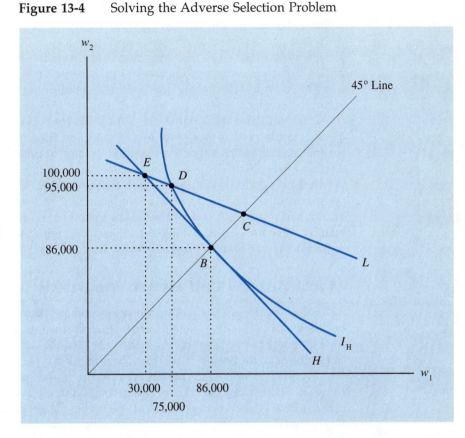

When the insurance company can offer different policies to different individuals, it can offer a policy with $70,000 of coverage and a $14,000 premium to the high-risk individuals, resulting in the wealth distribution at point B. This is the best fair insurance policy for high-risk individuals. To see why, notice that all the wealth distributions consistent with fair insurance for high-risk individuals lie on the budget line H. The high-risk indifference curve I_H is tangent to H at point B, showing that B is the best the high-risk individuals can do. Since B is on the 45-degree line, high-risk individuals are getting full insurance.

Fair insurance for low-risk individuals yields the budget line L. They would like to be at point C, where they get full insurance. But then all of the high-risk individuals would buy this policy, too, which causes an adverse selection problem. The best point on L for low-risk individuals that high-risk individuals won't also choose is point D. Because of adverse selection, low-risk individuals can only buy fair insurance policies with partial coverage.

D on the low-risk budget line. Of these, the low-risk individual likes D the best.

At point D, the low-risk individual's wealth is $75,000 in state 1 and $95,000 in state 2. This means that the insurance premium is $100,000 − $95,000 = $5,000, which pays for $50,000 in coverage. Low-risk individuals are only able to buy insurance policies that cover $50,000 of the possible

$70,000 loss. High-risk individuals are able to buy full insurance, but low-risk individuals are able to get only partial insurance. This unequal treatment is a consequence of adverse selection: Because insurance companies are unable to distinguish high-risk customers from low-risk customers, they must offer less insurance to the low-risk customers. Low-risk individuals are unsatisfied with the outcome because they would prefer to purchase full insurance.

This result also shows up in the national debate about health insurance. Young people usually have low health risks, but they have trouble getting insurance. The policies that are inexpensive do not provide enough coverage to satisfy them. Full-coverage policies are available, but they are not worth it because they charge the high-risk premium. So, relatively healthy people wind up having trouble getting satisfactory levels of health insurance. They are driven out of the health insurance market by people with health problems. This is just like what happened with the used car example of Section 13.1: Good cars were driven out of the market by bad cars.

Moral Hazard and Health Insurance

Moral hazard poses a different problem for health insurance. Moral hazard occurs when one party's actions are hidden from the other party, leading the first party to provide less effort than the second party would like. What does this mean for health insurance? There are two types of health care. One is preventive care, usually undertaken by the individual. It includes such things as eating right, exercising, and getting regular physical checkups. The other type of health care is treatment. When people get sick or injured, they require medical treatment. Health insurance covers the cost of treatment, but not the cost of preventive care. But treatment and preventive care are substitutes, and when the cost of one falls, it gets used more and the other gets used less. In this case, health insurance causes the cost of treatment to fall dramatically, so individuals expend less effort avoiding illness or injury and get treatment whenever they need it.

This presents a problem for health insurance providers. When an individual gets health insurance, he stops taking such good care of himself and becomes more likely to get sick or injured. So, when an individual gets health insurance, he is more likely to require treatment that is paid for by the insurance company. This is a classic moral hazard problem: Health insurance removes the incentive for the individual to expend effort on preventive care, so he doesn't. Insurance companies need to take this behavior into account when setting their premiums.

To see this, suppose that Dave spends an average of $500 per year on treatment. What would happen if the insurance company provided full coverage for a $500 annual premium? Because of moral hazard, Dave would expend less effort on preventive care, and his expected treatment cost would rise to, say, $600. The insurance company's expected benefit payment is $600, but it only collects $500 from the premium. It loses $100 on Dave's policy. The correct premium would take Dave's behavioral change into account, and the fair premium would be $600. But notice what happened here. The existence of comprehensive health insurance raised both the amount spent on treatment and the insurance premium. The fact that health insurance causes moral hazard is one reason why medical costs are so high.

Summary

- **Adverse selection** occurs when one side of the market has different information about quality than the other side of the market. For example, in a used car market, owners of used cars have better information about the quality of their cars than potential buyers do.

- In the used car market example, since buyers cannot tell good used cars from bad ones, if both types of cars are sold on the market they must sell at the same price. This makes owners unwilling to sell good used cars, and only bad used cars are traded on the market. There is no market for good used cars.

- If middlemen can distinguish between good and bad used cars, they can build reputations for selling only good used cars, thereby permitting a market for good used cars to exist. The adverse selection problem is avoided through use of the reputations of middlemen.

- Another method of avoiding adverse selection problems is through use of a **signal,** which is an action that the better-informed party can undertake to reveal the quality of the item. In the education example, high-productivity workers earn a college degree and low-productivity workers do not. Even though education does nothing to enhance productivity (in this example), it still allows high-productivity workers to distinguish themselves from low-productivity workers.

- **Moral hazard** occurs in an agreement when one participant has no incentive to exert the amount of effort intended by the other participant. For example, if someone pays a jeweler up front for a piece of custom jewelry, the jeweler has no further incentive to work hard on the piece of jewelry.

- Health insurance markets exhibit both adverse selection and moral hazard. Adverse selection occurs because high-risk individuals attempt to get the same insurance policies as low-risk individuals, driving low-risk individuals out of the market. Moral hazard occurs because people with health insurance have less incentive to take care of themselves than people without health insurance.

Problems

1. State whether the following situations are better characterized as adverse selection, moral hazard, or neither, and explain your reasoning.
   a. A tutor gets paid by the semester instead of by the hour.
   b. A driver needing gas must choose among four adjacent gas stations, and all four have posted their prices.
   c. An individual gets a phone call from someone trying to sell insurance.
   d. A tourist in New York thinks about buying a Rolex watch from a street vendor.

2. When pawn shops loan money to people, they require the borrowers to leave one of their possessions with the pawn shop, and the borrower cannot get it back until the loan is repaid. Explain how this solves the adverse selection problem.

3. Suppose that there are three kinds of cars: good, medium, and bad. Owners value good cars at $20,000, medium cars at $15,000, and bad cars at $10,000. Forty percent of all cars are good, 40 percent are medium, and 20 percent are bad. Buyers cannot tell the quality of a car before they buy it.
   a. Explain why there is no market for good used cars.
   b. Explain why there is no market for medium used cars.
   c. Is there a market for bad used cars? Why or why not?

4. In the discussion of middlemen in Section 13.1, we set the middleman's discount factor at 0.95 and showed that there was an equilibrium where the middleman only sells good cars. Find a lower discount factor for which the middleman has an incentive to cheat and so no market for good cars exists.

5. In the signaling model of Section 13.2, we showed that if the cost of education is just right, high-productivity workers can signal their productivity by getting an education.
   a. Show that if the cost of education to high-productivity workers is too high, there is no equilibrium in which high-productivity workers use signals.
   b. Show that if the cost of education to low-productivity workers is too low, there is no equilibrium in which high-productivity workers use signals.

6. The signaling model of Section 13.2 assumed that workers spend only four years in their jobs. What is the outcome of the model if workers spend five years on the job instead of four?

7. Some manufacturers provide warranties for their products. When a product is covered by a warranty, the manufacturer promises to repair for free any defects for a certain length of time after the original purchase. Explain how manufacturers can use warranties as a signal of quality.

8. From time to time consumer advocates argue that certain vehicles are prone to flipping over, and that automobile manufacturers should be forced to fix the problem. But if drivers are sufficiently careful, the vehicles are unlikely to flip over in the first place.

   a. If the law states that the manufacturer must pay all damages whenever the vehicle flips over, what will be the effect on how people drive?

   b. What will be the effect on the price of the vehicle?

   c. If, instead, the law states that the manufacturer must pay *half* of all damages whenever the vehicle flips over, does the moral hazard problem disappear? Why or why not?

9. In Section 4.3 we saw that one reason for insurance policies having a deductible is that insurance companies use a loading factor when calculating premiums, so that insurance is not actuarially fair. A second reason for deductibles is that they can be used as a signal to distinguish between high- and low-risk individuals, and this works even when insurance is actuarially fair. Using the health insurance example of Section 13.4, explain how offering policies with deductibles would solve the adverse selection problem.

10. Another problem with health insurance is that when insured people do not have to pay the full cost for doctor visits, they tend to visit the doctor too often. Use supply and demand analysis to show why this is. What effect does this behavior have on health insurance premiums?

11. If the government passes a law in which the government pays for health insurance for all citizens using tax dollars, would the adverse selection and moral hazard problems be alleviated? Explain your answers.

14

AUCTIONS

Overview

So far in this book we have discussed several mechanisms through which prices are set in markets. First we studied supply and demand, which works well in competitive markets, and then we expanded the analysis to include other market structures, specifically monopoly and oligopoly. Then, in Chapter 12, we studied bargaining situations. There is one more mechanism of interest—auctions. Auctions are used in a variety of settings. They are used to sell antiques, art, wine, stamps, and other collectible items. The Treasury Department uses auctions to sell government bonds. The Resolution Trust Corporation auctions off failed banks, savings and loans, and real estate. The government also uses auctions to sell the rights to drill for oil on tracts of government land. Construction contracts are awarded by auction, even when the construction contract is for something relatively small, such as a house. A person who wants to get a house built typically solicits bids from a number of different builders and chooses the builder with the lowest price.

There are two basic questions regarding auctions. First, from the bidder's point of view, what is the optimal bidding strategy? Bidders want to win the auction, but they also want to pay as little as possible for the prize. Bidders should not bid too low, however, because then they risk being outbid by someone else and losing the prize. For example, when Shell Oil bids for the right to drill for oil on a particular offshore tract, it must consider not only the price it will pay if it wins, but also the likelihood of winning. If Shell submits a low bid, it increases the size of its profit if it wins the auction, but it reduces the probability of winning, since a low bid makes it easier for other oil companies to win the auction. The optimal bidding strategy must account for this trade-off between paying less for the prize and risking losing the prize.

The second question concerns the seller of the prize. The seller's goal is to make as much money as possible from the auction. How should the seller design the auction to maximize profit? The U.S. government took this question very seriously in its recent auctions of spectrum channels suitable for personal communication devices, such as pagers and mobile telephones. Many of the leading economists involved in auction theory were consulted to design the auction that would generate as much revenue as possible for the government. Other economists were employed by telecommunications firms to help them bid appropriately. This is, perhaps, the best example of how economic theory has been used to guide behavior in the real world.

Auctions are analyzed using the tools of game theory. It is typical in auctions to have only a fairly small number of people bidding on any given item. These people behave strategically, with their optimal actions dependent on the behavior of their opponents. How we analyze auctions depends on two things: what type of auction it is, and what the characteristics of the prize are. In this chapter you will learn:

- How bidders behave in equilibrium in four different types of auctions.
- How the seller can decide which type of auction to use.
- How bidders behave when the prize has the same value to all bidders but the value is unknown.

14.1 PRIVATE VALUE AUCTIONS

How we analyze auctions depends on the characteristics of what is being sold. For example, when the government sells the right to drill for oil on a certain piece of land, the value of the right to drill is the same to every firm that bids. The value depends on how much oil can be extracted from the land. The problem is that nobody knows exactly how much oil there is, so nobody knows the true value of the oil lease. This is the case of a **common value auction.** The value of the prize is the same for all bidders, but the bidders do not know exactly what the value is. In contrast, consider the case of an art dealer auctioning a not particularly rare painting. The value of the painting to an individual is determined by how much that individual likes the painting. Since different people have different tastes in art, each individual has his own specific valuation of the item. Because the painting is not a terribly important work of art, the investment potential is negligible. The only value of the painting is the enjoyment the owner gets from hanging it on the wall. When valuations differ across individuals, the auction is a **private value auction.**

In the real world, most auctions have both a private value component and a common value component. For example, when builders bid on construction contracts, each builder has his own relationship with subcontractors, so each builder has different costs. This generates the private value component. All of the builders bid to build exactly the same building, however, so the costs should be approximately the same. This generates the common value component. By separating auctions into the two types, we simplify matters greatly. By understanding the two types, however, it is possible to get an understanding of auctions that are a combination of the two. In this section we analyze private value auctions, and in Section 3 we turn our attention to common value auctions.

The Private Values Assumption

The private values assumption states that each bidder has his own value of the item being auctioned and that bidders' valuations are private information. That is, each bidder knows his own valuation, but not the valuations of the other bidders. Moreover, the auctioneer does not know any of the valuations. What we eventually do in this section is describe how people behave in auctions. To do this, we must come up with a way to handle all of the things that the bidders do not know. That is, we must come up with a description of how the different values are generated.

In reality, the different values probably arise because different people have different preferences and different levels of income. Valuations are generated when each individual performs a consumer optimization problem, as in Chapter 3. We do not want to talk about indifference curves and budget constraints here, however. All we want to talk about is valuations and how people bid given their valuations. So let's think about valuations another way.

Consider the case of several people bidding for a not particularly rare painting. The value of the painting to each person depends on the person's characteristics, such as his tastes in art. Each person knows how much the painting is worth to him, but not how much it is worth to the other bidders. Since each individual bidder does not know the other bidders' valuations, it is natural for him to treat the other valuations as if they are random. For example, suppose that bidder A thinks that each of the other bidders values the painting somewhere between $3,000 and $6,000, with each possible valuation in this range being equally likely. Essentially, bidder A's beliefs are consistent with each of her opponents' being presented with a jar containing pieces of paper inscribed with every possible number between $3,000 and $6,000. Each bidder draws a number out of the jar, and the number is the bidder's valuation. Since each of the numbers is equally likely, the average, or expected, draw is $4,500.

Treating valuations as if they are random draws from some mysterious jar may seem like a rather strange way to describe how valuations are generated, but it really isn't so strange. Consider the art auction. The value of the painting to a bidder depends on such things as that bidder's taste in art, her preferences over art versus other consumption goods, her income, and her ability to pay that much money at the time. Now suppose that the number of potential bidders is large and that a randomly chosen group of them shows up for the auction. Since valuations are determined by the characteristics of the bidders, drawing the characteristics of the bidders randomly from the population is no different from drawing the valuations randomly. We are just cutting a step out of the process.

Now that bidders have their private valuations and their beliefs about their opponent's valuations, we can discuss what it is bidders try to do when they participate in an auction. Bidders try to maximize **expected surplus.** If the bidder loses the auction, the surplus is zero. If the bidder wins the auction, the bidder gets the item and must pay some price. The surplus generated by a winning bid is the value of the item minus the price the bidder must pay. So, for example, if a bidder values the item at $5,000, wins the auction, and pays $4,500, the bidder's surplus is $500. Since bidders do not generally know whether or not they will win the auction, they must calculate the probability of winning with a given bid. They can then calculate the expected surplus for each alternative bid and choose the bid that generates the highest expected surplus. Notice that the assumption that bidders maximize expected surplus has a hidden implication: Bidders are risk neutral. The behavior of risk-averse bidders is analyzed in the next section.

Four Types of Auctions

Four types of auctions are typically used to sell items. Two of them are likely to be familiar, and two are probably unfamiliar. One of the familiar auctions is the one in which an auctioneer calls out successively higher prices, bidders keep raising their bids until only one is left, and the high bidder gets the item for the price he bids. This auction is known as an **English auction.** One reason English auctions are familiar is that most of the auctions shown in television shows or movies are English auctions. They have a bit more drama than the other types of auctions. Another reason they are familiar is that they are commonly used to sell such things as art and antiques. The other familiar auction is the one in which bidders all submit bids secretly at the same time, and then the seller awards the item to the highest bidder, who pays his bid. This is known as a **first-price (sealed-bid) auction.** The term *sealed-bid* is used because bidders know only their own bids, and not the bids of the others. To preserve the secrecy of bids, participants often place their bids in sealed envelopes. First-price auctions are used in a variety of business situations, including the sale of oil leases and the awarding of construction contracts.

The unfamiliar auctions are variations on the familiar ones. One of the unfamiliar auctions has all the bidders submitting sealed bids at the same time, with the high bidder winning, just as in the first-price auction. This time, though, the winner pays the *second-highest* bid, not the highest bid. This auction is called a **second-price auction.** First- and second-price auctions differ only in the price that is paid by the winner, but, as we will see, this small difference has a big impact on how bidders behave. Second-price auctions may seem a bit strange, but they are actually used to sell stamps to collectors. The final type of auction is similar to the English auction, except that instead of going up over time, the price falls over time. All bidders start with their hands down. The price falls until one of the bidders raises his hand, the item is awarded to that bidder, and the price is determined by his bid. This type of auction is used to sell tulip bulbs in the Netherlands, and it is called a **Dutch auction.** The four types of auctions are summarized in Table 14-1.

Equilibrium Behavior in English and Second-Price Auctions

To analyze bidding behavior in the different types of auctions, we begin with the simplest to analyze and end with the most difficult. The simplest one is the English auction. Suppose that bidders are competing for a painting. Each time the auctioneer calls out a price in an English auction, an individual bidder must make a decision like the following. The auctioneer calls out the price p, and the bidder must decide whether or not to bid at this price. If he bids and wins, he receives the painting, which is worth, say, $5,000 to him. He must pay the bid p, so his surplus is $5,000 − p$. If he does not bid, he gets nothing. It is pretty clear that he should bid whenever the price is below $5,000, and should drop out of the bidding as soon as the price exceeds his valuation.

What happens in equilibrium? Each bidder is willing to bid up to his own valuation of the item and drops out as soon as the price rises above the valuation. The bidding stops when there is only one bidder left, which is when the bidder with the second-highest valuation drops out. At this point, there is no reason for the bidder with the highest valuation to bid any higher. Thus, the bidder with the highest valuation wins the auction and pays the valuation of the second-highest bidder. When the auction awards the painting to the bidder with the highest valuation, the auction is said to be **efficient.** English auctions are efficient.

Now consider second-price auctions. Bidders submit their bids, and the auctioneer awards the item to the highest bidder, who then pays the second-highest bid. A bidder's payoff in the auction, then, depends on the highest bid submitted by the other participants. Let b denote the highest other bid. Suppose that the bidder values the prize at $5,000, and let's see what happens if he bids $5,000. If $b < \$5,000$, he wins the auction, pays b, and receives a surplus of $5,000 − b$. If $b > \$5,000$, he loses the auction and gets zero surplus.

Table 14-1   Four Types of Auctions

Type of Auction	Sealed or Open Bids	Method of Bidding	Who Wins	How Much Is Paid
English	Open	Ascending	Last bidder	Last bid
Dutch	Open	Descending	First bidder	First bid
First-price	Sealed	Simultaneous	Highest bidder	Highest bid
Second-price	Sealed	Simultaneous	Highest bidder	Second-highest bid

Table 14-2   Bidding in a Second-Price Auction

Range of Highest Other Bid	Surplus If Own Bid Is $5,000	Surplus If Own Bid Is $5,010
$b \leq \$5,000$	$\$5,000 - b \geq \$0$	$\$5,000 - b \geq \$0$
$\$5,000 < b \leq \$5,010$	$\$0$	$\$5,000 - b < \$0$
$b > \$5,010$	$\$0$	$\$0$

Could he do any better by bidding more than $5,000, such as, for example, $5,010? To answer this question, we can separate possible values of b into three ranges. If $b < \$5,000$, he wins the auction, pays b, and receives surplus of $\$5,000 - b$. This is exactly what would have happened if he had bid $5,000. If $b > \$5,010$, he loses the auction and gets zero surplus. This, too, would have happened if he had bid $5,000. The only time something different happens is when $\$5,000 < b \leq \$5,010$. This time the bidder wins the auction, since his is the highest bid, he pays b, and his surplus is $\$5,000 - b < \$0$. If he had bid $5,000 instead of $5,010, he would have lost the auction and received zero surplus. Table 14-2 summarizes all of this information. No matter what the highest other bid is, the individual's surplus from bidding $5,000 is at least as high as when he bids $5,010. This means that bidding $5,010 is a *dominated strategy*. Similar reasoning shows that any bid above the bidder's valuation is a dominated strategy.

What about bids below the valuation? Suppose he bids $4,990 instead of $5,000. Table 14-3 shows what happens in this case. The surplus is the same from the two bids unless the highest other bid is between $4,990 and $5,000. If the individual bids $5,000 and b is in this range, the bidder wins the auction and gets a positive surplus. If, instead, he bids $4,990, he loses the auction and gets nothing. Bidding below the valuation is a *dominated strategy*. Combining this argument with the previous argument shows that a player's dominant strategy in a second-price auction is to bid his valuation. Because each player bids his valuation, the second-highest bid will be the second-highest valuation. Thus, in the dominant strategy equilibrium, the bidder with the highest valuation wins the auction and pays the second-highest valuation. This means that second-price auctions are also efficient.

Table 14-3   Bidding in a Second-Price Auction

Range of b	Surplus If Own Bid Is $5,000	Surplus If Own Bid is $4,990
$b \leq \$4,990$	$\$5,000 - b > \$0$	$\$5,000 - b > \$0$
$\$4,990 < b < \$5,000$	$\$5,000 - b > \$0$	$\$0$
$b \geq \$5,000$	$\$0$	$\$0$

Equilibrium Behavior in First-Price and Dutch Auctions

The third type of auction we consider is the first-price auction. In this auction bidders submit bids and the auctioneer awards the item to the highest bidder, who pays his bid. Notice that it is no longer optimal for the bidder to bid his own valuation. Suppose that he values the painting at $5,000, and he bids $5,000. If he wins his surplus is $5,000 − $5,000 = $0. If he loses, his surplus is also zero. No matter what happens, he gets a surplus of zero. Look what happens if he reduces his bid to $4,999. He is almost as likely to win the auction, since he reduced his bid only a little bit, but if he wins he gets a surplus of $1. This gives him a positive (though small) expected surplus instead of a zero expected surplus. So, in a first-price auction participants bid less than their valuations.

How much less should they bid? Before answering that question, let's do a mental exercise. Suppose that everyone knows all the bidders' valuations, and that bidder A has the highest valuation. There exists an equilibrium in which A bids just slightly over the second-highest valuation and his opponents bid their own valuations. Let's check that this is an equilibrium. If A bids more, he still wins the auction but gets less surplus. If A bids less, the bidder with the second-highest valuation can beat him. So then A loses the auction, which reduces his surplus. Thus, A has no incentive to deviate from the equilibrium. The other bidders are indifferent about what they do since they lose the auction and get zero surplus anyway, so they have no incentive to deviate either. This establishes that we have an equilibrium.

Now let's get back to the situation in which the opponent's valuations are unknown. Suppose that bidder A values the item at $5,000, with valuations evenly distributed between $3,000 and $6,000. How should he formulate his optimal strategy? First of all, he should behave as if he is going to win the auction. If he is wrong, so what? The only time he actually has to make any financial transaction is if he wins the auction, which is if he has the highest valuation. Otherwise he gets zero. The assumption that his is the highest valuation narrows down the range of his opponents' valuations. Instead of being between $3,000 and $6,000, bidder A behaves as if his opponents' valuations are between $3,000 and $5,000. There is nothing special about bidder A or his $5,000 valuation. Every bidder should behave as if his own valuation is the highest, and should revise his beliefs about his opponents' valuations accordingly. Each bidder, then, should determine what is the *expected second-highest valuation* relative to his valuation. By bidding the expected second-highest valuation, each bidder maximizes his expected surplus.

This said, let's propose an equilibrium and see whether it works. Each bidder assumes that his own valuation is the highest, and revises his beliefs accordingly. He then bids the expected second-highest valuation, calculated using the revised beliefs. For example, suppose that there are only two bidders, and the range of valuations is $3,000 to $6,000. Bidder A's valuation is $5,000, so he behaves according to the assumption that bidder B's valuation is between $3,000 and $5,000. According to A's beliefs, the expected value of B's valuation is $4,000, so A bids $4,000. What if A's valuation is $5,500? He revises his beliefs so that the range of B's valuation is between $3,000 and $5,500, with an expected value of $4,250. This would be A's equilibrium bid. The higher A's valuation, the more he bids.

Let's return to the assumption that A's valuation is $5,000, which implies a bid of $4,000, and let's calculate A's expected surplus. Since bidder B uses the same decision rule that A uses, if B's valuation is less than $5,000, B bids less than $4,000, so A wins the auction. If B's valuation is more than $5,000, B bids more than $4,000 and wins the auction. Remember that the complete range of valuations is evenly distributed between $3,000 and $6,000. Therefore, the probability that A wins the auction is 2/3, since this is the probability that B's valuation is between $3,000 and $5,000. The probability that A loses the auction and gets zero surplus is 1/3, since that is the probability that B's valuation is between $5,000 and $6,000. Bidder A's expected surplus is $(2/3)(\$5,000 - \$4,000) = \$667$.

Let's check to see whether bidder A has any incentive to deviate from this strategy, given that bidder B follows the proposed strategy. If A bids more than $4,000, he increases the probability of winning but reduces his surplus if he wins. Suppose he bids $4,100 instead of $4,000. In this case he beats everyone with a valuation below $5,200. Why? A bidder with a valuation of $5,200 assumes that A's valuation is between $3,000 and $5,200, so bids the midpoint of this range, or $4,100. The probability that the opponent's valuation is below $5,200 is $(5,200 - 3,000)/(6,000 - 3,000) = (2,200/3,000) = 0.733$. Bidder A's surplus if he wins is his true valuation minus his bid, or $5,000 - $4100 = $900. His expected surplus is $(0.73)(\$900) = \$657$, which is lower than $667. Repeating this analysis for other bids above $4,000 shows that A does not want to bid more than $4,000.

What if A bids less than $4,000? Suppose he bids $3,900. This reduces his probability of winning but increases his surplus if he does win. His opponent bids less than $3,900 if his opponent's bid is less than $4,800. (Can you figure out why?) This means that bidder A wins with probability 0.6. If he wins, his surplus is $1,100, so his expected surplus is $660. He would be better off bidding $4,000 and receiving an expected surplus of $667. Repeating the analysis for other bids below $4,000 shows that A maximizes expected surplus by bidding $4,000. This process establishes that bidding the expected second-highest valuation, under the assumption that each bidder's own valuation is the highest, is an equilibrium strategy.

The example just given shows how bidder A selects a bid when there is only one opposing bidder. He adjusts his bid downward from his valuation by half of the difference between his valuation and the lowest possible valuation. The same sort of formula works when there are more opposing bidders. For example, if there are three opposing bidders, for a total of four bidders, bidder *A* adjusts his bid by one-fourth of the difference between his valuation and the lowest possible valuation. If his valuation is $5,000 and the lowest possible valuation is $3,000, his equilibrium bid is $4,500, the expected second-highest valuation relative to bidder *A*. If there are nine other bidders, for a total of ten, he adjusts his bid downward by one-tenth of the difference. His optimal bid is $4,800. With a total of 100 bidders, the optimal bid is $4,980. As you can see, as the number of bidders rises, the equilibrium bids rise. This implies that the seller should try to get as many bidders as possible. More bidders mean higher bids, which means more revenue for the seller.

Finally, we get to the Dutch auction, in which the auctioneer calls out successively lower prices until a bidder stops the auction at a particular price and agrees to pay that price. Strategically, a Dutch auction is exactly the same as a first-price auction. Each bidder should behave as if his is the highest valuation. If he is wrong, someone will bid before him, and he will lose the auction. As the price falls, bidders do not learn anything except for the fact that nobody has a valuation above the current price. But, if every bidder assumes that his is the highest valuation, the fact that nobody has bid at a higher price has no effect on his behavior. He has already assumed that nobody would bid before him. Since the falling prices do not convey any information, the bidder might as well write down his equilibrium bid ahead of time and just hand it to the auctioneer, who will look at all the bids, award the prize to the highest bidder, and make him pay his bid. But this is exactly a first-price auction. So, in a Dutch auction a bidder should stop the auction when the price reaches the expected second-highest valuation, under the assumption that his own valuation is the highest.

Table 14-4 summarizes the equilibrium strategies for risk-neutral bidders in the different types of auctions.

14.2   WHICH TYPE OF AUCTION IS BEST?

We have introduced four types of auctions. Someone who wants to sell something through an auction would naturally want to use the auction that generates the highest price. The somewhat surprising result is that if all bidders

Table 14-4   Equilibrium Strategies in Different Types of Auctions

Auction	*Equilibrium Strategy*
English	Bid up to own valuation
Second-price	Bid own valuation
First-price	Bid expected second-highest valuation, under assumption that own valuation is highest
Dutch	Stop auction at expected second-highest valuation, under assumption that own valuation is highest

are risk neutral, it doesn't matter which type of auction is used. They all generate the same expected price. This result is known as **revenue equivalence.**

Revenue Equivalence

In all four auctions, the bidder with the highest valuation wins. What we need to do is compare the price he pays in the four auctions. Begin with the English auction. Bidding stops when the individual with the second-highest valuation drops out, which is at the second-highest valuation. The price expected in an English auction, then, is the expected second-highest valuation. In a second-price auction, the bidder with the highest valuation wins and pays the second-highest valuation. Once again, the expected price is the expected second-highest valuation.

Now consider the first-price auction. Since bidders behave the same way in the first-price auction and the Dutch auction, what we find for the first-price auction will also be true of the Dutch auction. The optimal behavior for a bidder in a first-price auction is to bid what he expects to be the second-highest valuation, assuming that his own valuation is the highest. Thus, the final price in the auction is the bid of the person with the highest valuation, and his bid is just his expectation of the second-highest valuation. But before the auction starts, the auctioneer does not know who the highest bidder is, or how much he values the item, or what he expects to be the second-highest valuation. So the auctioneer must formulate her own expectations about these expectations. She forms an expectation about what the highest valuation will be, and she forms an expectation about what the second-highest valuation will be. The price she expects to arise in the auction is the expected second-highest valuation.

In all four auctions, then, the expected price is the expected second-highest valuation. Since one unit of the good is sold at this price, the expected revenue is also the second-highest valuation. All four auctions generate the same, or equivalent, expected revenue.

Risk Aversion

Up to this point, our analysis of the first-price and Dutch auctions has depended on the assumption that bidders are risk neutral. Since most people are not risk neutral, let's see what difference risk aversion makes. We want to check two things. First, do risk-averse people bid any differently than risk-neutral people with the same valuations? Second, do the four auctions generate the same expected revenue when bidders are risk averse?

We begin by looking at first-price auctions using a specific example. Suppose that someone values the prize in a first-price auction at $5,000 and knows the probability that his bid will be highest. If he bids $4,400, he wins the auction with probability 0.4. If he bids $4,500, he wins the auction with probability 0.5. If he bids \$4,600, he wins with probability 0.6. These alternatives are presented in Table 14-5. If the bidder is risk neutral, which of these three bids does he prefer? The goal of a risk-neutral bidder is to maximize expected surplus. Of the three bids presented above, the one that yields the highest expected surplus is \$4,500. This is the optimal bid for a risk-neutral person.

What about a risk-averse bidder? To answer this question, begin by considering a person with a specific utility function. Suppose that the utility function is $u(x) = x^{1/2}$. This is the same utility function we used in most examples of risk aversion in Chapter 4. The expected utility of a particular bid is the probability of winning times the utility of the surplus. For example, when the bid is \$4,400, the probability of winning is 0.4 and the utility of the surplus is $u(600) = 600^{1/2} = 24.5$. The expected utility is $(.6)(24.5) = 9.8$. The expected utilities generated by the other bids are shown in Table 14-5. A risk-averse bidder selects the bid that maximizes his expected utility, which means that, of the three choices presented in the table, he bids \$4,600.

Why do risk-averse people bid higher than risk-neutral people in first-price auctions? Recall from Chapter 4 that, unlike risk-neutral people, risk-averse people are willing to pay to reduce risk. Operationally, this means that, compared to risk-neutral people, risk-averse people are willing to accept alternatives with lower expected values as long as they also have lower risk. A bidder in a first-price auction can reduce risk by increasing his bid. By bidding more he increases the likelihood of winning the auction, but he reduces the surplus if he wins. A risk-averse bidder is willing to take a reduction in the expected surplus in order to reduce the riskiness of the auction, so he bids more. Of course, he could completely eliminate the risk just by bidding his value of the prize. If he wins his surplus is zero, because he must pay the value, and if he loses his surplus is zero. He gets the same surplus either way, so there is no risk. Even so, no risk-averse bidder would want to do this, because even some small chance of a positive surplus is better than no surplus at all. So, we know that risk-averse people bid more than risk-neutral people with the same valuations, but they do not bid all the way up to their valuations.

This has an implication for revenue equivalence. If you look back at the derivation of the equilibrium strategies for English and second-price auc-

Table 14-5   First-Price Auction with Risk-Averse Bidder

Bid	Surplus If Wins	Probability of Winning	Surplus If Loses	Expected Surplus	Expected Utility
4,400	600	0.4	0	240	9.8
4,500	500	0.5	0	250	11.2
4,600	400	0.6	0	240	12.0

tions, you will notice that the derivations did not require risk neutrality. Regardless of risk attitudes, people should bid up to their valuations in English auctions, and they should bid their valuations in second-price auctions. So, even when bidders are risk averse, the expected revenue from English and second-price auctions is the expected second-highest valuation. When bidders are risk neutral, the expected revenue in first-price and Dutch auctions is also the expected second-highest valuation. But risk-averse people bid more than risk-neutral people with the same valuations, so expected revenue in a first-price auction is higher when bidders are risk averse, compared to when bidders are risk neutral. When bidders are risk averse, revenue equivalence no longer holds. First-price and Dutch auctions generate higher revenue than English or second-price auctions.

14.3   COMMON VALUE AUCTIONS

Auctions often involve a prize whose value is the same no matter who wins it. Examples include auctions for oil leases, where the amount of oil recovered is the same no matter which firm is doing the recovering, and construction contracts, where the actual cost of building the project does not depend on who is doing the building. In both of these auctions the bidders do not know the true value of the item. In this section we examine equilibrium bidding behavior in common value auctions.

The Common Value Assumption

In a common value auction, bidders know that the prize is worth the same amount to everybody, but they do not know exactly what that amount is. Each bidder has his own private information about the value of the prize, though, and the information is known only to the bidder. The information is not perfect; that is, it does not tell the bidder exactly what the prize is worth. For example, Shell Oil hires geologists to do seismic surveys of oil leases, and these surveys provide information about how much oil is underground. Seismic surveys are imperfect, because they do not tell exactly how much oil is in the ground, and sometimes they give false readings of what is oil and what is not. Also, seismic surveys do not always tell how easily the oil can be recovered, even if it's there. In spite of this, the surveys do provide some indication about how much the drilling rights are worth. Shell can use the information provided by the surveys to generate an estimate of the true value of the lease.

Let's do a numerical example. Suppose that Shell estimates that the value of the oil lease is $5,000. It knows that this estimate is not exact, but it is sure that the estimate is within $1,000 of the true value. This means that the true value could be anywhere between $4,000 and $6,000. Other bidders make their own estimates of the value of the lease. If their estimates are only accurate to

APPLICATION

How *Not* to Run an Auction

In the past when governments wanted to assign the rights to radio or television frequencies, or pay-television licenses, they would let a committee review applicants and assign the item to the one the committee decided was best. In recent years, however, governments have begun auctioning the rights to run communications services. For example, in 1990 New Zealand auctioned the rights to use different radio, television, and cellular-phone frequencies; in 1993 Australia auctioned two licenses for satellite-television services; and in 1994 the United States auctioned the spectrum rights for some newly invented personal communications devices, such as pocket telephones and portable fax machines. Some lessons can be learned from these auctions.*

First, why use auctions to sell these rights? One reason is that auctions are efficient: They sell the item to the bidder who values it most. Second, auctions provide revenue to the seller—in this case the government. The problem still arises of what form of auction to use. Should the government use a first-price, second-price, or English auction? There are other issues to consider as well, as the experiences of New Zealand and Australia illustrate.

New Zealand chose to use a second-price auction, with some politically embarrassing results. In one case, a firm that bid NZ$100,000 (about US$55,000) won and paid the second-highest price, which was NZ$6. In another case, the highest bid was NZ$7 million and the second-highest bid was NZ$5,000. In a third case, a college student bid NZ$1 for the television license for a small city and won because nobody else bid. The second-highest bid was zero, so he got the television license for free. What went wrong? The problem faced in New Zealand was that there was a relatively small number of bidders competing for a large number of licenses. In some cases there was only one serious bid, leading to the anomalous results just stated. But the government could have avoided this problem by setting a **reserve price,** which is a lowest price at which the item will be sold. In a second-price auction, if no one bids above the reserve price, the government keeps the license. If only one bidder bids above the reserve price, that bidder wins and pays the reserve price. If two or more bidders exceed the reserve price, the highest bidder wins and pays the second-highest bid. A reserve price would have helped the government in two ways. First, it would have guaranteed that no licenses sell at embarrassingly low prices. Second, it would have helped the government raise more revenue.

Australia learned from New Zealand's mistake and used a first-price auction to avoid the problem of low second-highest bids. But Australia made a different mistake. The two licenses were won by two previously unknown firms, both of which submitted extraordinarily high bids and beat out more established competitors. These firms had no intention of paying these high bids, however. Instead, after learning that they had won they defaulted on their bids, which meant that the licenses would be awarded to the second-highest bidders. Firms in this auction were allowed to submit more than one bid for the same prize, and the same two firms were also the second-highest bidders! What they had done was submit several different bids at small intervals, including some very high bids. After winning the auction they defaulted on all of the bids except for the one that was just above the highest bid by a rival. This way they guaranteed winning the auction but paying a low price. After all was said and done, one firm had originally won with a bid of A$212 million (about US$144 million), defaulted on a succession of bids, and paid a final price of A$117 million. The process of defaulting on bids delayed the final sale of the license by four months. The sale of the other license took even longer, a total of nine months. What happened? In designing the auction the Australian government neglected one detail. They neglected to require a deposit from the bidders, so they had no way of penalizing bidders for withdrawing bids. If there had been a deposit, the firms would have lost the deposit when they defaulted on the bids.

These experiences provide two lessons for designing auctions. First, reserve prices should be used to guarantee that the item does not sell for a ridiculously low price. Second, some method must be used to ensure that bids are binding, or at least to penalize bidders for defaulting on bids. When the U.S. government designed an auction mechanism to sell spectrum rights in 1994, it took both of these potential problems into account.

* This material is derived from John McMillan, "Selling Spectrum Rights," *Journal of Economic Perspectives,* Summer 1994, pp. 145–162.

within $1,000 of the true value, the range of possible estimates is quite large. Remember that bidder Shell's estimate was $5,000, which means that the true value could be anywhere between $4,000 and $6,000. If the true value is $4,000, bidders' estimates could be as low as $1,000 below the true value, or $3,000. If the true value is $6,000, bidders' estimates could be as high as $7,000.

Before going on, let's introduce some terminology. The information a bidder receives about the true value of the prize is a **signal.** The bidder then uses the signal to estimate the value of the prize, with the ultimate goal of formulating a bid that maximizes expected surplus. Since different bidders receive different signals, they make different estimates of the value of the prize. But now this is just a private value auction. The bidders have different estimates of the value, and they bid according to their estimates. The equilibrium bids are the same as they were in the two previous sections. The big difference between private and common value auctions, then, is where the valuations come from. In private value auctions the valuations are determined by the preferences and incomes of the bidders. In common value auctions the valuations are determined by information signals. What we need to do is figure out how bidders should use their signals to estimate the value of the prize.

The Winner's Curse

To talk about equilibrium behavior, let's restrict attention to one particular type of auction, the second-price auction. This auction is nice because the equilibrium behavior is simple: Bidders bid their valuations. Also, since everyone submits bids at the same time, there is no way for one bidder to find out another bidder's information. The first task is to see what happens if everyone simply bids his signal. In particular, is bidding the signal an equilibrium strategy? Suppose that the true value of the oil lease is $4,000 and this fact is unknown to Shell Oil, which receives a signal of $5,000. If signals are accurate to within $1,000 of the true value, Shell receives the highest possible signal. This means that if Shell bids $5,000, it wins the auction. No other company bids more than $5,000, because no other company receives a signal that the lease is worth more than $5,000. For the sake of the example, suppose that the second-highest bid is $4,500. What is Shell's surplus? It gets a prize worth $4,000, but pays the second-highest bid of $4,500. Its surplus is −$500. By winning the auction Shell actually loses money.

The problem is that Shell overbid. If bidders bid their signals, who wins the auction? The bidder with the highest signal. If the signals are dispersed both above and below the true value, however, the highest signal is likely to be above the true value. This means that the winning bidder probably bids too much for the prize. The phenomenon that the highest bidder overbids and loses money in the auction is known as the **winner's curse.** The existence of a winner's curse means that bidding the signal cannot be an equilibrium in the above example. To establish that it is not an equilibrium, all we must do is find a bidder that would like to change its strategy. Remember that bidders behave under the assumption that they are the highest bidders. So, when Shell assumes that its valuation is the highest, if it knows about the winner's curse it knows that the strategy of bidding its signal will most likely cause it to lose money. Shell would like to reduce its bid to avoid this problem. Because it would like to bid less, the bid leading to the winner's curse cannot be an equilibrium, and the winner's curse cannot occur in equilibrium.

How does a bidder avoid the winner's curse? The answer lies in the bidder's assumption that it will be the highest bidder. Look back at Shell, whose signal is $5,000. If Shell behaves under the assumption that its own bid is the highest, it must also behave under the assumption that its signal is the highest. This realization provides Shell with a little more information. Suppose that there are three bidders, including Shell, participating in the auction. Each bidder receives a signal that is within $1,000 of the true value of the prize. The range of possible signals is shown in Figure 14-1. Letting *V* denote the true value of the prize, the lowest possible signal is $V - 1{,}000$, and the highest possible signal is $V + 1{,}000$. If there are only three bidders, and if the signals are evenly dispersed in this range, what is the expected highest signal? The expected highest signal is $V + 500$. To see why, first look at what the average signal is. The average signal is V, and we would expect that the second-highest bidder, which is the middle bidder, receives a signal of V. His actual signal is almost surely different from V, but his *expected* signal is V. The highest signal is somewhere in the range from V to $V + 1{,}000$. The average value in this range is $V + 500$.

This tells us how Shell should optimally use its signal. If Shell wins the auction, it knows that its signal is the highest. The highest signal is, on average, $500 above the true value of the item. So, if Shell wins it knows that, on average, the true value of the item is $500 less than its signal. Shell should, therefore, base its bid on an expected valuation $500 below its signal. So, for example, if its signal is $5,000, Shell should base its bid on an expected valuation of $4,500.

How does this avoid the winner's curse? The winner's curse occurs when a bidder does not account for the fact that if it wins the auction, its signal must be higher than all the other signals. Once the bidder finds out that its signal is the highest, the bidder immediately knows that its previous estimate of the value of the prize was too high. It would then like to change its bid. With the procedure we have outlined, though, the bidder already incorporates the information it receives if it wins the auction. If it wins, then,

Figure 14-1   Inferring Value from Signals

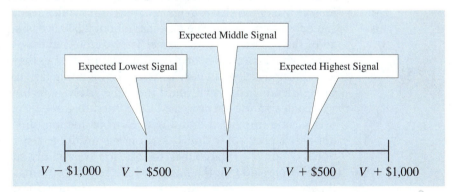

When there are three bidders and each bidder's signal is known to be within $1,000 of the true value of the prize, with each possible signal equally likely, it is possible to predict the highest, middle, and lowest signals. The expected middle signal is V, the true value of the prize, the expected high signal is $V + 500$, and the expected low signal is $V - 500$. This makes the expected signals evenly dispersed in the range from $V - 1{,}000$ to $V + 1{,}000$, as shown. If a bidder does not know V but believes his own signal to be highest, he can reverse these steps to figure out the expected value of the prize. The highest signal is expected to be $500 above V, so the expected value of the prize is the signal minus $500. Bidders can use this information to avoid the winner's curse.

there is no reason for it to change its bid. This brings up a point about equilibrium behavior in common value auctions. If bidders do not take the winner's curse into account when formulating their estimates of the value of the prize, the resulting bids are not equilibrium bids. This is because once a bidder finds out that it is the winner, that bidder would like to change its bid. If bidders do take the winner's curse into account, then it is *possible* for the resulting bids to be equilibrium bids. For the bidding behavior to be equilibrium behavior, the bidders must still behave according to the equilibrium strategies devised in Section 14.1 for the various types of auctions.

One type of auction is particularly useful for helping bidders avoid the winner's curse. In an English auction, bidders get to see when their opponents drop out of the bidding. The price at which a bidder drops out provides information about that bidder's signal. Even the fact that a particular bidder has not yet dropped out provides some information. These extra bits of information help bidders refine their beliefs about the true value of the item, and the better informed bidders are, the smaller the winner's curse is.

14.4 GAME THEORY IN ACTION: THE FCC SPECTRUM AUCTIONS

In 1993 the U.S. Congress passed a law allowing the Federal Communications Commission to auction use of the electromagnetic spectrum for personal communications services, such as mobile telephones, two-way paging, and portable fax machines. The legislation also specified some goals the FCC must follow in designing the auctions. The highest priority was the efficient and intensive use of the electromagnetic spectrum, while raising of revenue was assigned a low priority. The FCC had about 2,000 licenses to auction, and not all of the licenses were the same. They differed in bandwidth (which determines what kinds of personal communication devices they can accommodate), location, and size of the service area. The daunting task faced by the FCC was to design an auction that could reach the goals set forth in the legislation.

To design the auction, the FCC turned to game theorists. The game theorists came up with a brand new form of auction, different from the ones discussed previously, but based on the intuition generated by those auctions. By almost all accounts, the auction was wildly successful. For example, *Fortune* said that the auction was the "most dramatic example of game theory's new power. . . . It was a triumph, not only for the FCC and the taxpayers, but also for game theory (and game theorists)."[1] We now describe the auction and how well it worked.[2]

---

1 *Fortune*, February 6, 1995, p. 36.

2 This discussion is based on "Analyzing the Airwaves Auction," by R. Preston McAfee and John McMillan, *Journal of Economic Perspectives*, Winter 1996, pp. 159–175.

APPLICATION
The Winner's Curse in Construction Contracts

The way construction contracts are usually awarded is that the architect or owner of the project opens the project up for bid, and interested construction companies can submit bids.* The time and date for the closing of the bidding process are also announced. After bidding has closed, the winner is announced. In the construction business, the contractor's job is to get the materials and hire subcontractors. The subcontractors do most of the construction work, with different subcontractors doing electrical work, plumbing, foundation, heating and air conditioning, and so on. The general contractor also supervises all of this work. In large construction jobs, about 90 percent of the final price goes to material suppliers and subcontractors. Construction contracts are a bit different from the auctions studied in the rest of this chapter, because the buyer auctions off the right to sell. In art auctions, on the other hand, the seller auctions off the right to buy. In construction contracts, the low bidder wins, and the contractor is paid the bid amount to build the project. The winner's curse in this setting, then, is that the bidder bids too low.

It has been found that construction contractors are usually able to avoid the winner's curse. There are several methods by which this is done. First, most of the contractors have bid on enough projects that they have learned how to adjust their bids to avoid the winner's curse. Second, most states and municipalities have laws stating that low bidders can withdraw bids on public projects when the bids contain arithmetic errors. The interpretation of "arithmetic errors" has become quite liberal, and contractors do use this mechanism to withdraw bids that are far below everyone else's, thereby avoiding the winner's curse. If the contractor does withdraw his bid, he is not allowed to issue a revised bid, so there is a penalty to withdrawing a bid. The private sector also allows contractors to withdraw bids because of arithmetic errors. It makes sense that this is done. The buyer (the owner or architect) does not want to work with an unhappy contractor, because when the contractor is unhappy the quality or speed of the work can suffer.

A third method of escaping the winner's curse is that if the contractor bids too low, he can try to renegotiate with the subcontractors, trying to get their prices lower. The subcontractors have an incentive to renegotiate because if the contractor is going to lose money, the contractor may choose to withdraw his bid by claiming an arithmetic error. If the contractor withdraws his bid, the subcontractor is out of work. The fourth way of escaping the winner's curse is through change orders. It is almost inevitable that once a construction project begins, the original plans will need to be changed in some way. The contractor can recoup losses by charging a lot for change orders.

* This material is based on Douglas Dyer and John Kagel, "Experienced Bidders in Common Value Auctions: Behavior in the Laboratory versus the Natural Habitat," unpublished manuscript, University of Pittsburgh.

Designing the Auction

Because licenses divide the country up into regions, efficiency requires that some firms get several licenses covering contiguous geographic regions. Moreover, the value to a firm of any one license depends on whether that firm owns licenses for the same wavelength in nearby areas. Auctioning all of the licenses at once using, say, a sealed-bid auction would make it difficult for firms to get licenses for the same wavelength in contiguous areas. A firm might get lucky, but it might also win a license for one wavelength in one region and another wavelength in the next region. A better auction method would give bidders a chance to figure out which licenses they are likely to win, so that they can win compatible sets of licenses. Therefore, the auction must give bidders time to try to assemble sets of licenses and to switch to back-up sets if their first choices become too expensive.

This does not mean that the licenses should be auctioned one by one. If they are, a firm might win a desired license early in the auction but fail to win a nearby license later in the auction, reducing the value of the first license. To avoid this possibility, the auction designers decided to use a *simultaneous ascending-bid auction*. All of the licenses with the same bandwidth and the same region-size were auctioned simultaneously. Accordingly, the licenses were divided into five groups, and the smallest group was auctioned off first (to see how the auction design would work). Nationwide narrowband licenses were sold in July 1994, regional narrowband licenses in October 1994, and broadband licenses covering large geographic regions were sold from December 1994 to March 1995 (these auctions take a long time). The remaining two auctions sold broadband licenses with smaller geographic coverage. All of the auctions were run by computer, with bids entered online. Bidders could enter higher bids as long as there was some bidding on any of the licenses. This way if one license became too expensive, bidders could switch to other licenses even if those alternative licenses did not have much recent bidding activity. The bidding on all licenses in each auction closed when there was no more bidding on any of the licenses.

This auction form has several advantages. First, by allowing bids on all of the licenses at the same time, it increases the efficiency of the resulting allocation: Bidders can maneuver to buy desirable groups of licenses. Second, the auction reduces the winner's curse by allowing bidders to respond to each others' bids. Because they can see when other bidders stop, naive bidders do not bid the price up beyond the license's actual value. Third, since all similar licenses are on sale at the same time and since bidding is open for a while, licenses that are close substitutes for each other tend to sell for similar prices. If one license has high bids and a close substitute is going for a low price, some bidders can switch to the lower-priced license and bid up its price.

Performance of the Auction

The performance of the simultaneous ascending-bid auction can be assessed along a variety of dimensions. Here we talk about three of them. First, if the auction performs well, it should raise a lot of revenue. Second, it should fetch similar prices for similar licenses. Third, bidders should be able to assemble beneficial groups of licenses. It turns out that the FCC auction performed very well by all three of these criteria.

In terms of revenue, before the auction the Office of Management and Budget estimated $10 billion in revenue would be generated by the last three auctions. Industry executives thought this estimate was wildly optimistic, but it turned out to be too low: The last three auctions raised about $21 billion.

Revenue was not a major goal in the legislation authorizing the auction, however. The primary goal was an efficient allocation of licenses. It appears that bidders were successful in assembling desirable communications networks by winning regional licenses. For example, in the second auction (regional narrowband licenses) the FCC divided the country into five regions and sold six licenses in each region. Four bidders won licenses in all five regions, assembling nationwide networks. In the third auction (large-region broadband licenses) three bidders came close to filling all of the gaps in their existing cellular networks, and PacTel managed to win the network it stated that it wanted to win—both northern and southern California.

The third performance criterion is that similar licenses should fetch similar prices. For example, licenses covering the same region but with different wavelengths should sell for about the same price. Again the auction design performed very well. For example, in the first auction (nationwide narrowband licenses) there were five licenses that were very close substitutes, and they all sold for exactly the same price. So, by designing an auction to fit the specific circumstances, game theorists succeeded in meeting the efficiency and revenue goals set down by Congress.

Summary

- In a **private value auction,** every bidder has a different valuation of the item being auctioned than every other bidder. In contrast, in a **common value auction,** the item is worth the same amount to every bidder, but the true value of the item is unknown, and the bidders have different information about the true value.

- Bidders attempt to maximize **expected surplus.** The surplus is the value of the item minus the price paid for it. Expected surplus is the probability of winning times the expected value of the difference between the value of the item and the price paid.

- There are four main types of auctions. In an **English auction** the auctioneer calls out successively higher prices, and bidders drop out until only one is left. In a **first-price (sealed-bid) auction** bidders submit their bids secretly, and the highest bidder wins and pays his bid. In a **second-price (sealed-bid) auction** bidders submit their bids secretly, and the highest bidder wins and pays the second-highest bid. Finally, in a **Dutch auction** the auctioneer calls out successively lower prices, and the first bidder to accept a price wins the auction and pays that price.

- In an English auction, the dominant strategy for a bidder is to bid up to his valuation of the item.

- In a second-price auction, the dominant strategy for a bidder is to bid his valuation.

- In a first-price auction, the Nash equilibrium strategy for a bidder is to bid less than his valuation. How much less depends on the number of other bidders. More precisely, the Nash equilibrium strategy for a bidder is to assume that his valuation is the highest and to bid the expected second-highest valuation.

- In a Dutch auction, the Nash equilibrium strategy for a bidder is very similar to the equilibrium strategy in a first-price auction. The bidder should assume that his valuation is the highest and bid when the price falls to the expected second-highest valuation.

- All four of the auctions generate the same expected revenue for the seller. This result is known as **revenue equivalence.**

- In a common value auction, bidders receive signals about the value of the item. If bidders behave as if the signal is the same as the value of the item, they will overbid. This is the **winner's curse.** To avoid the winner's curse, a bidder must account for the fact that if he wins, his signal must have been higher than everyone else's, suggesting that the true value is lower than the highest signal.

Problems

1. Suppose that there are only two bidders in a first-price auction and the item they bid on is a ten-dollar bill. What are the equilibrium bids?
2. Suppose that there are only two bidders in a first-price auction and that there are only two possible valuations of the item. A bidder could value the item either at $10 or at $20. Each bidder knows his own valuation, but not his opponent's valuation.
   a. What is the equilibrium strategy of a bidder who values the item at $10?

   b. Is it an equilibrium strategy for a bidder who values the item at $20 to bid $10? Why or why not?

   c. Is it an equilibrium strategy for a bidder who values the item at $20 to bid $20? Why or why not?

   d. Is there any equilibrium pure strategy for a bidder who values the item at $20? Why or why not?

3. Sometimes auctioneers set reserve prices—that is, prices below which the item will not be sold. In a first-price auction, for example, if the highest bid is above the reserve price, the high bidder gets to purchase the item, but if the highest bid is below the reserve price the item is not sold. Suppose that the auctioneer knows exactly how much each bidder values the item. What reserve price should he set? Why?

4. Explain why an auctioneer would like to have as many bidders as possible participate in an auction.

5. We found that in a private values auction, no matter which auction is used the seller's revenue is just the expected second-highest bid. Instead of going through the trouble of running an auction, the seller could simply place a price tag with this price on the item and wait for the buyer with the highest valuation to come along and buy the item at this price. Give a reason why the seller might not want to do this.

6. Sometimes auctioneers sell more than one unit of the same item. For example, the Treasury Department sells more than one government bond at an auction. Suppose that there are 10 units of the good being auctioned off, and the 10 highest bidders get the good and each pay the 11th highest bid. What is the equilibrium bidding strategy in this auction?

7. Suppose that there are two bidders in a common value auction and that signals are known to be within $200 of the true value of the item. Bidder *A* receives a signal of $1,600. What valuation should he base his bid on after adjusting for the winner's curse?

8. Suppose that valuations are distributed evenly between $1,000 and $2,000, that there are only two bidders, and that bidder *A* values the item at $1,500.

   a. Find the equilibrium bid in an English auction.

   b. Find the equilibrium bid in a second-price auction.

   c. Find the equilibrium bid in a first-price auction.

9. In Section 14.3 we devised a method by which bidders can avoid the winner's curse. Even so, bidders do not completely eliminate the possibility of losing money on the auction. That is, they still bid high enough that it is possible that if they win the auction, they pay more than the item is actually worth.

   a. Suppose that signals are within $1,000 of the true value of the prize, that there are three bidders, and that bidder *A* receives a signal of $5,000. If bidder *A* wishes to completely eliminate any possibility of losing money on the auction, what is the highest bid he can make?

   b. If bidder *A* is risk neutral, is such a bid consistent with an equilibrium? Explain.

15

NEGATIVE EXTERNALITIES AND PUBLIC GOODS

Overview

In previous chapters, we discussed the possibility of market failure. In Chapter 8, we saw that a firm with monopoly power generally sets its price above marginal cost, thereby creating a deadweight loss. In Chapter 11, we saw that when firms form a cartel, they, too, set price above marginal cost. In Chapter 13, we saw how adverse selection and moral hazard can lead to market failure. In this chapter, we examine two other possible reasons for market failure: negative externalities and public goods.

A **negative externality** is when one individual (or firm) imposes a cost on another individual. When an individual acts in his own self-interest, and there is nobody bothered by his actions, no negative externality can exist. It's when someone is bothered by another's actions that there is an externality. For example, if you smoke a cigarette in the privacy of your own home, you are not directly bothering anyone else. If you smoke in a restaurant, however, your smoke may bother others. In this situation, if you ignore the cost you impose on others when you smoke, you may be smoking too much from a social welfare point of view. Smoking in public, however, is generally not a marketable good. In other words, you don't see smokers paying nonsmokers for the right to smoke, just as you don't see nonsmokers paying smokers to stop smoking. There is really no market for second-hand smoke. But that doesn't mean there can't be! In this chapter, market *and* nonmarket solutions will be considered as methods for dealing with negative externalities.

Another form of market failure exists in the case of **public goods.** Without being too specific at this point, a public good is basically one that anyone can consume without affecting the consumption of the good by others, and there is no way to exclude people from consuming it. For example, if you turn on a radio you can listen to any station you want to without affecting anyone else who wants to listen to a radio. Furthermore, as long as you have a radio, all you have to do to listen to it is to turn it on. Once a radio station's signal is sent out over the airwaves, there is no way to prevent anyone from listening to it. Radio stations survive in the market place, however, because they can sell advertising space—a private good. If one advertiser buys the 8:00 A.M. slot, no other advertiser can use that precise slot. Also, the radio station can exclude any advertiser not willing to pay the station's advertising rate. In general, public goods cannot be priced in a market. As a result, too little or too much of a public good may be provided.

In this chapter, you will learn:

- How market forces may control a negative externality.
- How to control a negative externality when market failure exists.
- How to control pollution with standards or fines.
- How to determine the optimal provision of a public good.
- How to design a tax system to get individuals to truthfully reveal how much they are willing to pay to have a public good provided.

15.1   NEGATIVE EXTERNALITIES, PROPERTY RIGHTS, AND THE COASE THEOREM

Loud Music and Neighbors: An Example

A very common negative externality, especially if you live in a dorm, is when one individual plays loud music that can be heard by others. Let's look at a simple numerical example, shown in Table 15-1. Jeff likes to listen to rock 'n roll music. How much he enjoys his music depends on how loud he turns the volume up on his stereo. In this example, the amount of activity undertaken by Jeff is measured in units of volume. In column 1 of Table 15-1, eleven levels of volume are listed, from $V = 0$ to $V = 10$.

When Jeff listens to music, he doesn't care about anyone else. His objective, then, is to maximize the total benefit *he* receives from undertaking

Table 15-1   Negative Externality by Type

Volume	Jeff's Total Benefit	Jeff's Marginal Benefit	Toby's Total Cost	Toby's Marginal Cost
0	0	—	0	—
1	.50	.50	.10	.10
2	.90	.40	.25	.15
3	1.20	.30	.45	.20
4	1.40	.20	.70	.25
5	1.50	.10	1.00	.30
6	1.40	−.10	1.35	.35
7	1.20	−.20	1.75	.40
8	.90	−.30	2.20	.45
9	.50	−.40	2.70	.50
10	0	−.50	3.25	.55

the activity. In column 2 of Table 15-1, Jeff's total benefit for each level of volume is listed, measured in dollars. The maximum total benefit, $1.50, is at a volume level of 5. In other words, the *value* Jeff places on listening to his stereo at $V = 5$ is equivalent to receiving $1.50 in cash.

Column 3 lists Jeff's marginal benefit of turning up the volume. As can be seen, as Jeff begins increasing the volume, his marginal benefit is positive. As the volume increases, however, his marginal benefit decreases. Starting at $V = 0$, each increase in volume increases Jeff's total benefit, but by a smaller and smaller amount, until $V = 5$ is reached. At this point, the music is loud enough that if he increases the volume to $V = 6$, his total benefit decreases from $1.50 to $1.40. That is, the marginal benefit of moving from $V = 5$ to $V = 6$ is negative. By looking only at the marginal benefit column, we can still see that Jeff maximizes his total benefit at $V = 5$, since this is the last volume level at which his marginal benefit of increasing the volume is positive.

If there is no other individual in this story, our analysis is finished. Jeff sets the volume level at 5 to maximize his total benefit. In this case, however, Jeff is not imposing a negative externality on anyone. But what if Jeff has a neighbor—Toby. Toby hates rock 'n roll and is bothered by Jeff's loud stereo. The fourth column in Table 15-1 demonstrates exactly how much of a bother Jeff is to Toby. For each level of volume, Toby's total cost is listed in column 4. At $V = 5$, for example, Jeff's loud music imposes a cost of $1.00 on Toby. In other words, Toby is willing to pay up to $1.00 to avoid hearing Jeff's stereo. Column 5 of Table 15-1 lists Toby's marginal cost of increases in volume. Each additional level of volume is more costly to Toby than the last increase. From either column 4 or column 5, it is easy to see that if it was up to Toby, she would prefer the volume to be set at $V = 0$, where her total cost of the activity is minimized.

At this stage in the example, we have yet to assign property rights. We know that if Jeff had the right to make as much noise as he wanted to, he would set $V = 5$. If Toby had the right to have as much noise as she wanted, she would set $V = 0$. Thus, it appears that what level the volume is set at depends upon who is assigned the property right. But as we will now see, this is not necessarily true. The assignment of the property right may have no effect on the final level of volume.

The Coase Theorem

Let's begin by assuming that the property right over the noise level is assigned to Jeff. This implies that Jeff can make as much noise as he wants to. From Table 15-1, Jeff maximizes his total benefit at a volume level of $V = 5$. While Toby has no right to turn down the volume, she certainly can try to persuade Jeff to turn down the volume. Suppose Toby wants to get Jeff to turn the volume down from $V = 5$ to $V = 4$. If Jeff does this, his total benefit is reduced by 10 cents (from $1.50 to $1.40). Toby's total cost, however, is reduced by 30 cents (from $1.00 to 70 cents). Thus, Jeff loses 10 cents and Toby gains 30 cents. If Toby can pay Jeff at least 10 cents, but no more than 30 cents, it is in Jeff's best interest to turn down the volume to $V = 4$. In other words, there are *gains from trade* in turning down the volume from $V = 5$ to $V = 4$. Both Jeff and Toby can be made better off.

Once at $V = 4$, are there any more gains from trade to be exploited? If Jeff turns down the volume from $V = 4$ to $V = 3$, his total benefit is reduced by 20 cents (from $1.40 to $1.20), and Toby's total cost is reduced by 25 cents (from 70 to 45 cents). As long as Toby pays Jeff as little as 20 cents, but no more than 25 cents, they can both be made better off if Jeff turns the volume down to $V = 3$. Once at $V = 3$, however, there are no longer any gains from trade to be exploited. To reduce the volume from $V = 3$ to $V = 2$, Jeff would need at least 30 cents to compensate him for his loss (from $1.20 to 90 cents), but Toby would only have her total cost reduced by 20 cents (from 45 to 25 cents). Toby would not be willing to pay Jeff a minimum of 30 cents to turn the volume down to $V = 2$. At most, she would only pay 20 cents.

What we have seen so far is that Jeff has the property right, but Jeff and Toby can negotiate. They can work out a deal that has Jeff turn down the volume from $V = 5$ to $V = 3$, but no further. What happens if Toby has the initial property right and can control the volume level? From Table 15-1, Toby minimizes her total cost by setting the volume at $V = 0$. Although Jeff has no right to turn up the volume, he can try to persuade Toby to let him turn up the volume. If the volume level is turned up from $V = 0$ to $V = 1$, Jeff's total benefit increases by 50 cents (from 0 to 50 cents). Toby's total cost increases by 10 cents (from 0 to 10 cents). Thus, as long as Jeff can pay Toby a minimum of 10 cents, but no more than 50 cents, they can both be made better off when the volume increases to $V = 1$. There are gains from trade to be exploited from $V = 0$ to $V = 1$.

If we continue in this fashion, Jeff and Toby can exploit gains from trade up to the volume level of $V = 3$. Once it is at $V = 3$, however, there are no longer gains from to exploit. To go from $V = 3$ to $V = 4$, Jeff's total benefit increases by 20 cents (from $1.20 to $1.40), but Toby's total cost increases by 25 cents (from 45 to 70 cents). Jeff would have to pay Toby a minimum of 25 cents to turn the volume up to $V = 4$, which he isn't willing to do. But all in all, with the property right initially given to Toby, Jeff and Toby can work out a deal that has Jeff turn the volume level up to $V = 3$. But this is exactly the same volume level they end up at when Jeff is given the initial property right! Regardless of who is assigned the initial property right, we end up with the same volume level—$V = 3$. This result is commonly referred to as the **Coase Theorem.**

The Coase Theorem states, in essence, that as long as property rights are well-defined and there are no transactions costs, the allocation of resources is *invariant* to the assignment of property rights. What does this mean in terms of our loud music example? A well-defined property right means that the right to control the volume level is assigned to either Jeff or Toby. No

APPLICATION
Property Rights Over Sunlight

The following two legal cases illustrate two different solutions to similar negative externalities. In the first case, two neighboring luxury hotels in Florida had to go to court to settle a property dispute.* The Fontainbleau hotel began constructing a 14-story addition that, when completed, would cast a shadow in the afternoon over the swimming pool of the Eden Roc Hotel. The Eden Roc Hotel sued to prevent construction from continuing, but was unsuccessful. The court ruled that no property right could be assigned to the free flow of light and air. A similar case in Wisconsin was resolved differently.** In *Prah v. Maretti*, Prah was the owner of a solar-heated house. Maretti planned to build a neighboring house that would block sunlight reaching Prah's house. The court ruled that the use of sunlight as energy was important enough to assign a property right to Prah. Even though these cases were decided differently, the lesson of the Coase Theorem is that as long as the disputing parties face low transactions costs, it doesn't matter how the courts assign the property right.

* *Fontainbleau Hotel Corp. v. Forty-Five Twenty-Five, Inc.* District Court of Appeals of Florida, 1959.
** *Prah v. Maretti.* Supreme Court of Wisconsin, 1982.

transactions costs means that Jeff and Toby can freely negotiate to exploit any gains from trade that exist. The allocation of resources in this example is the different volume levels that can be set. And finally, the allocation of resources being invariant to the assignment of property rights means, as we have shown, that the final volume level ends up at $V = 3$ regardless of whether it is Jeff who has the property right over the volume level or it is Toby who has that right.

The Socially Efficient Outcome

There is a further implication of the Coase Theorem that we have only implicitly discussed. In the loud music example, we have seen that as long as the property right is assigned to one of them, Jeff and Toby will exploit all the gains from trade and the volume will be set at $V = 3$. Not only is the final volume level invariant to the assignment of property rights, but $V = 3$ is also the *socially efficient* level of volume. Table 15-2 helps demonstrate this point.

Table 15-2   Total and Marginal Social Benefit

Volume	Total Social Benefit	Marginal Social Benefit
0	0	—
1	.40	.40
2	.65	.25
3	.75	.10
4	.70	−.05
5	.50	−.20
6	.05	−.45
7	−.55	−.60
8	−1.30	−.75
9	−2.20	−.90
10	−3.25	−1.05

Table 15-2 is derived from Table 15-1. Jeff and Toby are the only individuals in our example. To find the total social benefit at each level of volume, we subtract Toby's total cost from Jeff's total benefit. For example, at $V = 3$, Jeff's total benefit (from Table 15-1) is $1.20 and Toby's total cost is 45 cents. The total social benefit, then, is 75 cents. From a social point of view, we are looking at the net benefit of the activity—and this net benefit is maximized at $V = 3$. The final column of Table 15-2 lists the marginal social benefit. This is found by subtracting Toby's marginal cost from Jeff's marginal benefit at each level of volume in Table 15-1. At $V = 3$, the marginal social benefit is positive, but at $V = 4$, it is negative. Thus, the socially efficient level of volume is $V = 3$.

As we saw in Chapter 7, social welfare is maximized when all the gains from trade are exploited. As long as the property right is well defined, individuals can negotiate an agreement that exploits all the gains from trade. From a policy perspective, the Coase Theorem suggests a simple solution to dealing with negative externalities: Assign a property right to either the individual creating the harm or the individual being harmed, then do nothing else. The individuals themselves will negotiate to reach the socially efficient outcome.

A Graphical Analysis

Figure 15-1 presents a graphical analysis of a negative externality. (This analysis is very similar to the one shown in Figure 7-15.) Individual A undertakes an activity that yields him a positive, but diminishing, marginal benefit (depicted by curve MB_A) until Q_A is reached. At Q_A, individual A maximizes his total benefit. (Recall from Chapter 7 that the area under a marginal curve, be it benefit or cost, is the total benefit or cost, respectively.)

Figure 15-1   Gains from Trade

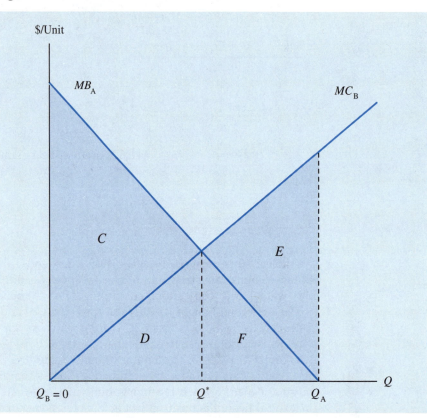

If given the property right, individual A maximizes his total benefit at activity level Q_A. To reduce his activity from Q_A to Q^*, individual A needs a minimum of area F, and the individual B is willing to pay a maximum of area $E+F$. Area E represents the gains from trade of moving from Q_A to Q^*. If individual B is given the initial property right, her total cost of the activity is minimized at $Q_B = 0$. To move from 0 to Q^*, individual B needs a minimum of area D, and individual A is willing to pay a maximum of area $C+D$. Area C represents the gains from trade of moving from 0 to Q^*. As long as the individuals can freely negotiate, the activity level will end up at the socially efficient level, Q^*.

The activity in question, however, creates a negative externality that imposes a cost on individual B (depicted by curve MC_B). If individual B could control the activity, she would minimize her total cost at $Q_B = 0$. The socially efficient outcome is where $MB_A = MC_B$ at level Q^*.

 If individual A is given the property right, he would need to be paid a minimum amount equal to area F to reduce his activity level from Q_A to Q^*. Individual B would be willing to pay a maximum of area $E+F$ to reduce A's activity level to Q^*. Thus, area E represents the gains from trade available when individual A is given the initial property right. Similarly, if individual B is given the initial property right, she would need a minimum of area D to allow A to increase his activity level from 0 to Q^*. Individual A would be willing to pay a maximum of $C+D$ to move to Q^*. Thus, area C represents the gains from trade available when individual B is given the initial property right. As long as the individuals can freely negotiate, the activity level will end up at the socially efficient level, Q^*.

15.2   HIGH TRANSACTIONS COSTS AND PROPERTY RIGHTS

Although the lesson of the Coase Theorem appears simple—assign a property right and all will be well—there may be complications. One of the key assumptions of the Coase Theorem is that there are no transactions costs associated with negotiations. If there are transactions costs, however, gains from trade may not always be exploited. One source of transactions costs involves the number of people affected by the negative externality. If a factory's pollution imposes an external cost on hundreds of home owners, it may be difficult to simply assign a property right and allow the factory to negotiate with each home owner. If the factory has the right to pollute, any single home owner has an incentive to let his neighbors try to negotiate with the factory, hoping that his neighbors will pay to reduce the pollution and he won't have to. If each home owner has the right to no pollution, the factory will have to negotiate with many separate individuals, each of whom has an incentive to hold out. If the home owners have an association, however, the problem may be reduced to negotiations between just two parties.

When there are only two parties involved in negotiations, it still may be difficult for them to exploit all the gains from trade. Even two people may have difficulties arranging a meeting to negotiate. In addition, what if Jeff and Toby hate each other? They may refuse to negotiate. When high transactions costs prevent all the gains from trade from being exploited, simply assigning a property right is not sufficient to reach the socially efficient outcome.

Protecting Property Rights

Let's return to the loud music example of Tables 15-1 and 15-2. Jeff's loud music bothers Toby, and Toby's solution is to sue Jeff. Assume that the judge in this case, Judge Gallaway, is concerned with social efficiency and realizes that Jeff and Toby will never be able to negotiate to reach the socially efficient outcome. For whatever reason, Jeff and Toby's high transactions costs prohibit gains from trade from being exploited. It is Judge Gallaway's role to assign a property right and then to protect it. What is meant by protecting a property right is that once the right is assigned, rules are set that govern any change in the activity level. Judge Gallaway's ability to achieve a socially efficient ruling depends upon what information he has.

Property Rules

Assume that Judge Gallaway assigns the property right to Toby and protects that right with a **property rule.** Under a property rule, Toby can do whatever she wants. In this case, she prefers the volume level to be set at $V = 0$. The only way the volume level can be changed is if Jeff negotiates an agreement with Toby. A property rule, then, is quite simple. All Judge Gallaway has to do is assign the property right to Jeff or Toby. Unfortunately, in this case, Judge Gallaway knows that a property rule will not yield the socially efficient outcome.

Judge Gallaway knows that Jeff and Toby face high transactions costs and will not negotiate with each other after the property right is assigned. If he assigns the right to Toby, she will control the volume without any concern for the benefit Jeff receives. If he assigns the right to Jeff, Jeff will set the volume at $V = 5$ without any concern for the cost imposed on Toby. Thus, if Toby gets the right, too little volume will be set. If Jeff gets the right, too much volume will be set. In a high transactions costs setting, a property rule does not allow for the efficient allocation of the resource.

There is another solution for Judge Gallaway to adopt. If he knows what the socially efficient outcome is, ($V = 3$ in this case), he can assign the property right to Jeff to set the volume at *no more* than $V = 3$. With this intermediate property right, under a property rule the only way the volume can be changed is if Jeff and Toby negotiate a change. Even if we drop the assumption of high transactions costs, there is no room for negotiation: At $V = 3$, there are no gains from trade to exploit! In a high transactions costs setting, a property rule is efficient if the property right is set exactly at the socially efficient level. Of course, for this to work the socially efficient outcome must be known to the judge.

Liability Rules

Suppose that Judge Gallaway assigns the property right to Toby. She prefers the volume to be set at $V = 0$. Because of high transactions costs, Jeff and Toby will not negotiate any change in volume. But if Judge Gallaway protects Toby's right with a **liability rule,** a change in volume may occur. A liability rule allows Jeff to pay Toby if he wants to increase the volume. This payment, however, is not negotiated between Jeff and Toby. Instead, Judge Gallaway determines a payment schedule Jeff must adhere to if he wants to increase the volume.

For example, assume that Judge Gallaway does not know the socially efficient outcome, but he does know Toby's marginal cost schedule. He can impose the payment schedule on Jeff shown in Table 15-3.

How will Jeff respond to this schedule? Remember, Jeff does not have to negotiate with Toby, and Toby has no control over Jeff if he adheres to the payment schedule. Starting at $V = 0$, Jeff's marginal benefit (see Table 15-1) of increasing the volume to $V = 1$ is 50 cents. His payment would be only 10 cents. Therefore, Jeff still has a net gain of 40 cents, making it worth-

Table 15-3   Liability Rule with Marginal Cost Schedule Known

To Turn the Volume Up From	Jeff Must Pay Toby
$V = 0$ to $V = 1$	10 cents
$V = 1$ to $V = 2$	15 cents
$V = 2$ to $V = 3$	20 cents
$V = 3$ to $V = 4$	25 cents
$V = 4$ to $V = 5$	30 cents
$V = 5$ to $V = 6$	35 cents
$V = 6$ to $V = 7$	40 cents
$V = 7$ to $V = 8$	45 cents
$V = 8$ to $V = 9$	50 cents
$V = 9$ to $V = 10$	55 cents

while for him to turn up the volume. His net gain remains positive until $V = 3$ is reached. At this point, to turn up the volume to $V = 4$, Jeff would have to pay Toby 25 cents, but his marginal benefit is only 20 cents. Under this payment schedule, then, Jeff pays Toby until $V = 3$, the socially efficient outcome, is reached.

Under the liability rule shown in Table 15-3, Judge Gallaway has *perfectly internalized the negative externality.* In other words, Judge Gallaway has made Jeff precisely responsible for the external cost he imposes on Toby. By setting Jeff's payment schedule equal to Toby's marginal cost of the activity, there is no longer any external harm. Toby is exactly compensated for her damages. This liability rule provides Jeff with the incentive to set the volume at the socially efficient level, without any need for negotiations with Toby.

Another way to use a liability rule is to assign the property right to the individual creating the external harm and impose a payment schedule on the individual being harmed. For example, Judge Gallaway can assign the property right to Jeff, knowing that Jeff would set the volume at $V = 5$, but not knowing exactly what harm is imposed on Toby. He then can impose the payment schedule on Toby shown in Table 15-4.

Table 15-4   Liability Rule with Marginal Benefit Schedule Known

To Turn the Volume Down From	Toby Must Pay Jeff
$V = 5$ to $V = 4$	10 cents
$V = 4$ to $V = 3$	20 cents
$V = 3$ to $V = 2$	30 cents
$V = 2$ to $V = 1$	40 cents
$V = 1$ to $V = 0$	50 cents

How will Toby respond to this schedule? To get Jeff to turn the volume down from $V = 5$ to $V = 4$, Toby must pay 10 cents, but she saves 30 cents (see Table 15-1). Her net gain, then, is 20 cents. Her net gain remains positive until $V = 3$ is reached. At $V = 3$, to get Jeff to further reduce the volume to $V = 2$, Toby must pay 30 cents, but she saves only 20 cents. The payment schedule in Table 15-4 encourages Toby to pay Jeff to set the volume level at $V = 3$—the socially efficient outcome.

With both liability rules presented in Tables 15-3 and 15-4, Judge Gallaway does not know the socially efficient outcome. In one case, he knows the harm the activity imposes on Toby. In the other case, he knows the lost benefit Jeff suffers from turning down the volume. It is important to notice that *both* individuals can be harmed. Toby is harmed from increases in the volume, but Jeff is harmed from decreases in the volume. Depending upon what information Judge Gallaway has, he can assign the property right to either Jeff or Toby and impose a payment schedule on the other.

Property and Liability Rules Compared

The ability of either property or liability rules to promote efficiency depends upon the settings to which they are applied. When transactions costs are so high that no negotiations will take place, a property rule is only efficient if the property right is assigned precisely at the socially efficient level of the activity. If not, there will too much or too little of the activity. A liability rule, however, with an appropriate payment schedule, can lead to the socially efficient outcome.

In any high transactions costs setting, it is the information available to whoever assigns and protects property rights that determines the efficiency of the rule. It is unlikely that a judge will know the socially efficient outcome, making property rules difficult to use. If a judge has some idea of only the costs imposed by the activity, he can assign the property right to the individual being harmed and set a payment schedule that follows the marginal cost of the activity. If the judge has some idea of only the benefits created by the activity, he can assign the property right to the individual undertaking the activity and set a payment schedule that follows the lost benefits as the activity is being reduced. If a judge has no information about the costs or benefits of an activity, social efficiency will only be achieved by chance.

In a low transactions costs setting, the beauty of the Coase Theorem is that a judge does not need any information to achieve the socially efficient outcome. Simply by assigning the property right to either party, he can ensure that negotiation will lead to the efficient outcome. Another advantage of having a low transactions costs setting is that the individuals themselves do not need to know the socially efficient outcome to achieve it. Jeff does not need to know the extent of the costs he imposes on Toby, and Toby does not need to know the extent of the benefits Jeff receives. If they can negotiate freely, regardless of who has the property right, all gains from trade will be exploited. If you are negotiating with a car dealer over the price of a new car, you may not know his minimum selling price, just as he may not know your maximum offer. But as long as your maximum offer is greater than his minimum selling price, eventually trade will take place.

15.3   POLLUTION CONTROL

Pollution is an obvious example of a negative externality. There are many types of pollution, and many settings in which pollution can occur. Some are low transactions costs settings, such as a neighbor's noisy lawnmower early on a Sunday morning. Others are very high transactions costs settings, such as an oil spill that affects an entire coastline. As we have already discussed, property rules tend not to be efficient in high transactions costs settings, and liability rules may also be difficult to use, especially when many individuals are involved. In these cases, regulations are often used to control pollution. Unlike assigning a property right and then protecting it, government regulators often just set standards that polluters must adhere to and/or impose fines to control pollution.

Standards Versus Fines

Figure 15-2 can be used to illustrate the differences between a regulator's use of standards or fines to control a firm's pollution level. The horizontal axis measures pollution *control*. At zero, the firm is not controlling its level of pollution at all. At the No Pollution level, the firm is completely controlling its pollution. Because the firm's private gain of controlling pollution is zero but its private cost is positive as measured along the marginal cost curve, the firm has no independent incentive to control its pollution level. We will also assume that the pollution affects so many people that assigning and protecting property rights will not be effective. Without regulator intervention, then, the firm provides zero pollution control.

From a social point of view, for each level of pollution the firm controls there is a social benefit of reduced pollution. This benefit is measured along the marginal benefit curve in Figure 15-2, which is assumed to be horizontal in this example. The efficient level of pollution control is where $MB = MC$, at level PC^*. If the regulator imposes a standard of PC^* on the firm, the firm incurs a total cost of area A (the area under the marginal cost curve) to maintain that standard. For the standard to be effective, the firm must be punished if its control level falls below PC^*. As long as the punishment fine is above the marginal cost curve, it will be in the firm's best interest to maintain the standard and avoid the fine. This is true because if the firm reduces its control by one more unit, it saves the marginal cost of controlling that unit. The fine, then, must outweigh that cost saving.

Figure 15-2   Pollution Standard Versus Fine

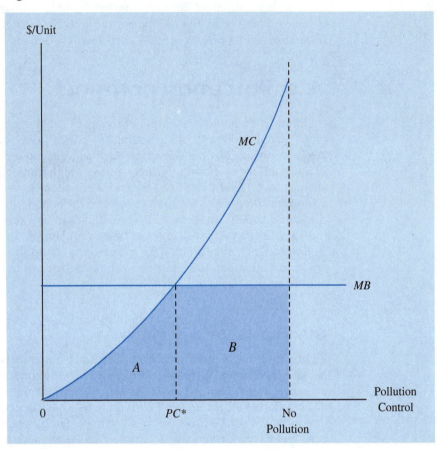

If the regulator sets a standard of *PC** to control pollution, the firm incurs a total cost of area *A* to maintain that standard. If the regulator uses a fine set at the rate of the marginal benefit curve when starting at the No Pollution level, the firm will pay the fine until level *PC** is reached. At this point, it is less expensive for the firm to control the next unit of pollution than to pay the fine. The total cost to the firm of maintaining level *PC** in this case is the total cost of the fine, area *B*, and the total cost of controlling level *PC**, area *A*. The firm prefers the standard to the fine.

Another way for the regulator to control pollution is to fine the firm for each level of pollution control it *does not* undertake. For example, the regulator can fine the firm at a rate given by the *MB* curve, starting at the No Pollution level. As the firm relaxes its control, *moving from right to left*, it must pay a fine of *MB* for each unit not controlled. In this case, the fine is cheaper than the marginal cost of pollution control to the right of the efficient level, *PC**. Once at *PC**, however, the fine along the *MB* curve is greater than the marginal cost of control along *MC*. The total fine the firm pays is equal to area B, but the firm also incurs the cost of controlling pollution at level PC^* equal to area A. The fine, then, is a more costly method of control for the firm than the standard is.

The choice of using a standard as opposed to a fine is similar to the choice of using property rules as opposed to liability rules. If the regulator knows the correct standard, it can be set directly with fines only being used to punish a firm that does not adhere to the standard. If the correct standard is not known, but the marginal benefit of pollution control is known, the regulator can internalize the negative externality with a precise fine set at the rate of the lost marginal benefit as the control is relaxed. Notice in this case that the fine is paid to the regulator, and not to the individuals being directly harmed by the pollution. If the fine could be paid to these individuals, it would then simply be the equivalent of a liability rule.

Marketable Permits

With more than one firm polluting, it becomes difficult for regulators to set the appropriate standards for each and every firm. This is because firms are very different, and they face different marginal costs of pollution control. And along with many individuals harmed by pollution, the more firms there are the more difficult it is to control pollution by assigning and protecting property rights. But even in a high transactions costs setting, with government regulations in place, the logic of the Coase Theorem can be helpful.

Figure 15-3 presents two firms and their marginal costs of pollution control. Figure 15-3 has a strange feature that distinguishes it from other figures in this book: Firm 1's level of pollution control is measured on the horizontal axis from left to right, and Firm 2's is measured from right to left. At the extreme left, Firm 1 has no pollution control, and Firm 2 has 10 units of pollution control. At the extreme right, it is just the opposite—Firm 1 has 10 units of pollution control, and Firm 2 has none. With no regulatory standards in place, Firm 1 controls zero at the extreme left, and Firm 2 controls zero at the extreme right. When each firm has zero pollution control, we will assume that each firm creates 10 units of pollution; therefore, a total of 20 units of pollution is being emitted.

The first issue a regulator must deal with is how much pollution control in total is needed. Assume that the efficient level of pollution control is determined to be 10 units. The second question that must be addressed is how much pollution each firm should control. If the firms are different, it may not be efficient for them to face the same pollution control standard. For example, at 5 units of control each, Firm 1's marginal cost is shown at point B, and Firm 2's is shown at point A. Because point A is above point B, $MC_2 > MC_1$. In other words, Firm 1 is more efficient at controlling pollution than is Firm 2. We saw in Chapter 11 that when two firms form a cartel, they maximize profit by equating their marginal costs of production. Similarly, in this case, efficient pollution control requires that $MC_1 = MC_2$.

Figure 15-3   Marketable Permits

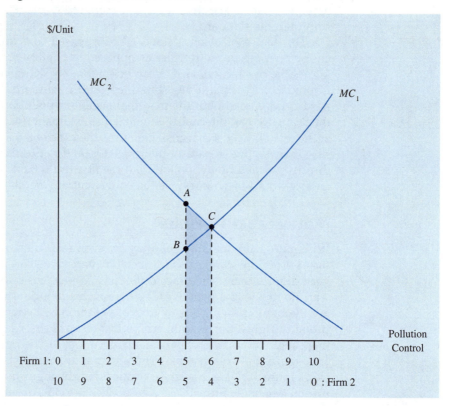

Firm 1's pollution control level is measured from left to right, and Firm 2's is measured from right to left. With no regulatory standards, Firm 1 controls zero units of pollution at the extreme left, and Firm 2 controls zero units at the extreme right. With no pollution controlled, a total of 20 units of pollution is emitted. If the regulator distributes 5 marketable permits to each firm, each firm is initially allowed 5 units of pollution and must control 5 units. At 5 units of control each, Firm 1 has a lower marginal cost of control than does Firm 2, as seen by point B being below point A. Thus, there are gains from trade to exploit. At 6 units of control for Firm 1 and 4 units of control for Firm 2, pollution is controlled efficiently, since $MC_1 = MC_2$ at point C.

When the firms are at 5 units of pollution control each, a savings is created if Firm 1 controls one more unit and Firm 2 controls one less unit. At point C, then, with Firm 1 controlling 6 units of pollution and Firm 2 controlling 4 units, the marginal costs are equal.

If a regulator cannot determine how to set separate standards for each firm, there may be another option that takes advantage of the results of the Coase Theorem. While a property rule may be ineffective in a high transactions costs setting between the firms and the individuals who are harmed by the pollution, there may be low transactions costs between the firms themselves. In this setting, a regulator may issue **marketable permits** to the firms. A marketable permit allows a firm to emit one unit of pollution. The more permits a firm has, the more pollution it can emit, and the fewer units it has to control. Furthermore, these permits can be sold to other firms. Why would a firm want to sell a permit?

If a firm sells a permit, it must control one more unit of pollution. The cost of this additional control is the firm's marginal cost of pollution control. If a firm buys a permit, it can control one less unit of pollution and save the marginal cost of controlling that unit. A firm with a high marginal cost will be willing to buy a permit from a firm with a low marginal cost, and the firm with the low marginal cost will be willing to sell. As long as the marginal costs of control are not equal, there are gains from trade to exploit. This can be illustrated with the help of Figure 15-3.

If the regulator wants to control 10 units of pollution out of the total of 20 emitted, he must allow for 10 marketable permits to be distributed to the firms. Let's say the permits are initially distributed equally, with each firm getting 5. This means that each firm can emit 5 units of pollution and, therefore, must control the other 5 units. We have already seen that at points A and B each firm controls 5 units, and Firm 2 has a higher marginal cost of control than does Firm 1. With $MC_2 > MC_1$, it is in Firm 1's best interest to sell one permit to Firm 2. If Firm 1 sells one permit, it must increase its control from 5 to 6 units of pollution. If Firm 2 buys one permit, it can reduce its control from 5 to 4 units. Because Firm 1 can control a unit of pollution at a lower marginal cost than can Firm 2, there are gains from trade for the two firms to exploit. When trade occurs, Firm 1 is left with 4 permits and must control 6 units of pollution, and Firm 2 has 6 permits and must control 4 units of pollution. Furthermore, the efficient division of pollution control is achieved, where $MC_1 = MC_2$ at point C.

Marketable permits provide an interesting merging of regulatory and market forces. Regulation may be needed to control the pollution level of the firms involved, but market forces may assist regulators in allowing firms to achieve the efficient levels of pollution control. Exactly as with the Coase Theorem, for marketable permits to lead to an efficient outcome, the property rights over the permits must be well defined, and there must be low transactions costs between the trading firms. These assumptions may not always hold in practice, as the next application illustrates.

15.4 PUBLIC GOODS

Throughout this book, we have always considered goods that are *private*, as opposed to *public*, in nature. There are two key distinctions between private goods and public goods. The first distinction is that public goods are **nonrivalrous** in consumption. If you eat a hamburger, nobody else can eat that particular hamburger. Hamburgers, then, are rivalrous in consumption. If you're listening to a radio station while eating your hamburger, anyone else

APPLICATION
Controlling Pollution in Southern California

In 1994, the RECLAIM program (Regional Clean Air Incentives Market) was initiated in Southern California in an attempt to control polluting firms' nitrogen oxide and sulfur dioxide emissions. Over 37,000 marketable permits (referred to as Reclaim Trading Credits) were distributed to many polluting firms. The objective of the program was to allow the firms to trade the permits so that an efficient division of pollution control would evolve. Unfortunately, very few permits were ever traded, and the program appeared to be a failure.

Why did little trading occur? One explanation is that maybe the initial distribution of permits was already efficient. If there were no gains from trade to exploit, no trading would occur. Given the tremendous differences between the firms, however, this is an unlikely explanation. A second explanation is that transactions costs between the firms may have been high. This explanation is more difficult to rule out, but so few permits were traded (less than 5 percent of the total number available), it may be worth looking for an additional explanation. The explanation that makes the most sense is that the property rights over the permits were not well defined at all. The regulatory rules specifically stated that

> An RTC (Reclaim Trading Credit) shall not constitute a security or other form of property . . . . Nothing in District rules shall be construed to limit the District's authority to condition, limit, suspend, or terminate any RTCs . . . .*

In effect, the firms did not really own any of the permits. Trading under these conditions was very risky. With a lack of well-defined property rights, it is not surprising that little trading occurred.

*James L. Johnston, "Pollution Trading in La La Land." *Regulation*, Number 3, 1994, pp. 44–54.

with a radio can also listen to the station. Radio stations are nonrivalrous in consumption. There is a simple way to determine whether a good is rivalrous or nonrivalrous: If a good is nonrivalrous, the marginal cost of providing it to an additional consumer is zero. A radio station does not produce discrete units of its signal, but McDonald's produces discrete units of hamburgers, each with a positive marginal cost of production.

The second characteristic of a public good is that it is **nonexcludable.** National defense is the classic example of a nonexcludable good: If a country defends its citizens, it defends *all* of its citizens. If I benefit from national defense, so does my neighbor. With a nonexcludable good, if one person consumes it, there is no way to prevent others from consuming it as well. But with hamburgers, for example, McDonald's can exclude anyone who isn't willing to pay the price of a hamburger from consuming it.

To clearly distinguish between the two characteristics of public goods, it is useful to consider goods that satisfy one of the characteristics, but not both. For example, premium cable channels such as HBO and Showtime are nonrivalrous in consumption, but they are excludable. Unless you pay for the premium service, the signal will be jammed and you will be excluded. But if you subscribe to the service, your consumption does not affect the consumption by others who subscribe to the service. As another example, picnic tables in state parks are nonexcludable—anyone can use them—but they are also rivalrous. If one family is using a picnic table, another family can't use the same table.

The Efficient Provision of a Public Good

With a private good that is competitively produced, we saw earlier that the efficient level of production is where the social marginal cost curve intersects the demand curve. For a public good, we have basically the same result. The difference is in how the market demand curve is derived for a public good versus a private good.

In Chapter 3, Figure 3-10, a market demand curve for a private good is derived. Recall that a market demand curve is a *horizontal* sum of the individual demand curves. *At each price*, each individual's quantity demanded is summed. Also recall from Section 7.4 that a demand curve is a marginal willingness to pay schedule. At any given price, an individual consumes a total quantity where the marginal willingness to pay for the last unit is equal to the price. Thus, at a given price for a private good, each individual has the same marginal willingness to pay. This is not true for a public good.

Because a public good is nonrivalrous and nonexcludable, at whatever level it is provided, all individuals consume the same amount. With a private good, individuals consume different amounts but have the same marginal willingnesses to pay. With a public good, all individuals consume the same amount, but have different marginal willingnesses to pay. To derive a market demand curve for a public good, the individual demand curves must be summed *vertically*.

Figure 15-4 demonstrates how to derive a market demand curve for a representative public good. Assume that there are three individuals with demand curves D_1, D_2, and D_3. At output level Q^*, for example, each individual has a marginal willingness to pay for the last unit of V_1, V_2, and V_3, respectively. The market demand at level Q^*, then, is $V_1 + V_2 + V_3$ at point E. When the marginal willingnesses to pay at each output level are verti-

Figure 15-4   The Efficient Provision of a Public Good

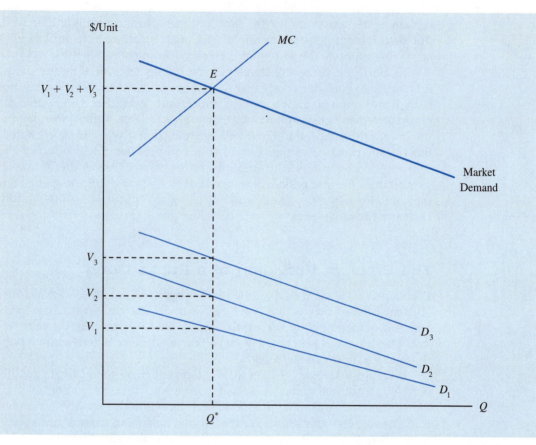

The market demand curve for a public good is derived by vertically summing the individual demand curves, D_1, D_2, and D_3. At output level Q^*, each individual has a marginal willingness to pay of V_1, V_2, and V_3, respectively. The market demand for Q^* is $V_1 + V_2 + V_3$ at point E. When the marginal willingnesses to pay are vertically summed at each output level, the market demand curve is mapped out. The efficient provision of a public good is where the market demand curve intersects the marginal cost curve, at point E and output level Q^*.

cally summed in the same way, the whole market demand curve is mapped out.

Once the market demand curve is derived, the efficient level of production is found where the marginal cost of providing the public good intersects the demand curve. In Figure 15-4, this is found at point E at output level Q^*. At any output level less than Q^*, the *market's* marginal willingness to pay for the good exceeds the marginal cost of providing the good, and it is efficient to provide more of the good. At any output level greater than Q^*, the market's marginal willingness to pay for the good is less than the marginal cost, and it is efficient to provide less of the good.

Preference Revelation and the Clarke Tax

Throughout this book, we usually have assumed that the demand curves are known to the firms that produce goods. This allows each firm to precisely determine its profit-maximizing level of production. A competitive firm only has to know the market price to determine its perfectly elastic demand curve. A firm with monopoly power, however, faces a downward-sloping demand curve. In the real world, this firm can only guess the position of its demand curve. But this firm has the ability to make good guesses! At any price the firm calls out, it can observe how many units are sold at that price. If the firm experiments with several prices, it can eventually map out its demand curve. But determining the market demand curve for a public good is much more difficult to do.

By their nature, public goods cannot be priced in a market. The demand for a public good depends upon what individuals are willing to pay for the good. If one unit of a public good costs $100 to provide, it is only efficient to provide that good if the sum of the individual willingnesses to pay is at a minimum $100. But how can this be known? Simply asking people to reveal their true preferences will generally not work. Depending on who bears the burden of paying for the public good, people have an incentive to misrepresent their true preferences. For example, if everyone who benefits from a public good has to pay an equal share of the cost for the provision of the good, and the good will only be provided if the revealed value of the good outweighs the cost, every individual who values the good has an incentive to overstate its true value. In this section, we present an example of a preference revelation scheme that can yield truthful responses when individuals are asked to state a value for a public good.

As an example, assume that Jim, Susan, Bob, and Amy each own one of four houses on a dark street. They have been petitioning the city to build a street lamp that costs $2,000 to install. For the street lamp to be provided efficiently, the sum of the four individuals' values for the street lamp must exceed $2,000. The objective of the city tax collector is to design a tax scheme that can give each individual the incentive to reveal the true value he or she assigns to the street lamp. This scheme is known as a **Clarke tax,** and it consists of the following rules:

1. A fixed tax burden of $500 is assigned to each individual to recover the exact cost of the street lamp if it is installed.
2. Each individual bids a *net* value for the street lamp. This may or may not be the individual's true net value.
3. The bids are summed. If the sum is positive, the street lamp will be installed. If the sum is negative, the street lamp will not be installed.
4. Any individual whose bid is *pivotal* in the decision to install or not install the street lamp must pay an additional Clarke tax to the city. The Clarke tax is the absolute value of the sum of the *other* individuals' bids.

Table 15-5   Clarke Tax Example

Individual	Fixed Tax Burden	Value for Street Lamp	Net Value for Street Lamp	Clarke Tax
Jim	$500	$200	−$300	0
Susan	$500	$400	−$100	0
Bob	$500	$700	$200	0
Amy	$500	$1,000	$500	$200

How the Clarke tax is calculated, and why it creates the incentive for each individual to truthfully reveal the net value he or she assigns to the good, is explained with the help of the numerical example shown in Table 15-5.

Table 15-5 lists each individual's true value for the street lamp. For example, Jim values the street lamp at $200. If it is installed, his fixed tax burden is $500, leaving him with a net value of −$300. In other words, Jim is willing to pay up to $300 *not* to have the street lamp installed and save the fixed tax burden. In contrast, Amy's true value is $1,000, and, therefore, her net value is $500. This means she is willing to pay $500 more than the fixed tax burden to have the street lamp installed. Jim and Susan have negative net values; Bob and Amy have positive net values. The sum of the net values is $300. Because this is positive, it is efficient to install the street lamp (that is, the total cost is $2,000 but the total value is $2,300). If the sum of the true net values were negative, it would not be efficient to install the street lamp. Whether or not the street lamp is actually installed, however, depends on the sum of the net values that are *revealed* by the individuals, and not on the sum of the true net values. Will the individuals reveal their true net values?

To illustrate how the Clarke tax works, we will begin by assuming that all the individuals know each other's true values, and that each individual believes the others truthfully reveal. Of course, this is an extreme assumption. But for now, all we are interested in showing is that if one individual believes the others truthfully reveal, that individual also has an incentive to truthfully reveal. In other words, truthful revelation is a *best response* to the others' truthful revelations.

Let's begin with Jim. Because he has a negative net value, he prefers not to have the street lamp installed. Therefore, he never has an incentive to bid higher than −$300, since this would only increase the chances that the street lamp would be installed. Does he have an incentive to bid lower than −$300 to try to prevent the street lamp from being installed? Assuming that Jim believes the other three individuals each bid their true net values, the sum of these other net values is $600 ($500 + $200 − $100). For Jim's stated net value to prevent the street lamp from being installed, he has to bid less than

−$600, say −$700. If he bids −$700, the sum of the net values is −$100, and the street lamp is not installed. Sounds like a good deal for Jim. But it isn't.

Without Jim's bid of −$700, the sum of the other net values is positive. With Jim's bid of −$700, the sum of the net values is negative. Therefore, Jim is *pivotal*. His bid alone of −$700 prevents the street lamp from being installed. But because he is pivotal, he will be assessed a Clarke tax equal to the sum of the other net values—$600. The street lamp isn't installed, but Jim is out $600. Had he bid truthfully, he would not have been pivotal and his final net value would have been −$300, which is better than −$600. Jim is better off not lying to prevent the street lamp from being installed.

Susan faces the same problem Jim does. She prefers not to have the street lamp installed, so she never bids more than −$100, but she also doesn't want to be the pivotal vote and be assessed a Clarke tax that would make her worse off than if she bid truthfully. If she is pivotal, her Clarke tax will be the sum of the other truthful net values—$400. She'd be better off bidding truthfully for a net value of −$100.

Bob and Amy both have positive net values and, therefore, have no incentive to understate their true net values. They both prefer to have the street lamp installed. If Bob believes the others bid truthfully, he cannot be pivotal and he will not be assessed a Clarke tax. Without Bob's bid, the sum of the other net values is $100, and the street lamp will be installed. Bob has no incentive to overstate his true net value. Amy, on the other hand, is pivotal. If the other three bid truthfully, the net values sum to −$200 ($200 − $300 − $100). Without her bid, then, the street lamp will not be installed. If she bids truthfully, she alone affects the outcome. Her Clarke tax is the absolute value of the sum of the other net values, $200. Her total tax burden is $700, leaving her with a final payoff of $300 ($1,000 − $700). Because her tax burden does not depend on how she bids, she has no incentive to overstate her bid.

To summarize, in this example we have seen that if an individual believes the others bid truthfully, that individual has no incentive to lie. If it is efficient for the street lamp to be installed, the two individuals who prefer not to have it installed do not want to overstate their net values, since this would increase the chances that the project will be undertaken. They also don't want to lie to try to block the project. The only way to block the project is to bid low enough to be pivotal, and then they would be faced with a high tax burden. The two individuals who prefer to have the street lamp installed have no incentive to understate their net values, since this would lower the chances that the project will be undertaken. They also cannot gain by overstating their net values, because their tax burdens do not depend on their individual bids.

The reason the Clarke tax leads to truthful revelation is because it places a burden only on pivotal bidders, and the amount of the tax is independent of the pivotal bidder's own bid. If an individual lies to change the outcome, the Clarke tax is a severe burden. If an individual tells the truth to change the outcome, the Clarke tax is not severe. From Table 15-5, Amy is the only one who pays a Clarke tax because she is the only pivotal individual when they all reveal their true net values. But even with the Clarke tax, Amy's final payoff is positive and she still prefers to have the street lamp installed.

So far in this example, we have assumed that each individual knew the other bids and believed the others were bidding truthfully. This assumption was maintained to help explain how the Clarke tax works. Even if each individual is uncertain about the other bids, the Clarke tax still leads to truthful revelation.

Consider Jim, whose true net value is −$300. Jim believes the sum of the *other* bids is an unknown variable, X. How should Jim bid? Because Jim's net value is negative, he never has an incentive to bid higher than his true net value since this only increases the chances that the street lamp will be installed. Can he gain by lying and bidding lower than −$300? If Jim believes X is negative, the street lamp will not be installed even without Jim's bid. (Remember, if the sum of all the bids is negative, the project is not undertaken.) Jim is not pivotal when X is negative, so he has no incentive to understate his true net value. If Jim believes X is positive but less than $300, his truthful bid is pivotal since it prevents the street lamp from being installed ($X − \$300 < 0$ when $X < \$300$). By being pivotal, Jim pays a Clarke tax of $X < \$300$, which is better than having a net value of −$300 when the street lamp is installed. Jim pays the same Clarke tax no matter how low he bids, so he has no incentive to lie. Finally, if Jim believes $X > \$300$, his truthful bid is not pivotal: The street lamp will be installed and his net value will be −$300. The only way he can block the project is to bid less than −$300, but then he would be pivotal and face a Clarke tax of $X > \$300$. He'd rather have a net value of −$300 than pay a Clarke tax greater than $300. No matter what Jim believes is the value of X, he has no incentive to lie about his net value.

What about an individual who has a positive net value? Consider Amy, who never has an incentive to understate her true net value of $500. Does she have an incentive to bid higher than $500? If Amy believes X is positive, the street lamp will be installed even without her bid. Since she will not be pivotal, she has no incentive to lie. If Amy believes X is negative but greater than −$500, her truthful bid is pivotal in having the street lamp installed. Her Clarke tax will be $X > -\$500$, which still leaves her with a payoff of ($\$500 − X$). This will be her payoff even if she bids higher than her true net value. Finally, if Amy believes X is negative but less than $500, the only way for her to be pivotal is to bid greater than her true net value of $500. But if she does lie, her Clarke tax will be $X > \$500$, making her worse off than if she truthfully bids and the street lamp isn't installed. As with Jim, Amy never has an incentive to lie about her net value.

The Clarke tax, then, is an amazing mechanism. By providing the incentive for every individual to truthfully reveal his net value, it guarantees that the public good will be provided when it is efficient for it to be provided. It also guarantees that the public good will not be provided when it is inefficient for it to be provided.

Summary

- A **negative externality** is when one individual (or firm) imposes a cost on another individual.

- The **Coase Theorem** states that as long as property rights are well defined and there are no transactions costs, the allocation of resources is *invariant* to the assignment of property rights. This implies that an activity that yields a negative externality will end up at the same level if a property right is assigned *and* if individuals can freely negotiate, regardless of to whom the property right is assigned. The Coase Theorem further implies that the allocation of resources will be *socially efficient.*

- Once a property right is assigned, there are two basic ways of protecting the right. That is, there are two basic rules that govern any change in the activity level—a **property rule** or a **liability rule.** Once a property right is assigned, a property rule allows the parties involved to negotiate any change in the activity level they see fit. A liability rule, however, imposes a damage schedule upon one of the individuals; the activity level may be changed if the individual adheres to the schedule and compensates the other individual.

- In high transactions costs settings, the allocation of resources is not invariant to the assignment of property rights. Specific property or liability rules may be needed to achieve the socially efficient outcome in high transactions costs settings.

- There are two key distinctions between private goods and **public goods.** The first distinction is that public goods are **nonrivalrous** in consumption. This means that the marginal cost of providing this good to any additional consumer is zero. The second distinction is that public goods are nonexcludable. With a **nonexcludable** good, if one person consumes it, there is no way to prevent others from consuming it as well.

- A market demand curve for a public good is derived by *vertically* summing the marginal willingnesses to pay at each output level for each individual. The efficient level of production is found where the marginal cost of providing the public good intersects the demand curve.

- By their nature, public goods cannot be priced in the market. To determine whether a public good should be efficiently provided, a **preference revelation scheme** may yield truthful responses when individuals are asked to state a value for a public good.

Problems

1. Consider a factory that produces a good but also creates pollution that affects a neighboring resident. The total and marginal benefits to the factory and the total and marginal costs to the resident are depicted in the following table:

Output	Total Benefits to Factory	Marginal Benefits to Factory	Total Damages to Resident	Marginal Damages to Resident
0	0	—	0	—
1	500	500	25	25
2	900	400	75	50
3	1200	300	175	100
4	1,400	200	325	150
5	1,500	100	575	250
6	1,550	50	925	350

   a. Assume the factory and resident can negotiate without cost. If the courts assign the property right to the factory and protect it with a property rule, how much will be produced? Is this the socially efficient amount? Explain, using the numerical example.

   b. Assume the factory and the resident cannot negotiate. If the courts assign the property right to the resident, how would you design a liability rule that will allow the factory to produce the efficient amount? Explain, using the numerical example.

2. In the property rights over sunlight application, the court in *Prah v. Maretti* argued that sunlight for energy was more important than sunlight for tanning and leisure. Thus, they argued that the assignment of the property right depends on the importance of the resource being allocated. Evaluate this argument.

3. Using the graphical analysis in Figure 15-1, show how a property right assigned to individual B protected with a liability rule affects the activity level of individual A. Graphically demonstrate a liability rule that leads to the socially efficient level of the activity, Q^*.

4. Compare two ways of dealing with the negative externality of second-hand smoke smokers impose on nonsmokers in public places. Assign the property right to nonsmokers (that is, smoking is not allowed), or assign the property right to smokers (that is, smoking is allowed). Does your answer depend on where the externality is occurring (for example, a privately owned restaurant versus a government office building)? Does your answer depend on the extent of the externality (for example, second-hand smoke is simply annoying to nonsmokers versus second-hand smoke causes cancer in nonsmokers)?

5. Another type of externality is a **positive externality.** In this case, someone's action imposes an external *benefit* on another. Give examples of positive externalities. Discuss the social welfare consequences of a positive externality in both a low and high transactions costs setting.

6. Provide more examples of goods that satisfy one of the characteristics of public goods, but not both characteristics. Are there potential market failures associated with the provision of these goods?

7. In Table 15-5, change Susan's net value for the street lamp from −$100 to −$500. How does this affect the Clarke tax imposed on each individual?

8. What difficulties would there be in actually implementing a Clarke tax in the real world?

GLOSSARY

Actuarially Fair Insurance: When the insurance premium is set equal to the expected benefit payment.

Adverse Selection: Occurs when one side of the market has different information about quality than the other side of the market.

All-or-Nothing Demand Curve: Represents a consumer's average willingness to pay for each output level.

All-or-Nothing Pricing: The monopolist sets a price for a specific quantity of its good and allows the consumer to buy only that quantity or nothing at all.

Allocation: Assignment of goods.

Average Fixed Cost: Total fixed cost divided by output; capital cost per unit produced.

Average Product of Labor: Total output divided by the amount of labor; the average output per unit of labor.

Average Revenue: Total revenue divided by the number of units of output.

Average Total Cost (ATC): Total cost divided by output; the total cost per unit produced.

Average Variable Cost (AVC): Total variable cost divided by output; variable cost per unit produced.

Backward Induction: Solving a game by starting at the end of the game and working backward to the beginning of the game.

Backward Unraveling: The players' failure to sustain the cooperative outcome in a finitely repeated game, even for a single stage.

Barriers to Entry: When entry into a profitable industry is deterred.

Bertrand Duopoly: A model in which the firms choose prices simultaneously.

Best-Response Curve: Shows the firm's most profitable choice for the level of the strategic variable, for each of its rival's choices.

Best-Response Function: A function that tells a firm's most profitable choice for the level of the strategic variable, given its rival's choice.

Budget Line: The outermost border of the budget set; it displays the set of alternatives in which all of a consumer's income is spent.

Budget Set: The set of affordable alternatives a consumer can purchase given his income and the prices of the goods.

Cardinal: Assigning meaningful numbers to a bundle of goods; for example, weight.

Cartel: Firms that explicitly collude to act in unison.

Clarke Tax: A tax scheme that gives each individual the incentive to reveal his or her true value.

Coase Conjecture: The inability of a durable good monopolist to set its price above the competitive price.

Coase Theorem: States that as long as property rights are well defined and there are no transactions costs, the allocation of resources is invariant to the assignment of property rights.

Cobb-Douglas Production Function: A commonly used production function that is useful for discussing returns to scale.

Common-Value Auction: The item is worth the same amount to every bidder, but the true value of the item is unknown, and the bidders have different information about the true value.

Competitive Fringe: The set of price-taking firms in a dominant firm model.

Competitive Industry: One in which all firms produce the same product; consumers know the prices charged by every firm in the industry; each firm's output is small relative to the total output of the industry; and firms may enter and exit the industry freely. An industry in which firms are price takers.

Complements: A situation in which an increase in the price of one good causes a decrease in the demand for another good.

Completeness: A property of preference orderings: Preferences are complete when, for any pair of goods, either one is preferred to the other or the individual is indifferent between them.

Constant-Cost Industry: A situation in which an increase in output in the industry has no impact on the prices of its inputs.

Constant Returns to Scale: When doubling all inputs leads to exactly doubling output.

Consumer Surplus: The total amount that consumers are willing to pay for a certain number of units in excess of what they actually have to pay to buy the units.

Corner Solution: A situation in which the optimal consumption point is at the corner of the budget set, so that the individual does not consume some of every good.

Cournot Duopoly: A model in which the firms choose output levels simultaneously.

Credible: Believable.

Cross-Price Elasticity of Demand: Measures the percentage change in the quantity demanded of one good brought about by a one percent increase in the price of another good.

Deadweight Loss: Unexploited gain from trade.

Decreasing-Cost Industry: A situation in which an increase in output in the industry causes input prices to fall.

Decreasing Returns to Scale: When doubling all inputs leads to less than doubling output.

Deductible: The set amount someone must pay for a claim before the insurance company pays.

Diminishing Marginal Rate of Substitution: When an indifference curve is downward sloping and bowed toward the origin. This property implies that as an individual has more and more units of one good, he is willing to give up fewer and fewer units of the other good to remain on the same indifference curve.

Discount Factor: A number, typically close to one, that measures an individual's impatience, or willingness to trade consumption today for consumption in the future; see also *Discount Rate*.

Discount Rate: A number similar to the interest rate that measures an individual's impatience, or willingness to trade consumption today for consumption in the future; see also *Discount Factor*.

Distortionary Taxes: Taxes that alter individuals' decisions at the margin.

Diversifier: An investor whose portfolio contains a variety of types of assets, risky and riskless.

Dominant Firm: Firm that acts as the industry price setter.

Dominant Firm Model: When one firm acts as the industry price setter and many firms act as price takers.

Dominant Strategy: The player's best response to all of its rival's strategies.

Dominant Strategy Equilibrium: The strategies players choose when every player has a dominant strategy.

Duopoly: Market structure in which there are exactly two firms in the market.

Durable Goods: Goods that last for several periods.

Dutch Auction: The auctioneer calls out successively lower prices, and the first bidder to accept a price wins the auction and pays that price.

Economic Bad: A commodity that people prefer not to consume.

Economic Profit: Total revenue minus total cost, where total cost includes opportunity costs; accounting profit minus the next best alternative return on capital.

Economies of Scale: When the average cost of production decreases with increases in output.

Efficient Auction: When the item goes to the bidder with the highest valuation.

Efficient Input Combinations: Combinations of inputs for which it is impossible to produce more output than the desired level of output, so that nothing is wasted.

Elastic Demand: When a one percent increase in price brings about a greater than one percent decrease in quantity demanded.

Endowment: The amount that a consumer must consume if he or she does not participate in a market, and therefore cannot exchange one good for another.

English Auction: The auctioneer calls out successively higher prices, and bidders drop out until only one is left.

Equilibrium: A situation in which no individual has any reason to change behavior.

Equilibrium Wage: Equates the quantity of labor supplied by workers in the market and the quantity of labor demanded by firms in the market.

Excess Demand: When the quantity demanded by consumers exceeds the quantity producers are willing to supply at a particular price.

Excess Supply: When the quantity producers are willing to supply is greater than the quantity demanded by consumers at a particular price.

Expected Utility: Multiply the utility of a payoff by its probabilities, and then sum over all of the possible outcomes in the prospect.

Expected Utility Maximizer: An individual who always chooses the prospect with the highest expected utility.

Expected Utility Representation: When an individual's preferences can be represented by an expected utility function.

Expected Value: A mathematical measure of the average payoff from a prospect.

Expected Value Maximizer: An individual who always chooses the prospect with the highest expected value.

Explicit Collusion: When firms formally agree to coordinate their activities to increase their joint profit.

Extensive-Form Game: Form of game that presents the players' moves in the order in which they are taken.

Facilitating Practices: Practices that aid a cartel in achieving and maintaining the cartel outcome.

Finitely Repeated Game: A game in which a stage-game is repeated a finite number of times.

Firm: A single entity producing goods or services from inputs.

First-Best Price: The price that minimizes deadweight loss.

First-Mover Advantage: The player who gets to make the first offer in the infinite-period bargaining game gets to keep more than half of the surplus.

First-Price (Sealed-Bid) Auction: Bidders submit their bids secretly and simultaneously, and the highest bidder wins and pays his bid.

Fixed Inputs: Inputs that cannot be varied in the short run.

Fixed-Proportion Production Functions: When inputs must be used in specific proportions, and it is impossible to substitute one input for another.

Full Insurance: A policy that covers the full loss.

Gains from Trade: When both parties to a transaction are made better off.

Game Theory: The study of behavior in situations in which each party's payoff directly depends on what another party does.

Giffen Good: A good that consumers buy more of when its price rises or less of when its price falls.

Grim (Trigger) Strategy: Strategy that cooperates until punishment is triggered, in which case the punishment lasts forever.

Group Insurance: Employer-purchased insurance that covers all employees, not just the high-risk ones.

Human Capital: The knowledge and skills accumulated by workers.

Income Effect: Measures the change in consumption of a good caused by the change in the consumer's purchasing power brought about by the change in the price of the good, holding the price ratio constant.

Income Elasticity of Demand: Measures the percentage change in quantity demanded brought about by a one percent increase in income.

Increasing-Cost Industry: A situation in which an increase in output in the industry causes input prices to rise.

Increasing Returns to Scale: When doubling all inputs leads to more than a doubling of output.

Incumbent Firms: Firms that already exist in a market.

Indifference Curve: When graphing preferences, points on an indifference curve represent bundles among which an individual is indifferent.

Indifference Map: Shows a set of the individual's indifference curves.

Indifferent: Finding two or more alternatives equally appealing.

Industry: A collection of all firms producing a single good or service.

Industry Long-Run Supply Curve: Shows how much is produced by the industry at every possible price when all inputs are variable and firms can enter or exit freely.

Industry Supply Curve: The horizontal summation of all the individual firms' supply curves; the total output produced by all of the firms in the industry at every price; also called *Market Supply Curve*.

Inelastic Demand: When a one percent increase in price brings about a less than one percent decrease in quantity demanded.

Inferior Good: When the demand for a good decreases as income increases.

Infinitely Repeated Game: A game in which a stage-game is repeated a (potentially) infinite number of times.

Initial Node: The first node of an extensive form game.

Inputs: Goods and services used in the production of another good or service.

Insurance Benefit: The amount the insurance company pays.

Insurance Coverage: The amount the insurance company promises to reimburse for a loss.

Insurance Premium: The price of insurance.

Iso-Cost Line: Shows all the combinations of inputs that cost a set amount.

Iso-Expected Value Line: The line in state-payoff space showing all points with the same expected value.

Isoquant: A curve showing all combinations of inputs that can be used to produce a given constant amount of output.

Isoquant Map: A graph showing a set of isoquants for a firm.

Iterated Dominance: The technique of eliminating strategies from a game.

Last-Mover Advantage: In single- and two-period bargaining games, the player proposing in the final period gets more than half of the surplus.

Law of Diminishing Returns: The property that the marginal product of an input begins to decrease after some point, and as the number of workers increases, the firm gets less and less output from each additional worker.

Lerner Index: Measures the proportion of the profit-maximizing price that is not attributable to marginal cost; used to measure monopoly power.

Liability Rule: A way of protecting a property right that imposes a damage schedule upon one of the individuals—the activity level may be changed if the individual adheres to the schedule and compensates the other individual.

Loading Factor: The factor by which the insurance company increases a premium.

Long Run: Period when all inputs are variable.

Long-Run Equilibrium: When no firm can gain by changing its output or exiting, and there is no incentive for new firms to enter.

Marginal Analysis: The comparison of marginal benefits and marginal costs.

Marginal Benefit (MB): The extra benefit generated by producing or consuming one more unit of a good.

Marginal Benefit of Search: The expected benefit of one more search.

Marginal Cost (MC): The extra cost of producing one more unit of output.

Marginal Cost of Search: The total cost of searching for a job one more time, including travel expense and opportunity cost.

Marginal Product of Labor: The extra output generated by one additional unit of labor.

Marginal Rate of Substitution (MRS): The negative of the slope of an indifference curve; the quantity of the vertical-axis good that the individual gives up to get one more unit of the horizontal-axis good while remaining on the same indifference curve.

Marginal Rate of Technical Substitution (MRTS): The negative of the slope of an isoquant (a positive number); measures how much capital is needed to make up for the removal of one unit of labor when output is kept constant; tells how a firm can substitute capital for labor.

Marginal Revenue (MR): The extra revenue generated by one more unit of output.

Marginal Revenue Product of Labor (MRPL): Additional revenue generated by the last unit of labor.

Marginal Utility (MU): The extra utility generated by one additional unit of a good, holding all else constant.

Market Demand Curve: The horizontal sum of all the individual demand curves; measures the total quantity demanded for a particular good at a specified price.

Market Failure: When the market is unable to exploit all gains from trade; some (or all) gains from trade are unrealized.

Market Labor Demand Curve: Shows the total amount of labor desired by all firms at a given wage.

Market Labor Supply Curve: Shows how much all of the workers desire to work at a given wage.

Market Price: The price at which market supply equals market demand.

Market Price Discrimination: When a firm divides consumers into different market groups and charges different prices to each group.

Market Supply: The total amount of a good that all firms in a given industry are willing to produce.

Market Supply Curve: A graph depicting the market supply of a good for every conceivable price; also called *Industry Supply Curve.*

Marketable Permit: Allows a firm to emit one unit of pollution.

Markup Pricing Formula: Tells how much a firm should increase price over marginal cost.

Meeting Competition Clause (MCC): A facilitating practice that guarantees a firm will match the lowest price available or release its customers and allow them to buy from another firm at the lower price.

Microeconomics: The study of individual decisions made by people, firms, households, etc., and how these decisions interact.

Mixed Strategy: When a player selects an action randomly.

Mixed-Strategy Nash Equilibrium: An equilibrium in which one or more players play mixed strategies.

Money Pump: A sequence of choices through which an individual willingly gives up money.

Monopolist: The only firm in an industry.

Monopolistic Competition: Market structure in which there are many price-setting firms in the market and in which there is free entry and exit.

Monopoly Power: The ability of at least one firm to set its profit-maximizing price above its marginal cost.

Monotonicity: A property of preference orderings stating that more is better.

Moral Hazard: Occurs when one participant of an agreement has no incentive to exert the amount of effort intended by the other participant.

Most-Favored-Customer (MFC) Pricing: A price protection policy that guarantees current consumers a rebate of the price difference if the firm sells to future consumers at a lower price.

Nash Equilibrium: A strategy combination in which no player has an incentive to change his or her strategy, holding constant the strategies of the other players.

Natural Monopoly: When all the profitable levels of output can be most efficiently produced by just one firm.

Negative Externality: When one individual or firm imposes a cost on another individual or firm.

Nonexcludability: A characteristic of a public good, when it is impossible to prevent an individual from consuming the good.

Nonrivalry: A characteristic of a public good, when the marginal cost of providing the good to an additional consumer is zero.

Normal-Form Game: A list of players in the game, a list of strategies each player can choose, and a list of the payoffs each player receives for each combination of strategies he or she chooses.

Normal Good: When the demand for a good increases as income increases.

Odds Ratio: The probability that state 1 occurs divided by the probability that state 1 does not occur.

Oligopoly: A market structure that includes more than one firm, but less than "very many" firms.

Opportunity Cost: The value of the best forgone alternative.

Optimal Search Rule: The search rule that maximizes the searcher's expected utility; accepting the first offer at or above the reservation offer.

Ordinal: Ranking bundles of goods in order of preference, as in utility functions.

Outcomes: Possible payoff combinations in a game.

Payoff: The amount of utility a player can earn in a game.

Perfect Complements: Pairs of goods that must be consumed together in a fixed proportion; one is never consumed without the other.

Perfect Price Discrimination: Extracting as revenue the consumers' total willingness to pay for a good, allowing the monopolist to earn the greatest amount of profit available in a market.

Perfect Substitutes: Goods that are willingly exchanged in the same fixed ratio.

Perfectly Elastic Demand: When elasticity is infinite and quantity demanded is completely sensitive to changes in price.

Perfectly Inelastic Demand: When elasticity is zero and quantity demanded is completely insensitive to changes in price.

Perishable Goods: Goods that perish after a single period.

Players: Participants in the game.

Plunger: An investor who puts all of his money into a single asset—the risky asset.

Preference Function: Utility function representing the individual's preference ordering.

Preference Ordering: A list of every conceivable pair of combinations of goods and stating a preference for each pair.

Preference Revelation Scheme: To determine whether a public good should be efficiently provided, individuals are asked to state a value for a public good.

Present Value: The value of a future income stream presented in today's dollars.

Price Elasticity of Demand: Measures the percentage change in quantity demanded brought about by a one percent increase in price.

Price Takers: When firms must take the price determined by the market.

Principal of a Loan: Amount of money originally borrowed.

Prisoner's Dilemma: Games in which the equilibrium is not the outcome the players would choose if they could perfectly cooperate.

Private-Value Auction: Every bidder has a different valuation of the item being auctioned.

Producer Surplus: The amount producers receive above the minimum they need at a minimum to produce.

Product Differentiation: Product differences that give firms some power over price, but not complete monopoly power.

Production Function: A mathematical function telling how much output is produced for a given combination of inputs.

Profit: Total revenue minus total cost.

Profit-Maximization Condition: When marginal revenue equals marginal cost.

Property Rule: A way of protecting a property right that allows the parties involved to negotiate any change in the activity level they see fit.

Proportional Loading: When the insurance company charges a loading factor that is proportional to the expected benefit payment.

Prospects: The alternatives when payoffs in risky alternatives are amounts of money.

Public Good: A good that anyone can consume without affecting the consumption of the good by others, and there is no way to exclude people from consuming it.

Pure Strategy: When a player selects a particular action with probability equal to one.

Quantity Demanded: The amount of a good consumed at a particular price.

Quantity Supplied: The amount of a good produced at a particular price.

Reservation Offer: The least amount that a person is willing to accept for a job.

Reserve Price: The lowest price at which the seller is willing to sell the item.

Residual Demand Curve: The portion of the demand curve that lies below the price.

Returns to Scale: A measure of how much output changes when the amounts of labor and capital are varied in the same proportion.

Revealed Preferred: Commodity bundle A is revealed preferred to bundle B when both are affordable but the individual chooses A.

Revenue: The total amount paid by all the firm's customers for its products or services.

Revenue Equivalence: The property that all four types of auctions generate the same expected price.

Risk Aversion: When an individual prefers a riskless prospect to a risky prospect with the same expected value.

Risk Loving: When a person prefers a prospect to its expected value.

Riskless: A situation that has only one possible outcome.

Risky: A situation in which the outcome of a choice is uncertain.

Satiation Point: When individuals consume the amount of a commodity that is most preferred.

Second-Best Pricing: Minimizing deadweight loss subject to a break-even constraint; giving the firm at least zero profit while trying to keep the deadweight loss as small as possible.

Second-Price Auction: Bidders submit their bids secretly and simultaneously, and the highest bidder wins and pays the second-highest bid.

Short Run: Period when some inputs are fixed, while others are variable.

Short-Run Labor Demand Curve: Shows how much labor the firm hires at each wage rate; given by the firm's marginal revenue product curve.

Short-Run Total Cost Function: Measures the lowest possible total cost of producing different levels of output when the amount of capital is fixed.

Signal: In signaling, an activity that has no productive value but conveys information. In auctions, the information a bidder receives about the true value of a prize.

Social Welfare: The sum of consumer surplus and producer surplus.

Solving a Game: Figuring out what strategies the players choose in a game, usually relying on some equilibrium concept.

Stackelberg Duopoly: A model in which the firms choose their output levels sequentially.

Stackelberg Follower: The firm that chooses its output level second.

Stackelberg Leader: The firm that chooses its output level first.

State of Nature: A randomly determined event.

State-Payoff Space: The space on a graph showing the payoff in different states of nature.

Strategic Variable: The variable set by oligopolistic firms, such as price in Bertrand duopoly or quantity in Cournot duopoly.

Strategies: Complete plans for playing a game.

Strictly Dominated Strategy: A strategy that a player never chooses, regardless of what the other player does.

Subgame: A part of an extensive-form game that begins at a node (not the initial node) and continues to the terminal node.

Subgame-Perfect Nash Equilibrium: A Nash equilibrium not only for the complete game, but also for every subgame.

Substitutes: A situation in which an increase in the price of one good causes an increase in the demand for another good.

Substitution Effect: Measures the change in the consumption of a good when its price changes but the individual remains indifferent; see also *Income Effect.*

Sunk Cost: A cost that is irretrievable. Once incurred, a sunk cost is not part of the opportunity cost of an activity.

Supply Curve: The amount of output a firm desires to sell at every price.

Tacit Collusion: When firms do not formally agree to act in unison, but still implicitly act interdependently to improve their profit level relative to the competitive outcome.

Tangent: A situation in which two curves have the same slope at the point where they intersect.

Terminal Node: The last node of an extensive-form game.

Total Benefit: The benefit generated by all produced or consumed units of a good.

Total Cost (TC): The sum of total fixed cost and total variable cost.

Total Fixed Cost (TFC): The combined cost of all fixed inputs.

Total Product Curve: The graph of the production function.

Total Revenue (TR): The amount of money a firm collects from selling its output, equal to the price of the good times the number of units sold.

Total Variable Cost (TVC): The cost of all variable inputs used to produce the desired quantity of output.

Transitivity: A property of preference orderings: When alternative A is preferred to alternative B and alternative B is preferred to alternative C, then A is preferred to C.

Trigger Price: An agreed-on cartel price used as a punishment trigger. If any firm lowers its price below the trigger, all the other firms immediately lower their prices to some predetermined level for some amount of time.

Two-Part Pricing: Setting two prices, a per-unit price and a fixed fee.

Unit Elastic Demand: When the price elasticity of demand is exactly equal to 1.

Utility Functions: Mathematical formulas that can be used to represent preferences; that is, they can be used to determine whether an individual prefers one commodity bundle to another.

Value of Time: Opportunity cost of time; its value in its best alternative use.

Variable Inputs: Inputs that can be varied in the short run.

Weak Nash Equilibrium: A Nash equilibrium in which one player is indifferent between two or more actions given the equilibrium strategies of his or her opponents.

Winner's Curse: The phenomenon in which the highest bidder overbids and loses money in an auction.

INDEX

Note: The symbols *f*, *t*, and *b* after page numbers indicate figures, tables, and boxes, respectively.